Inside Hitler's Greece

Inside Hitler's Greece

The Experience of Occupation, 1941–44

Mark Mazower

Yale University Press • New Haven and London   1993

First published in paperback 1995
Reprinted 1997, 1998

Set in Bembo by Best-set Typesetter Ltd., Hong Kong.
Printed in Great Britain by St Edmundsbury Press Ltd.

Library of Congress Cataloging-in-Publication Data

Mazower, Mark.
    Inside Hitler's Greece: the experience of occupation, 1941–1944/
by Mark Mazower.
        p.   cm.
    Includes bibliographical references and index.
    ISBN 0–300–05804–7 (hbk.)
    ISBN 0–300–06552–3 (pbk.)
    1. World War, 1939–1945 – Greece.   2. Greece – History – Occupation,
1941–1944.   I. Title.
D802.G8M39   1993
940.53'37 – dc20   93–13363
                                                                  CIP

A catalogue record for this book is available from the British Library.

Frontispiece: German anti-aircraft gun stationed in front of the Temple of Olympian
Zeus, Athens, 1941.

for Deb

Contents

List of Illustrations ix

Introduction xiii

Acknowledgements xx

Abbreviations and Foreign Terms xxiii

Prologue: Swastika over the Acropolis I

PART I: The Chaos of the New Order: 1941–43

1 Venizelos's Funeral 11
2 The Occupation Begins 15
3 The Famine 23
4 Black Market Axioms 53
5 'An Atmosphere of Imminent Catastrophe' 65
6 Greek Workers in the Reich 73
7 Dreams of a New Europe 79

PART II: 'This Heroic Madness': 1941–43

8 The Resistance of Daily Life 85
9 Prudence or Bravery? The Old Politicians 97
10 Becoming Organised 103
11 Urban Protest 108
12 'Freedom or Death!' 123
13 Politics of the Andartiko 138
14 The End of Italian Rule 144

PART III: The Logic of Violence and Terror: 1943–44

15 The Logic of Violence 155
16 Anatomy of a Massacre: 16 August 1943 190
17 'The Loveliest Time': the Behaviour and Values of the German Soldier 201
18 The SS and the Terror System 219
19 Greek Jewry and the Final Solution 235

Contents

PART IV: A Society at War: 1943–44

20   *People's Democracy in Free Greece*   265
21   *ELAS: the People's Liberation Army*   297
22   *'A Cemetery Awash in Blood': the Counter-Revolution*   322
23   *'Tired Out by History': Athens '44*   340

Epilogue: 'No Peace without Victory'   355

Notes   378

Archival Sources   415

Note on Sources   423

Index   429

List of Illustrations

Frontispiece: Anti-aircraft gun: Athens, 1941.   ii
1.   German troops enter Salonika.   2
2.   German troops enter Athens.   5
3.   German tanks beneath the Acropolis.   6
4.   Field Marshal von Brauchitsch visits the Acropolis.   7
5.   Signing the surrender.   17
6.   Soup kitchen: Athens, 1941.   29
7.   Buses in Athens, 1941.   34
8.   Food queue: Athens, 1941.   35
9.   A man collapses from hunger in central Athens.   38
10.   The municipal mortuary in central Athens.   42
11.   Malnourished children: Athens, 1941.   45
12.   A requisitioned caique.   59
13.   The 1942 5,000 drachma note.   66
14.   A German propaganda photo.   81
15.   Vasilis Tsitsanis.   91
16.   Chrysa Chadzivasileiou.   105
17a.   Anastasia Siouli.   110
17b.   Maria Manthopoulou.   110
18.   Demonstrators in Jannina.   115
19.   Palamas's funeral.   118
20.   An EAM rally.   119
21.   Aris Velouchiotis.   126
22.   A group of ELAS *andartes*.   128
23.   *Andartes* around a camp fire.   130
24.   German soldiers pose by the ruins of a sabotaged viaduct at Isari in
        the Peloponnese.   136
25.   Napoleon Zervas.   139
26.   Soldiers visit the Acropolis.   158
27.   Lieutenant Glitz interrogates a shepherd.   168
28.   Planning operations against the *andartes*.   171
29abc. The mass execution at Kondomari on 2 June 1941.   174
30.   A ruined village near Athens, 1944.   182
31.   Refugees living in the mountains.   184
32.   Children: Mikro Chorio, central Greece, 1943.   187
33.   Women mourning.   189

34.	Colonel Josef Salminger, 1943.	193
35.	Alexandros Mallios: Komeno, 1988.	196
36.	German soldiers pose for a photograph.	202
37.	A donkey race: Peloponnese, August 1943.	205
38a.	The destruction of Distomo, 1944.	213
38b.	Survivors: Distomo, 1945.	213
39.	The SS in Greece: Hans Dörhage, Jürgen Stroop, Walter Schimana, Walter Blume and Paul Radomski.	221
40.	A Purim play in Chalkis, 1928.	237
41.	Anti-semitic measures in Salonika, 11 July 1942.	239
42.	Jews being deported, place unknown.	242
43.	Errikos Sevillias (1901–74) and family.	258
44.	Jewish orphans leave Greece for Palestine, 1945.	260
45.	In the mountains of 'Free Greece'.	266
46.	People's Court, 1944.	272
47.	A village council in Epiros, 1944.	275
48.	Resistance graffiti: Epiros, 1944.	278
49.	A woman delegate speaking at a public meeting.	280
50.	The Little Eagles.	281
51.	A resistance school book.	282
52a.	Village farmers listen to a speech.	286
52b.	An ELAS orator: Epiros, 1944.	287
53.	Delegates to the National Council.	292
54.	ELAS *kapetans* in Epiros, 1944.	300
55.	*Andartes* on the march.	306
56.	New recruits to ELAS.	307
57.	Two of Aris's bodyguards.	319
58.	Rallis (on the right) reviews the Evzones: Athens, 1944.	323
59.	Security Battalionists under British guard after Liberation.	333
60.	Colonel Poulos in a northern Greek village, 1944.	338
61.	The blocco at Kokkinia, Athens, in August 1944.	343
62.	Security Battalions raid a factory.	344
63.	Hanged resistance fighter is displayed in Athens.	347
64.	Taking down a swastika on Samos at Liberation.	356
65.	The Liberation of Athens.	361
66.	Greek villagers in Xylokastron welcome a British jeep.	363
67.	A new pair of shoes: Athens, 1945.	367
68.	Civilians rush a wounded man to safety. A British sniper fires from the Acropolis.	369
69.	*Andartes* learn about the demobilisation terms.	373

Photo credits

Bundesarchiv (cover, frontispiece, 1–5, 12, 26–7, 36, 42, 63); Benaki Museum (6, 11, 38b, 44, 65, 67); Kostas Paraschos (7, 9); Spiros Meletzis (10, 16, 21, 24, 32, 46, 53, 56); Kostas Balafas (18, 25, 38a, 47–8, 50, 52a–b, 54–5, 69); Liddell Hart Centre for Military Archives, King's College, London (22, 45, 49, 62); Imperial

War Museum, London (23, 30–31, 57, 59, 64, 66, 68); Berlin Document Centre (39); Jewish Museum of Greece (40–41, 43).

Apologies are extended to owners of those photographs where it proved impossible to trace the copyright.

ROMANIA

YUGOSLAVIA

Nis

Pleven

BULGARIA

Varna

BLACK SEA

Pristina

Sofia

Stara Zagora

Maritza

Skopje

Axios

ALBANIA

Durazzo

Tirana

Shkoumbi

Bitolj

L. Doiran

Doiran

Nestos

Mesta

Adrianople

Istanbul

L. Ochrida

L. Prespa

Florina

Edessa

Kilkis

Kavalla

SEA OF
MARMARA

Devoli

Koritza

MACEDONIA

Kozani

Verria

Salonika

Alexandroupolis

Delvina

EPIROS

Samarina

Konitza

Grevena

Katerini

THASOS

LEMNOS

Dardanelles

CORFU

Metsovo

Jannina

Trikkala

Larissa

AEGEAN
SEA

MYTILENE

TURKEY

IONIAN IS.

Philiata

PINDOS MTS.

Preveza

GREECE

Volos

LEFKADA

Thermopylae

EVVIA

CHIOS

Izmir

CEPHALONIA

Amphissa

ATTICA

Argostoli

G. of Patras

Thebes

Patras

G. of Corinth

Eleusis

Marathon

ANDROS

SAMOS

ZANTE

Corinth Canal

Corinth

Athens

Piraeus

Porto
Raphti

TENOS

Nauplia

Saronic Gulf

PELOPONNESE

CYCLADES

LEROS

IONIAN SEA

Kalamata

NAXOS

AMORGOS

Monemvasia

MELOS

Astypalaea

STAMPALIA

C. Matapan

KYTHERA

DODECANESE
(ITALIAN)

RHODES

Chief roads

CARPATHOS

Chief railways

CASO

0   50   100 miles

Suda B.

Herakleion
(Candia)

Kandanos

Canea

Sitia

0   160 kilometres

Rethymno

Sphakia

CRETE

Greece and the Balkans, 1939

Introduction

You will find a spring to the left of Hades' halls,
and standing by its side, a white cypress tree.
Do not approach this spring.
But you will find another spring by the Lake of Memory,
with cool water flowing from it. There are guards in front.
Say . . .
'I am parched with thirst and I perish. Give me quickly
the cool water flowing from the Lake of Memory'.
And of their own accord they will give you to drink from the holy
  spring.
        'Instructions for the Journey of the Dead', 4th cent BC

It was Kurt Waldheim who aroused my interest in occupied Greece. Almost fifty years after the young Wehrmacht lieutenant served there, I went to Athens to try to find out what he had known and done. Studying the files that had passed through his hands, I read about how the Wehrmacht had requisitioned food while people died of hunger; how its financial demands upon the Greek state caused a rampant inflation in which olive oil became the chief currency and a loaf of bread cost 2 million drachmas; how mass resistance led to bloody reprisal operations and the shooting of civilian hostages. In the first year of the occupation alone, over 40,000 people starved to death. By Liberation, the Wehrmacht's unsuccessful efforts to defeat the guerrillas had cost the lives of another 25,000. Greece's Jewish communities, among the most ancient in Europe, were virtually wiped out.

Slowly I came to realise that the question of whether or not Waldheim himself was a war criminal betrayed a lack of understanding of the nature of Nazi rule. As a junior intelligence officer at Army Group headquarters, Lieutenant Waldheim had few opportunities to kill people. But he was in the best possible position to understand the realities of life inside Hitler's Europe. Not only in the camps but throughout the Nazi empire conventional distinctions between criminal and lawful activity had collapsed. This book aims to show what it was like to live in such a world. By focusing on individuals, their stories, and the struggles of day-to-day existence, I have tried to depict a small part of Hitler's empire in a way which illuminates the experience of Nazi occupation as a whole.

*

In Britain, we tend to remember the Second World War as a sequence of epic battles – Dunkirk, El Alamein, Salerno and Normandy: first comes the heroic retreat from the continent, then the triumphant return. Unconquered, the Sceptered Isle never entered the Grey Zone of the Nazi New Order. Today, we gaze speculatively at photographs of a Wehrmacht band marching past a branch of Lloyds Bank in Guernsey; it takes the genius of Len Deighton in a book like *SS-GB* to conjure up a world where Heinrich Himmler controlled Scotland Yard.

Across the Channel, however, the memory of occupation lingers and it is more evident that the brief episode of Nazi rule helped to shape Europe's political evolution. Like a tidal wave, occupation swept away old structures, and changed the entire landscape. It forced upon Europe a regime whose brutality it had inflicted on other continents, but had not expected to suffer at home. The shock caused established systems of rule and thought to disintegrate. In this way Nazi rule acted as the catalyst for a series of unpredictable political and social reactions. Nowhere perhaps were the consequences more tragic than Greece, where occupation merged almost imperceptibly with a civil war which devastated the country till the end of the 1940s.

*

A few days after the Germans left, in late 1944, an American OSS agent drove across the Peloponnese, filming whatever he found. In contrast with the waving, jubilant crowds who greeted Allied troops in France, the people he met in Greece seemed tense and exhausted. The clothes hung off their bodies, and many were barefoot. Everywhere he found signs of malnutrition, disease and destruction. Because village schools had been burned to the ground, children attended lessons in the open air, using rocks for desks. Viewing his film today in the comfort of the National Archives in Washington, one sees women trying to prepare food in the ruins of a house, amid charred timbers and piles of rubble. In the coffee-shops, the camera pans unsteadily across rows of gaunt and expressionless faces. Perhaps the eeriest sequence shows a small town in the mountains. Although there is relatively little sign here of physical destruction, the streets seem oddly empty. A line of women, dressed in black, can be seen moving slowly down a road shaded by cypresses. From the cameraman's notes, we find that this was

Kalavryta, in the northern Peloponnese, almost exactly one year after all the men of the town had been shot by Wehrmacht soldiers.

Lasting from 1941 to 1944, the 'long night of barbarism' (to use Churchill's phrase) had brought together farmers, village widows and black-marketeers, frightened Italian deserters and Waffen-SS teenage conscripts in provincial garrisons. Its backdrop included the empty shops in Salonika left abandoned by their Jewish owners, the damaged caiques on island beaches, the burned villages with their rotting harvests, the bodies left dangling from trees by a road in Arkadia after 'mopping-up' actions and reprisal killings. Among the leading characters were informers and spies, the Poulos squad and the Security Battalions, the police and the guerrillas. Caught up in a total war, society itself had become the battlefield.

This world of unfamiliar moral choices and incessant, unpredictable dangers confronts people on the outside with the inevitable question: how would *you* have coped? 'D. was this type. He always sailed with the wind,' writes one Greek to a friend in 1944. 'He was looking prosperous and getting fat when everyone else was slowly fading away.' But how much does strength, and weakness, of character explain? Was it predictable that 'Jason, son of P.' should serve the Italians on his island so well that 'they carried out all his desires'? What made him denounce thirty fellow-Greeks as pro-British? What combination of character, class, and sheer chance explains why one of his intended victims was out of town when the Italians made their arrests, with the result that he never returned home, but went to 'join the patriots in the mountains'?[1]

Even during the war, people living in relative freedom found such a world difficult to imagine or comprehend. A British woman who lived in Izmir, in neutral Turkey, met up with some friends who had just escaped from Athens, and could hardly believe what they told her. Learning about people who had been murdered for a few gold sovereigns and then 'cut to pieces', she confessed herself 'astounded beyond words on hearing all this'. It is perhaps even harder for us, returning to these events after many years, to put them into some sort of perspective and context.[2]

For all its horrors, however, the occupation did not happen in a historical or social void; it formed part of the continuum of European history, reaching back and forwards over time. As Robert Paxton showed many years ago in an exemplary study of Vichy France, people living under Nazi rule were deeply influenced by events that had occurred before the war.[3] In Greece, the memory of an unpopular dictatorship (1936–41) was fresh in people's minds when the Germans and Italians arrived. To make sense of occupation, then, means setting it in the context of Europe's experience of the 1930s. In turn, the occupation helped shape what was to come. A close connection exists between the conditions of life in Nazi-occupied Europe and the subsequent polarisation of politics throughout the continent in the 1940s: this is where the Cold War began, as German diplomats and SS officials – contemplating a future without Hitler – were not slow to appreciate. The task confronting historians of the Occupation period is to demonstrate this by linking the world of high policy to the social, military, cultural and economic influences upon the lives and beliefs of ordinary people.

*

In a recent bestseller, an American intellectual equated the ending of the Cold War with 'the End of History'. To European eyes, however, the dissolution of the Soviet empire and the reunification of Germany suggest, if anything, History's resurrection: former polemics have suddenly been forgotten, as a new order of questions poses itself. Today we are able to appreciate just how powerfully the Cold War impressed itself upon our understanding of the past.[4]

Even before the German occupation ended in Greece, the Cold War loomed over the country. Wartime clashes between nationalist and left-wing resistance groups were followed after Liberation by the Civil War (1946–49), when forces of the official government, aided by the British and Americans, combated and eventually defeated the communist-led guerrillas of the Democratic Army. Not surprisingly, many of the first studies of the occupation period focused upon the role played by the Greek Communist Party in monopolising the wartime resistance: this, according to a powerful body of opinion during the early phase of the Cold War, had been designed to clear the path for an eventual communist takeover in Greece, which only decisive British intervention in favour of non-communist forces had averted.[5]

When the intellectual pendulum swung in the other direction, the Anglo-American role in wartime Greece was cast in a completely new light. Now it was not the Left but the Allies who looked like the villains, undermining a genuinely popular resistance movement to lay the foundations for a succession of right-wing and even fascistic Greek puppet regimes which culminated in the Colonels' *coup d'état* of 1967.[6]

Recent research on British and American foreign policy towards Greece, together with the publication over the last few years of the memoirs of former guerrilla leaders, at last provides a more subtle and plausible picture of the origins of the Civil War. Just as resistance fighters in the left-wing movement EAM/ELAS were not all either fervent communists or pathetic dupes, so too British diplomats and military personnel were not engaged in a massive plot to turn Greece over to right-wing authoritarian hands. The truth was less mechanical and more tragic.[7]

As this whole debate draws to a close, its underlying assumptions have come to the surface. Among the most important of them, though rarely defended explicitly, is the view that Axis policies were of only secondary importance, compared with relations between the British and the Greeks. Occasionally we gain a glimpse of a small German or Italian detachment, at the far end of a remote valley, whilst British agents and Greek resistance fighters in their mountain sanctuaries haggle over the future of the country. Alexandria, Cairo and London rather than a land under enemy occupation provide the customary backdrop for these accounts. But was the nature of Axis rule really so benign as to exert no significant influence over developments in wartime Greece? To ask the question is to answer it, for the scale of famine, inflation and physical destruction there had few parallels in Europe. In this book, therefore, it is the Axis rather than the Allied powers who are in the spotlight, and readers who want a highly detailed account of British policy can turn to one of the studies recommended in the Note on Sources at the end of this book.

A second equally implausible assumption has been that wartime developments inside occupied Greece were determined within the realm of high politics. Ambassadors, generals, senior mission officers, Greek politicians and resistance leaders flit across the pages in a variety of colours, according to the author's sympathies. The existence of the mass left-wing resistance movement EAM/ELAS is taken for granted, or attributed to the actions of a small nucleus of dedicated communist activists who dragged a mass of anonymous followers in their wake. By focusing on the last year of the occupation, when EAM/ELAS had established itself as a major political force, most writers pass over the question of how a movement of mass resistance came into existence in the first place. This is fertile terrain for conspiracy theories and heroic epics. Neither genre, however, offers a satisfactory basis for understanding what was essentially the product of turbulent social change.

Since other writers have provided excellent accounts of the politics of the resistance – whether between the Allies and the Greeks, or between the different Greek organisations themselves – I have let this subject take a back seat to the question of the social origins of resistance activity.[8] This has meant concentrating on EAM/ELAS, and giving less attention to smaller groups like EDES. In the complexity of its structure, ideology and of course in its size,

EAM/ELAS overshadowed its rivals. It was something unprecedented in modern Greek history – a mass ideological movement in a country of clientilist factions and charismatic leaders.

It was, in fact, one of the most startling manifestations of the radical break with established political traditions that the Second World War inspired inside and outside Europe (the resistance movements in Yugoslavia, Italy, French Indochina and the Philippines provide parallels). Why did wartime lead to mass radicalisation? What sort of people joined the resistance? And what, more generally, was the impact of the occupation on the structure of politics, and the way people thought about their society? These questions have a relevance beyond the borders of Greece, for they raise fundamental issues in the European experience under Nazi rule.

*

The catalyst for events in wartime Greece was the power vacuum created by the Axis conquest in 1941. Reflecting Hitler's own tendency to view the subjects of his European New Order as sources of raw materials, food and labour rather than as potential political associates, Berlin and Rome sought to govern Greece through the existing administrative machinery headed by a designedly weak political leadership. But the Greek state bureaucracy, never impressive for its efficiency, seized up in the face of exorbitant Axis demands, and was pushed towards an acute fiscal and monetary crisis within a few months. Inflation, black-marketeering, food shortages and eventually famine itself marked the collapse of the national economy. Athens could no longer feed itself, still less rule the country.

For ordinary Greeks worried by the prospect of hunger and economic breakdown, it became vital to band together. When the official state lost its authority, alternative social groupings emerged. As the sociologist Jan Gross suggests in the case of wartime Poland, mass resistance movements were, in origin, social phenomena. EAM's rapid growth in Greece stemmed *both* from forces pushing from below – notably the innumerable 'People's Committees' which were formed in the provinces (often initially in ignorance of one another's existence) – *and* from above, through the work of communist activists sent out from Athens. In the mountains of 'Free Greece' a surrogate state emerged to challenge the faltering legitimacy of the Athens government.[9]

The Wehrmacht responded with a series of anti-guerrilla operations, based upon reprisal killings and the arrest of civilian hostages. Violence, to put it simply, became the chief way of reasserting German control over the countryside. Terror became the basis for rule in urban areas. Not solely the response of nervous soldiers in the field, the logic of violence and terror reflected the core values of the National Socialist *Weltanschauung*. But these policies proved incapable by themselves of wiping out the resistance and may have even been counterproductive. By 1944, EAM/ELAS was claiming that its support extended to more than one million members.

EAM/ELAS was determined to monopolise the resistance, and terrorised its opponents. Yet at the same time it was unquestionably popular. Wartime radicalism was a complex and paradoxical phenomenon, a revulsion from the past as much as a dream of the future. War kept many guerrillas too concerned about their day-to-day existence to think very long about what would happen after Liberation. Though communism became more popular than ever before, it remained the allegiance of a minority. At the top of the movement, EAM's social achievements were accompanied by political indecision. At lower echelons, regional and village realities continued to predominate over national ones. Local conditions, geography and personalities obstructed any possibility of strong central direction.[10]

Fear of the forthcoming revolution, on the other hand, was a great unifier: in the last year of the war, nationalists of various backgrounds came together, under German auspices and often with tacit British approval, and prepared to take on the Left. The composition of this increasingly vicious counter-revolutionary coalition of forces was as diverse as the resistance it was pitted against, and often drawn from the same social groups. Over the final months of the occupation the middle ground in Greek politics disappeared: two armed camps faced one another, most dramatically in Athens. There lay the origins of the bitter feuding and street battles which led after Liberation to outright civil war.

Acknowledgements

I am deeply indebted to the many librarians and archivists who have helped me: Valentina Tselika of the Benaki Museum, Ioanna Tsoumeri of the Bank of Greece library, the late Joseph Lovinger and the staff of the Central Board of Jewish Communities in Greece, Nikolaos Depastas and General Mourgelas of the Greek Army History Directorate, the staff at the Newspaper Division of the Parliament Library, and Christos Loukos at the Academy of Athens; in Germany, Oberstaatsanwalt Willi Dressen and his colleagues in the Zentrale Stelle der Landesjustizverwaltungen at Ludwigsburg, the staff of the Staatsbibliothek at Stuttgart, Dr Maria Keipert of the Auswärtiges Amt, Bonn, Dr David Marwell of the Berlin Document Centre, Frau Monica Mayr at the Institut für Zeitgeschichte in Munich, Herr Bauer of the Bundesarchiv at Koblenz, Herr Dr Detlef Vogel of the Militärgeschichtliches Forschungsamt and Herr Moritz and his colleagues at the Bundesarchiv-Militärarchiv in Freiburg.

My thanks also to the archivists of the Archives Diplomatiques at Nantes, the staff at the Public Record Office in London, as well as David Cesarani, Alexandra Weissler and their colleagues at the Wiener Library, Stephen Walton and Philip Reed at the Imperial War Museum Library (Foreign Documents Division), John Harding of the Army Historical Branch (Ministry of Defence), Rosemary Campbell of St Antony's College, Oxford, the Librarian of Christ Church, Oxford, the staff of the Foreign and Commonwealth Office Library, the British Library, and the Liddell Hart Military Archives at King's College, London. At the US National Archives in Washington I received the courteous assistance of Will Mahoney and John Taylor. The Inter-Library Loan department of Firestone Library at Princeton University obtained American, Italian and German documents with great efficiency.

Jack Stroumsa, the 'violinist of Auschwitz', told me the story of his own odyssey from Salonika to Jerusalem, and smoothed my path into the archives at Yad Vashem. The late Arthur Wickstead provided me with material from his period of service as a British Liaison Officer in northern Greece and generously discussed his experiences with me. Patrick Gray readily made available the papers of his father, and Margaret Wilkes allowed me to see an unpublished memoir by her late husband: my thanks to them both. Professors Steve Bowman, Richard Breitman and Dr Jonathan Steinberg very kindly shared materials with me which they had acquired in the course of their own research. Dr Rainer Eckart was good enough to send me copies of two valuable dissertations – his own and Dr Anke Weppler's – at a time of turmoil in his own country. Marion Sarafis gave me an entrée into the papers of the League for Democracy in Greece, as well as the benefit of her intimate knowledge of modern Greek history. This book grew out of a TV investigation into the wartime career of Kurt Waldheim, and it is a pleasure to thank producers Jack Saltman and Ed Braman and my co-researchers Ariana Yiakas, Alexandra Weissler, Richard Mitten and Hans Safrian for their support.

Many individuals tolerated my questioning. Sture and Clio Linner, whose humanity and strength of purpose were reflected in their work for the Red Cross during the war, offered the warmth of their friendship as well as their recollections over many meals in Athens and Spetsai. I am also deeply indebted to Alexandros Mallios and his wife, as well as other inhabitants of Komeno, for their hospitality, patience and trust. Others who allowed themselves to be interviewed or questioned included Georgios Bageorgios, Jacob F., Prof. Peter Fraser, Prof. Nicholas Hammond, Dr Reinhold von K., General Mario Maniakis, Brigadier and Mrs Edmund Myers, Theodoros Sarantis, Dekan Rudolf Schwarz, Edgar Thomashausen, Dr J. Wilkinson, the Hon. C.M. Woodhouse and Prof. Alexandros Zaoussis. I am grateful to them all and to others who prefer to remain unnamed.

I was generously helped in my search for photographs by Fani Constantinou of the Benaki Museum, Photograph Archive; that brilliant and still youthful photographer of the *andartiko*, Kostas Balafas; Kostas Megalokonomou, Spyros Meletzis, Kostas Paraschos, and the staff of the Imperial War Museum, Photograph Collection.

At the start of my work, the Dean and Students of Christ Church, Oxford supported me with leaves of absence and travel funds. Princeton University's Research Grants Committee also provided financial assistance, while Dimitri Gondicas and Mike Keeley gave willing and warm support and arranged for the Trustees of the Stanley J. Seeger Fund to aid my work through the award of a University Preceptorship. I only wish I could have found a better way to testify to the strengths of the Hellenic Studies Program they have created. In Dickinson Hall I received an education, friendship and inspiration from the members of a remarkable History Department. Stephen Kotkin and Gyan Prakash, in particular, have been deeply appreciated companions and critics. At the very end of my research, a grant from the German Academic Exchange Service made a second trip to Germany possible.

First in Princeton, then in Highbury I count myself especially fortunate to have enjoyed the generous and affectionate judgements of Peter Mandler. I am also indebted to John Campbell, Philip Carabott, John Hyman and Rod Kedward each of whom made time to read all or part of the manuscript closely, offering many valuable suggestions. And I would like to thank my youthful great-great-uncle Adam Spiro who told me stories round his kitchen table in Wayne, New Jersey, about his own experiences across wartime Europe which helped to bring the realities of occupation home to me. Bill Hamilton was instrumental in finding the manuscript a home, while Robert Baldock and his colleagues at Yale University Press have been sympathetic and delightful collaborators. My greatest debt of all, however, is to Deb: I dedicate this book to her, *yia panta*. . . .

Abbreviations and Foreign Terms

andarte	resistance fighter
archigos	a political or military leader
ADAP	*Akten zur Deutschen Auswärtigen Politik*
AO	Abwehroffizier – *military counter-intelligence officer*
BA/K	Bundesarchiv, Koblenz
BA-MA	Bundesarchiv – Militärarchiv (Freiburg im Breisgau)
BDC	Berlin Document Centre
BG	Bank of Greece archives
DDI	*Documenti diplomatici italiani*
EA	Ethniki Allilengyi – *National Solidarity*
EAM	Ethniko Apeleftherotiko Metopo – *National Liberation Front*
EASAD	Ethnikos Agrotikos Syndesmos Antikommounistikis Draseos – *National Agricultural Federation of Anti-Communist Action*
EDES	Ethnikos Dimokratikos Ellinikos Syndesmos – *National Republican Greek League*
EEAM	Ethniko Ergatiko Apeleftherotiko Metopo – *National Workers' Liberation Front*
EEE	Ethniki Enosis Ellados – *National Union of Greece*
EK	*Efimeris Kyverniseos* (Athens)
EKKA	Ethniki Kai Koinoniki Apeleftherosi – *National and Social Liberation*
ELAS	Ethnikos Laikos Apeleftherotikos Stratos – *Greek People's Liberation Army*
EOKA	Ethniki Organosi Kyprion Agoniston – *National Organisation of Cypriot Fighters*
EPON	Eniaia Panelladiki Organosi Neon – *United Panhellenic Organisation of Youth*
EV	*Eleftheron Vima*

FO	Foreign Office files (Public Record Office, Kew, London)
GFP	Geheime Feldpolizei – *Secret Field Police*
Gray Coll.	Christ Church Library, Eric Gray Newspaper Collection
HSSPF	Höherer SS-und Polizeiführer – *Higher SS and Police Commander*
IWM	Imperial War Museum (London)
KKE	Kommounistiko Komma Ellados – *Communist Party of Greece*
kafeneion	café
kapetan	the leader of a guerrilla band
laokratia	People's Rule (EAM/ELAS slogan)
macaronades	lit. macaroni-eaters – a wartime Greek term for the Italians
MFA/AD	Ministère des Affaires Etrangères, Archives Diplomatiques (Nantes)
MFA/ASD	Ministero degli Affari Esteri, Archivio Storico Diplomatico (Rome)
NSFO	Nationalsozialisticher Führungsoffizier – *National Socialist Guidance Officer*
OKW	Oberkommando der Wehrmacht – *Armed Forces Supreme Command*
OPLA	Organosi Perifrourisis tou Laikou Agona – *Organisation for the Protection of the People's Struggle*
OSS	Office of Strategic Services
PEEA	Politiki Epitropi Ethnikis Apeleftherosis – *Political Committee for National Liberation*
RG 59	US National Archives, State Dept files
RG 165	US National Archives, US 7th Army files
RG 226	US National Archives, OSS files
RHSA	Reichssicherheitshauptamt – *Reich Security Head Office*
Rochlitz	*The Righteous Enemy: Document Collection* (Rome, 1988)
Säuberungsunternehmen	mopping-up operations
SiPo/SD	Sicherheitspolizei/Sicherheitsdienst – *Security Police/Security Service*
SME US.DS	Stato Maggiore dell'Esercito V Reparto, Ufficio Storico (Rome)
SOE	Special Operations Executive
SSGM	*Actes et documents du Saint Siège relatifs à la seconde guerre mondiale*

StA.	Mussolini Papers (formerly held at St Antony's College, now at Foreign and Commonwealth Office, London)
Sühnemassnahmen	lit. atonement operations – reprisals
USNA	US National Archives (Washington, DC)
WO	War Office files (Public Record Office, Kew, London)
ZSt.	Zentrale Stelle der Landesjustizverwaltungen (Ludwigsburg)
IC	Military Intelligence
IVB4	The RSHA bureau for Jewish affairs

PROLOGUE

'Swastika over the Acropolis'

'What are we waiting for, gathered in the market-place?'

'The barbarians will come today.'

'Why is there no activity in the senate?
Why are the senators seated without legislating?'

'Because the barbarians will come today;
What laws can the senators pass now?
The barbarians, when they come, will make the laws.'

In April 1941, as the Greeks waited nervously for the Germans to arrive, the writer Theotokas recalled these lines of Cavafy in his diary.[1] To the north, the front had collapsed and Greek, British and Australian soldiers, who had been cheered on their way to fight just days earlier, were now returning in retreat down the same dusty roads. The civilians who watched them go past knew that the Wehrmacht was not far behind.

The preceding months had been a time of great euphoria in Greece. Over that winter Mussolini had tried, and failed, to invade the country. The Greek army had pushed back the Italians with astonishing success. Throughout Europe the news spread of this setback to Axis prestige. Even reports that Hitler had decided to come to Mussolini's aid failed to dampen public enthusiasm; in the streets of Athens excited crowds shouted insults against the Axis, while wounded soldiers convalescing in hospital sang the national anthem and demanded to be sent back north to fight.[2]

It took just a few days into the German invasion for the mood to change. Field Marshal List's 12th Army launched its assault at dawn on 6 April. Three days later, German units entered the northern port of Salonika. As the Wehrmacht pushed towards Athens, defeat and enemy occupation loomed. On 18 April, in despair at the

1

1.   German troops ask directions from a Greek policeman, Salonika, April 1941.

course of events, the Greek Prime Minister shot himself. The country remained leaderless while the King, the politicians and the generals squabbled over his successor. Wealthy families with good connections weighed up whether to leave the country. The German airforce intensified its attacks on ports and cities. People fled the towns for the hills.

Through the second and third weeks of April, the front moved southwards across the country. Greek and Allied forces fell back before the last successful blitzkrieg of the Second World War. In the port of Patras, exhausted Yugoslav officers arrived with news of the sudden defeat their own country had suffered days earlier. Stukas screamed in periodically to attack the docks, destroying caiques, ferries and steamers. Afterwards, shoals of dead fish were left floating belly up in the harbour.

Like many other towns, Patras was devastated by the continuous bombing. Its scared inhabitants took refuge inside the bomb shelters, newly equipped with icons and incense. Food prices soared, for peasants no longer entered the town to sell their produce. Following a bombing raid on 23 April, shops and tavernas remained closed. Xavier Lecureul, the French consul, grew used to a spartan diet of bread, oranges and dried figs: even eggs became a luxury. Patras, he wrote, was virtually abandoned; it had become 'a lugubrious cemetery . . . I remain one of the few inhabitants of a strange town where the least noise provokes terror.' Military discipline began to break down. Small groups of British soldiers from the 14th Hussars nervously patrolled the deserted streets. Greek troops from the local barracks refused to obey orders to march off to prepare new defences in Corinth. Senior officers issued leave-permits to their men so that they could return home.[3]

There must have been many people who longed for this ordeal to be over, who were growing impatient for order to be restored and even perhaps for a first glimpse of the conqueror. 'In truth,' wrote the novelist George Theotokas, 'we have reached the point of hoping that they will come as soon as possible to free us from our waiting.'[4] And unlike Cavafy's barbarians, of course, eventually 'they' did.

On Saturday, 26 April 1941 there was a bombing raid at 2.10 in the afternoon; around 5 p.m. the last Greek lorries rumbled south to join the retreating forces; at 6.45 the final British convoy drove out of the town, firing into the air in a farewell salute. For just half an hour, the town square stood deserted in the evening sun. Then the first German officers made their appearance, followed a little later by a motorcycle with two camouflaged junior officers in a sidecar. 'A poignant sadness completely possessed the town,' wrote Lecureul, who watched the scene from his window, 'and the few people who were about did not realise exactly what was happening.'[5]

Next morning Patras's occupation began in earnest. Detachments of the Leibstandarte Adolf Hitler marched into the town. The elite SS troops made a frightening impression on bystanders: 'The men in helmets and carrying over their uniform light camouflage tunics, green, brown and black, armed to the teeth. Marching with a heavy but quick step, human "robots" forming two rectangles of iron, they give an impression of invincible force.' The city now filled up with army cars, trucks and motorcycles, whose din ended the nervy silence of the previous days. 'From now on there will be a continual racket from these noisy machines. The occupation goes on, and becomes organised,' Lecureul wrote.[6]

In the hamlets, islands and valleys which lay outside the combat zone, the occupation arrived less obtrusively. The island of Syros surrendered after a brief bombardment from the air: three Austrian soldiers and a junior officer rowed into the harbour and raised the swastika at the entrance to the port. A couple of friendly locals came to the quay to offer them the use of one of the island's few cars.[7] Not until the evening of 2 May did German troops on the SS

Norburg, escorted by two Italian destroyers, reach Chios. The Greek administration there decided, after some argument, that it would be futile to put up any resistance. The island's prefect, Themistokles Athanasiades, and the military commander waited at the quayside near the Moschouri coffee-house for Major Winkler, the German battalion commander, to disembark.[8]

In Athens itself, rumours had reached fever pitch thanks to a secret German transmitter, 'Fatherland', which had started up on 18 April. 'Athenians! Don't drink the water! Death awaits you!' it warned, accusing the British of having poisoned the Marathon reservoir with typhoid baccili. 'Fatherland' spread many other scare stories, and called on the capital's inhabitants to loot the food stores.[9]

As German bombers roared overhead to attack Piraeus harbour, the Athenians became desperate for news of the German advance. Unsure how close the Germans were, they saw them everywhere. On the city outskirts, a priest carrying an umbrella had a narrow escape from angry farmers and conscripts who took him for a lone German parachutist. Any information brought by refugees from the north was eagerly devoured. 'They all asked us: "Will the front hold?"; "Where's the front now, where's the attack?"' recalled one teenage Red Cross nurse, in the capital for the first time in her life. The spirit of solidarity which had appeared so suddenly at the time of the Italian invasion vanished again as the end approached. Panic buying left the shops empty of food. The banks were surrounded by crowds hoping to withdraw their savings. 'The transitory nature of these last days,' wrote one Athenian, 'when one lot are already gone and the others not yet here is pitiful for everyone. . . . We are on the verge of anarchy.'[10]

At 8.10 a.m. on 27 April, with the sun already up, an advance group of two armoured cars of the 6th Armoured Division entered the capital from the north. They were followed by a long line of tanks, motorbikes and cars, driving in single file down Vasilissas Sofias Avenue towards the centre of town. Keeping off the main streets, which were patrolled by the city police, the curious Athenians clustered in the side roads and stood at their windows. Walking down Akadimias Street in the morning sunshine, the writer Theotokas noticed a swastika hanging ostentatiously from one of the houses. On Stadion Street pedestrians ignored the efforts of the Greek police to disperse them. From the balcony of his office opposite the Hotel Splendid the young lawyer Christos Christides saw the onlookers standing on the pavement and the balconies watching the occasional German motorbike with its red pennant pass down the empty boulevard. One came from Syntagma Square

2.   The first German troops enter Athens, 27 April 1941.

in the direction of Omonia; it stopped in front of the Parliament building and turned around. 'Looks like he's lost,' quipped an onlooker. 'He must be looking for something.' 'He's after a taverna.' The jokes ran along the balconies. But then a column of thirty motorbikes, with a car at their head, approached and came to a halt. Faces vanished behind their shutters.[11]

Passing the Wehrmacht column in the other direction, on their way to a rendezvous with the German commander, General von Stumme, were the mayors of Athens and Piraeus, the prefect of Attica, and the commander of the Greek army garrison in Athens. At 10.45 they met von Stumme at the 'Parthenon' coffee-house in a northern suburb of the city and officially handed over the city. The national anthem which Athens radio had been broadcasting was interrupted and a German officer proclaimed the capture of Athens in Hitler's name. It was, wrote Theotokas, 'as if time had been cut with a knife. Here ends a chapter of our lives.'[12]

*

For others, however, a new, exciting life seemed about to begin. Landesgruppenleiter Walter Wrede was a lanky forty-one-year-old

5

3. German tanks parked beneath the Acropolis, April 1941.

archaeologist and head of the Nazi party organisation in Athens. He
and other members of the city's German community had taken
refuge in the German Archaeological School from the upsurge of
anti-German feeling of the previous weeks. 'The Greek press has
devoted itself since 6 April to the rudest insults against Germany.
The Führer, *Volk* and Army are most evilly mocked,' he had noted
in his diary. 'People call us Huns and barbarians.' On 18 April he
wrote: 'The night was deathly quiet. Hardly any cars about. . . .
The streets heavily patrolled by police detachments. In our house
too the watch was strengthened. By day only a few Germans
go out to reconnoitre. The disturbances begin around evening.
The loudest din comes from the direction of Omonia Square.
Twice groups of 30–40 drunken youths come our way singing
anti-Mussolini songs and shouting: "Down with the 5th Column!"
The police tell us to stay calm; we needn't get alarmed, they're only
singing patriotic songs.'[13]

For Wrede and his companions, Sunday the 27th was a day of
fulfilment and jubilation:

A police official comes to the door at 9.30 and tells us that
German troops are making their way to the Acropolis. There

4. Field Marshal von Brauchitsch (on the left) and his entourage visit the Acropolis, May 1941.

they will hoist the German flag. I spring to our lookout post on the upper floor. Correct! From the mast of the Belvedere of the city shines the red of the Reich's flag! The cry: 'Swastika over the Acropolis!' rings through the house. In a few minutes we are all gathered together to give thanks to the Führer. The national anthem carries through the now open windows into the streets outside. The front door stands wide open. Flowers and cigarettes are quickly found, and thus prepared we stand at the windows waiting for the first German soldiers. There is not long to wait. One of the legation cars draws up and four or five *Gebirgsjäger*, unshaven, sunburnt, dirty but beaming, jump out into a hail of flowers and cigarettes.

For Wrede there now began a period of hectic activity. He rushed to and fro across Athens, greeting newly arrived officers, helping out at talks with the Mayor, Plytas. He organised the local party members, and assigned Hitler Youth boys and girls to guide the tired and dusty troops to their quarters. Even his professional skills were drawn upon, when he was summoned to guide Field Marshal von Brauchitsch around the Parthenon.[14]

7

A year later a photograph of the two men would appear in a book commemorating the Balkan campaigns: it showed the Wehrmacht Field Marshal and the Nazi archaeologist as they strolled around the ruins of the Acropolis in the strong sunlight of a Greek spring morning, savouring that moment of triumph when the representatives of the Third Reich – Army and Party together – took possession of what Hitler himself called the symbol of 'human culture'.[15]

PART I

The Chaos of the New Order: 1941–43

In all the occupied territories I see the people living there stuffed full of food, while our own people are going hungry. For God's sake, you haven't been sent there to work for the well-being of the peoples entrusted to you, but to get hold of as much as you can so that the German people can live. I expect you to devote your energies to that. This continual concern for the aliens must come to an end once and for all. . . . I could not care less when you say that people under your administration are dying of hunger. Let them perish so long as no German starves.
Goering to Reich Commissioners and Military
Commanders of the occupied territories, 6 August 1942

CHAPTER ONE

Venizelos's Funeral

In April 1936, thousands of mourners packed into the narrow streets of the old port of Chania for the funeral of the great statesman Eleftherios Venizelos. They knew they were witnessing the end of an era in Greece's history. From Paris, where he had died in exile, his body had travelled by train through Italy, and then home to Crete on the ship which was now moored by the quay. His coffin was carried through the weeping crowds by tall, elderly mountaineers, former guerrillas who had fought with him at the turn of the century to liberate Crete from the Ottoman empire.

In his time Venizelos had gained a worldwide reputation. His skilful statesmanship earned Greece not only Crete and islands in the eastern Aegean but also vast territories in the north – Epiros, the port of Salonika, the wheat plains of Macedonia, and rich tobacco lands in Thrace. All these formed part of Greece's imperial dream, the Great Idea of a fantasy kingdom extending to Constantinople itself. In the century since the small country had won independence in 1830, most politicians had talked of little else. After he arrived in Athens from Crete in 1909 Venizelos made much of the dream a reality. But in 1922, as Constantinople seemed within their grasp, the Greeks fell at the final hurdle. A Turkish army officer, Mustafa Kemal – later known as Ataturk – inflicted a shock defeat on the Greek expeditionary force in Anatolia. Greek troops retreated across the Aegean, followed by hundreds of thousands of refugees, members of the Greek communities of Asia Minor who had been uprooted by the demands of an aggressively nationalistic world. In Greece people referred to these events simply as 'the Disaster'.

The Disaster cast its shadow over the entire interwar period. Robbed of the imperial, nationalist mission which they had been taught at school and fought for, many Greeks felt humiliated and unsure of what the postwar world held in store for their country. The poet Palamas gave up his stirring national epics and retreated into a melancholy, often nostalgic, quieter world of private emotions; his successors were men like the restless Kazantzakis, who roamed vaguely between Buddhism, Nietzsche and Marxism, moving away from the nationalistic certainties of the past. Karyotakis, a younger writer, suspicious of all rhetoric and bombast, encapsulated the mood of disillusionment with uneasy brief satires of provincial Greek life before committing suicide at the age of twenty-eight.

Like everything else, politics fell under the Disaster's shadow, splitting the country in two. The new territories and the Asia Minor refugees were staunch supporters of Venizelos. It was his eloquence and vigour, they argued, which were responsible for the lands Greece had won; to his absence in the crucial years 1921–22 they attributed the defeat in Asia Minor. They called him Leader of the Nation, the One, Our Father, and worshipped him with messianic zeal. But in the Peloponnese and Attica, the nineteenth-century heart of the kingdom, the white-bearded and dapper Cretan was regarded as nothing less than the embodiment of Satan himself. He had schemed against the monarchy during the First World War, and it was his over-ambition which had been responsible for the Disaster, for the masses of wretched, barefoot, politically suspect refugees in their shanty towns, who had destroyed the 'poetic calm' of prewar Athens, crowding the pavements with their wares.

In the cafés and the political salons of Athens talk would always come back to this one theme: who was to blame for the Disaster? Venizelos himself was one of the very few politicians able to escape from the cul-de-sac of nostalgia and recrimination into more constructive avenues. He knew that with further territorial expansion out of the question, the Greeks needed to concentrate their energies on other matters, cultivating practical rather than martial virtues, pursuing above all the social and economic reform of their existing institutions. Their roads were the worst in Europe, their fields cultivated in medieval fashion without fertilisers or machinery; in the workshops which made up most of Greece's primitive industry ten-year-olds worked underground twelve or fourteen hours a day. Patching up relations with Turkey, Venizelos devoted himself to the task of reconstruction. His Liberal Party supervised a sweeping land reform which turned Greece into a country of smallholders, and encouraged foreigners to invest in public works and industry. In four years, he promised the electorate in 1928, he would make Greece 'unrecognisable' and turn its corrupt, creaking and vastly over-manned bureaucracy into the motor of a modern state.

It was not to be: the world depression put an end to Greece's economic reconstruction, and in 1932 forced Venizelos to resign. His efforts to keep Greece on the gold standard pushed the economy into recession and alienated many of his poorer supporters. When he eventually lost his self-proclaimed 'battle for the drachma', and devalued the currency, his credibility suffered a further blow. His supporters reacted nervously to opposition after a decade in power, while his royalist opponents took over a republic whose legitimacy they questioned.

In Parliament the constitutional issue remained the axis around which all else revolved. But while the political world of Athens discussed whether King George, exiled since 1923, should be allowed to return, it paid little attention to the acute social and economic crisis that gripped the country. In the Peloponnese, currant growers were rioting, tearing up rail tracks and burning public buildings, in protest at the lack of state support. Industrial action swept the country from Kalamata to Kavalla. The usual response from Athens was to declare martial law and send in the troops.

In 1935 Venizelos tried to lead a pre-emptive republican putsch against the royalists. It was an ill-prepared and shortsighted débâcle which the government managed to suppress. Venizelos and other leading republicans fled into exile abroad; their supporters were purged from the armed forces. The end result was the opposite of what Venizelos had intended. Royalism was now triumphant; at the end of the year King George was invited back and the republic was abolished.

This was the point at which the whole constitutional issue began to be overshadowed by the country's social problems. Now in exile, a tired Venizelos appealed to his supporters to accept the King. Parties which had identified themselves in terms of the republican–royalist vendetta broke up into squabbling factions, as the vendetta lost its meaning. Both sides increasingly saw their task as defending what they called the 'bourgeois status quo'. As the Greek Left grew in strength, republicans and royalists alike were attracted to anti-communism as a new rallying cry. Many began to question the value of parliamentary democracy itself, and gazed admiringly at Nazi Germany and Mussolini's Italy.

King George himself was certainly not a committed democrat, and he had grave doubts about the abilities of the politicians he was forced to work with. In April 1936, following a period of parliamentary deadlock, he chose the loyal General Ioannis Metaxas, a veteran royalist, as caretaker Prime Minister. Metaxas had been a brilliant staff officer during the First World War, and one of the few men to argue against the Asia Minor campaign on military grounds. He had then led a small nationalist party through the years of the republic, and had become increasingly contemptuous of parliamentary democracy. Metaxas's Interior Minister was actually a well-known admirer of the Third Reich. That spring the new government clamped down on industrial unrest with unprecedented harshness. Faced with the threat of a general strike in August 1936, Metaxas declared martial law, inaugurating a regime which would last until his death on the eve of the invasion in 1941. King George himself had paved the way for this course by giving Metaxas permission to suspend Parliament indefinitely.

In the dictatorship of the Third Hellenic Civilisation (1936–41), the First Peasant and First Worker (as the stocky General liked to be known) introduced Greece to such totalitarian phenomena as fascistic salutes, a national youth movement and a vigilant and brutal security service; but there was one notable absence: Metaxas had no mass party along the lines of the Italian Fascists or the National Socialists in Germany. His power base remained small, linked uneasily to his relationship with the King. Far from being a genuine *mass* movement of the Right, Metaxas's 4 August regime was deeply conservative, a last means of controlling the urban masses in a country with no tradition of mass politics. If social discontent could not be dispelled by the charisma of a Venizelos, or by legislative reform, it would have to be curbed by force. For almost five years this strategy seemed to be working, for there was little overt opposition to the dictatorship. But in retrospect, Metaxas's regime was little more than a holding action – postponing more enduring solutions to Greece's problems. In January 1941, three months before the German invasion, Metaxas died. Occupation would magnify existing social and economic strains and bring to the surface popular demands for a fundamental reshaping of Greece's political system.

CHAPTER TWO

The Occupation Begins

Hitler did not really want to invade Greece. He attributed the defeat of the Central Powers in the First World War at least in part to Balkan entanglements, and hardly wished to divert troops to a risky sideshow during the build-up to the invasion of Russia. Through trade, the Third Reich held south-eastern Europe in a powerful embrace, and there seemed little reason to add the burdens of military occupation. Yet ironically, it was Hitler's own actions which led to the German intervention in Greece.

In the late summer of 1940, the Romanians had agreed to let German soldiers, unconvincingly masquerading as 'advisers', into the vital Ploesti oilfields. For Mussolini this was a further sign of a dangerous expansion of German influence into south-eastern Europe, and he decided, in a fit of anger, to launch the invasion of Greece. But what had begun as an assertion of Italian independence quickly turned into a humiliating check to the Axis as Greek forces held the Italians on the Pindos mountains and even pushed them back into Albania. To Hitler it was unthinkable that he could allow his partner to be defeated, and he decided to come to Mussolini's aid. In December 1940 he issued the orders for Operation Marita, by which German troops would attack Greece from across the Bulgarian border.

The Greeks had no illusions about their chances against the Wehrmacht. Old and sick as he was, Metaxas desperately tried to convince Berlin that the Greeks had not wanted a conflict with Italy, and that the country would remain neutral in the larger international struggle. He hoped that instead of attacking Greece, the Germans might mediate with the Italians to end the hostilities in Albania. Thus he permitted discreet approaches to be made to Berlin through the German military attaché in Athens. At the same time, several of his political rivals also tried secretly convincing the Germans that their leadership would ensure a benevolently pro-Axis neutrality.[1]

Greece's generals, too, wanted to avoid hostilities with Germany, and in the weeks before the invasion, King George was forced to dismiss several of them for defeatism. Among their approaches, one in particular acquires significance in the light of later events. On 12 March the German consul in Salonika informed his superiors that he had been approached by a Colonel Petinis seeking his help in ending hostilities in Albania. The consul noted that Petinis was not acting alone: behind him was believed to be a certain General Tsolakoglu, a close associate of one of the generals the King had dismissed.[2]

When the Wehrmacht launched its attack on Greece on 6 April, Tsolakoglu was commander of 3 Army Corps in the Greek Army of Western Macedonia. His men were caught between the Italians on the Albanian front to the north-west, and the Germans advancing rapidly from the north-east. By 20 April their position was hopeless. Field Marshal List had sent the Leibstandarte Adolf Hitler south-west over the thinly defended Metsovo Pass. Racing forward to beat the Greek troops that were being rushed up as reinforcements, the Leibstandarte reached the vital northern town of Jannina on the morning of 20 April, Hitler's birthday. So fast was their advance that the British were still sending messages to the Greek staff there, only to receive the reply: 'Hier ist das deutsche Heer' (This is the German Army).[3]

Next day, General Tsolakoglu capitulated to the Germans, apparently on his own initiative. His communications with the general staff in Athens were constantly interrupted, and he appears to have hoped that by reaching an agreement with List he could hold the line against the detested Italians in Albania. At first he was not disappointed, for List agreed that the Italian forces should not be allowed south across the border into Greece. Some detachments of the Leibstandarte, impressed by the brave performance of the Greek army, went so far as to block the Italians by stationing themselves between Greek and Italian units at a border crossing called Ponte Berati.

But to the Italians these developments came as an unwelcome and most humiliating blow, for Mussolini had been desperately anxious to beat the Greeks before the Wehrmacht arrived. As news of the terms of the Greek capitulation came through, he was enraged. He warned the German military attaché in Rome that he would observe a ceasefire only if the Greeks came to terms with the Italians too. Otherwise the 'perfidious' Greeks would later boast – as, quite justifiably, they indeed did – that they had not been beaten by the Italians. On learning that List had negotiated a surrender, not just a ceasefire, the Duce became even more incensed. Rintelen, the German attaché, drily reported their exchange: 'He alone had been

5. General Tsolakoglu signs the final surrender document in Salonika, 23 April 1941.

ready for the Greeks. If 500,000 hadn't done it, he'd have sent a million. He regarded it as impossible to accept that the Greek surrender was a result of the German attack. I assured the Duce that this was certainly not the German view, nor no doubt that of the Greeks either.'[4]

Most reluctantly Hitler decided to help Mussolini once again, even though this meant publicly humiliating List and the other Wehrmacht officers who had negotiated the original terms with Tsolakoglu. On 23 April, with the Italians present, a second surrender document was signed. In a feeble effort to exploit the propaganda potential of the occasion, Mussolini decided to anticipate the agreed public announcement of the surrender by broadcasting the news earlier that morning. According to Italian radio, the surrender had been tendered to 'the commander of the Italian Eleventh Army' and details would be worked out together with 'our German allies'.[5]

This broadcast further embittered relations between the two Axis armies. The Wehrmacht now felt utter contempt for their allies. The Italians were 'just like children, wanting to gobble up everything', observed Field Marshal Keitel. And when men of the Leibstandarte marched past some Italian women outside Patras, the soldiers responded to their greetings with shouts of 'Brutta Italia! Heil Hitler!'[6]

*

It soon emerged that Mussolini had launched the invasion of Greece without any precise war aims at all. On 21 April his Foreign Minister told the Germans vaguely that he thought the Duce's demands would eventually include the annexation of territories in northern Greece and the Ionian islands. But as the Italian army had already found to its cost, much of this proposed new Roman empire in Greece consisted of poor upland villages linked by mule tracks and snowbound paths. Such goals made little strategic or political sense. No Greek government could have handed these territories over and retained a shred of credibility. Suspecting that his country's ill-prepared claims would not receive a sympathetic hearing from their Axis partner, the Italian military attaché in Berlin actually urged Rome to 'accelerate our occupation even by sea to forestall the German troops'.[7]

At the second surrender negotiations in Salonika, the Germans brought the Italians down to earth. Benzler, the chief Foreign Office delegate with List's 12th Army, wanted the whole question of Italian territorial claims shelved until after the war. The task of the Italian delegation, he stated bluntly, was simply to help form a new Greek government to serve the Axis in the wartime administration of the country. Anfuso, his Italian counterpart, floated the idea of inserting a clause in the surrender protocol mentioning future territorial adjustments. Benzler's response was firm: they should not frighten General Tsolakoglu with such formulae. All Anfuso could do was to respond weakly that given the 'total defeat' Greece had now suffered, he would have preferred a 'pure and simple' occupation, as had occurred in Poland.[8]

But Greece and Poland were very different cases so far as the Germans were concerned. Greece was less important strategically, less contemptible racially. From Hitler downwards there was nothing but admiration on the German side for the way the Greeks had fought. The Germans had no long-term plans for the country, and Hitler had already decided that a domestic puppet regime would be the least expensive drain on German energies and resources as the invasion of the Soviet Union came closer. The day after Anfuso and Benzler's conversation, the establishment of a government under General Tsolakoglu was officially announced.

On 26 April Tsolakoglu proclaimed his readiness to serve the

'Führer of the German People'; a government that he headed, he assured the Germans, would be supported by all the senior generals of the Greek army. Such an offer, made even before Athens had fallen and while Greek and Commonwealth troops were still fighting their way southwards through the Peloponnese, struck Hitler as 'a gift from heaven'.[9] It was not as though the Führer had many other options. The official government and the King were barely an hour away on Crete, and in Athens most influential politicians were biding their time before committing themselves. Detached from active politics by the Metaxas dictatorship, they hardly wished to make their re-entry into public life at such a moment.

Before the war, Tsolakoglu's career had been respectable but undistinguished; nothing in his background had equipped him for the responsibilities he now took on. As though to emphasise the narrowness of his political vision, his initial Cabinet contained no fewer than six other, equally inexperienced generals. The civilian ministers too were an unimpressive group – among them a professor of medicine, Constantine Logothetopoulos, whose main qualification for office seemed to be that he was married to the niece of Field Marshal List, and Platon Hadzimikalis, an obscure merchant with German business connections, whose wife eventually left him in disgust at his political activities.[10]

'The business of rebuilding the Greek government,' reported Benzler on 29 April, 'has been very difficult up till now, because it is very difficult to persuade qualified civilians to participate in any form.' Archbishop Chrysanthos gave the lead by refusing to swear in the new government. A number of possible candidates declined to take office because they suspected that Germany was about to withdraw from Greece, leaving them under the thumb of their despised enemies. 'What emerges from all my conversations,' wrote Benzler, 'is how deeply the Greeks hate the Italians.'[11]

From the start Tsolakoglu was boxed in by the Italian question. 'We are known to you,' ran his first proclamation to the Greek public, 'as soldiers and patriots.' But service under Italian authority undermined his claims to patriotism. Less than a week after joining the government, his civilian ministers were already threatening to resign if the Italians took over. Tsolakoglu himself warned of a breakdown in law and order if the Italians came in and started behaving 'like tyrants'.[12]

The philhellenic German military attaché in Athens advised that Greece could be held by minimal German forces provided there was no occupation by Italian troops. Altenburg, heading the German diplomatic team, confirmed that handing Greece over to the Italians would be viewed as a 'moral and political defeat' for the Germans and would turn Greek public opinion against them. Desperately Tsolakoglu tried to persuade Hitler that such a move would 'completely undermine the authority of the Greek government'.[13]

Hitler, however, ignored all these warnings. He wanted to transfer German troops northwards as fast as possible, and on 13 May, before the battle for Crete, he announced his intention of leaving the country to the protection of the Italians. The Germans were not to succumb to the temptation of acting as intermediaries between the Greeks and the Italians: 'It is none of our business whether the Italian occupation troops can cope with the Greek government or not,' insisted the Führer: it was the German–Italian relationship that was of paramount importance.[14]

After failing to drive a wedge between Rome and Berlin, Tsolakoglu fell into line, dutifully submitting ministerial nominations to both the German and Italian plenipotentiaries for their approval. Suspicious of the Greeks' capacity for making trouble, the Axis decided to withhold international recognition from the new regime, which remained without a Foreign Minister for its entire lifetime. The government itself was racked by internal disputes and held in low esteem by the Greek public, especially after the Italians replaced the Germans throughout much of the country in June.

Yet was this not – in a way – the outcome the Axis sought? The German Foreign Office observed that replacing Tsolakoglu with 'more energetic' persons might create more problems than it solved. In their eyes, the sole function of the new government was to keep the administration of the country going in accordance with Axis wishes. Events soon demonstrated, however, that the government's very weakness would prevent it from carrying out that task.[15]

*

The first devastating blow to Tsolakoglu's credibility came when the fertile regions of eastern Macedonia and western Thrace were occupied by Bulgaria, Hitler's ally. This humiliation at the hands of the hated Bulgarians affronted the nationalist sentiments of every Greek, especially as in an early example of 'ethnic cleansing' the Bulgarian authorities immediately began to drive out the Greek inhabitants amid scenes of great brutality, and encouraged Bulgarian settlers to move in. Over 100,000 Greek refugees fled westward from the Bulgarian zone.

Nor was Tsolakoglu's authority bolstered by the way the rest of the country was also divided up, provisionally, into a patchwork of areas under German and Italian control. The Germans retained a few strategically important zones – Crete, Piraeus, Salonika and its Macedonian hinterland, the border strip with Turkey, the islands of

Zones of Occupation in Greece, 1941

Lemnos, Lesbos and Chios – and granted the Italians so-called 'predominance' throughout the rest of the mainland, as well as in the Ionian islands and the Cyclades. During May and June Italian units replaced Germans in these areas to the undisguised dismay of the Greek inhabitants. In the Ionian islands, and on Samos, where the Italians appointed a civilian governor, it looked as though the Italians, like the Bulgarians, might try to annex Greek territory. But no formal announcement of annexation was ever made, and both territories remained in communication with Athens.

Needless to say, the new Greek government was kept under strict Axis control. The two Axis plenipotentiaries, Günther Altenburg and Pellegrino Ghigi, who had the power to recommend the appointment and dismissal of Greek officials, were the key civilian figures in shaping Axis policy towards Greece. At the same time, neither man could ignore the interests of the substantial German and Italian armed forces in the country, since the exorbitant occupation costs demanded by the latter were to become perhaps the most bitterly disputed political issue facing the civil authorities. In practice, no rigid distinction between the civil and military spheres of administration was really possible. Worse still, not even the military spoke with one voice, for while the commander of the Italian 11th Army held supreme military authority in the Italian zone, his counterpart, the commander of the German 12th Army, was responsible for the area around Salonika, while 'Fortress Crete' was administered quite separately.

The stage was set for bureaucratic infighting of Byzantine complexity: Italians pitted against Germans, diplomats against generals, the Greeks trying to play one master off against the other. Even in the Third Reich the realities of National Socialist administration were far removed from the smooth efficiency implied by the Führer principle; in Greece, the New Order had brought nothing less than administrative chaos.

While Ghigi and Altenburg saw the need to re-establish the Greek government's jurisdiction in some form over the entire country, if law and order were to be maintained, the priorities of the Axis military were local rather than national, and involved above all taking whatever measures were required to feed their troops. The combination of military requisitioning on a large scale, the exaggerated but widely believed rumours that ran swiftly though the villages of still worse pillaging to come, and the economic disruption which the war had already brought to Greece turned administrative chaos into economic catastrophe; in a matter of months, Athens was to endure the worst scenes of starvation seen in occupied Europe outside the concentration camps.

CHAPTER THREE

The Famine

Plunder and the Collapse of the Market

'I wish to digress to ask you to recall how a prosperous and industrious city, almost . . . without physical change, has become the abode of hordes of destitute, starving people,' wrote Burton Berry, an American diplomat from the Athens legation. 'Of course the answer is the German army of occupation.'[16]

The troops appeared undernourished, tired and even 'half-starved' when they first arrived. Though the occupation itself proceeded with little violence, the soldiers took food and requisitioned what they liked. 'The Germans have been living off the country,' wrote an informant who left in July, 'They brought no food for the troops with them and no soldiers' messes; the troops simply ate in restaurants. The troops were not in camps, to avoid bombing, but in private houses. Many were thoroughly looted.' German soldiers reportedly stopped passers-by in Omonia Square to demand watches and jewellery. A Greek harbour official returned to his office a few weeks after the occupation had begun to find that 'there is nothing left of my old office. Everything which could be of use to the German authorities, desks, chairs, safe etc. has been taken off by them. The rest has been destroyed or used as firewood.'[17]

By the time the Wehrmacht entered Greece, a string of victories across Europe had given the troops a sense of almost superhuman invincibility. Their behaviour fascinated one young American in Athens. He wrote that morale and discipline had been replaced by 'a corporate realisation of power which runs through the German army from generals to privates. They all appear to have a mass sense of undeviating strength (with almost sadistic overtones) which creates a psychology difficult for outsiders to understand.' The musicologist Minos Dounias was simply shocked: 'Where is the traditional German sense of honour? I lived in Germany thirteen years and no one cheated me. Now suddenly with the New Order they have all become thieves. They empty houses of whatever meets their eye. In Pistolakis' house they took the pillow-slips and grabbed the Cretan heirlooms from the valuable collection they have. From the poor houses in the area they seized sheets and blankets. From other neighbourhoods they grab oil paintings and even the metal knobs from the doors.'[18]

Strong criticism of the Wehrmacht was also coming from internal German sources. On 25 May, plenipotentiary Altenburg warned Berlin in alarm of the 'catastrophic supply situation' in Greece, and advised that the army should be bringing food into the country rather than taking it out.[19] He was backed up by an Abwehr report which drew an unflattering contrast between the British, who had distributed food stocks to the Greeks before their retreat, the Italians, who were apparently distributing pasta and oil, and the Wehrmacht which was busy confiscating all means of transport as well as food. 'Because German troops had to keep themselves alive off the land during their rapid march into the country,' the report concluded, 'They should use [their reserves] to compensate the inhabitants.'[20]

However, alongside plundering by individual soldiers, supply officers were requisitioning much larger quantities of goods: 25,000 oranges, 4,500 lemons and 100,000 cigarettes were shipped off Chios within three weeks of occupation. The steamer *Pierre Luigi*, which left Piraeus in June, carried a typical cargo – hundreds of bales of cotton goods, jute, and sole leather which had been seized from Greek warehouses to be shipped north on behalf of the Wehrmacht High Command. Army officers also seized available stocks of currants, figs, rice and olive oil.[21] James Schafer, an American oil executive working in Greece, summed it up: 'The Germans are looting for all they are worth, both openly and by forcing the Greeks to sell for worthless paper marks, issued locally.'[22]

Reflecting the high degree of planning behind these policies, businessmen, often with Balkan expertise, were seconded to the Economics Staff of the Wehrmacht High Command from firms such as Krupps and I.G. Farben. Sonderführer H. Heine had been seeking access to Balkan chrome supplies on behalf of Krupps before hostilities broke out. Now in Wehrmacht uniform, he marched into the offices of Greek mining concerns and secured several long leases at favourable rates. Another Krupps employee drew up the contracts. 'During the period 1–10 May 1941 in Athens,' he reported with satisfaction, 'the entire output of Greek mines of pyrites, iron ore, chrome, nickel, magnesite, manganese, bauxite and gold was obtained for Germany on a long-term basis.'[23]

Members of the Economics Staff handled electricity firms, the Vasileiades shipbuilding works, textile plants and the Bodosakis munitions works. Shell was forced to sell its Greek plant to the Germans after being warned that unless it agreed to the sale it would be charged with sabotage and its property confiscated. Tobacco stocks lying in the warehouses of northern Greece, leathers, cotton cloth and silk cocoons were all confiscated or bought up at prewar prices and sent north to the Reich. The French managing director of the Lavrion silver mines was told by the Germans to hurry up and sign a new contract before the Italians took over![24] Thus in the first weeks of the occupation, assets passed into German hands at an incredible rate. 'After the end of the war,' stated a German Foreign Ministry memorandum, 'the Italians will have to accept the fact that the victory in the Balkans, which was won with German blood, will offer economic benefits to the Reich.'[25]

Naturally, the Italians did not share this view. Spokesmen for Italian business interests in Greece, men like Mussolini's former Finance Minister Count Volpi, were soon *en route* to Athens. On 8 May, which was before the Italian Foreign Ministry had got around to sending a permanent representative to Athens, Volpi arrived with a large entourage to pressure Greek industrialists to deal with him instead of the Germans. The same day, his associates visited the National Bank in Athens to demand blocks of shares in Greek electricity corporations. Their visit coincided with further demands from Walter Deter, of the Wehrmacht Economics Staff (and formerly an employee of Rheinmetall-Borsig), for the Bank's holdings in major industrial concerns.[26]

By late May the race to seize Greece's assets was clearly hurting Axis co-operation and a chill had settled over dealings between the two sides. Foreign Minister Ciano warned that 'this "plundering" by certain private German parties of the principal economic activities of the country we have conquered is certainly not in harmony with the co-operation . . . so vital to each country, which ought to exist between Rome and Berlin'.[27] To avert a more serious deterioration in relations, the Germans relaxed their stance. Generously, they allowed an Italian firm to buy up shares in the Lokris nickel mines – with which it had in fact held an exclusive contract before the war![28] The Axis partners split the country's stocks of leathers between them, whilst cotton, resin and other goods useful to the Italian war effort were shipped across the Adriatic. But German generosity had its limits. Berlin turned a deaf ear to Rome's suggestions that a 'totalitarian solution' to the Greek problem ought to extend Italian control to the Salonika region as well. The Germans had several good reasons to want to stay in Salonika: nearby lay mines, which they hoped might satisfy up to 30 per cent of the Reich's chrome needs, as well as fertile valleys producing wheat, cotton and tobacco.[29]

*

These policies of expropriation and plunder – the reflection of an ultimately self-defeating tendency in Berlin to see the economic benefits of conquest before the political ones – had a catastrophic impact in Greece. The effects were soon visible in the sharp rise in unemployment, and the sudden drop in industrial output, as factories closed for lack of raw materials, or because their equipment and stocks had been sent out of the country. But worst of all was the effect on the supply of food.

In his detailed study of the causes of food scarcity, the economist Amartya Sen has shown that few famines are caused solely by natural disaster. Human actions and social forces – the type of farming system, the structure of the market, popular attitudes to basic rights and the response of officialdom – often determine whether a people will eat or starve. In the Bengal famine of 1943, Sen found that 'powerful inflationary pressures, vigorous speculation and panic hoardings' contributed to the widespread starvation. His analysis showed how a relatively small drop in the size of the harvest turned into an 'exceptional shortfall in market release'. Something similar lay behind the terrible famine that Greece was about to endure.[30]

Because of wartime disruptions, the 1941 harvest of most crops was between 15 and 30 per cent lower than it had been before the war.[31] Even these totals might have ensured the survival of the population at subsistence levels had the state managed to collect, distribute and ration the grain supply. Grain and other foodstuffs needed to be collected from the farmers in surplus regions, transported to the key deficit areas, notably Athens and Piraeus, and distributed through a rationing system there. As Sen remarks, the complexity of such operations, and the challenges they pose a state apparatus, should not be taken for granted; under the strains of occupation, they were to prove beyond the power of the Tsolakoglu regime.

One crucial difficulty was that in Greece grain was not produced on large, accessible farms which local officials could easily control. After the First World War Venizelos's land reform had turned Greece into a nation of smallholders. Grain was grown by thousands of peasant farmers, each of whom normally marketed only a small proportion of his output. Prewar collection policies by the

Greek state had been voluntary, designed to support farm prices, and the availability of grain largely hinged upon the readiness of Greek smallholders to offer their crops for sale. Once they became reluctant to sell, it was costly and difficult for the state to force them.

State collection policies also depended on a stable system of prices. Farmers would sell into 'concentration' as it was known, when state support prices were high relative to those in the free market. Inflation reduced the real value of the support prices and encouraged farmers to sell privately. Hyperinflation made it almost impossible for civil servants to 'concentrate' the country's wheat stocks.

The economic policies which the Axis authorities followed in the first weeks of the occupation threw the prewar collection system into disarray. Both the Wehrmacht and the Italians set up road-blocks, checked warehouses and seized crops for the use of their troops. Such actions, together with the rumours they generated, made farmers hesitate to bring their crops to market, or even to declare the size of harvest they anticipated. At the same time, the requisitioning of pack-animals increased the cost of transporting foodstuffs from farming areas to the towns where they were needed.[32]

Prices rose steadily, fuelled by the money printed to cover the demands of the occupation authorities. Inflation led producers and retailers to withdraw their goods from the market, and hoarding became widespread. Ignoring the official purchase price for wheat set by the authorities in June, farmers sold at double the price or more to the military supply officers and dealers who were touring the countryside. They paid little attention to decrees which ordered them to deliver fixed amounts to the state marketing agency and penalised black market sales with death. The Tsolakoglu government tried sending demobilised army officers out to help collect produce. But these officers often sided with the farmers as they did not believe that the crops would go to feed their fellow-countrymen and suspected that they would be shipped to North Africa for Axis troops instead: sabotaging the government's efforts to collect grain thus became an act of resistance. Shepherds refused to hand over their milk to state authorities at what they regarded as inadequate prices. A provincial daily reported in disgust: 'The [shepherds] regard the milk as theirs to be distributed as they wish. In other words, the shepherds are completely indifferent to any state decree.'[33]

As a result the harvest slipped beyond the reach of the government. In the vital grain-producing areas of Macedonia, where there was intense hostility towards the Athens regime, farmers with 'guns in hand' refused to deliver their crops to the authorities; it was even reported that 'they find a certain complicity in their opposition from the gendarmerie who participate in the gains from black market deals and lose no opportunity to undermine the public authorities supported by the Germans'. Lorries sent out to collect the harvest drove back from the fields around Salonika almost empty, and so dangerous were these trips that the Governor-General of Macedonia exempted civil servants with children from taking part. The overall result was that the government managed to collect barely one-quarter of its grain target.[34]

Transportation and distribution posed further problems for the bureaucrats. Where the Greek Ministry of Supply did succeed in concentrating stocks of vegetables and fruit, it was often unable to find ways of transporting these goods to the towns. Local Italian commanders tried to keep produce in their region. The military commander at Argos and the Italian High Command in Athens clashed in August over efforts to transport soft vegetables and fruit from the fertile Argos plain.[35] The Germans were tougher: there was no question of surplus produce being shipped legally to the Italian zone from the regions under their control. Consequently Athens was almost entirely deprived of the excellent olive oil harvest that year on Crete and Mytilene.[36] Nor could the traditional wheat surplus from Macedonia be moved south. Greece was disintegrating into a patchwork of isolated regional units. The various provinces – as an Italian administrator put it – had become 'stagnant compartments, with no logical relationship to the geographical, economic and demographic situation of the country'.[37]

In Athens itself, the Italians, not wanting to start by creating a bad impression, kept the bread ration high as long as possible. Even so, it fell from its pre-occupation level of over 300 grams daily to under 200 grams by the end of June. Soon there were stretches when no bread was distributed at all, or only on alternate days. Its quality deteriorated as well. By the autumn the ration was dropping fast, and in the middle of November there was only a three-week supply at a ration of less than 100 grams per day.[38]

While the increasingly meagre official rations testified to the public authorities' failure to control the food supply, soup kitchens and other private initiatives tried to provide alternative sources of foodstuffs for the urban population. In Athens and other towns, charitable and religious bodies assisted the refugees, homeless ex-servicemen and unemployed. Wealthy housewives in the port of Volos publicised lists of participants in a scheme to 'adopt' and feed a child from the poor quarters. In Salonika, where Greek soldiers

6. Children wait to be served soup during the famine: Athens, 1941.

had been reduced 'to an indescribable misery', and where numerous
amputees begged in the streets, a soup kitchen was set up by French
nuns based in the city.[39]

But although these voluntary groups showed up the incompetence of the Tsolakoglu administration, their efforts were no
substitute for concerted public action. Unlike the government they
had no fiscal or coercive powers, and they lacked the funds to
purchase food on a large scale. 'No organisation of public assistance
or social welfare,' stated a Red Cross report, 'could have managed
to save all those who suffered from the famine.' In the soup kitchens
of the capital, less than a quarter of the people who needed such

assistance were fed there. The portions served contained minimal nutritional value or fat content.[40]

The other unofficial source of food, of course, was the black market. Though its full significance will be discussed in detail below, we must note at this point simply that the black market spread its benefits unevenly. It worked no better than the soup kitchens for the people who most needed help. Poor families could not afford high prices for food, and lacked assets to sell or exchange. The League of Nations estimated that for the majority of the Greek population the daily calorie intake from all sources, including the black market, was about one-third of standard nutritional requirements. For a large proportion of the working class in Athens it was lower still.[41]

The Diplomacy of Food

To Ghigi and Altenburg, the Axis plenipotentiaries, the army's expropriation policies were evidently contrary to Axis interests as well as morality. The lack of bread had led to riots in Argos, angry demonstrations by housewives in other towns and raised the spectre of a complete collapse of law and order. 'Greece belongs today to the European space controlled by Germany and the Axis Powers,' Altenburg cabled in protest to Berlin. 'It must therefore be brought into the economic planning for this area. Greece must not be allowed to fall into political and military chaos.'[42]

In July Altenburg did succeed in attracting Hitler's attention to the problem. But barely a month into the invasion of the Soviet Union, his supreme gamble, the Führer did not pay much attention to what he must have regarded as a rather marginal matter. He issued vague orders that help should be provided if possible, at least in the zones still occupied by German troops. In Berlin, however, the Ministry of Food and Agriculture was against giving any assistance to Greece at all. The Foreign Ministry tried arguing that the Italians had originally agreed to take responsibility for provisioning Greece. But as Italy had no surplus of its own and was in fact increasingly dependent on German food imports, this stance virtually condemned Greece to starvation.[43]

As the summer ended Italian and German diplomats did draw up a schedule for the monthly provisioning of Greece until the end of June 1942. Once again, however, no grain was to be made available for export from the Reich. The Germans simply agreed to transport 10,000 tons of grain from other occupied regions, so long as the Italians would ship over the same amount. Another 40,000 tons were to be delivered during the last three months of 1941, 15,000 tons in January and February. This grain too was to come, not from the Reich itself, but from Greece's neighbours. Bulgaria was earmarked as the most likely source since she was not at that time supplying Germany. Yet Bulgaria was still an independent state and not one traditionally friendly towards Greece, some of whose northern territories she was currently despoiling. Her government wasted little time in making it quite clear to Berlin that her own food requirements left none over for Greece.

By October, Berlin had evidently lost interest in the Greek food problem. So far as officials in the Ministry of Food were concerned, no grain could be shipped out to Greece without jeopardising Germany's own supply. Ribbentrop at the Foreign Ministry declared that there were no pressing foreign policy reasons to worry about Greece at the Reich's expense. And from Field Marshal Goering's Four-Year Plan Ministry came the *coup de grâce*: if food supplies were to be sent anywhere in occupied Europe, Belgium, Holland and Norway should receive priority over Greece. In the Nazi pecking order she was near the bottom of the list.[44] Meanwhile the Armed Forces Supreme Command announced that the rail line from Salonika to Athens was badly damaged. This meant that trains were subject to long delays and could not be used to carry grain supplies south.[45]

Charting the amount of food the Axis powers actually sent in this period into Greece underlines Berlin's indifference to what was happening. In the period from 15 August to 30 September the Italians sent in 93,000 quintals of grain, most of it to the Ionian islands, Epiros and the Cyclades. This total was not much short of the 100,000 quintals they had pledged to send. The Germans, however, sent only 50,170 quintals before bluntly informing Rome that 'for the future the Italian government must take the responsibility for provisioning Greece, since Greece lies in Italy's sphere of influence'.[46]

The Italians were appalled. They argued that they had fulfilled their side of the bargain, sending grain to the Ionian islands and Epiros; Athens and Piraeus, on the other hand, were within the German zone. They pointed out that although the Wehrmacht had pledged to release all stocks seized after 1 September, it had failed to do this. In the middle of November, as winter approached, an increasingly desperate plenipotentiary Ghigi remarked bitterly that Germany could not continue to be an 'exploiter' of the Greek economy. If Italy was to be made responsible for the overall food supply, then she should have control over *all* parts of the administration, setting advisers in Greek ministries, and building up a government able to take the sweeping and urgent measures now required.[47]

Thus the food issue raised the question of who was actually in charge in Greece. As things stood, the Germans were taking goods out of the country and putting nothing in. When it came to sending food into the country, the Germans left matters to the Italians. As Ghigi observed, this was an arrangement which offered the Germans the benefits but none of the responsibilities of victory. 'The Germans have taken from the Greeks even their shoelaces,' Mussolini complained to Ciano, 'and now they pretend to place the blame for the economic situation on our shoulders.'[48]

Mussolini's verdict might have been more forceful had it not come from the one man whose impulsive actions had led the Axis into Greece in the first place. But his concern was justified. The Reich had obtained the lion's share of the spoils, whilst giving back less than the Italians. This was the logical consequence of policies which aimed to use the resources of occupied Europe to cushion the Master Race from wartime deprivation. In the winter of 1941–42, whilst thousands of people died of starvation in Greece, the level of food consumption in the Reich itself remained virtually the same as it had been before the war.[49]

The Famine in Athens

'One can of course say that the Greek problem is the problem of Athens,' wrote General Geloso, commander of the Italian 11th Army. As wartime food experts observed, it was urban areas which were worst hit by food shortages, and Athens, together with its adjacent port of Piraeus, had housed one-fifth of the country's population before the war. Since then, the city's population had actually increased, perhaps by as many as several hundred thousand with ex-servicemen searching for a way home, refugees from other parts of Greece, and Axis troops. Occupation thus saw the urban population rising at the same time as the availability of food shrank.[50]

In these circumstances, it did not take long to see the spectre of famine on the horizon. One Greek expert was anxious about the supply situation as early as 4 May, just a week after the Germans entered Athens. The combination of plundering and inflation led shopkeepers to withdraw their goods from sale, and encouraged hoarding. By July, queues of 300–400 people stretched outside the diminishing number of shops that still had supplies. The lines for cigarettes were so long that people brought along chairs. The response of Wehrmacht troops was disquieting. 'Germans say: "Oh, you have not seen anything yet; in Poland 600 people die every day from starvation,"' reported a young American, who left on 25 July.[51]

So far as civilians – as well as food – were concerned, all the normal systems of transportation had broken down. To travel from the capital to the Peloponnese required a permit from the *carabinieri* and a booking several days in advance; the journey by train to Salonika took thirty-six hours. The voyage by caique from Piraeus to Chios took fifteen to twenty days, and could only be managed at a price beyond most people's reach. Over the summer people queued for over an hour for trolley rides within Athens; shortage of fuel forced the authorities to cut services, or sometimes to suspend them completely. On 14 July, for example, the musicologist Dounias decided to walk into Athens from his home in the suburbs because each time a bus passed, people were packed inside like 'sardines in a barrel'. Within a few months, all public transport in Athens would have ceased, forcing people to walk to work through the snow.[52]

For some the summer hid these problems and life in the capital retained its charms. Having just described the fall in the bread ration, the absence of oil, butter and soap, the long queues and soaring prices, an American, Mrs Homer Davis, went on to reassure a friend: 'In spite of all this, you would be surprised to see how normal life seems in general. We had lunch at Bessie's just before we left, and everything was as always.' Life for the German colony seemed so promising that its numbers increased as people arrived from the Reich, fleeing the Allied bombing raids. One German woman, the widow of a Greek civil servant, wrote happily to her son:

> Greece has become for me a piece of my fatherland, it is quite incredible how everything has changed. In the big house on Kifissia where Mr Forbes lived, on the Tatoi road, lives a Major with his officers. We became friends and I have them nearly every day at my house. I have three motorcars at my disposition. I live as a little queen. Very respected and beloved, I refresh [sic] myself from the Greek rabble, I live at least in my ambience, among strong men, very well educated, cleanly dressed, with the best manners.[53]

Before long, however, even the privileged and well-connected were feeling anxious. September was very hot and dry. People looked ahead fearfully to the coming winter. From the island of

7. As fuel becomes scarce, the buses run less frequently and become more crowded: Athens, 1941.

Aegina, a Mrs Constantakos reassured her daughter in Zurich that the food situation was better than in the towns, with fish, figs and vegetables available – 'but I predict a tragic winter for the poor and the children in the towns'. Another American, Ralph Kent, suggested that 'there might be something after the style of the French Revolution in Greece, since the poor were literally starving to death'.[54]

For those sections of the urban population who depended on official assistance the outlook was bleak. The trickle of foodstuffs entering Athens over the summer did not give the Ministry of Supply much room for manoeuvre. In addition to bread, it also rationed rice, olive oil and sugar in May. In June there was one distribution of meat, one of rice and one of sugar. In July there were two small rations of meat and one of rice. In August and September no foodstuffs were rationed at all, apart from bread and a small quantity of rice. Thereafter meat became a fond memory, and isolated distributions of olive oil, currants and sugar were all the Ministry of Supply could manage until the following spring.[55]

A world away from the fashionable boulevards of central Athens,

8. Queuing for food: Athens, 1941.

it was the slums on the city's outskirts which bore the brunt of the famine. In the interwar period, shanty towns had sprung up or been constructed at a convenient distance from the heart of the city to house thousands of the refugees who had fled from Asia Minor after the 1922 'Disaster'. Their inhabitants, who had arrived with few personal possessions, lived in shacks made of tin and boards, which were difficult to heat or keep clean. Families of four or five people shared a single room; often, instead of proper plumbing, there were open sewers running behind the muddy alleys. Unlike other Greeks, these newcomers had no family home in the provinces to return to when times were hard. They were the country's first genuine urban proletariat, and they had been badly neglected by the state.

Before the war, they and their children had earned a living in poorly ventilated factories for low wages; others worked as street vendors or domestic servants. When the occupation began, thousands of them lost their jobs as industrial plant and stocks were requisitioned and fuel shortages halted economic activity. Major prewar employers like the textiles and chemicals sectors were forced to reduce output to 10–15 per cent of their usual levels.[56] Desperate to earn money, people turned to peddling goods or begging. At the docks in Piraeus, a crowd of odd-job men occupied the quayside: 'Ex-clerks, workers, chauffeurs and cashiers, whose jobs have been scrapped, have become porters and try to earn their miserable daily bread carrying bags and shopping on carts or on their backs.'[57] Street vendors sold dirty-looking pieces of carob cake, figs and other fruit, or matches, cigarettes, old clothes. Beggars lay on the pavement. In the centre of Omonia Square, stretched out on blankets above the warm air vents of the Metro, there were people of all ages, holding out their hands to passers-by.

There are no official figures for the extent of unemployment in the poorer quarters, but Marcel Junod of the Red Cross reckoned that over half of the working-class population was out of work. Two-thirds of these families were enrolled in local soup kitchens; but they were not fed more than two or three times a week, and even then not all members of the family were catered for. Junod observed that women in particular tended to go without food, to leave some for their children.

For many, the only means of survival was to gather wild grass and other weeds from the countryside around the city. These were then boiled, if there was fuel available, and eaten without oil. But these grasses had virtually no nutritional value: 5 kilos were needed to produce the daily dose of hydrocarbons required by the human body. Children searched through rubbish bins for scraps of food, or waited near the service entrances of large hotels. Others clustered around the doors of restaurants. Some German officers tormented urchins by throwing them scraps from balconies and watching them fight among themselves. Soldiers eating olives in the street attracted a crowd of children. As soon as one spat out an olive stone, the children rushed for it: the fastest would put it in his mouth and suck it clean.[58]

Though malnutrition enfeebled the body and made work increasingly exhausting, working families had little choice if they wished to stay alive but to continue as though nothing was happening. Chrysa P., a widow, went out to work three days a week to earn food for her tubercular children, even though she was ill herself. Gregorios M., who had been laid off work, walked several hours each day into the hills to pick wild plants to bring home. He already showed the oedemas that were signs of severe malnutrition, but he had a mother, wife and child to feed.

To make matters worse, the hot, dry summer was followed by an unusually harsh and prolonged winter: there was snow in the streets of Athens, and at night the temperature fell below freezing.

Because coal and wood had become very expensive, and sometimes unobtainable, houses were not properly heated, and people succumbed to colds, flu and TB. After several weeks of malnutrition, people weakened quickly. Vitamin deficiency caused tumours and boils to appear on their hands and feet, and, unless cured, these spread on to the body and the face. Around half the families in the poor quarters showed these symptoms by the beginning of 1942.

The final stage before death was a state of physical and mental exhaustion. This was the point at which people simply collapsed, and were unable to raise themselves up again. A builder working on a house in the suburb of Psychiko suddenly fainted in the summer heat. A woman, who had been walking with her two undernourished children through central Athens, collapsed in the street, leaving the children to cry. Demobbed Greek servicemen, veterans of the Albanian campaign, lay in doorways or propped against walls. One freezing December evening, a young man collapsed in Skoufas Street. 'Get up! get up or you're done for,' someone said to him. 'My God! Why have you brought me to such a state?' the young man whispered. 'Why am I not at home, instead of crawling like a dog through the streets at night. Why, my God? What did I do to you?' He was a conscript from the island of Zakynthos, one of many who had been unable to return home following the end of the fighting, and now begged in the streets without any government support.[59]

In a shack in the refugee quarter of Dourgouti, forty-year-old Androniki P. lay slumped by the door, covered in an old blanket, having sold the rest of her possessions to buy food. Her husband, who had died several days earlier, lay inside. Her three children sat crying, but she was too weak to help them. In another hut in Ayios Georgios, an unemployed worker lay unable to move, while his children clustered around his bed, asking for bread. Many of the people enrolled in the soup kitchens were too weak to make the journey there. In the working-class district of Dourgouti, which may be regarded as a typical example of the poorest quarters, 1,600 out of the 2,200 families needed urgent medical attention and proper nutrition.[60]

Numbers

Neither national nor municipal mortality statistics are completely reliable. Though the figures obtained by district councils were more conscientiously compiled than national ones, all statistics tend to

9. Outside the National Library a man collapses from hunger and passers-by gather round to help: Athens, 1941.

underestimate the actual rate of mortality – how badly we cannot say – since many deaths were not announced to the authorities. Families dumped the bodies of deceased relatives in the public cemeteries at night so that they could hold on to their ration cards. Sometimes they buried them in hastily dug unmarked graves. The municipal services ended up collecting hundreds of anonymous corpses, and these too did not figure in the official data.

We might take as a minimum figure the official estimate for the Athens–Piraeus conurbation in the year following October 1941, which gave a total of 49,188 deaths, compared with 14,566 deaths the previous year. As an upper limit, we should note the clearly exaggerated reports of Greek and British propagandists, which led the BBC, for example, in April 1942 to cite the figure of 500,000 victims.[61] By keeping in mind these two extremes, and looking at monthly figures at the local level, it is possible to gain a more accurate impression of the famine's scale and duration.

For example, the monthly mortality figures for the Ayios

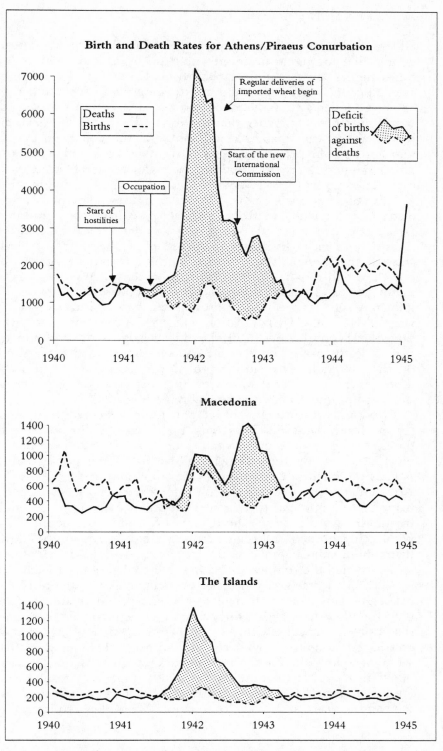

Birth and Death Rates for Athens/Piraeus Conurbation

Deaths ———
Births – – – –

Regular deliveries of imported wheat begin

Start of the new International Commission

Occupation

Start of hostilities

Deficit of births against deaths

Macedonia

The Islands

Source: B. Helger, *Ravitaillement de la Grèce pendant l'occupation 1941–1944 et pendant les cinq mois après la libération* (Athens, 1949), pp.614–15.

Georgios quarter show that in August 1941 the rate was already double that for the same month in 1940; by October it was four times higher and eight times higher in December. In December 1940 40 people were reported dead. In August 1941 the number was 58, in October 123, November 225 and in December 1941 – the worst month – 323. After that the total fell, to 146 in April, and remained between 90 and 120 in the months that followed. In other words, the cold period between November 1941 and April 1942 saw a staggering rise in the death rate which was far in excess of that suggested by the year-on-year figures for the city as a whole.[62]

This conclusion is supported by other figures. Data from certain districts of Piraeus and from hospitals in Athens show mortality rates in the winter of 1941–42 between five and seven times that of the previous year. Estimates published by the Ministry of Health showed that hunger was reported as the direct cause of between one-third and one-half of all deaths. Indirectly it was the cause of many more, as malnutrition increased people's exposure to TB, influenza and other illnesses. From these figures Piraeus, with its largely working-class population, emerges as the worst-hit part of the Athens conurbation. In all, the official estimate of approximately 35,000 deaths from famine in the Athens–Piraeus area appears to be on the low side. The famine probably caused more than 40,000 deaths there in the year following October, in addition to several thousand deaths in the months before October itself.[63]

Two highly disturbing demographic trends emerged from Ministry of Health data. First, 1941 and 1942 were years in which – for the first time since records began – the mortality rate exceeded the birth rate, leaving the city with a sharply falling population. In Athens the birth rate fell from 15 per thousand in 1940 to 12.5 in 1941 and 9.6 in 1942. The death rate rose over the same period from 12 per thousand to 25.8 in 1941 and 39.3 in 1942. A similar trend, though less pronounced, was evident in the country as a whole. In addition, mortality among children rose more slowly than among adults. Junod visited several households in the Piraeus area in which the mother and father had died, leaving the children to fend for themselves. On many occasions this was the result of a deliberate choice by the parents to give their children any food that they found. Adults above forty years old seem to have been most susceptible, particularly males. The famine, in other words, was creating thousands of widows and orphans. Though the effects were complex and took time to work themselves out, it seems likely that the destruction of the family unit as a result of the famine profoundly influenced the response of Greek society over the coming years to the Axis occupation. We will return later to the newly assertive role of teenagers and women as the resistance took shape; but our comments must be largely speculative, for this is a subject on which little has yet been written.[64]

The BBC's figure of 500,000 deaths in the winter of 1941–42 was clearly too high. But the final death toll from hunger throughout the occupation may not have been far short of that number. The Red Cross, which commissioned its own study, estimated that about 250,000 people had died directly or indirectly as a result of the famine between 1941 and 1943. Taking into account the short-fall in the number of births over the same period, it reckoned that the total population of Greece was at least 300,000 less by the end of the war than it would otherwise have been, as a result of food scarcity.[65]

Famine Mentalities

It hardly need be pointed out that the famine was much more than a statistical problem; its psychological dimensions were at least as important for future developments during the occupation as the death toll itself. The hell of that winter marked the consciousness of all those who lived through it, changing them mentally, morally and politically.

Death itself – its associations, rituals and significance – was dramatically affected. Greek Orthodoxy and popular tradition dictated that the living adopt certain procedures to honour and take care of the dead. But on many occasions these now had to be abandoned, causing bereaved families additional grief and shame. 'The biggest headache you can cause your dear ones is to die,' wrote one Athenian bitterly. A decent burial was hard to arrange. Private transportation to the cemetery was costly and undignified: 'Whoever can find the large sum necessary to pay for the petrol fastens the bier to the bumper of some ancient car which carries it like merchandise, like wood to the graveside.' Many people simply gave up the effort and buried their dead themselves wherever they could in the frozen earth. Burial sites were dug round Athens without the permission of the Church, even though to the Orthodox Greeks such acts raised the deeply disturbing possibility that the souls of the deceased would not find peace and might even return to haunt this world as *revenants* or vampires.[66]

Having failed the living, the public authorities were also unable to take care of the dead. Emaciated corpses were left for hours in the streets before the municipal carts came round. Then they were

10. A passer-by watches council employees deliver corpses to the municipal mortuary in central Athens during the winter of 1941.

thrown on top of other bodies and taken away to the nearest cemetery. In the port of Volos there was – in the words of the local newspaper – a 'queue at the cemetery' during the winter: 'If one should be jealous of the dead, it is that they are at peace. . . . But their living relatives are not.' Only rich families could afford single graves; the rest made do with mass burials. The gravediggers were too weak from malnutrition to dig into the icy soil and the mayor had to provide them with special additional rations. According to the local paper, a visit to the cemetery, which once provoked 'a certain melancholy', now caused the visitor 'terror' at the sight of the carts bearing coffins and corpses wrapped in old sheets. Most were dumped in a far corner of the grounds where they were blessed *en masse* if a priest happened to be present. The paper could provide reassurance on only one point: reports that the corpses were stripped at night by robbers were untrue. Most of them had nothing left to steal.[67]

People became deranged by what they had experienced. One widow Junod met muttered nonsense, as she busied herself trying to care for her sick daughter. Another woman had become insane watching members of her family die at home. Others could not stop themselves weeping continuously. 'Many people are psychologically affected by starvation,' Junod found. 'They talk to themselves, they rave and have visions.' Clemm von Hohenberg, the philhellenic military attaché at the German Embassy in Athens, summarised the numerous and often contradictory psychological consequences of extreme hunger as: 'paralysis of initiative, dislike of work, listlessness and resignation or neurotic irritability . . . unrestrained hedonism'. One middle-class Athenian couple actually split up following a violent quarrel which started after the husband helped himself one day to some prewar marmalade that his wife was keeping for emergencies.[68]

The sight of corpses in the streets shook people deeply. 'I saw a dead little boy on the right-hand side of Constitution Square on Christmas day,' wrote one man, 'There cannot be a more tragic image of horror.' People noticed, however, that they got used to death disturbingly quickly and began to worry at their own growing emotional hardness and selfishness: 'the instinct for self-preservation deafens all other sounds'.[69]

Many felt that they were engaged in a personal struggle for their life with Charon, the personification of death in the popular imagination. The war had given this vivid and commonly encountered motif of the Greek oral tradition a new immediacy. 'Buy raisins. A handful will save you from Charon!' shouted the hawkers as they trudged round the suburbs, and it was common to see pedestrians chewing compulsively on a handful of currants. One little boy appeared in a soup kitchen wearing earrings, because all the other boys in his house had died – to cheat death he had decided to disguise his sex: 'If Charon tries to seize me, he'll think I'm a girl and let me go.'[70]

Despite such defiance, panic spread swiftly, for few people could feel entirely confident of escaping starvation. One Athenian wrote later: 'The first dead person I encountered, swollen from hunger, frightened me because I was hungry too.' '"Will we live?"', was the question on their minds. They scrutinised each other's faces carefully. 'The agony appears in their eyes, which still show signs of life. Their faces, however, have already acquired the colour of death,' one wrote. To Roger Milliex, the faces of dead children – shaven and distorted by hunger – had lost all semblance of humanity.[71]

Rumours of imminent salvation spread like wildfire through the streets. They were one expression of popular desperation – an early one in Salonika in December 1941 claimed the British would be arriving that spring – and they were invariably followed by even greater despair as the truth sank in. In September 1942 it was said that the Swedish ships which were on their way to Athens with grain would also be bringing a gift parcel for every inhabitant of the city; there was widespread disappointment when no gift parcels arrived.[72]

Rumours that food had arrived on the shelves of a neighbourhood shop sent people rushing to stand in line for hours. Their behaviour changed noticeably, and they became more quarrelsome. Fights broke out in queues and at the soup kitchens. One man confided to his diary, at the famine's height: 'We are all quick to anger. I feel faint when I'm in a crowd. I want to hit whoever is in front of me.' People felt hungry even after they had eaten several meals a day.[73]

Food became an obsession, dominating conversations and invading people's dreams. 'Nothing has any importance today apart from the question of food – or rather hunger,' Christides wrote. 'Cold, snow, hunger,' Ioanna Tsatsou noted in her diary on 25 November. Married to a university professor, with a house in a prosperous suburb, she too was shivering. Her work helping to organise relief for the capital's children had brought her face to face with the plight of the poor. One night she had a dream: 'A large table laid with the most beautiful food and drink. At its head the Christ child was seated, and round him countless little Greek children. All ate compulsively and with gusto, smearing their faces. Among them many of my little friends . . . I awoke with the feeling of coming out of paradise and sinking slowly but consciously into a familiar nightmare. My room is icy. I am hungry.'[74]

Ironically, not even the German colony in Athens escaped. The files of the Nazi Party's Auslands-Organisation contain a desperate report which Landesgruppenleiter Walter Wrede, whom we last saw in Athens on the day German troops took over the city, sent to Berlin on 10 January 1942. He wrote that the German community had been deprived of meat and green vegetables for the last two months; they had lived off offal and scraps left over from Wehrmacht supplies. Hans Dörhage, the head of the Security Police, was not immune either. During the autumn he had brought his wife and children out from the Reich to be with him. But it was discovered that he had been feeding them from official rations to sustain them through the famine. In March 1942 he was posted back to the Reich and demoted. He probably felt lucky to be out of Greece.[75]

Outside Aid

An early resistance proclamation, dating from October 1941, warned that 'famine and misery have reached their final stage . . .

11. Malnourished children in the care of the Red Cross: Athens, 1941.

our whole race is threatened with complete extinction'. This would not have been regarded as hyperbole at the time, for it was generally believed that behind the starvation lay a deliberate German policy of genocide. Still shocked at what she had seen, a Swiss woman who left Salonika in December 1941 reported that 'Greeks . . . accuse [the Germans] of destroying food rather than letting Greeks have it; they are convinced that hunger is the Germans' "secret weapon" and that this is being systematically used against them for the purpose of their deliberate extermination.' She warned: 'The spectre

45

of a contrived extermination of a whole population cannot be dismissed as an illusion conjured up by starved stomachs but rather viewed as a logical appraisal of German behaviour in Greece since the invasion of Russia.'[76]

In reality, there was no deliberate German plan of extermination. But equally the Germans, particularly those outside Greece itself, were not prepared to do much to help the starving Greeks. A German archaeologist returned from a visit to Athens in May 1942. Warning that pro-German sentiment, formerly strong, had declined as a result of the famine, he reminded civil servants of the Greeks' unique importance in the coming peace as 'the only people of non-Slavic stock able to fulfil the European mission against the Slavs of the East'. Unimpressed by such arguments, Berlin continued to regard occupation as a matter of profit and loss for the occupying power. Goods were still exported from Greece to help the Reich war effort during the worst months of the famine. The Italians also expropriated what they could, but they were readier to help. This did not do much good, as they had less to offer than the Germans.[77]

The Axis powers presented the famine as a problem caused by the British sea blockade and suggested that it should be lifted to enable grain to reach Greece from outside Europe. Though a convenient solution for them, such a move would be painful for the British, who were relying upon the blockade at a time when they had little else to use against their enemies. Had matters been left to British civil servants, it is doubtful whether the blockade would ever have been lifted. But there was a vital difference between the Axis powers and the Allies. Public opinion in Britain and the USA was aroused by the news of the famine. Slowly and belatedly, the British came round to the idea of supporting an international relief effort for Greece.[78]

The Greek Legation in London had first requested British assistance over the blockade as early as 25 April 1941. Whitehall recognised that Greece could be considered a special case both because of her extreme dependence upon food imports, and because of her contribution to the Allied cause. For this reason the Foreign Office did not reject subsequent approaches by King George and his *émigré* government out of hand.[79]

The British suggested turning to Turkey for relief supplies. Because Turkey was defined as lying 'within the blockade zone', this option did not involve breaching the blockade itself. Anxious that a total refusal to help the Greeks would anger public opinion in the USA, which was well informed about the famine thanks to extensive lobbying by Greek organisations, Whitehall hoped that Turkish grain would do the trick. This proved to be wishful thinking. The Greek War Relief Association in the USA provided funds, which were channelled through London to Turkey. But bureaucratic delays meant that it was not until October 1941 that the SS *Kurtulus*, a Turkish vessel, sailed for Piraeus, where the International Red Cross took charge of receiving and distributing the food. Between October 1941 and January 1942 the *Kurtulus* made five voyages before it was sunk. In this time it managed to transport 6,735 tons of supplies, too small a quantity to have had much impact on the situation in Athens.

In practice, the Turkish option was unworkable. Although the Turkish government had granted permission for up to 50,000 tons to be shipped to Greece, the grain was hard to find in Turkey, and the military authorities there began to clamp down on sales. Whitehall's nightmare – a relaxation of the blockade itself – came to seem the only way out for the Greeks. British officials insisted publicly that it was the duty of an occupying power under international law to feed the civilian population under its control. Behind the scenes, however, an extremely delicate round of negotiations began.

The Vatican had approached the British on 20 September about lifting the blockade. The British response was uncompromising; they accused the Italians of letting the Germans rob Greece 'by pillage and extortion'. The British believed that the Vatican was acting on behalf of the Italian government, who were desperate to find a way out of the mess in which the Germans had landed them. Subsequent approaches from the Vatican in November met with a similar response. The Vatican also approached the Germans, however, and established that they were willing to allow relief to be sent to Greece. They would also guarantee that this would be made available solely to the Greeks.[80]

The hunger was at its peak when the British agreed, for the first time, to permit the blockade to be broken. Public opinion in Britain and the USA, together with worries about the effects inside Greece on popular sentiment towards Britain, pushed Whitehall down this path. On 16 February the British Cabinet agreed to allow shipments of wheat, provided that they were sent under neutral supervision. For several months London, Berlin and Rome wrangled discreetly over the composition of the proposed relief commission. An International Red Cross mission had been established in Athens in October 1941 to supervise the *Kurtulus* shipments. Eventually this was expanded to include Swedish representatives. The new committee issued new ration cards to the civilian population and controlled the distribution of imported grain shipments inside the country.

Agreement was finally reached between all parties in early June

1942, and the first shipments of wheat left Canada for Greece in early August. The food situation for the Greek population improved immediately. Although the mortality rate throughout 1942 remained at a high level, there was no repetition of the famine of the first winter in the capital. Predictions made during the summer of 1942 that there would be one million deaths the next winter turned out to be completely false.

The Geography of the Famine

Although relief operations by the Red Cross initially focused on the Athens area, famine conditions also prevailed in other parts of the country. In some they persisted right through the occupation, and they spread later in the war to areas that had not lacked food in 1941.

During the winter of 1941–42 many provincial towns endured actual starvation. Mortality rates were lower than in Athens, but higher than those of most farming areas. As any semblance of a national, unified economy vanished to be replaced by a patchwork of disconnected and isolated regional trading areas, so the towns' traditional means of extracting a food surplus from the farmers collapsed too. The fuel and transportation shortage simply compounded the city-dwellers' plight. Acute vitamin deficiency was observed in the port of Kalamata. Refugees in Salonika died of malnutrition, despite the proximity of the rich alluvial plains to the west of the city. In the industrial port of Volos, one daily paper advised its readers that the only means of escape from the famine was 'to return to the villages: whoever has parents, relatives, or land should head for them'.[81]

In much of the countryside, however, conditions in 1941 and 1942 were little or no worse than they had been in earlier years. Farmers survived as they had done during the First World War, or in the 1930s, when many rural communities had retreated to a measure of self-sufficiency. Hill villagers hoarded their maize, potatoes and barley, looked after their sheep and goats, and made it through the winter at a safe distance from the military supply officers in the valleys.

In northern Greece conditions would only worsen as a result of the growth of the resistance. From 1943 Axis anti-guerrilla operations affected mountain areas which had escaped the starvation in 1941–42. When Red Cross delegates began travelling out of Athens into the provinces, in 1943 and 1944, they found that the destruction caused by 'mopping-up' operations against the resistance had disrupted regular farming. So the last phase of the occupation saw a partial reversal of the food balance: by 1944 an effective rationing system protected the cities from hunger; but villagers in the Peloponnese and the Pindus mountains were increasingly malnourished, vulnerable to disease and in a few cases suffering from actual starvation.

By then, however, Red Cross delegates had also become aware of the calamity that had swept across the Greek islands, some of which had suffered higher mortality rates even than Athens, and starved for longer, since Red Cross assistance was more difficult to arrange and was never as effective. Cut off from the mainland, islanders were forced to live off whatever they could coax from the arid, stony soil.

On Ikarya, near the Turkish coast, for example, there were no cattle and only a few vegetables, figs, grapes and apricots. Before the war, one-third of the islanders' food had come from fishing, two-thirds from imports: now, during the occupation, fishing was forbidden and imports shrank almost to zero. The island of Naxos had previously obtained 30 per cent of its food from Athens, using six large caiques. Not only was the food no longer available, but four of the boats were sunk.[82]

The resulting sense of isolation, helplessness and anger emerge vividly from the diary of Mario Rigouzzo, the honorary French consul on the island of Syros. Living in its capital Ermoupolis, a town of splendid villas, a graceful theatre and spacious squares, he tells the story of a small, provincial society in the throes of disintegration. For him what happened there was bound up with the events taking place on the world stage. Commenting on that ubiquitous phrase 'the new order of things in Europe', Rigouzzo wrote in February 1943:

> I have seen nothing up till now since the occupation of Greece by the Axis powers which could make me accept that this new order of things will be something just, moral and human. On the contrary, in everything that these renewers of humanity have done one sees injustice, immorality and inhumanity, thieving, the plundering of every living thing by the invaders in order to make the population die of hunger, administrative injustice, terror and police brutality daily.[83]

His pages allow us not just to chart the progress of the famine across the island, but also to observe its social, moral and political consequences.

The Syros Experience

The first Italians arrived on Syros on 5 May 1941 to the surprise of the islanders, and took over from the Germans. Parading in front of the town hall, they raised the Italian flag alongside the swastika. First they tried to obtain goods by flooding the market with lire. Then after a month these were withdrawn and replaced by a new currency, occupation drachmas. Soldiers began to requisition goods outright, including the island's entire crop of potatoes, olive oil, fat and butter.

By August it was clear that not everyone on the island was suffering to the same degree. Rich shipowners, often pro-British in their sympathies, had accumulated large stocks of goods over the previous months, with the connivance of the Greek authorities and Italian officers. In the hills outside Ermoupolis itself, wealthy farmers were buying up the land of small producers. By the end of August, Rigouzzo's own family had gone twenty-five days without eating anything but some onions from the nearby island of Andros. With nothing on their shelves, many shopkeepers shut their doors despite police orders to remain open. Although there was a nominal bread ration, actually no bread was distributed for a month until a boat docked from the Dodecanese near the end of September. No butter or meat was available for months, and cigarettes were obtained only through the black market, which was administered by the police themselves.

Apart from the town's magistrates, local civil servants had lost any sense of civic duty and followed a policy of *sauve qui peut*. The prefect in office at the start of the occupation was soon replaced; but after just three days the new appointee left too, worried at the shortage of food, and Athens failed to send a replacement. With only junior officials in the prefecture, the Greek state had more or less abandoned the island.

The Italians were aware of the apathy and corruption of the Greek authorities and made efforts to bring in food, but it was not enough. The island's death toll rose sharply from 435 in 1939 to 2,290 in 1942. In 1939 births exceeded deaths by 52; in 1942 the deficit of deaths was an incredible 964.[84] A large ditch had to be dug just outside the town to accommodate the corpses. By March 1942 it had been widened, and other trenches added. Rigouzzo watched some men burying a young girl:

> The bearer of the coffin, who was none other than the father of the little girl, a victim of our common fate, helps the digger at the burial of his own famished darling, then pulls out of his

pocket a note which he hands to the priest who accepts it and another for the gravedigger who refuses, telling him: 'I want nothing, my good Iannis, you are as poor as me.' The priest and the father leave and the digger turns to me and says: 'You know, sir, that is the fourth child the unhappy man has buried like this since the occupation.'

Hunger was slowly ripping the social fabric apart, but it also made the islanders aware of their common predicament. The selfishness of the speculators and certain rich notables turned people's thoughts to the need to help each other. Even the Italians on the island could be included within such an embrace, especially the conscripts, who generally behaved well towards civilians and seemed tired of the war. They attended mass regularly and talked about their families to anyone who would listen. 'Rather than tell us their military exploits, their naval victories over the English, as their twice-weekly journal does, they find pleasure and consolation in showing us photos of their wives, babies, fiancées, even their entire family,' wrote Rigouzzo. 'The soldier who brought me an invitation to the anniversary of the March on Rome, a boy of 22, said: "Alas, it's that march on Rome which led us into this war today!"'

Italian officials, town professionals and wealthy notables continued to play the old games of pomp and propaganda, but against the backdrop of the famine these took on an almost surreal dimension. In May 1942, for example, there was a ceremony to mark the visit of Admiral Inigo Campione, the governor of the Aegean. He flew into the small harbour by hydroplane, reviewed the Italian guard in the main square and decorated several soldiers for their exploits on the Albanian front. A few Greeks present, not knowing Italian, clapped enthusiastically. Later there was a soirée at the Hotel Hellas in Campione's honour. Some prominent Greeks from the town had been invited to give an impression of harmony on the island. But as soon as the sumptuous buffet was revealed, a grotesque free-for-all followed, as Greek lawyers, doctors and professors plundered the dishes, stuffing food in their mouths with both hands and refusing to move away from the table. When the Italian dignitaries eventually left the building, they were accosted by crowds of children begging for bread.

Like the town notables at Campione's reception, other islanders were driven by hunger to throw social niceties out of the window. 'If our prayers go unanswered,' wrote the Metropolitan bishop and the mayor in desperation, 'We decline all moral responsibility before God and history.'[85] Rather than wait for divine help, some parents sent their daughters out after the Italian soldiers for food.

Popular resentment grew against profiteers and speculators – the merchants who had joined forces with Italian officers in importing goods illegally, the relatives of the Catholic clergy, who were reputedly amassing enormous riches thanks to Italian support, the farmers whose daughters now wore silk dresses and boasted of their grand pianos recently acquired from starving town-dwellers.

At the end of his diary, Rigouzzo tried to sum up the famine's winners and losers. Two groups had suffered the worst – those on fixed salaries, like the civil servants whose monthly wages were now equivalent to the price of a pair of shoes, and the workers, whose pay had lagged behind the rate of inflation. Many peasants, on the other hand, had benefited from high food prices, and had been able to pay off their prewar debts in depreciated drachmas. In the town of Ermoupolis itself, the entire working class and most of the bourgeoisie had shifted politically far to the left during the years of occupation. Only a few capitalists and rich notables had resisted this tide. The overall shift would have been less extreme, Rigouzzo concluded, if the public authorities had been better organised and demonstrated a social conscience. Instead they had simply looked after themselves and indulged in speculation. Here in miniature was the link between food scarcity and political radicalism which was emerging throughout occupied Greece. Everywhere the hunger intensified people's alienation from the state and radicalised large sections of the population, including many white-collar workers and middle-class professionals, former bastions of the old bourgeois order, who looked in vain to the established political world in Athens for guidance and leadership in their daily struggle for survival.

CHAPTER FOUR

Black Market Axioms

Rigouzzo's journal suggests that the black market was at the centre of the social changes brought about by the occupation. The scope and importance of a black market stand in inverse proportion to the power of the state, and in few countries was the state weaker than in occupied Greece. Where no consistently enforced set of official prices exists, a black market functions more freely than where rationing is relatively efficient. In Greece enforcement was extremely haphazard, and eventually abandoned altogether.

Challenging the authority of Axis rule, the black market was an economic, a political and a social pathology all at once, highlighting the state's inability to secure the resources it needed to preserve the lives of its citizens. It could be seen – ambiguously – as the triumph of individual enterprise over state control. For better or worse, the black market had its own morality, its own rules, and most people had to learn these if they were to survive.

First Axiom

The black market is a necessity. Junod noted: 'If all the Greeks based their hopes of being fed solely on the efforts of the Government, no one would remain alive for this report. . . . An important part of the population manage to obtain small quantities of requisitioned goods by two methods, i.e. a) through relatives living in the provinces, and b) through the black market.' Major A. Tsaousopoulos, director of transport for the International Red Cross Commission in Greece, was still more emphatic: 'Although it has permitted villainous exploitation and the enrichment of persons of doubtful moral standards, the Black Market has undoubtedly saved from certain death by starvation the greater part of the middle classes in the big urban centres.'[86] A group of leading young economists, in a memorandum on the food situation written in

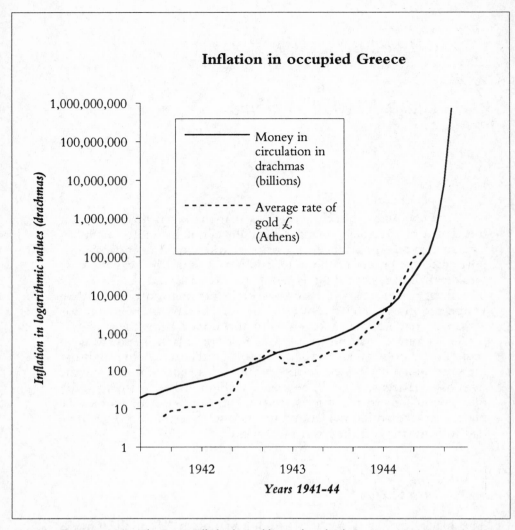

Inflation in occupied Greece

Inflation in logarithmic values (drachmas)

Money in circulation in drachmas (billions)

Average rate of gold £ (Athens)

1942   1943   1944

Years 1941–44

Source: D. Magriotis, *Thysiai tis Ellados kai enklimata katochis kata ta eti 1941–44* (Athens, n.d.), p.35.

May 1942, described the official market as non-existent, and insisted that 'it is only the "Black Market" which has been supplying the population of Athens and Piraeus' even if 'at exorbitant prices'.[87]

As has been observed in other cases of famine, the very rumour of food difficulties tended to dry up the normal flow of goods through the country, as food-producing localities hoarded their crops and prevented their sale elsewhere.[88] Region was pitted against region. In Argos, local Italian garrisons prevented produce being sent to Athens, as their own superiors in the capital wished.

In Larissa Greek officers temporarily employed by the government to collect the harvest for transportation to Athens colluded with villagers in preventing wheat leaving the Thessaly plain. 'Larissa isn't sending us wheat,' complained the *Messenger* in nearby Volos. Wrangles over fuel allocations and shipping space slowed down the transport of foodstuffs from surplus to deficit areas. So did security measures, like the Italians' prohibition on trade between islands in the Aegean and the notoriously strict surveillance of fishing boats, which could carry information or even passengers as well as fish.[89]

Down in the Mani, the fertile district of Pyrgos Dirou had food for sale, while less than a day's march away around Gerolimena there was great distress. On the island of Samos conditions were better than on nearby Chios, where bread had disappeared and children could be seen on the quayside, eating the heads and bones of fish.[90] Black market trade was one way of bringing food from one region to another. Prices diverged substantially across the country, inducing the marketeers to move goods over large distances. Suitcases of clothes belonging to Jews from Salonika were being sold in the southern Peloponnese only weeks after their owners had been deported.[91]

The career of one black-marketeer with a practised eye for the main chance illustrates the value as well as the moral complexities of his occupation. Thirty-nine-year-old George Petropoulakos went into the fishing business in June 1943, after a busy few years in which he had bought and sold a café in Piraeus, fought in Albania, worked in the family grocery and managed a gambling joint. He and his brothers decided to buy a caique, the *Ayia Sotira* and several smaller boats to go fishing because, he was to claim later, 'he did not wish to be engaged in Black Market activities'. Maybe this was true at first. But then came a series of disasters: he was arrested by the Germans for fishing without permission and had to bribe his way out of jail; next he lost his other boats in a fire after German troops burned the village where they were moored.

By this time he needed money. Thirty thousand drachmas he received from selling off a plot of land did not last long. Early ventures to the islands of Kea and Kithnos to exchange oil and soap for livestock were not a success. Shipping Jews to the Middle East paid rather better – 20 million drachmas for a party of eighteen. Another good source of income was smuggling people in and out of Greece for the British: the shortage of caiques made men like Petropoulakos in demand for secret operations. Combining 'resistance' activity with a little barter trade on his own account, Petropoulakos stocked up on foodstuffs in Turkish ports, and swapped lambs and calves on Tinos for wheat and beans. On one occasion he exchanged 100 okes of soap and 140 okes of oil for 15 gold sovereigns. Eventually he chose, or was obliged, to flee to Turkey, where the British interrogators who debriefed him were understandably cautious in taking his story at face value. But the central place which deals, trading and black-marketeering occupy in his testimony is convincing. Without the chance of profit, few caique *kapetans* would have risked shipping Jews across the Aegean, or carrying papers and agents for the British. Although the islanders they met were, if they had any sense, cautious in dealing with such men, they knew very well that only on Petropoulakos's caique, or those of others like him, would they get *any* soap, meat or thread at all on their island during the war.[92]

Second Axiom

The black market is not confined to one social group. There were markets in different commodities catering for all needs and tastes. In the town of Chalkis, for instance, the area around the public marketplace, including the side roads, squares and small alleys, was crowded with carts and stalls: 'People of all classes and ages, men, women, children, clean and dirty, tricksters and fools, old men with worn hands and women wearing gloves and shabby blouses, young "Don Juan" spivs with slicked-back hair – all of them make up the black market, which begins its work at the crack of dawn, and ends just as the first shadows embrace the town.'[93]

Most hated by the common people, as we saw on Syros, were the notables who abused their power to connive with the *xenous*, the foreigners, and ignored the plight of the poor. 'When we see Greece despoiled by the invaders, why shouldn't we save what we can for ourselves?', one minister was reported as saying. It was taken for granted that figures in authority, from cabinet ministers downwards, took advantage of their position to enrich themselves. The notorious Ioannis Polychronopoulos, a senior police official in the Ministry of Public Security, was reported to have turned his own house into a base for black market operations. The Bishop of Mytilene stood accused of diverting Red Cross relief towards his friends. The chief of police there, Nikolaos Katsareas, had a finger in food and fuel rackets, helped 'supervise' allocations of flour to the island's bakers, and finally fled at an opportune moment by caique to the Middle East so weighed down with large quantities of British tinned goods that he had to ask his fellow-passengers to help him carry them on board.[94]

Families with personal connections with the Germans were especially well placed for instant enrichment. The Athens police noted with interest the changing fortunes of Dionysos P., a poor bank clerk, whose mother was of German descent. Shortly after the occupation, he opened a bureau with his German uncle in the centre of Athens and acquired a series of profitable contracts, helping for example to recover the Greek warships which had been sunk in Piraeus harbour. He also ferried olive oil from Mytilene, beating the official embargo. By 1944 he owned three houses – one by the sea at the resort of Glyphada, one in a good neighbourhood of Athens, and a third in Mytilene. As for Emma O., a German woman married to a Greek, police informers noted simply that she and her husband 'were very poor and are now rolling in money'.[95]

By far the largest group to profit from the black market were the producers of food. After the agricultural depression of the interwar years, the occupation saw the countryside take its revenge on the towns. In the provinces, among the townsfolk, fishermen and shepherds, enormous bitterness was felt against the farmers. In Crete there was 'a feeling approaching hatred' in the towns against the peasants 'who exploited so ruthlessly their advantageous position as producers'. A fisherman on the rocky islet of Dhenousa, with no farm or garden, and unable to fish because his boat had been taken, could survive only by buying bread from a better-off neighbour in exchange for his household possessions. With no future for him on the island, he escaped to the Middle East. There he expressed his outrage at his neighbour's callous behaviour, and threatened to take back his goods when the war is over 'at exactly the same rate in loaves of bread'.[96]

At the end of June 1941 Tsolakoglu launched a bitter attack on the farmers, threatening strict measures to ensure their compliance: 'They must remember the sacrifices which the city population and the workers made when times were difficult for them, to support the prices of agricultural goods. Now we have the right to demand that the cities' misfortune is not ignored by the producers. They must pursue, not just their own advantage, but that of the community too.'[97] This was strong language from the head of a government which in Roncalli's words 'counted for nothing' and possessed 'neither authority nor dignity'. Tsolakoglu's warnings needed to be repeated rather often: in March 1942 farmers were reminded of their responsibilities 'towards the Nation'; later they were chided that 'the war is not an opportunity for enrichment'.[98]

The farmers themselves, of course, saw their actions in a more positive light. Hiding crops from the tax-collector was virtually a duty for most peasants. Villagers from Playia on Mytilene, critical of the rich black-marketeers in the island's capital, felt their own activities to be quite different. They hid as much of their olive oil as possible from the authorities; then, forming a secret co-operative, each family put in 100 okes of oil and chartered a boat to smuggle the lot across to the Chalkidiki peninsula, where it was exchanged for enough food to last them through the year.

The high prices marketeers charged often simply reflected the dangers of their business. The Germans, for example, had banned the export of olive oil from Mytilene and Crete. Chartering a vessel was therefore often illegal and also expensive: it might be sunk by the Allies or requisitioned by the Axis. Many boats had been deliberately damaged by their owners to stop them being taken by the authorities and few were available. Bribes were demanded everywhere. Experienced black-marketeers smoothed their way past the checkpoints that ringed the major towns with a packet of cigarettes or a few eggs for the more exorbitant soldiers. The list of officials to be paid off was a long one: harbour-masters, gendarmes, the Germans who issued passes and fishing permits, and most of all their Greek translators.[99]

Sometimes the involvement of the authorities in the black market took on such dimensions that it becomes impossible to describe the economic life of the area except by reference to it. On the small island of Sifnos, for example, the Italian garrison of 120 men controlled the entire olive oil business. They forced local producers to declare their expected harvest in advance on the basis of the number of trees they possessed. After the harvest, they allowed each family a certain ration and commandeered the surplus at low prices, distributing some to the non-producers on the island, and keeping the rest. Officially they claimed this was to barter for imports of goods from neighbouring islands, such as potatoes, broad beans and wine, but in fact most of it was put in the hands of a local olive oil merchant, who sold it at six times the compulsory purchase price on Sifnos and split the profits with the Italians.[100] On Chios, the officials of the German Wirtschaftskommission enriched themselves and a few local dealers through their monopoly of the trade in oil, citrus fruits and mastic. In Salonika many soldiers were selling their rations plus any foodstuffs they could obtain from Germany on the black market for gold. 'These trans-actions are often – perhaps normally – undertaken as a means of accumulating capital . . . for the eventual purchase of a place to live back home,' concluded an army report, which noted with alarm that up to 60 per cent of soldiers' letters discussed nothing else.[101]

Most of the marketeers, however, were Greeks. Some were rich merchants; others small farmers, or their relatives. Poverty and unemployment turned clerks, labourers, writers and lawyers into

12.   A requisitioned caique in German service in the Aegean.

petty traders. They sold newspapers, or wandered the streets as vendors, advertising perhaps a couple of cigarettes, poor-quality pocket torch batteries, or a tiny heap of currants.[102] Demobbed soldiers who had not been able to get home stood at street corners selling odds and ends. Finally, even the middle classes were pushed into the marketplace. Down in the muddy alleys of Asyrmato, hoping to buy oil and eggs, Ioanna Tsatsou found herself surrounded by 'some dirty, unshaved men' who cautiously showed her samples of their wares, beans and chick-peas. Civil servants piled up their furniture, their pots and pans, even their shoes on the pavement and waited for a customer. Greece's former ambassador to Italy sold off his rugs and *objets d'art*, yet still could not avoid losing several stones in weight. The professional classes were now desperately selling off carpets, furniture, paintings and clothing before reaching the final item, their bed. By 1942, pedestrians were walking past the bed-frames lined up for sale along one of Athens's main streets.[103]

Everyone seemed to be buying and selling. Second-hand merchants placed advertisements in the daily press. There were numerous public auctions where dealers and newly wealthy farmers bought up whatever they could. Sales of property rose and fell in tandem with the timing of the famine, revealing that many people were being forced to sell their homes to survive.[104] And if the vast majority were motivated by desperation and necessity, there was also a core of speculators who were simply out to make their fortune by playing the market.

Hoarding evidently took place on a massive scale, because on a couple of occasions rumours of an imminent improvement in the food situation brought black market prices tumbling. In the spring of 1942, for example, the arrival in Piraeus of the *Radmanso*, with a supply of wheat, led prices to slump in the grain market. The same thing happened the following winter after news of the Axis defeats in North Africa caused a wave of Liberation rumours to sweep across the country. Suddenly the narrow streets of central Athens were packed with goods that had been unavailable for months.[105]

As food prices plummeted, one foreign observer drew the bitter moral:

Meat: from 20 or 25 to 6 thousand (drachmas). Potatoes from 8 to 3 thousand. Beans from 15 to 4 or 5 thousand. The same for clothes, cloth, shoes etc. The conclusion of this phenomenon is evident. . . . While the entire world anguished over the fate of the Greek people, the Greeks got rich on the blood of their brothers.

This does not mean that the relief of these unhappy Greeks should be cut back: for side by side with the numerous sharks a multitude of poor continue to scrape a living. But we have turned a new and grim page in the dishonourable history which the world war is writing.[106]

But was this speculation really the prerogative of a new class, created by the war? That was certainly the dominant view, and everyone talked readily about the 'new rich' who had risen to the top. 'The new rich,' wrote Theotokas, 'are adventurers who act as if in a jungle and each grabs what he can.'[107] In a striking account of the famine, a Viennese newspaper described how old wealth in Greece was being replaced by a new, more vulgar set: 'Usually of poor heritage, and with a shocking lack of education, they give the impression to foreigners that they are debasing Greek cultural life completely.' It depicted 'the wife of the "nouveau-riche" sitting at the coffee house showing off her newly-acquired jewels, while a beggar stretches his hand out timidly for alms'.[108]

Newcomers there were, to be sure. One Athenian of an old bourgeois family wrote to a friend that their former gardener, Stavros, had 'blossomed into a successful black marketeer'; he had become a 'great capitalist' and a defender of the status quo against the Left.[109] But such accounts were often tinged with snobbery. Wealthy peasants and jumped-up labourers were only part of the problem. People with established fortunes also managed to ride out the occupation, and even to profit from it. Outside Athens, local notables found themselves in a strong position to 'assist' isolated Italian or German garrison commanders. In the capital shipowners and industrialists were active in the black market for gold sovereigns. The notorious 'Group of Georges' – five of Athens' most prominent speculators – included three well-known and well-off prewar government ministers, and united erstwhile Venizelists and their opponents. Perhaps all that we can say by way of generalisation is that there were two positions which helped ensure enrichment – proximity to the dwindling supply of goods, and proximity to power. This penalised many previously comfortable families, whose skills were not wanted, whose rental income had fallen, and whose friends and patrons were out of power. But it was not the 'new faces' alone who lacked scruples and managed to manoeuvre themselves to their own advantage. The fundamental political fact was simply that the number of those impoverished and humiliated by economic collapse was far larger than that of those who gained.

Third Axiom

The black market is immoral. On this there was almost universal agreement, from the Axis authorities to their most vehement opponents.

As early as 8 May 1941 Tsolakoglu's government announced that special courts would be set up to try speculators. 'Speculators' of course provided the authorities with a badly needed scapegoat, for it was easier to blame food scarcity on the immorality of a few individuals than on the combination of official mismanagement, Axis rapacity and market structure which was really responsible. But in November the new courts came into the glare of publicity when Tsolakoglu announced the arrest of a group of import merchants accused of selling sugar on the black market. Though the Prime Minister himself demanded a speedy prosecution of the trial, endless delays underlined the Greek authorities' own ambiguous stance on the issue.[110] There were widespread rumours that government ministers were implicated and that to 'clean out the Augean stables completely', senior civil servants would have to be dismissed. Tsolakoglu's wife was reputedly one of the great *rousfetisti* (corruptibles); her unaccustomed influence and power had gone to her head.[111]

There was certainly some foundation to stories of official corruption. The two economics ministers, Hadzimikalis and Karamanos, who resigned in the spring of 1942, were widely suspected of having been forced out of office by German disgust when 2,500 tons of olive oil which the Germans had sent specially for public consumption in Athens mysteriously found their way on to the black market. After his resignation, Hadzimikalis continued his lucrative involvement in the financing of Greece's pitiful import trade. The president of the Merchants' Association of Salonika was arrested for illegal trade in livestock and raw materials; his acquittal – which made 'an enormous and gloomy impression' among the city's inhabitants – was attributed to sweeteners amounting to 'no few millions of drachmas'. The Governor-General of Macedonia himself was regarded as 'a hoarder of the first class' together with the president of Salonika's Chamber of Industry and other notables. A former director of the Food Provisioning Service, arrested on twenty-five counts of profiteering, was reckoned to have made £300 sterling a day in office. Commenting on the reluctance of Greek tribunals to act with any severity against such men, the Italian consul-general in Salonika observed that 'this impunity of the grand profiteers is received with a sense of dejection by the great starving mass of the population'.[112]

Not surprisingly, the pledges of Tsolakoglu and his Finance Minister, Sotirios Gotzamanis, to eradicate the black market failed to convince the Athenian public. As an effort to gain support for the government, their tactics were clearly a failure. Yet, oddly, they spoke in terms which many of their most hostile opponents probably accepted, and which indeed would be used by the Left in the coming months. Gotzamanis, for example, blamed the country's economic woes on the 'plutocrats' and announced that the government had placed itself at the head of all poor and starving Greeks in its battle with the profiteers. Later he described the black market in more theoretical terms as an aspect of the struggle between liberal individualism and the interventionist state. The fight to control the distribution of goods, he argued, underlined the need to abandon 'the old methods of economic liberalism' and to push ahead towards 'a managed economy'. People had to move beyond considerations of individual advantage, to see themselves within the social whole.[113]

Meanwhile, the rich had a 'holy duty' of charity towards the poor; the farmers should help their brothers in the towns: 'whilst profit once oiled the economic machinery, now what is required is working together, discipline and obedience to the interests of the collectivity. . . . This is not the time to acquire new fortunes or increase old ones.'[114] Through the language of a debate which dated back to the time of the 1929–32 depression, the occupation was helping to discredit *laissez-faire* capitalism. On this, unexpectedly, quislings and resistance militants were in agreement. Similar policies, backed up by similar rhetoric, would later be introduced to considerably greater effect by the main resistance organisation, EAM, in the areas it controlled.

So it was certainly not only on Syros that the black-marketeers aroused feelings of disgust by their unprincipled greed and unrestrained self-interest. One of Greece's most popular lyricists, Kleon Triantaphyllou, better known as 'Attic', wrote a song called 'Money' which he dedicated 'by way of consolation to all those who have nothing'. Composed shortly before 'Attic' himself committed suicide, its bitter tone was in sharp contrast to the easy banter which was his trademark:

> As you walk out each evening
> You hear 'I'm hungry' on every corner
> It's the poor who bug you, rich man,
> So you walk a little faster
>
> And sweat, because you're plump and round!

> Who's to blame if in this world
> There's misery? . . . Money! . . . Money!

With the famine came the possibility of social breakdown in its most violent form. Beggars broke into the basements of suburban houses or dug up vegetable gardens at night in the search for food. The musicologist Dounias wrote: 'One came to our house and said aggressively: "Sir, I'm starving, I haven't eaten for three days, give me something to put in my mouth." He was so threatening – if I'd refused to help him, he would have attacked me!' And when the professor descended from leafy Psychiko to the miserable quarter of Kokkinia to buy some wheat he felt even more alarmed: 'In their despair their hatred turns against anyone who looks properly fed. They have declared a war of the "have-nots" against the "haves". The "haves" are those who have anything more – however little – than they do.'[115]

Old women were attacked and robbed in broad daylight in the suburbs of Athens. Volos was hit by a crime wave, brought on – according to the local paper – by the 'apathy of the state'. The journalist insisted that there was no connection with the prevailing hunger, yet the main targets for thieves were tavernas, restaurants, confectioners, food factories and warehouses. Fifty-one cases of currants were stolen from the stores of the Bank of Athens. The town of Larissa was shocked by news that two men had killed a family in the village of Ossa for a sack of flour. Villages had become more dangerous places since the local field guards, who were traditionally fed by the community, went hungry. Government decrees increasing their pay, and stiffening the sentences for theft and robbery, had little effect.[116]

For over a year the frustrations of the starving poor were manifested sporadically in assaults, thefts and pilfering, but without political expression. The language of communal solidarity – the discontent with the selfish values of prewar capitalism – seemed hollow and fraudulent slogans in the mouth of Tsolakoglu or Gotzamanis. But they were to appear again in the public arena, and next time, coming from the underground Left, they would find an immediate response from a society radicalised by an economic collapse of unprecedented dimensions.

CHAPTER FIVE

'An Atmosphere of Imminent Catastrophe'

The 5,000 drachma note of 1942 featured designs by a young engraver called Alexandros Koroyiannakis. Koroyiannakis had a preference for the heroic and the statuesque – images of the human form ennobled by work – in that ideologically ambiguous classicising style which was shared by a wide range of artists in the 1930s, from Picasso to Mario Sironi or Carrà in Fascist Italy.[117] Now, as the Greek economy collapsed in chaos, the Greek artist produced his own version of the corporatist idyll. On one side of the banknote was a rural scene – the farmer tilling the soil, a sturdy moustachioed peasant casting the seed, and surrounding them a framework of tobacco and olive leaves, an ear of wheat, and clusters of grapes; on the other side, two workmen in the shade of a wingless Victory, a view of modern, industrial (still unbombed) Piraeus and a fishing scene.

Money, these images suggest, is both the symbol and the foundation of a well-ordered society. It brings the different elements of the labouring world together in productive harmony. The costly stabilisation policies, which Greece like many other countries had pursued after the First World War in an effort to return to the gold standard, had been prompted by the conviction that a stable currency indicated not merely creditworthiness in the eyes of foreign investors, but also the deeper moral credibility of the bourgeois state. Yet the confidence suggested by Koroyiannakis's idealised figures was fast becoming a confidence trick. In June 1941 there had been 24 million drachmas in circulation, a year later there were 109.8 millions. In the same period the price of bread – the *official* price – had risen from 70 drachmas to 2,350, soap from 65 to 3,100, dried beans from 90 to 2,900.

In many parts of the country, money was no longer a reliable measure of value. In Volos people counted in cigarettes, in the mountains in olive oil, down in the plains in wheat. Once the Red Cross started distributing quinine tablets in the malarial areas of central Greece, these too started circulating as currency, be-

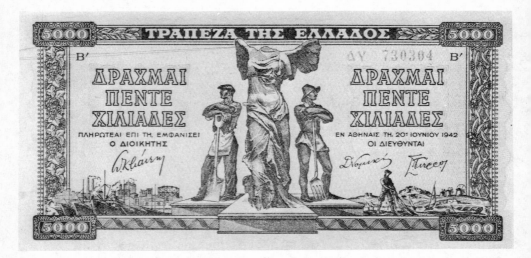

13. Alexandros Koroyiannakis's design for the 5,000 drachma note, 1942.

coming too valuable to swallow. Fees published in June 1942 by the Doctors' Association of Chios did not bother to refer to money at all: 'I oke of corn, oil or dried vegetables for an appointment at a doctor's surgery; for treatment at the patient's house 1.5 okes if he lived in Chios town, 2 okes if he lives outside.'[118]

Fuelling the inflation were the so-called *Besatzungskosten* (occupation costs) levied by the Axis. After requisitioning foodstuffs and other valuable commodities, the Axis forces stationed in Greece adopted a more sophisticated means of extracting the country's resources; just as they did elsewhere in Europe, they levied enor-

66

mous 'occupation costs' to cover their expenses from the Greek authorities. Unable to raise the required sums through taxation – normal methods of taxation could not function when the authorities themselves were forced to secure produce from the farmers through barter – the government turned to the Bank of Greece and printed notes. With each issue of banknotes, a new twist was added to inflation's upward spiral, causing the next month's occupation costs to be set at a higher level. 'Greece is completely squeezed dry,' warned Ghigi in mid-1942.[119]

Briefly, it seemed that help might come from an unexpected quarter. On the morning of 20 July 1942, Mussolini flew in to Athens on his way back from a tour of North Africa. It was the Duce's only visit to Greece during the war, and on his brief inspection of the Acropolis he seemed in a lively mood. But what he heard, in the course of conversations with the Axis plenipotentiaries, Prime Minister Tsolakoglu and Finance Minister Gotzamanis, disquieted him. Explaining the scale of the economic crisis facing the country, Gotzamanis insisted that the Wehrmacht must scale down its financial demands.[120] Mussolini promised to take up the matter with the Germans and he was as good as his word. Soon after his visit to Athens he sent a letter to Hitler, warning him in no uncertain terms that 'Greece is on the brink of financial – and therefore economic and political – catastrophe.'[121]

Hitler's response was enlightening. Writing from his HQ in the East, he envied Mussolini his visit to the Acropolis: 'I perhaps better than anyone else can share your feelings with regard to a place where all that we today call human culture found its beginning.'[122] But the expression 'occupation costs' was, insisted the Führer, a misnomer. German troops were in fact *rebuilding* roads, bridges and rail-links, which would serve the Greeks as well as the Axis. In his view, the Greeks had not contributed enough to this effort! To his subordinates in Berlin, Hitler was blunter: the Italians had to be made to realise the 'true nature' of the war effort in Greece, and its military significance as a stepping-stone for troops and supplies to North Africa. He recommended that the word *Besatzungskosten* be replaced by the more positive *Aufbaukosten* – for these were not 'occupation costs' but 'construction costs'![123]

But Hitler's peremptory denial that the problem existed, and his characteristic belief that a change of word would efface reality, proved an inadequate response. Just a year into the occupation of Greece, the Tsolakoglu administration was to be torn apart by the economic crisis.

*

As early as the previous autumn, the Greek Finance Ministry had warned of 'complete collapse' if the whole system of occupation costs was not rethought. In June 1942 Gotzamanis warned Ghigi that exorbitant occupation costs were leading the country 'to ruin'. 'Prices and values move in an atmosphere of imminent catastrophe,' he wrote. 'In Greece for a while now all the foundations of a healthy economy have been overturned. There can be no stability, neither in economic equilibrium nor in monetary or financial affairs.' The budget for 1941/42 had finished with a deficit of 14 billion drachmas (against revenues of 16 billion drachmas), and as the Wehrmacht scaled up its monthly demands from 17 billion drachmas in June to over 30 billion in October the deficit was certain to increase. Prices diverged by 100–500 per cent between different regions. Food and tax collection was hindered by local military authorities stopping foodstuffs leaving their region. Since the government had announced plans that spring to collect and distribute food in the towns in return for wage and rent freezes, such local bans jeopardised Gotzamanis's entire economic policy. He now publicised his negotiations over occupation costs in the press, emphasising his belief that the Greek case would be favourably received by the Axis authorities.[124]

While the Italians, as Mussolini's reaction suggested, were genuinely worried by Greece's financial crisis, it was the Germans who needed to be persuaded. Initially, Altenburg's advocacy of the Greek position was not well received even in his own Ministry. But then the political stakes were suddenly raised. In the middle of August a group of Greece's prewar political leaders – making a rare public intervention into occupation politics – urged the Prime Minister to be firm on the issue of future occupation costs; otherwise, they claimed, the country was destined for 'full economic collapse'. Conscious of the need for their backing, Tsolakoglu notified the Germans that without financial concessions he would have to resign.[125]

Few Greeks, unsurprisingly, were keen to follow in the General's footsteps and Altenburg warned Berlin of the difficulties involved in finding a successor. They were back to the old problem: should the Axis take direct control of affairs in Greece? The Germans could not, for Hitler had agreed to let the Italians have the 'preponderance' in Greece; the Italians might, but only at the price of removing an area of strategic importance uncomfortably far from German reach. Hence Altenburg urged making some concessions to the Greeks over the *Besatzungskosten* for the sake of keeping Tsolakoglu in place.[126]

At the time when the vital German offensive through the Caucasus was petering out, and Paulus's 6th Army was on the outskirts of Stalingrad, the political situation in Greece did not rank high on Hitler's list of priorities. Even so, with Rommel's North Africa campaign nearing its climax, the country's strategic importance was obvious. Altenburg's long telegram was sent on to Hitler. And it was just a few days later, on 4 September, that the Führer issued the instructions we have already referred to: the subject was redefined, the Italians and Greeks were to be made to see sense, OKW and the Foreign Ministry in Berlin were to get together and sort the matter out. Hitler's one concession to the Greek government was to agree that Gotzamanis should be invited to Berlin.[127]

In Athens people expected the Finance Minister to win substantial concessions from the Germans. In actual fact he was in a very weak position. Berlin was by now deeply suspicious of the aims of Italian policy in the Balkans, and Gotzamanis's reputation as a favourite with the Italians did not help him. In Berlin, he was allowed to present various memoranda stating the Greek government's case to officials at the Foreign Ministry, but his talks with German and Italian civil servants petered out inconclusively.

In retrospect, the most significant thing about his mission was its failure. It was not that the Greek financial crisis could be ignored; nor that the Greek Finance Minister lacked the wit or intelligence to present his case. It was simply that no Greek politician carried enough weight to be heard seriously in Berlin. Gotzamanis's failure underlines one of the main features of Nazi foreign policy: the reluctance to permit any concentration of real power, however circumscribed, in the hands of satellite politicians. 'To stabilise the existing state of affairs via negotiations with the Greek authorities is not possible,' wrote Foreign Minister Ribbentrop shortly afterwards. 'That is our conviction.'[128]

As an alternative, Ribbentrop proposed to find a German or Italian 'personality' with 'special powers in economic and financial matters' who would take 'draconian measures' in co-operation with the local Axis authorities and the Greek state. It was a typical attempt to cut through the tangled undergrowth of Nazi bureaucratic rivalries by creating a *new* post or agency to solve an inter-ministerial conflict, such as was now visible on the horizon between Ribbentrop's Foreign Ministry and OKW. And of course it also suggested that the Germans saw Greek politicians as puppets, not interlocutors.[129]

The man Ribbentrop had in mind was the impressively qualified, charming and loquacious Hermann Neubacher, a former mayor of Vienna and one of the 'old guard' of Austrian Nazis. Still only in his forties, Neubacher was 'a slight blond man with the profile of a tired eagle'. He had an outstanding reputation as an economic expert, and had been associated with I.G. Farben, whose Balkan interests were extensive, before the war. He was able, extremely self-confident and possessed powerful friends in the Nazi establishment.[130] Any Italian reservations about the appointment were brushed aside and on 16 October 1942 Neubacher was nominated Reich Special Plenipotentiary for Economic and Financial Questions in Greece. Over the next two years he was to emerge as the most tireless and resourceful advocate of a moderate policy towards Greece, keen where possible to bolster rather than weaken the authority of the Greek state.

Swiftly he now embarked upon the twin tasks of putting some order into the Greek administration and curbing the appetite of the German military. Before leaving Berlin, he conferred with Economics Minister Funk and Backe at the Ministry of Agriculture, and obtained their support for the general course he intended to follow. In what could only have been interpreted as a critical commentary on Wehrmacht thinking he noted: 'Purely technical financial operations of whatever sort are doomed to absolute failure. An economic and social solution with all the political consequences can only be fought for with any hope of success if the problem is approached in its totality.' In other words, the political effects of economic policies would be ignored by the Axis at their peril.[131]

Neubacher secured the promise of increased food deliveries into Greece from Romania, Germany and elsewhere, ordered an end to food exports from Greece, and insisted that the Wehrmacht scale down its financial demands. Although these were certainly steps in the right direction, Neubacher benefited in his anti-inflationary campaign from two fortuitous developments for which he could claim little credit. The first was that the International Red Cross began shipping supplies into Greece from the autumn of 1942 onwards, greatly easing the food situation in Athens. The second was the course of the war in North Africa. The failure of Rommel's campaign in Libya, followed by the Anglo-American landings round Casablanca, aroused hopes of an early end to the war in the Mediterranean. Black market speculators panicked and began to unload their stocks of food, with the result that inflation slowed down after October, food prices slumped dramatically, and the drachma rose against gold.[132]

This 'good start' (as one of his colleagues described it) put Neubacher in a strong position to cope with the political crisis which now broke inside the Greek government. For some time it had been obvious that the exhausted and disillusioned Tsolakoglu was reluctant to remain in office. His original decision to form a government had been prompted by the fierce nationalism that was characteristic of his generation and milieu. Yet he had been unable to prevent the dismemberment of Greece. That summer he had toured Macedonia and made a series of embarrassing speeches urging the refugees from the Bulgarian zone not to lose heart: 'Hitler abhors the idea of servitude,' he told them. 'He will not allow us to lose *any* territory. Have heart, you refugees from East Macedonia and Thrace, you will soon return.' Invariably he ended with the slogan: 'Long live greater Greece!'[133]

By mid-November both Italians and Germans felt it might be better to let him go: he had become 'untrustworthy'. Neubacher's new policies had won back some support for the Axis in certain Greek political circles. 'In view of the latest developments, it is now perhaps not inconceivable to reach agreement with Greek politicians,' observed Altenburg. When Tsolakoglu made several exorbitant demands as the price of his remaining in office, he was allowed to leave. His interim successor was the Vice-Premier, Constantine Logothetopoulos, a large, verbose and self-important university professor from the Athens medical school. 'I never mixed in politics, but always in scholarship, at which – I venture to believe – I was not unsuccessful,' was the typically maladroit opening of his first address to the nation. 'But I was forced by the indifference of others to guide this helpless country.'[134]

Logothetopoulos had only agreed to assume the premiership provisionally. But noting the Allied victories in North Africa, several potential successors, notably Ioannis Rallis – in whom the Foreign Office placed high hopes – were more cautious as November ended than they had been when it began. Altenburg warned that 'what appeared in October as an act of generosity and broad-mindedness, now looks like weakness or an expression of anxiety to the Greek public'.[135] Worse still from Neubacher's point of view, the loss of North Africa changed Greece's military role from forward supply base to a likely centre of operations in its own right. Expecting an Allied invasion somewhere in the Aegean in 1943, the Wehrmacht began a massive military build-up in Greece. Further increases in the *Besatzungskosten* were demanded and this time it was more difficult for Neubacher to argue against their importance.[136]

His conflict with the military was approaching a critical point. Inflation had led to a 'proletarianisation' of the population. The Greeks were now reported to be '95 per cent' hostile to the Axis. Yet the Wehrmacht still refused to scale down its financial demands on the Greek state.[137]

In an effort to resolve the disagreements between the diplomats and the military, a high-level discussion of the Greek problem was held in Berlin on 5 February 1943. Field Marshal Keitel, the head of OKW, started off by congratulating Neubacher, who 'had made the impossible possible in stabilising the situation in Greece'. But when a senior Foreign Ministry official raised the question of the 'new situation' that would arise if Greece became a combat zone, Keitel emphasised that there would be no military interference in Neubacher's work only so long as the situation remained unchanged. Put less diplomatically, OKW and the Foreign Ministry were on a collision course.[138]

Though they continued to tussle over financial policy for the duration of the occupation, the gradual approach of the Allies towards southern Europe during 1943–44 inevitably gave the Wehrmacht the upper hand. The course of the drachma–gold exchange rate over the next months revealed that Neubacher's success had been temporary. After February 1943 the price of gold began to rise once more; it regained its previous high point in August and went on climbing. The money supply expanded from 402 million drachmas in February to 4 billion the following January, and 68.6 billion by the summer of 1944.[139] Neubacher had merely checked, not ended, Greece's financial and fiscal crisis.

By 1944 the main topics of conversation among ordinary Greeks were the rise in food prices and the spread of barter, which had become 'the only way of acquiring the various commodities needed for life'. Money was useless for even the smallest transaction. In Karditsa an oke of corn cost 25 million drachmas. On the island of Kastellorizo, at the end of July 1944, an oke of oil cost 12 million drachmas, bread 2 million. Landlords in Athens asked their tenants to pay them in vegetables and fruit. Gendarmes on Samos found the wages they were issued by the local bank worthless, since farmers refused to accept money for their produce. Ironically, even the efficiency of the Wehrmacht was impaired: on Corfu, where a barter economy flourished, the going rate for one hand grenade was a gold sovereign, three eggs for a round of ammunition; when local German soldiers wanted a good meal they simply exchanged a number of grenades for a sheep with a local shepherd.[140]

With prices diverging substantially across the country, central control of administration became impossible, and wages had to be set locally. Private industrial and commercial firms were able to do this better than the public sector. So quite apart from the psychological and political impact of hyperinflation on people's lives – the restlessness and insecurity which led many to question the justice of the established order and made radical action increasingly popular – the economic crisis had effectively paralysed the machinery of state.

CHAPTER SIX

Greek Workers in the Reich

Dear listeners, many of you have relatives, friends and acquaintances working in Germany, and you must often wonder about the kind of life they live there. Now listen:

It is afternoon. The workers are streaming from the workrooms and go laughing and talking towards the canteen. There are many thousands of workers. We see the Greek group over there. Let us go near them and ask them: 'Hey, boys!'
Worker: Are you Greek?
[Babble of talk in Greek. Several Greek workers talking.]
Announcer: We want to know how you are getting on here.
Worker: It's now three months since I left Greece and came here. . .
Announcer: How about food?
Worker: Quite good. We get . . . bread, margarine, eggs, marmalade, macaroni. . . . We lack nothing.
Announcer: But look here, you seem to be getting much more than we get.
Worker: Yes, we do. Heavy workers get twice as much as others.
Announcer: And how is work?
Worker: No hardship there, believe me . . .
Announcer: And are you taken care of otherwise?
Worker: As for care and welfare. . . they can't do enough for us. Let my chum here tell you what happened to him the other day.
2nd Worker: I had a toothache so I went to have my tooth extracted. The doctor extracted it and told me to go straight to bed. Me go to bed for a tooth I could have extracted with my bare fingers? So I went back to work laughing at the idea, and a little after, what do you think, a man came from the hospital and said he had orders to take me to bed. . . . So I went to the hospital for the night, I tell you, for a tooth I could have extracted with my bare fingers. Just think what they'll do if you are really taken ill.

Announcer: *But boys, these things are not known at home. They would like to hear all about it.*
Workers: *Well then, you who are educated, tell them how it is with us. Tell them we are fine, never better.*[141]

This radio broadcast, preceded by a talk on socialism in Europe, and followed by a Suppé overture and a denunciation of the Katyn massacre, was part of a German propaganda drive to encourage Greeks to volunteer for work in the Reich. Greece's economic value to Berlin did not lie only in foodstuffs and minerals. One of the most valuable resources that the subjugated lands of Europe offered the Third Reich was labour, and even a small country like Greece had many unemployed workers.

Nazi utilisation of foreign labour in Fortress Europe had begun in an uncoordinated fashion. Anticipating a quick victory, the German leadership originally failed to see the value of its newly acquired labour force. There was an ideological split between technocrats who wanted the conquered territories to provide a cheap stream of *Untermenschen*, and racial purists who feared the contamination of Aryans from inferior stock. By the winter of 1941 about a third of the 3.5 million foreign labourers in the Reich were Poles; the rest were West Europeans who had come to the Reich as volunteers. At the same time the 3.9 million Soviet POWs who had been captured by the Wehrmacht in the first months of 'Barbarossa' were starving to death, and by February 1942 only 1.1 million were still alive.[142]

That this appalling crime was also an act of economic folly took time to register in Berlin. But early in 1942 Albert Speer was appointed to boost armaments production as the Eastern campaign entered a second season. With Hitler vetoing the use of German women for factory work, the Reich desperately needed foreign labour and Fritz Sauckel, the newly appointed Plenipotentiary for Labour, began a series of recruitment 'actions' across Europe in an effort to find workers for Germany.

Before Sauckel's appointment, Axis efforts to attract Greek workers abroad had been a miserable failure. According to the OKW, out of the 3.5 million workers employed in the Reich in October 1941 only 550 were Greek! Yet there were 109,000 from former Yugoslavia and 14,600 from Bulgaria, which was not even occupied.[143] In January 1942 the Commission for the Recruiting of Greek Workers for Foreign Work invited applications at its Salonika office from interested workers. When only 15–20 people responded, the German military ordered a civilian draft, and spread the rumour that those who waited to be drafted would be sent to the Russian front as auxiliary workers. But there were carrots too, and Greek workers were promised high wages and transportation expenses for their families. Letters appeared in the Greek press purporting to be from workers in Germany, praising the abundance of food, beer and medical care. By the end of 1942 around 10,000 Greeks are reported to have registered with the Commission, including workers from Athens and Patras, as well as Salonika. Farewell ceremonies were laid on at the railway stations to see them off, and they were saluted with speeches comparing Hitler's fight against Asiatic barbarism with the exploits of Alexander the Great. Then, carrying their two suits, two pairs of shoes and three days' provisions, they began their journey.[144]

Whilst the numbers were far higher than the previous year's level, they fell short of the 30,000 the authorities had expected to raise. 'Is it worth while to go on being ceremonious with the Greek people?' asked an exasperated correspondent in *Donauzeitung*. In an article entitled 'France–Germany–Greece' the pro-Axis daily *Nea Evropi* – whose collaborationist boss had just been appointed mayor of Salonika – reflected worries at the disappointing results of the labour drive. The French, it reported, had responded warmly to German appeals for help on the front and in the factories in the war against Bolshevism. But – 'we must confess' – the Greeks had been slower. The paper outlined the benefits of going to work in Germany; it was much more advanced than Greece, and Greek workers could learn a lot: 'You don't have to fight; just come and work.'[145]

Such appeals made little impact on their readership. Indeed the Greeks' reluctance was apparent at almost every level. Civil servants at the Greek Ministry of Labour did not want to recruit for Germany, forcing one of Sauckel's representatives to come to Greece to supervise the drive himself. Greek workers who were summoned to his office for examination to establish what type of work they might best be assigned claimed ignorance of any trade at all; others stated bluntly that they did not want to leave Greece and work for the Axis.[146] At the end of the year recruiting had to be suspended. In early 1943, following rumours that the Germans intended to resort to compulsory civil mobilisation, massive protest demonstrations and strikes rocked Athens and forced the Logothetopoulos government to deny that the idea was being considered.

Of the workers who went to the Reich, few lived up to German expectations. If not actually coerced, many had gone only as a last resort to escape starvation. Scares that prospective workers were carrying infectious fevers delayed the transports from Athens on several occasions and in fact a high percentage of the new arrivals proved to be, or claimed to be unfit for work. Of 500 who reached Gau Oberdonau in the summer of 1942, 272 were reported to have malaria, 66 trachoma, 22 syphilis, 70 gonorrhoea; another 17 had tuberculosis and 18 – an implausibly high number – claimed they had epilepsy. This was the Greek contribution to Speer's total war economy! On a transport which reached the Tirol that September, 80 per cent of the newcomers were found to be physically unfit. It is not clear whether the foreign labour option was attracting particularly unhealthy workers or whether, more probably, they simply reflected the deterioration in the general standard of health in Greece as a result of malnutrition and inadequate medical facilities.[147]

Among German employers the Greek labourer soon established a distinctive reputation. 'The manner and performance of the Greeks is especially poor and . . . they stand out as the worst of the foreign workers,' noted one report. The use of Greeks, according to another, was 'a failed experiment.' From Linz it was reported that 'from the beginning the Greeks set a record for absenteeism, reluctance to work and idleness'. And an agent at Reichenberg wrote that 'the works supervisor has stated that the Greeks are the biggest good-for-nothings he has ever heard of'. There were also accusations that they loitered in public places, begging and stealing, and sometimes even picked fights with Germans.

'Among the population the Greeks are often likened to Gypsies, on account of their dubious moral and political qualities,' reported a Gestapo officer. In the context of the racial values of National Socialism, and the ultimate fate of many Sinti and Roma, this was a sinister comparison to make. He went on to allude to their fondness for cards and dice, which supposedly impoverished them and led them into a life of crime. But what alarmed the Gestapo above all were the Greeks' anti-German sentiments. They caused more trouble than any other group, infecting other foreign workers with their unruliness and misbehaviour. They whipped up trouble in the labour compounds, and even argued quite openly that Germany was about to lose the war.

'The Greek agent at BBF Inc., who treats his fellow-countrymen absolutely objectively and correctly, is completely loathed in the Camp, because people regard him as a spy and even describe him as such,' stated a secret police report. 'They throw his pro-German attitude in his face, and even oppress him with threats and actual violence, so that on 26 January 1943 he received two stab wounds that sent him to hospital. At the workplace too, Greeks cause brawls, and are always picking fights even with German workers, usually over politics.' Such reports give a very different picture of the foreign worker's life abroad from that radioed back to Greece. So did the letters workers sent home: 'Please send me money and clothes,' wrote one. 'We are working 14 hours a day. Our salary is insufficient to buy food even from the people's kitchen.'[148]

Some Greek workers were equally ready to demonstrate their opposition to National Socialism outside the workplace. 'There has been a recent case in Furth, where around 9–10 p.m. a Hitler Youth member in uniform was attacked and beaten up in the street. According to the statement of this Hitler Youth member his assailant was a Greek worker. . . . So it has come to this, that Greek workers are able to . . . beat up German citizens – and youths too – during their nightly expeditions,' concluded a Gestapo report.[149]

But it was not only their violence that intruded upon the life of civilians in the Reich. Many workers supplemented their wages with a little bartering of foodstuffs and other goods, which they would hawk around the neighbouring countryside, or bring back to their camp to sell at a profit to their workmates. Some claimed to earn more like this than from their main employment. They would beg, cajole or even threaten householders and farmers for food. But there were also reports of Germans sympathising with them, and providing them with groceries. And what made the Gestapo very uneasy was that the Greeks had a habit of hanging round shops and farms where the menfolk were thought to be absent. For this, in a state structured upon the principle of racial segregation, raised the spectre of trade in the most unacceptable commodity of all – sex. An informant exclaimed: 'It is incomprehensible that German women and girls are often ready not only to run after the Greeks, but even to show themselves openly with them.' Numerous pregnancies were reported. The Greeks themselves were supposedly surprised at the behaviour of the German women. One said: 'All German women are whores. If a woman conducted herself like that in Greece, she would be delivered to a brothel.'[150] To the dismay of the authorities, the Reich's womenfolk continued to turn a deaf ear to their warnings.

No wonder the German police saw Greek workers as nothing but a headache and suggested that, since their productivity seemed so low, 'it might be considered whether in future it is worth going on with the work transports from Greece to the Reich'. In the words of another report, 'the difficulties that have occurred with the Greeks have been greater than the anticipated benefits'.[151] By late 1943, out of some 5.4 million foreign workers employed in the Reich only about 11,000 came from Greece. Many of those who had arrived on earlier transports had gone back to Greece on leave and stayed there. The following year the SS started rounding up civilians in Greek towns to make up for the shortage of volunteers.[152]

It is tempting to speculate why so few Greeks went to work in the Reich. Economic disaster at home was clearly not sufficient to drive them north, even though conditions were much worse in Greece than in other areas of Europe that provided proportionately higher numbers of recruits: many more Belgians, French and Czechs ended up working in Germany than Greeks. Nor does their ill-treatment within the Reich offer an explanation, for the Greeks' treatment at German hands was no worse than that of other foreign workers, and was probably better than that meted out to Poles, Ukrainians and Russians. Transport difficulties hardly explain the low numbers either, since when transports were laid on they were not always filled.

Wartime Allied propaganda suggested that the Germans had deliberately allowed the Greeks to starve in order to turn them into slaves. But it may be that the famine of 1941–42, together with the cruelty of Axis occupation policy generally, produced the opposite effect. The Gestapo reports suggest that the Greek population was more outspokenly anti-Nazi than, say, the Italians, French or Czechs.

The novelist Nikos Kazantzakis spent the occupation working on his novel *Alexis Zorbas*. After the war 'Zorba the Greek', a manual labourer, would come to symbolise a peculiarly Greek spirit of defiance and independence. Kazantzakis himself would write that he had learned from Zorba 'how to turn misfortune, bitterness and uncertainty into pride'. Here perhaps was a clue to the strength of national feeling which made a whole society reject the propaganda idyll of a New Europe.[153]

CHAPTER SEVEN

Dreams of a New Europe

One of the most revealing assessments of what the Nazi New Order in Europe really meant was written in the spring of 1943 by Sotirios Gotzamanis after he resigned as Greece's Finance Minister. The erstwhile 'economic dictator' had become deeply unpopular, but he was a man of considerable ability and political conviction. As a passionate admirer of Germany, he had been imprisoned during the First World War, and sent into internal exile in 1940. To General Metaxas he had argued that Greece should welcome the weakening of English 'plutocracy' and the reorganisation of Europe along totalitarian lines. Yet what reward had he received from Berlin for his convictions? The chance to preside over the economic demolition of his country. Humiliated at every turn, Gotzamanis illustrates the plight of the Greek Germanophile.

A revealing example of this humiliation took place when he visited German headquarters in Salonika in May 1942. Shortly after his arrival it happened that a German officer was found dead in the street by the Ionian Bank. The Germans immediately postponed his official dinner with General von Krenzski, and threatened to place machine-guns in the streets and shoot passers-by if the perpetrators were not captured. Only when the autopsy proved to their embarrassment that it was a case of suicide – the officer having thrown himself from an upper window – was the dinner rescheduled.[154]

Gotzamanis was taken no more seriously during his trip to Berlin and Rome in September 1942, when he had hoped he would have the opportunity to present the Greek case for reducing the occupation costs in congenial and sympathetic surroundings. For all the fanfare, the stay in the Hotel Adlon and the visits to performances of *Tannhäuser* and *Zigeunerbaron*, his official reception had been brusque. One of the senior Berlin civil servants he had met recorded later: 'In these discussions both in Rome and Berlin there were never any negotiations with Herr Gotzamanis. He was merely brought over so that we could demand certain information from him and invite him to prepare memoranda on certain topics.' His return empty-handed from Berlin precipitated a political crisis in Athens and ultimately led to his resignation. In April 1943 his first thought was to request permission, for reasons of 'personal security', to move with his family out of Greece.[155]

This was the background against which he now set out his thoughts on 'The New Europe' for Hitler and Mussolini. Grand schemes for the reorganisation of the continent under German leadership were currently being drawn up in Vienna, Paris and Milan, and at first sight the ex-Minister was simply imitating these. In fact, Gotzamanis offers many clues to his country's predicament, and indeed to the flawed premises of Hitler's whole European vision. His document masquerades as a statement of hope; but it is shot through with profound disillusionment. The sense of alignment with the course of history, which he had felt in 1940, was gone. In just three years, there had been a sea-change in his convictions.

Gotzamanis begins by reflecting on the purpose of the war and the future of Europe. The Axis must make it clear to the people of Europe what the war is about: that it is not the Anglo-Americans who will bring Europe peace, freedom and well-being, but the Europeans themselves. They are fighting for nothing less than the freedom of their continent against outside interference, against the centuries-long meddling of the British, the threat of American capitalism and Russian Bolshevism.

This external menace, however, is just the framework for his vision. For Gotzamanis, the aim of concentrating the continent's forces against the outside world is justified by the substance of the 'New Europe' that will emerge. Here he goes into considerable – and surprising – detail. The creation of a strong Europe depends upon its inhabitants coming to realise that nationalism, for all its glorious history, must be consigned to the past. 'We have arrived at the end of this stage of historical evolution.' It is amid the turbulence stirred up by national conflicts in the past that the cunning British have been able to spread their power throughout the continent. But this is not all that must be abandoned: 'It is further to be hoped that the European peoples, small and large, victors and vanquished, faced with the new ruins and misfortunes of the war, will be instructed by today's experience. . . . For them the criterion of force, gains through annexation, expansions at another's expense, must be abandoned.' Rather they must seek unification, co-operation, and search together for further 'living space' outside the confines of their continent.

Gotzamanis does not shy away from following his argument to its radical and surprisingly outspoken conclusion. 'In the new phase

14. A German propaganda photo. The original caption reads: 'The wishes of hill farmers are conveyed by the priest and noted down for the Occupation authorities. Insofar as military necessity permits, the German soldier is ready to help the population with their everyday needs.' Crete, 1944.

of international life', National Socialism of any variety is no longer strong enough in itself to secure its own aims; it requires the assistance of 'a larger and broader concept, of an enviroment which corresponds more closely to the necessity of international political-economic coalitions' – in a phrase, 'European continentalism'. The people of Europe, 'if they do not wish to be reduced to political-economic slavery, misery and ruin', must 'remake' their own history, in such a way that they shall be safe against external threats but also respectful of each other's national autonomy. For Gotzamanis does not propose an extreme federalism that would abolish national and regional differences; rather, he sets out a scheme whereby certain matters would be settled on a continental level, whilst others would come under the umbrella of a limited national sovereignty.

We may be impressed by the resemblance his 'New Europe' bears to the European Community almost half a century later, a resemblance heightened by his almost uncanny prefiguring of many of those institutions – a European monetary system, a customs union, forms of dual citizenship – which we see in the process of formation around us. But we should not lose sight of the fact that Gotzamanis's 'New Europe' is much less a prediction than a critique, and none too veiled, of the New Order he had seen imposed on Greece. For despite its respectful and even fulsome tone, Gotzamanis's memorandum does not fail between the lines to castigate the short-sightedness and rapacity of Axis policies. His message is clear: Greece finds itself not a free nation in a larger continental confederation but subordinate to larger powers pursuing their own national interests according to the traditional methods of force. Like the unhappy continent he envisages if his warnings are not heeded, Greece has been reduced to 'political-economic slavery, misery and ruin'. If her population has failed to give the Axis any support, it is because the latter have failed to provide any political motive for securing it.[156]

Gotzamanis's dream of a continental alliance of equal partners was shared by numerous collaborators throughout occupied Europe. They had all hoped to persuade Hitler of the advantages of co-operation over coercion. But like Laval in France, Mussert in Holland and Quisling in Norway, Gotzamanis and Tsolakoglu discovered that Germany's New Order was strictly hierarchical. Indeed, it had no room for politics at all, in the sense of a process of discussion and negotiation between autonomous partners. Economics, not politics, defined relations between states in the New Order. 'That which strikes everyone who comes into contact with the Germans,' wrote a young Italian diplomat in 1942, 'is their purely mechanical and materialistic conception of the European order. To organise Europe for them means fixing how much of this or that mineral should be produced or how many workers must be employed. They take no account of the fact that no economic order can survive if it is not based on a political order, and that to make the Belgian or Bohemian worker work it is not enough to promise him a given salary, but he must also be given the sense of serving a community, of which he forms an intimate part, of his own nature and in which he recognises himself.'[157]

In Greece famine, inflation and expropriation had produced a profound sense of alienation from the Axis cause. The sight of the emaciated figures who clustered each morning to search through the garbage behind the Grande Bretagne Hotel plainly revealed Greece's role in the New Order. The Germans had broken apart the existing structures of Greek society. They had failed to legitimise their presence or to create a new sense of solidarity in a common enterprise. It was to be left to the Greeks themselves to try and recreate the sense of community which would allow them in the first place to survive and then, perhaps, to find a new sense of purpose in resistance, mutual assistance and planning for the future.

PART TWO

'This Heroic Madness': 1941–43

God's wheat was loaded and hauled away
        on their giant trucks.
In the desolate and empty city
        only the hand remains
To paint across the great walls
        BREAD AND FREEDOM.

O. Elytis, *To Axion Esti*, translated
by E. Keeley and G. Savidis
(Pittsburgh, 1974), 78–9.

*Last winter – our journey into Hell. I dared not write about what
I saw – it was too burdensome & painful. . . . [Those who were
not there] will have the urge to relive it, perhaps indeed to discern
in the midst of that horror the magic of great historical moments.
All we ask is never to see such things again, to flee from them.
To flee – but in what direction?*

G. Theotokas, diary entry for 6 January 1943

CHAPTER EIGHT

The Resistance of Daily Life

On Friday, 2 May 1941, just a few days into the occupation, Panteli Georgiou was walking down Voukourestiou Street in central Athens when he heard the sound of people clapping. Thinking that pro-Nazi sympathisers were saluting German troops, he went to look. To his astonishment he found a crowd by the roadside applauding two lorry-loads of exhausted British POWs. The following Monday morning a similar incident took place: people surrounded a Wehrmacht lorry with four POWs inside, clapping loudly and offering the prisoners cigarettes. One man ran to an *ouzeri* and came back with two glasses of beer.[1]

Such demonstrations of sympathy for the POWs were frequent in the first days of the occupation. Responding swiftly, the Germans issued a decree punishing any 'contact with soldiers or civilian POWs under the guard of the German Army'. Listening to foreign radio broadcasts was also prohibited, as was any assembly or work stoppage designed to harm German interests. The new legislation prescribed the death penalty for anyone convicted of assault or sabotage against the German armed forces. These statutes provided the initial legal framework for the punishment of resistance activity.

The Germans had failed to round up all the Allied soldiers who had been left behind in Greece after the retreat to Egypt. In the summer of 1941 many were on the run. For the Greeks it was a small though dangerous step from saluting the POWs who were being driven out of the country to helping those who were still hiding. Few hesitated. 'British soldiers are universally well received,' reported two Americans who left Greece in late June. 'Many escape and the Greek population will always harbour them at whatever risk and however short they may be of food.' Another source estimated that there were hundreds of soldiers at large in Athens alone. Worried about endangering their Greek hosts, some tried to make a living by themselves, picking up a few words of Greek and roaming the streets as pedlars. Others went into 'partnership' with Cretan servicemen stranded in the capital.[2]

Even after one has taken into account the importance Greeks attach to *philoxenia* (hospitality), the extent of their support for these men is astonishing. When Constantine Altzerinakos returned from the front at the end of April to his village of Ayeranos in the Peloponnese, he found up to a hundred soldiers hiding there. Without the collusion of many civil servants and village policemen this obviously could not have happened. Altzerinakos helped form a unit with three Australians and two New Zealanders to guard and supply the remaining soldiers in the district. On Mount Taygetos a small band under a certain Captain Richard MacNabb was similarly protected by the villagers. Although the group had to disperse after a Greek gendarme was killed trying to arrest two soldiers, many of its members remained free for months. MacNabb himself became an almost legendary figure and was only captured a year later, in May 1942, in Athens.[3]

Spontaneous popular support was evident in the capital too. British soldiers were hidden in poor homes in the Ayia Varvara district. Educated women like Ioanna Tsatsou provided them with clothes, food and sheets of paper with basic phrases translated into Greek. Tsatsou explained her actions by saying simply: 'Every time we help an Englishman I have this additional satisfaction, that we are responding somehow to the force of the occupier. Because, whether by deceit, or by rebellion, we feel the need to answer their violence as a law of necessity.'[4]

One night at the end of May two young Greeks climbed up the Acropolis under the noses of the guards and took down the swastika. It was the most spectacular act of defiance so far. Athenians first heard about the incident the following day when the local German authorities threatened the culprits with the death penalty. In fact, the two boys were never arrested, even though they had been stopped and questioned by a Greek policeman on their way home. Judging from the Athens commandant's announcement, however, the theft of the swastika was merely the tip of the iceberg, as his proclamation listed many other Axis grievances against the Greek population: public opinion continued to exhibit excessive partiality for the English; demonstrations of sympathy for British POWs continued without the Greek police making any effort to intervene; public behaviour generally in Athens towards members of the German armed forces was 'not very friendly'. Greek readers seem to have found it all rather puzzling. What did the Germans expect? 'Do they truly imagine,' wrote Christides after the theft of the swastika, 'that there is a single Greek, however deeply and incurably Germanophile, who does not feel satisfied and proud at this heroic madness?'[5]

Anti-German feeling had spread into the state apparatus itself. Already the government had been forced to warn that any civil servant refusing to carry out his duties would face dismissal and lose his pension, and the Ministry of Public Security had actually dismissed several gendarmes for 'behaviour not in conformity with government policy'. When the Germans issued new ID cards in Crete in June, village policemen provided blank passes to British soldiers on the run, and even affixed their signature too. As hostility to the Germans grew – first because they had allowed in the detested Italians, then because of the famine – public professions of support for the Axis remained confined to a tiny minority of Greeks. The imitation National Socialists who eagerly offered their services to the Axis had no following at all, and the Germans never took them very seriously.[6]

Despite the growing strength of anti-Axis feeling, overt acts of resistance were sporadic. Most incidents in the first few months involved sabotage or intelligence-gathering – the work of isolated individuals or tiny groups – rather than mass action. Saboteurs, armed with British-supplied explosives, sank two ships in Piraeus harbour on 30 May; the next day there was an explosion at a munitions dump in Salonika. Similar acts continued throughout the summer, prompting the Germans to begin executing hostages in reprisal. They shot several Greeks for possessing firearms, and destroyed a number of homes.[7]

During the autumn, resistance briefly took on a new dimension with the appearance of armed bands in the mountains of northern Greece. There had been a clash in July near Kozani, in Macedonia, between a group of demobilised Greek soldiers and a German detachment, resulting in the burning down of two villages in reprisal. In September more bands appeared. The railway line from Salonika to Serres was the object of repeated sabotage efforts which produced a small number of German casualties. The forces of the Befehlshaber Saloniki-Aegais responded in a terrifying fashion: in the first mass reprisal killings of the occupation on the mainland, German troops burned two villages, Kato and Ano Kerzilion, in the estuary of the River Strymon, and shot over 200 men *en masse*. A week later, on 24 October, another 142 hostages were shot. In all some 488 civilian hostages were shot and another 164 seized in the month of October 1941 in the German zone around Salonika.[8]

The population of Macedonia was deeply shocked by the German reaction. The Governor-General of northern Greece, Alexandros Rangavis, a former ambassador to Berlin and a Germanophile of the old school, visited some of the burnt villages to see for himself what had happened, and then resigned in disgust, after a violent quarrel with the local German commander. In some cases, terrified villagers took arms from the Germans to keep the guerrillas out. Sporadic acts of sabotage continued; but in general the deterrent effect in northern Greece was swift, and resistance faded away in the winter months.[9]

It is tempting to assume that the reason for this, apart from the onset of winter, was the very ferocity of the German response. Yet to the north, in dismembered Yugoslavia, where German reprisal policy was, if anything, harsher than in Greece, widespread resistance sprang up in the early summer of 1941 and, far from dwindling away, intensified as the year progressed. Yugoslavia possessed many of the same elements of a potential mass resistance movement as Greece – a defeated army, economic collapse, a dismembered state, a small but active communist party. But there were in addition several crucial catalysts. One was ethnic disharmony: the bloody anti-Serbian policies of the new puppet Croat state set up by the Axis immediately drove thousands of frightened Serbs into the hills, where many joined either the Serbian nationalist chetniks, or Tito's partisans. In Greece there was no parallel to the disruption caused by the Croat Ustashe. The closest case was in Bulgarian-occupied Greek Thrace where the population did, indeed, rise up in the first few months before fleeing into the adjacent German zone. But Thrace was on the fringes of Greece, Croatia in Yugoslavia's centre.

Another peculiarity of the Yugoslav case was that under Tito's leadership the Communist Party made an early decision to ground the armed struggle in the rural areas, anticipating their Greek counterparts by over a year. Finally, under Mihailovic there was also a core of Serbian army officers who chose to lead a resistance movement in the summer of 1941; Greek army officers, on the other hand, either fled abroad to the Middle East – a more feasible journey from Greece than from Yugoslavia – or made their way home. Many of them only took up arms in 1942 when the Italians decided to intern them in camps in Italy. So far as Greece was concerned, the combination of localised German terror and more generalised Italian *far niente* kept the countryside quiet.

*

So in the first year of the occupation as the country slid into economic catastrophe, it was difficult to foresee the long-term effects on Greek popular opinion. The struggle for survival seemed to leave little time for other concerns. The hostility towards the Axis and their surrogates was evident, but against the background of Nazi Germany's overwhelming domination of Europe it was unclear what forms this hostility was likely to take or how intense it would become.

Some thought that the Germans' 'mad policy must inevitably provoke revolt'. One American talked of the likelihood of another 'French revolution'. Italian observers also believed they discerned the origins of a 'revolt psychosis'. In a report of January 1942 addressed to Mussolini, an Italian official put this in stark terms: 'The reasoning which pushes the Greek towards revolt is simple enough and straightforward. It tells him: "Come what may you cannot live". Your sons are condemned to die of hunger. All that is left to you is to revolt, kill and be killed honourably. All Europe, suffering like you, will follow your example and the country will have new heroes.' Foreign Minister Ciano reckoned that 'anything is possible, from epidemics to ferocious revolts on the part of a people who know they have nothing to lose'.[10]

Yet signs of a deep despondency and sense of resignation were also in evidence in those early months. Against the revolutionary prognosis, it was equally possible to argue that few people revolt in a state of physical exhaustion. According to this line of reasoning, put with his customary forcefulness by Josef Goebbels, active opposition lay some way off. 'The inhabitants of the occupied areas,' he wrote in his diary in February 1942, 'have their fill of material worries. Hunger and cold are the order of the day. People who have been this hard hit by fate, generally speaking, don't make revolutions.'[11]

With almost no encouraging news from abroad, what Theotokas called the 'grim ugliness of foreign subjection' seemed to have subdued the Greeks. They were leaderless and confused, neither King George in exile nor Tsolakoglu offering anything to rally round. 'They seem like people coming back from the cemetery after a funeral,' noted Roncalli, 'returning home to face new griefs.' This was what Theotokas called 'the great sadness of wartime Athens. The dead, deserted, weighty presence of foreign occupation.' One day he noticed that the clocks had stopped; in the streets and arcades, on public buildings – no one was bothering to wind them: 'It's like a universal epidemic of clocks. A melancholy and enigmatic symptom of the disintegration of the life of the community.'[12]

'A heavy silence' was what the empty streets of Athens conveyed to the American journalist, Betty Wason, broken only by 'the occasional screech of a Nazi military car . . . and the faint, whimpering cry of the starving, who beg in small voices from the corners where they have dropped, too weak to move further'. 'Landscape of death . . . only a boundless, dense, unwrinkled silence,' wrote the young poet Takis Sinopoulos. The sense of overwhelming deprivation and gloom was underlined by electricity cuts and water shortages, which made even the home life to which so many people retreated increasingly oppressive. The curfew drove people off the streets. 'In the silence and perfect obscurity of the night,' wrote a visitor to Salonika, 'one hears the measured tread of the sentry, as if the city had become an immense penitentiary.'[13]

Summing up this mood of almost claustrophobic oppression, Vasilis Tsitsanis, a young bouzouki player, wrote 'Cloudy Sunday', a song which as he later put it, 'came out of the "clouds" of the occupation, from the despair which gripped us all, a time when fear overshadowed everything and slavery held us down'. 'You're a day like the one when I lost my happiness,' ran the lines which remain familiar to Greeks today. 'When I see you bringing rain, I have no peace. You make my life black and I sigh deeply.'[14]

In response, perhaps, to the tribulations of daily life, people flocked to the theatre, the cinema and other entertainments of their own. While night-clubs and gambling dens opened up for Axis officers or black-marketeers – the Oasis in the Zappeion gardens, Argentina in Philhellinon Street, Kit-Kat ('das beliebteste Lokal in Athen mit dem besten Attraktionen') in Voukourestiou – open-air games of roulette were a common sight in the streets of the capital and signs hung in the kafeneia windows announcing 'The Great Roulette available within'. Nothing like this had been seen in prewar Athens. 'Round these tables you can see the boys who sell cigarettes, beggars, vagabonds, school-kids, clerks and policemen – everybody. An indescribable disgrace,' wrote the scandalised Christides. But for some (like Nina, the tough, loud-mouthed heroine of Taktsis's novel The Third Wedding Wreath) gambling became a diversion from the horrors and humiliations of daily life; for others, perhaps, it offered a chance to mimic the shattering of the prewar order, as fortunes collapsed and changed hands through inflation and starvation.

Nostalgia offered another escape route. The Amfissa taverna on Omonia Square, for example, advertised 'genuine prewar cuisine and excellent retsina at unbelievable prices.' Soon 'prewar' came simply to signify almost unimaginable quality. Another of Tsitsanis's songs, 'Arabian Girls', summed up male yearning for the pleasures of a past which now seemed to belong to a different world:

Magical nights, dreams of sensual loves, forgotten, in exile.
My mind runs back to those beloved evenings in Arabia.

I'll tell you sadly, with tears, of so many crazy women

15. A publicity shot of the young Vasilis Tsitsanis.

> I long for, sensual, erotic Arab girls, with whisky,
> sweet guitars, fun and drink....

*

While individual acts of defiance remained rare, anonymous messages to the occupiers began to spread across towns and cities. Anonymity is often, after all, a tool of the weak against the strong. In late July 1941 giant painted V's suddenly appeared on street walls in Athens. The Germans insisted that they stood for German victory, the Italians for 'Vinceremo' (We will overcome). The Greeks knew better. 'Yesterday I saw two wonderful signs with black paint on the marble of a house on Ave. Vasilissas Sofias,' wrote Dounias on 29 July, ' "Vinceremo" and next to it a capital "M" i.e. Mussolini. But someone had added to it the letters "erda". So today the Athenians are reading: "Vinceremo Merda"!' (We will overcome – Shit!) Often, so that there should be no misunderstanding, the 'V' was followed by the letters 'RAF'.[15]

The famous war-cry of 'Aera' (literally, 'Air') with which the Greeks had put the Italians to flight in the Albanian campaign inspired a whole repertoire of jokes at the expense of the detested

91

macaronades. German soldiers shouted it after Italians in the middle of Athens; so did urchins and shoeblacks. The story spread of the quick-witted *loustro* (shoeblack) who yelled 'Aera' at a *carabiniere* and then took to his heels. Seeing the irate Italian chasing after him, he stopped suddenly, turned round with his hands in the air and shouted: 'Bella Grecia!' – which was the phrase *Italian* soldiers had used in Albania when they surrendered to Greeks! When the USA entered the war, 'Aera' acquired a new meaning. Scrawled everywhere it had now turned into an acronym: 'Anglia/Ellas/Rossia/Ameriki' (England/Greece/Russia/America).[16]

In November 1942, when one of many rumours of imminent Liberation swept the country, slogans appeared daubed across the walls of the market in Piraeus mocking the local black-marketeers who had begun to panic and dump their goods: 'Telegram for General Alexander. Please delay your arrival. We are being ruined. Signed: the black-marketeers of Piraeus'! The reply followed: 'For the black-marketeers of Piraeus. Can't stop. Sell! Signed: General Alexander.' There were similarly ironical messages for Rommel, urging him to try harder to defeat the British.[17]

So ubiquitous was this graffiti, psychologically so important in reasserting the Athenians' sense of control over their own city, that the capital's appearance was completely changed. When Karl Rankin, an American diplomat, returned to newly liberated Athens on the heels of the retreating Germans in October 1944, he noted that 'the most striking innovation was the stupendous amount of paint which had been and was still being used, not to improve appearances, but to deface buildings and monuments and sidewalks, with slogans of various kinds'. Rankin perhaps did not realise what courage many of those responsible had needed: Wehrmacht files record, for example, that two months before Liberation an unnamed man, surprised in the act of daubing the words '5 Minutes to 12' on a wall in Piraeus, was 'shot in flight' by German troops.[18]

Air raids presented a further opportunity for Greeks to demonstrate defiance of the Axis, and when Allied bombing missions began, many of them reacted in an extraordinary way. During a large raid at the end of August 1941 Theotokas was at an open-air cinema on Stadion Street; to his surprise, people continued watching the film, pointedly ignoring what was happening above their heads. One woman whispered to herself 'Ah, my *Englezakia*, my *Englezakia*!' with what he records was 'an erotic excitement', to the delight of her neighbours.[19] 'Let's see,' says the starving little orphan boy in Julia Persaki's story 'The Boy Looks at the Heavens', 'perhaps they will come and drop their bombs? Perhaps the *Englezakia* will set us free this evening!' 'Do you remember,' wrote Eleni Vlachou in 1945, 'leaping out of bed and running to the terrace. . . . There above, close to us, free men lived and fought . . . English, Greeks, perhaps friends or acquaintances. The sky knew no occupation. It was a free battlefield above the enslaved city.' Significantly, 'sky' and 'heaven' are the same word in Greek: the bombers could be seen as a sign from God.[20]

Of course, not everyone saw them that way. Theotokas himself noted that at another open-air cinema there were scenes of panic, and the inhabitants of the badly hit area around the Piraeus docks cannot have shown the same sang-froid as those in the centre of Athens. Yet the impression remains that the air raids provided a welcome reminder of the Germans' own weaknesses, and kept hopes of Liberation alive. Axis propaganda efforts to use the bombing raids to turn public opinion against the Allies were mostly unsuccessful. As Dounias wrote, at the end of 1941: 'Above our national disaster, which assumes more terrible dimensions every day, one consoling thought alone takes wing, making our worst ills bearable: the hope and the certainty that at the end England will win! This hope of ours thrives a little more each time we hear the familiar hum of the English planes above our heads.'[21]

*

In these early months, before politics polarised everything, writers, artists and poets were also encouraging a spirit of resistance. During the Second World War Greek poets would produce a body of work comparable in quality to the British war poetry of 1914–18. Two Nobel laureates, Seferis and Elytis, and other major poets such as Ritsos, Engonopoulos and Sinopoulos wrote some of their finest poems in these years. None, however, made a greater impact at this time than Angelos Sikelianos. Despite financial and physical problems that made his friends despair, the mercurial fifty-eight-year-old poet still possessed the extraordinary vigour of his youth. Like Yeats perhaps, another great nationalist poet, Sikelianos found his instinctive aesthetic elitism and his total confidence in his own poetic powers justified by his ability to express popular concerns.

As if to point up the complacency in Goebbels's confident assertion that revolt was still far away, Sikelianos wrote a defiant epigram at the height of the famine which quickly made the rounds in Athens. In '25 March 1942' – a date which commemorated the 1821 War of Independence – he prophesied an imminent national Resurrection:

The swallows of death threaten to bring you
Oh Greece, a new spring, and from the grave a gigantic birth.

Vainly is the guard of the Romans on watch around you.
Soon you will rise up in a new Twenty-One.

Nor was this an isolated example of Sikelianos's attitude towards the Axis. The very title of his wartime collection, *Akritika*, which he published at the end of that first harrowing winter, reflected the increasingly defiant and patriotic direction of his work. The 'Akritika' was the name traditionally given to a body of Greek folk-poems which celebrated the Byzantine frontier hero, Digenis Akritas, the guardian of the eastern marches against the Muslim invaders. *His* poems too would be popular, martial and patriotic, tapping the various streams – the Byzantine, but also the classical and the Orthodox – which flowed together into modern Hellenism.

In January 1943 the novelist Theotokas would record his inability to describe 'the journey through Hell' of the previous winter. It was a sign of Sikelianos's sense of purpose that he attempted just this, and in 'Agrafon' ('The Unwritten') – perhaps the grimmest and most disturbing poem in his entire *oeuvre* – he hammered home the connection between the winter's suffering, the economic collapse and the need for a spiritual rebirth and a new social order.[22]

The poem opens with Jesus and his disciples walking outside the walls of Jerusalem. They come suddenly upon a rubbish dump, filthy and squalid, where crows are feeding off the debris and animal carcasses. When Jesus's followers shrink back, overcome by the stench, he walks straight ahead. One of the disciples asks him how he can stand the smell:

> Jesus, His eyes fixed on the carcass,
> Answered: 'If your breath is pure, you'll smell
> the same stench inside the town behind us.
> But now my soul marvels at something else,
> marvels at what comes out of this corruption.
> Look how that dog's teeth glitter in the sun:
> like hailstones, like a lily, beyond decay,
> a great pledge, mirror of the Eternal, but also
> the harsh lightning-flash, the hope of Justice!

As these lines suggest, Sikelianos had come to believe passionately that the pursuit of social justice was one of the chief goals of Christianity. In July 1941 he praised the newly appointed Archbishop of Athens, Damaskinos, as 'our national and heroic *social* Fighter!' Like poetry, Orthodoxy had to his mind above all a social function. During the famine, his views hardened. Writing near the end of the war on 'The Social Content of Christianity', he called for a return to the seriousness and devotion of the early Church. Citing an appeal which Damaskinos had made, attacking the food speculators who enriched themselves amid widespread starvation, Sikelianos too demanded 'an urgent economic egalitarianism among all Greeks' and an 'organic and viable national and social formation', whose guiding principles would be derived from 'the original social contribution of Christianity'.[23]

By 1944, with civil war breaking out between rival resistance factions, he was in despair. His own ecumenical vision of resistance had been overtaken by events, while his outspoken opposition to the greed of the wealthy led him to be mistakenly accused of belonging to the Left. As his wife Anna said: 'Some narrow-minded party hacks, with ready judgement, now saw a change in Angelos' political position. There was no change . . . he served Greece and the popular spirit in its struggles for Freedom and the honour of History, angrily rebutting recalcitrant individualism, un-controllable party bickering.'[24]

*

While Sikelianos pursued his own, largely apolitical course with his customary panache, other Greeks were approaching the task of resistance in a very different spirit. Motivated to a large extent like him by outrage at the social consequences of foreign domination, they began discreetly and anonymously applying themselves to the task of constructing an underground organisation which, though few realised it at the time, would revolutionise Greek politics.

One evening at the beginning of 1942 there was a knock on Ioanna Tsatsou's door. It was a friend: ' "I have come to request you officially to join EAM," he said. "They have asked for you specifically." "What is EAM," I asked. "Who is their leader?" "EAM is a Resistance Organisation," he replied. "They don't give names at a time like this." '[25]

'They don't give names': the very words are an important clue to something new in Greek politics. For the first question a prospective member normally asked before joining any group was the name of its leader. The klephts who had fought the Turks in 1821 had proudly publicised their names; so too had the great heroes in the Macedonian struggle against the Bulgarians at the turn of the century.

But these activists were different. A young army officer, Mario M., had a meeting one day in 1942 with an EAM contact in a house up in the hills above Agrinion. As he made his way down again, he was stopped by an elderly shepherd, a veteran of the Balkan Wars. 'What did they want?' enquired the old man with characteristic directness. 'They invited me to join their organisation.' The old man asked just one more question: 'Who is their *archigos* [leader]?' On being told that they did not have one, he advised the young man not to join them. 'Are they ashamed?'[26]

The shepherd's questions reflected many of the values of Greek mountain life – its focus on shame and pride, and its individualism. Several smaller resistance organisations in occupied Greece did conform to such traditional expectations, and based themselves on the influence and prestige of local notables. But EAM/ELAS, which developed into the largest resistance movement of all, was different, and in place of the usual *archigos* there was a committee. Its anonymity was bound up with an essentially new form of political activity in Greece, a process of mass social mobilisation. The old political system of patrons and clients, based upon personalised and publicly recognised links between individuals, now found itself outstripped by a resistance movement which boasted proudly that it was an 'organisation' of occupational groups. It drew upon the secretive methods of prewar communist activism but no less important in the long run than secrecy was its ability to recruit broadly across Greek society by appealing to ordinary people's daily concerns. In place of the territorial and constitutional preoccupations of the old political class, EAM – like Sikelianos – emphasised the need for 'social justice' and 'an urgent economic egalitarianism among all Greeks'. And its activists saw themselves precisely as the poet had described Archbishop Damaskinos, as 'national and heroic social fighters'.

CHAPTER NINE

Prudence or Bravery? The Old Politicians

EAM's meteoric rise underlined the bankruptcy of traditional politics in wartime Greece. To explain how a small, outlawed communist party like the Greek Communist Party (KKE) was able to assume the leadership of a mass movement in the space of a couple of years, we must first turn to the behaviour of the mainstream parties. For it was as much their weakness as the strength or deviousness of their successors that explains the subsequent pattern of events.

In the twenty years up to 1936 politics had revolved around the quarrel between Venizelists and anti-Venizelists over the issue of whether Greece should be a monarchy or a republic. Professional politicians found it more difficult to tear themselves away from this constitutional issue than the general public did. When King George returned to Greece in 1935, royalist politicians had almost as much trouble drumming up enthusiasm among their supporters as the republicans did in arousing any sort of active hostility. There was little protest and no serious resistance to Metaxas's dictatorship – the sort of democracy he had abolished had few defenders left.

Ideological differences were not what separated Venizelists and anti-Venizelists and they had not encouraged debate about the real issues that faced the country – the refugee problem, land reform, the expansion of industry, and the need for legislation on social security. The main parties had no roots at the base except for those secured through personal ties; and if such roots could extend far they were also weak. Once he lost his influence at the top, a politician risked seeing his clients and followers look elsewhere for help.

This process had already begun under Metaxas: if former deputies did not come to terms with the new regime – as many did, either by accepting ministerial office, or keeping up their *mesa* (connections) with acquaintances in government – they lost power quickly. By the time the Germans marched in, and Axis occupation began, the old patronage networks had been badly damaged. They

97

could not be repaired during the occupation except by the risky strategy of collaboration, a course few followed.

Yet there was another way of securing political power before – and after – 1941, and that was to start at the base. Making a virtue of necessity, the Greek Communist Party, the KKE, had adopted this strategy. Only the KKE – out of all the prewar parties – had managed to establish a permanent youth section, a feat which testified to its very different approach to politics and which hinted at its future growth. For a party which never managed to gain above 10 per cent of the vote between the two world wars, it developed surprising strength in the union movement and among students. Although the KKE was persecuted and almost destroyed by Metaxas and Maniadakis, his efficient Minister of Public Security, its members acquired expertise in a type of political practice well suited to the occupation period.

King George's decision to suspend Parliament indefinitely in 1936 had clearly been unconstitutional. After Metaxas's death in January 1941, however, he might have healed his rift with the politicians by forming a government of national unity. This could even have been presented as the prelude to an eventual recall of the 1936 Parliament. But the King's attempts to invite the Venizelists back brought a sharp reaction from senior army officers, who were by now in control of a thoroughly purged anti-Venizelist force and had no wish to share their power with their old enemies. King George gave way, and entrusted the government instead to a non-politician, the banker Koryzis. He thus rebuffed the country's democratic forces and confirmed the power of men who were at that moment holding out peace feelers to the Germans. With extraordinary incompetence, he moved further down the same road after Koryzis committed suicide. By rejecting calls to dismiss Metaxas's security chief, Maniadakis, George ensured he would be identified with the dictator's heritage. He departed from Athens for exile with a government headed by yet another non-politician, Emmanouil Tsouderos.

Left behind in occupied Athens, the old politicians were split into various factions, united only by their bitter feelings towards the King; even prewar royalists were alienated by his support for Metaxas and his continued associations with survivors of the regime. General Tsolakoglu tried to capitalise on this anger. Unabashed by his own formerly royalist views, he presented his government as one opposed to Metaxas and to the King, and announced his intention to prosecute some of Metaxas's former ministers. A press campaign was soon mounted to expose various 'scandals' which had occurred after 1936. Several prominent public figures, such as the writer and academician Spiros Melas, published attacks on the former dictator.

Although the leading political 'personalities' avoided taking office under Tsolakoglu, they could not help being seduced by his pleas for their advice. Several were convinced of the inevitability of an eventual German victory; others were attracted by his anti-Metaxas campaign. In early May he was able to announce that he had held talks with many important figures 'to hear their views on the new situation'; among them were most of the leaders of the anti-Venizelist side, and several of their former opponents, including George Papandreou. As Christides noted bitterly: 'What they said when they went there has no importance. The important thing is that they went. That was a terrible mistake.' At Tsolakoglu's trial after the war, it was to emerge that many of them had backed his decision to form a government.[27]

But it did not take long for most of them to realise the dangers of a close association with his government. No major politician agreed to serve the Axis until Ioannis Rallis in 1943, and even he was not in the first rank. Some, like General Pangalos, planted their followers in administrative positions in the state apparatus. Others retreated to local bastions. In general, however, the prewar political elite avoided implicating themselves very deeply with the Axis.

But they did little to oppose them either. In July 1941, for example, the elderly General Mazarakis, a conservative but independently minded Venizelist, called together a group of politicians and intellectuals to discuss what measures would have to be taken to maintain public order and prevent anarchy when the occupation ended. It is difficult to say whether we should admire their confidence in the final outcome or be astonished at their indifference to events around them. But to suggest that their time might have been more effectively spent organising soup kitchens or making arrangements for the support of demobilised soldiers would be to misunderstand their own conception of their role. Such practical matters were for women, priests, or well-intentioned foreigners. Politics, as they understood it, was about defending the country's borders, upholding public order, establishing a sound constitutional basis for government. For men like Mazarakis, the most worrying result of the German invasion was that it had prevented the political elite from re-establishing itself at 'the helm of the Nation' after Metaxas's death. Greece was 'a ship buffeted by the storm of European history' and the forces of anarchy were capable of capsizing it. By 'anarchy' Mazarakis and his generation meant not the Germans but communist rule. Even before the Greek Communist Party had recovered from the catastrophic effects of Metaxas's repression, the traditional politicians were already allowing their old anti-communist apprehensions to guide them.[28]

The members of Greece's political elite were confident that they alone embodied the popular will, and were uniquely positioned to establish what it was. 'True leaders . . . guide, inform, direct, they don't pander to the frequently inconsistent, unstable and wavering public opinion,' insisted Mazarakis.[29] Not the impersonal structures of party or state bureaucracy but direct personal contact and popular acclaim provided, in their view, the channel between the populace and their leaders. It was a view of politics which left them few options in the circumstances of the occupation.

The Communists, meanwhile, were active: in May they set up EA – National Solidarity – an underground relief organisation that expanded very rapidly during the famine and introduced many people to resistance work; in July they helped found EEAM – the National Workers' Liberation Front – and then, at the end of September, EAM – the National Liberation Front – itself. Unwilling to make their dominant role in EAM too visible, they encouraged several groups of fellow-travellers to join them. In addition, they sought the co-operation of the political mainstream.

As they had perhaps expected, the leading bourgeois politicians rejected their overtures. The elderly Venizelist Kafandaris doubted the value of resistance and wanted to wait and see what turn events would take. ('Kafandaris is so egocentrically minded, that for him the whole world catastrophe, with all its appalling consequences for Greece, is reduced to another war – the war of the Two Georges – between himself and the King', ran a later damning non-communist assessment of the republican boss.)[30] Another veteran Liberal, the elderly Themistoklis Sofoulis, was equally sceptical. For Mazarakis, talk of a 'national liberation struggle' was childish: the political world would lose all credibility if it took it seriously. And George Papandreou, a much younger man, justified a similar stance with the quip that 'a politician's primary virtue is prudence; bravery comes second.'[31]

Such doubts were not necessarily signs of cowardice: Papandreou and others were, for example, willing to pass on intelligence to the British. The obstacle lay rather in their anxiety that EAM represented a more impersonal form of political organisation which was ill-suited to their own style of activity. 'What is it which makes them rest content with *kafeneion* gossiping with their busy acolytes, who can't wait to lick the bone of power as soon as it is offered?' demanded Dimitri Glinos, a leading communist intellectual. He went on to supply his own answer: 'Because, above all, they fear the People. They fear their awakening, their active participation in the struggle for redemption; they fear that when people take their freedoms into their own hands, it will no longer be they who guide them in their future political life. Because till now they've been used to governing from above.'[32] Rather than becoming involved with a movement whose goals they mistrusted, most politicians preferred to look far ahead to the restoration of their own power.

This was an attitude which inevitably brought them up against the thorny question of the monarchy, for the British, and above all Churchill, insisted on standing by King George. For more than two years, Whitehall and Downing Street ignored a stream of advice which clarified in unmistakable terms the depth of anti-monarchist sentiment in occupied Greece. The King's association with Metaxas, his flight from the Germans, his failure to organise or set himself behind any form of resistance movement were all factors contributing to his unpopularity.

Reflecting the popular mood, a letter brought out to Egypt opposing the King's return carried the signatures of leading members of all the main prewar parties. It was, however, no coincidence that this first united action by the old political leaders took place soon after the formation of EAM. Stressing the constitutional question – their old obsession – in effect became part of an alternative political strategy to joining the new organisation. Among EAM's members there was a furious debate over whether or not to sign the declaration, and the organisation came close to disintegrating before it was decided that EAM must be kept open to people of *all* political affiliations, including supporters of the King. 'I can't understand you communists,' the veteran Liberal leader Sofoulis remarked to a communist emissary. 'While you have paid and continue to pay for the King's idiocies, you are prepared to work with royalists.'[33] Glinos's verdict on politicians like Sofoulis was that 'they forget nothing of their old bad habits and learn nothing from the new conditions'.[34]

But did the old politicians' intransigent republicanism just reflect their outmoded mental attitudes; or did it have a more considered, and even sinister, side as well? For where did it lead them? By abjuring active resistance against the Axis, and insisting on their hostility to the King, they took up a position very close to that of the Tsolakoglu regime itself. Venizelist figureheads like Generals Gonatas and Pangalos might argue that infiltrating their cronies into the state apparatus would make useful intelligence available, and put men in place who would turn against the Axis 'when the time came'; but unsympathetic critics found other, less creditworthy explanations for such tactics.

The apathetic attitude of the old 'political world', whether motivated by fear, reluctance or genuine doubt at the value of armed resistance, suited the quisling government. For so far as the dispute over the King was concerned, the focus of politics lay not in occupied Greece but in the Middle East. Gradually, the Greek politicians' antagonism to King George was tempered by the reflection that behind him lay the British, in whose hands the ultimate authority over postwar Greece would surely lie. Their rejection of any part in mass resistance left them in the position of having to choose between the Germans and the British; and since for most the decision was an easy one, they soon realised that they would have to come to terms with the government in exile. Panayiotis Kanellopoulos was one of the first to realise this. He avoided signing the protocol against the King, then unexpectedly fled from Greece in April 1942 and became Minister of War in the exile government, blazing a trail that many other politicians would follow. Soon the caiques would be ferrying party leaders across the Aegean to Turkey and the Middle East. Their thinking was clear: the future of postwar Greece would be decided outside the country.

CHAPTER TEN

Becoming Organised

It is now time to look more closely at the role of those activists on the fringes of – or indeed outside – the 'political world', who took a different view. Thanks to a recent flood of memoirs, biographies and other sources, we can appreciate how quickly members of the Greek Communist Party (KKE) moved to create the organisational basis of a mass resistance movement. And if there is a danger of taking this evidence too literally, and being accused of accepting the claims of the Left at their face value, the fact is that no one else acted with the same sense of purpose to harness the anti-Axis sentiment that existed among the population at large.

*

For the first few months the main concern of communist activists was the reformation of the Party itself. This was in terrible disarray following five years of highly effective repression by Metaxas's secret police. Immediately following the invasion, its general secretary, Zachariades, had been sent north to Vienna and then to Dachau, where he spent the entire war. Some 200 members escaped from prison or island exile in the confusion during April and May, but many more remained incarcerated. Agents of the Metaxas regime had to be weeded out, new appointments made. Before the German invasion of the Soviet Union, moreover, there was great debate over what line the Party should take, and those cadres who publicly called for resistance from as early as May were not immediately heeded. But 22 June – the start of Operation Barbarossa – swept away all doubts, and at the 6th Plenum, held in July, the basic decision was made to endorse national front tactics in the fight against the Axis. The Party proclaimed that it would struggle for 'social liberation' and the 'popular rule of workers and peasants'. In the same month the negotiations with various union representatives, which had been going on since mid-May, reached fruition in the formation of EEAM – the National Workers' Liberation Front. The signatories included the general secretary of the main national trades union confederation, and a representative of the rival communist union movement. Later they would be joined by the third major organisation, the Independents.

At the 7th Plenum, after the failure of its efforts to attract mainstream politicians, the Party decided to move ahead and formed EAM in September. The Central Committee member introducing the resolution stressed the need to draw broadly on popular support from all quarters, irrespective of political sympathies and, above all, to provide badly needed leadership:

> Popular anger grows daily, as in the mass refusal by farmers to hand over their crops to the thieving [state] collection organisations which give them to the foreign occupiers, the continued struggle in Crete . . . The terror tactics of the occupiers have led in Greece to an anti-Fascist ferment. If popular anger has not taken more widespread forms (strikes, sabotage, demonstrations etc.), this is due to the tardy organisation of national forces in a National Liberation Front, as a result of past errors by the 'political world' of our country. We must accelerate the rhythms of organisation of our national forces.

It was an ambitious and forceful analysis, couched in increasingly patriotic and national rather than class-based terms.[35]

The speaker on this occasion was Chrysa Chadzivasileiou, an unusual figure in the male-dominated world of Greek politics. The very presence of the thin, intense former schoolteacher, with her glasses and her tightly bound dark hair, her long experience of poverty, prison and island exile, epitomised the challenge which now faced the old politicians from the much broader social vision of the KKE. Not only was an effort made to incorporate as wide a range of social groups as possible within EAM, but these groups were identified, not as isolated individuals, but in terms of their social role. The emphasis, unusually for Greek politics, was firmly on the need for effective organisation. We find, for instance, that when an EAM cell was set up on Corfu, in the winter of 1941–42, it rapidly broadened around its initial nucleus, the Welfare Committee, to include a range of different departments: EAM for civil servants; EAM for workmen; EAM for women; EAM for students; EAM for high-school pupils. A similar development took place in Boeotia.[36]

The public announcement of the formation of EAM occurred on 10 October 1941, and was followed by a period of intense organisational activity. While talks with the bourgeois politicians continued, the structure of EAM was being consolidated. Local and

16.   Communist Party activist: Chrysa Chadzivasileiou.

regional groups were established. Many workers, civil servants and others were already members of EEAM or EA, the food distribution organisation, both of which were represented on the central committee of EAM and participated in its first full session in January 1942. Town and village committees were set up.

There is no doubt that the driving force behind these developments – on the organisational level, at least – was the KKE. Its own party machine was strong and well oiled, and far more powerful than those of its junior partners in EAM. The vacuum caused in its central committee by the absence of Zachariades was resolved by the appointment of a former tobacco worker called George Siantos, known as the 'Old Man', as acting general secretary over the winter. The leading figures in EAM, Apostolou and Chadzis, were both party members, and the latter admits to acting on Siantos's instructions when he approached bourgeois politicians on EAM's behalf. All this, however, was quite clear to the latter during their talks and did not necessarily rule out their co-operation; after all, these same Liberals had been prepared to work together with the communists in 1936. Now, though, instead of co-operating, they played for time.

In the autumn of 1941 a rival to EAM called EDES – the National Republican Greek League – was also set up in Athens. Supposedly under the leadership of the absent republican General Plastiras, it was in fact controlled by a shady but ebullient army officer called Napoleon Zervas. EDES's goals were announced as the establishment of a republic with a 'socialist form'; but Zervas's socialism was only skin deep. Even this, however, was more than his commitment to armed resistance against the occupiers, which found no place at all in his initial programme. When EAM representatives met Zervas to discuss the possibility of joint action, Zervas was extremely evasive. Well might he have been, for EDES's sponsors included ardent republicans like Generals Gonatas and Pangalos, who were determined not to alienate the Axis authorities. Zervas was not yet confident of the British backing which would eventually enable him to take to the mountains and play an extremely complex double game against EAM's military wing, ELAS.[37]

ELAS itself, which eventually became the most formidable armed resistance movement in the country, only took shape slowly. From October 1941, army officers sympathetic to EAM were encouraged to study the problems of organising and continuing an armed struggle. At the end of the year, *Rizospastis*, the party daily, called for the resistance to move forward under the inspiration of the bands that had appeared in Crete and Macedonia. Next month, Siantos called for armed units to be formed throughout the country. Andreas Tsimas, the young and highly intelligent Athens party secretary, was instructed to travel to central Greece, where the first armed units were officially approved by EAM in April. It is only then that we find the first formal mention of the Greek People's Liberation Army – ELAS.

By the spring of 1942 all the main elements of the EAM organisation were in place – the central organisation itself, its union arm, EEAM, its youth movement, which had also been formed during the winter, and, finally, ELAS. The membership of the KKE was expanding quickly – by March 1942 the Athens branch alone had over a thousand members – and it seems likely that the evolution of EAM followed a similar course. But we must not assume that this organisational achievement automatically translated into active resistance. It is as well to treat EAM claims for its leading role in the patriotic demonstrations of 28 October 1941 and 25 March 1942 with caution: it is often unclear whether EAM and its affiliates were leading or being led by the great upsurges of what Roncalli described as the Greeks' 'fervid nationalism'.[38]

Certainly the Italian authorities did not feel threatened for some time. General Geloso reported with satisfaction in the summer of

1942 that 'throughout Greek territory during one year of occupation public order has never been disturbed by events which could be seriously regarded as threatening the security of the troops and the population'.[39] British POWs at large had been efficiently rounded up, and substantial quantities of arms hidden after the armistice had been recovered. 'With the passage of time,' he went on, 'the population has become steadily more satisfied with our rule, recognising the virtues of fair, considerate and generous action.' With the terrible winter of 1941–42 behind them, and the prospect of Red Cross food supplies easing the situation still further, the Italians had good reason to view Greek popular feeling with equanimity. The senior Italian military officer in Greece was untroubled at this stage by EAM's existence.

One year later, though, the picture looked very different. In the spring of 1943 General Pièche, a senior Italian envoy, sent alarming reports back to Rome. Noting the boldness of the bands of *andartes* (guerrillas), he also referred to a flood of pamphlets inciting the population to take up the struggle against the Axis, and was clearly disquieted by the public response: 'the mass of the population, especially in the great city centres, is openly abandoning the obsequious and submissive attitude . . . which it showed in the past towards us, and in certain circles increasingly displays a tone of arrogance towards the occupation authorities'.[40] What had happened over the preceding months to cause such a change?

CHAPTER ELEVEN

Urban Protest

It was, in the first place, the acute shortage of food which created the conditions for widespread political mobilisation. Shifts in wealth and income generated by food scarcity, inflation and the black market amounted to a 'veritable social revolution'. According to one intelligence source, 'the public servant, the private employee, the small professional man, the lawyer, the state pensioner and the small businessman . . . are practically starving'. The same observer remarked the 'veering towards the Left of elements of the public who, before the war, were among the most conservative'.[41]

The result was clear enough in many provincial towns, where the government's inability to gain control of the harvest eventually forced local people to take initiatives of their own. Town mayors and bishops urged the rich to show charity to the poor by contributing to special relief funds. But 'fraternal philanthropy' was overshadowed in the winter of 1941–42 by more extensive, unprecedented forms of self-help, and in many places local labour centres, white-collar and professional organisations joined forces to form unofficial 'People's Committees'.

Their initial aim was simply to put pressure on the local civil servants to squeeze food and resources out of Athens. In Volos, for example, a 'People's Committee' was set up at the suggestion of the town's Lawyers' Federation in January 1942; it issued appeals to Athens for food, and recommended setting up a market control committee of citizens, headed by a civil servant, to supervise the movement of supplies. Alongside it was set up a 'Women's Committee', which invited the town's women to help feed children. A ten-man 'People's Committee' was set up in the town of Farsala in February 1942, with representatives of all the professional, business and workers' organisations of the town. Isolated mountain villages set up provisioning committees, usually headed by the priest or schoolmaster, to seek help from the market towns in the plains.[42]

Aside from a general disgust with the ineptitude of the Tsolakoglu regime, these 'People's Committees' did not start out with any specific political colouring. Very few of their founders were communists, and some would end the war firmly in the anti-communist camp. In early 1942 the Deputy Prime Minister actually met several groups of such concerned local notables during an official tour of the Peloponnese. But the war and the famine had radicalised popular opinion, and when the EAM Central Committee in Athens sent activists to spread the news of its existence, it found a sympathetic response. Nausicaa Papadakis was a young girl from the mountains of central Greece who – in her own words – 'hadn't a clue about Communism' when she began to distribute food to starving local children in her village church in March 1942; a year later, now nicknamed 'First of May', she was an EAM activist. The 'Liberation Organisation' founded on the island of Mytilene in January 1942 was the work of republican notables – an army major, a former Venizelist deputy, a landowner and a soap manufacturer. Such men were hardly typical radicals, yet they found their programme of moderate social reform chimed with EAM's programme, and early in 1943 they petitioned to enter EAM and adopted the title 'EAM Mytilene'.[43]

The extent to which the strains of war had broken down many of the old political divisions in the provinces and brought former rivals together could be seen, for example, in Thessaly, where communists and non-communists had jointly established an organisation called the 'National Front'. The Larissa branch was headed by a Liberal; the Kalabaka committee included an ardent royalist. Activists spanned a vast range of backgrounds and occupations – from bankers, army officers and agronomists to taxi drivers, tailors, tobacco workers and manual labourers.[44] When communist activist Kostas Gambetas arrived from Athens at the beginning of 1942 to publicise EAM he found that his most urgent task was not to persuade members of the National Front to join EAM – that was quickly done – but to explain to the local communist cadres why the Party had decided to co-operate with such 'bourgeois' forces.[45]

Gambetas himself was the sort of charismatic young figure who played a vital role in spreading EAM's influence outside the capital. Tall, thin and good-looking, nervous and quick-witted, he had already spent much of his life in Greek jails for his political activities. He, together with other dedicated activists, ran enormous risks as they travelled through the provinces. Gambetas exercised a decisive influence over the resistance in Thessaly, which was to become one of EAM's power bases, before travelling in disguise as a railway worker to Patras to take control of the local EAM movement there. He lived underground in the port for several months before being captured by the Germans and shot early in 1944.

17a. (*left*) The EAM activist: Anastasia Siouli (1909–44), a schoolteacher in the village of Katranitsa near Kozani from 1927. During the occupation she joined EAM and was put in charge of propaganda for the area around her village. Captured during a raid on 23 April 1944, she was executed together with six men the next day in the town of Ptolemaida.

17b. (*right*) Postwar photo of EAM village activist Maria Manthopoulou, who organised a network of child care centres in central Greece.

Courageous activists like Gambetas were indispensable to the development of EAM in the provinces; yet perhaps the most important single element behind the movement's popularity lay elsewhere: unlike other resistance groups, which made appeals in the time-honoured fashion to the public's sense of 'national honour' and patriotism, EAM focused on everyday grievances. It largely ignored constitutional or territorial issues and instead mobilised housewives in countless small towns to protest at the price of bread and oil. It publicised the fact that the prefect of Patras, for example, was enriching himself by siphoning off stocks of the crops that had been collected locally. When olive growers in the region refused to pay a new levy on sales of olive oil, and *carabinieri* were sent in to arrest the ringleaders, the authorities themselves were simply helping drive people into EAM. Farmers who had no previous affiliations with the Left now listened to party cadres with a new respect.[45]

What seems to have been crucial in this process was not simply that the occupation authorities should be seen by the population as enemies – even in peacetime the state simply meant the tax-collector and the gendarme so far as most farmers were concerned – but that they should have been acting in an increasingly arbitrary and violent way. While allowing some regions to starve, they were roaming through others, levying taxes in kind at the point of a gun. Thessaly offered the clearest example of this, for the local Italian commanders there had tried to exploit ethnic tensions by arming the Vlach minority and forming them into a 'Roman Legion' to help enforce order. In fact, the Legion became extremely unpopular even among the Vlachs for its arbitrary pillaging and its assaults on local merchants. Cattle breeders lost the right to sell their cattle if they did not support the Legionaries, and manual workers were thrown out of work if they refused to join up. Not suprisingly, the Legion formed the target of the very first armed bands to appear in the region, who could convincingly argue that when the so-called authorities were condoning extortion and pillaging, it was up to individuals to restore order themselves.[47]

More generally, as an official historian of the gendarmerie frankly admitted, the exactions of local civil servants 'distanced the citizen from the state'. Olive growers on the slopes of Pilion could not see why they should hand over their harvest when the state had failed to supply them with food throughout the winter. Shepherds in the Patras region felt the same way. Under the direction of Finance Minister Gotzamanis, the official response in 1942 was far tougher than the previous year and the courts punished farmers with heavy fines and periods of internal exile. Others were imprisoned. Once released, they often took to the hills and were recruited into guerrilla bands. Faced with tax demands which often exceeded the official limits – in some areas the local authorities took 50 per cent of the harvest instead of the 10 per cent laid down by Athens – the rural populations looked for a way of freeing themselves from govern-ment control. The path was mapped out by proud, resilient men like thirty-year-old Kostas Tassopoulos, who returned from the Albanian front to his farm in the southern Peloponnese determined to keep the spirit of 'the Albanian epic' alive. June 1941 saw him encouraging other villagers to resist the demands of the local Italian garrison for a new levy on flour. Within months, there was a price on his head and he was forced underground into EAM.[48]

By the end of 1942 EAM was reportedly 'the only active underground organisation on Samos'; it had branches and cells through the towns and villages of central Greece; it was 'the only resistance group in the Kalamata district', down in the very south of the Peloponnese, where it was organising guerrilla bands, issuing 'patriotic proclamations' and supporting passive resistance to Italian food confiscation. In October 1942 its influence with local syndicates and professional organisations in Levadia enabled it to get one of its own members appointed as sub-prefect of the town, putting the civil administration of Boeotia largely in its hands. Even before the spread of armed resistance, therefore, EAM had established its authority throughout much of rural Greece.[49]

*

On 12 April 1942 a clerk in the telegram office of the central post office in Athens fainted from hunger. This was not an uncommon sight near the end of the winter's famine. But it prompted a committee of workers to visit the manager to demand larger food rations. His ill-judged reaction was to threaten them with dismissal. As soon as word spread round the building the workers inside declared a strike. This was near the end of the blackest period of food scarcity in the capital – a month later the food situation would be much improved – and workers were desperate.

The following day, 13 April, the strike spread elsewhere. At first the government took an uncompromising line: strike leaders were arrested and threatened with the death penalty, while Gotzamanis argued that wages could not be permitted to rise, since that would simply push inflation out of control. But soon he began to back away from outright confrontation and agreed to the distribution of foodstuffs in part payment to civil servants.[50]

Up to this point EAM had played little part in shaping the workers' actions. But now the 'Organisation' intervened. EAM representatives persuaded the strikers to continue their action until they had forced the government to release those strike leaders who had been arrested. Capitulating completely, the government did so. A few days later the KKE's Political Office ran a post-mortem: the strike had shown that 'broad and well-organised mass popular pressure can win out even under the most fearsome conditions'.[51]

But the same document carried a warning: EAM's workers' arm, EEAM, had to be developed further into 'the general organiser and leader of the struggle of the working-class of our country'. The implication was that the labour movement was not yet fully under

EAM control. Nor was it ready to participate in an unequivocally political struggle against the Axis. There were few strikes over the next six months, and these were carefully presented as entirely economic in character.[52] The supply of food improved over the summer of 1942, and Gotzamanis tried buying off the workers with legislation that guaranteed them food in part payment of wages. Neubacher's radical economic measures also seemed to have slowed down inflation and brought a new sense of stability. By the end of November meat could be seen in the butchers' shops – 'a sight forgotten for many months'.[53]

The experience of mobilisation was a heady one, however, and the unrest in the capital was only temporarily quelled by the improved supply of food. In the late autumn and winter of 1942 several developments provoked a new militancy among the city's inhabitants, undermining Neubacher's hopes. The first of these was news of Rommel's retreat from El Alamein, which reached Athens in the first week of November and soon gave rise to rumours of imminent Liberation. Then the Allied landings in North Africa, the German occupation of Vichy France and the news from Stalingrad seemed to confirm that the tide of war had finally turned against the Axis. Many people expected the Second Front to be opened in Greece, after a feint against Italy, before the end of 1943. An exuberant optimism swept over the capital.[54]

Adding to all the excitement there were reports of guerrilla bands up in the mountains. 'An expansion of the *andartes*' struggle in the mountains of Roumeli [central Greece],' wrote Theotokas on 27 October. 'It is said that this extends into Thessaly and northern Greece, but concrete information reaches the capital from Roumeli alone and passes from mouth to mouth.' A month later came the news of the *andartes*' destruction of the Gorgopotamos viaduct, which caused fuel shortages and electricity cuts in Athens. It also exposed the vulnerability of the Axis position in Greece, which was dependent on a thin ribbon of rail and road snaking down the east coast of the country.[55]

But it was above all the fears that civil mobilisation was imminent that, as elsewhere in Europe, provoked an upsurge of discontent and outrage. By early 1943 the Germans' voluntary labour programme had clearly failed. Meanwhile, workers who had returned from the Reich for Christmas were spreading harrowing stories among their acquaintances, describing wretched living conditions, frequent beatings and occasional shootings by German overseers and police. Soon the walls of Athens were covered with graffiti: in prominent red letters one could read the EAM slogan – 'Mobilisation equals death: *andartes* everyone'.[56]

*

In the escalation of protest that now occurred, one crucial group should be mentioned: the young. From 1848 to 1989 they have played a prominent part in national uprisings throughout Europe, and wartime Greece is no exception. 'The youth of our country,' an intelligence source in Athens warned the Greek government in exile, 'of both sexes, almost in its entirety and especially in the towns, has aligned itself with the Leftists, and the enemy occupation has accustomed them to express their ideas fearlessly, and to uphold them by any means.' Disgusted with the inactivity of the established politicians, they now demanded 'young leaders' of their own, and started to take matters into their own hands.[57]

Looking for the causes of this youthful radicalism, the cynic might point to the time left on students' hands by the disruption of their normal studies. Certainly it is true that the school year in many regions in 1940–41 lasted only three months, and in 1941–42 barely twenty days! What is more, damage to school buildings and their confiscation for official use led tens of thousands of children to miss out on regular schooling altogether. But these disruptions were really aspects of a more profound social upheaval: by breaking the hold of traditional institutions of authority – whether the state itself, or the power of parents within the family – the war had opened up new opportunities and challenges for the young.

For some this took the form of an almost deliberate hedonism; the diaries of one teenager suggest that the war passed in a blur of parties and sex; for others, it involved entering the black market to support themselves and their families. A third possibility, not of course incompatible with either of the others, was political activism. Students had already taken the lead in demonstrating noisily on national holidays, or in favour of patriotic professors who had been sacked. With much to lose if civil mobilisation was introduced, they now participated actively in opposing it. Alongside them were youthful manual workers, like Theodoros X., an eighteen-year-old labourer from Piraeus, who joined demonstrations and protests, in his own words, 'with the enthusiasm of a young man who disregards pain and sacrifice'.[58]

This was a struggle which cut across the divide of gender in unprecedented ways. In EPON, the EAM youth movement, girls painted slogans on walls, or shouted defiant messages at night across the Athens rooftops through cardboard megaphones. Female voices were supposed to carry better than men's. Theotokas noticed the prominent part played in the demonstrations by university students and high-school pupils – 'boys and girls together', he remarked in surprise – who displayed 'an amazing bravery. While

18. The power of youth: young demonstrators take to the streets in Jannina, defying the Occupation authorities.

formerly in peacetime a few shots fired into the air were enough to break up a demonstration . . . now these kids don't scatter even at volleys or machine-guns shooting to kill or cavalry charges.' He observed that 'the young treat the whole thing as a playground prank, even though there are people falling dead'. Teenagers figured prominently in the casualty lists.[59]

Amid rumours of the planned mobilisation, the unrest spread. On 7 February, for example, 500 students gathered in the church of Agios Pandeleimon in Acharnon Street for a service commemorating Dimitri Constantinidis, who had been killed during a demonstration in December; two days later, about a thousand civil servants gathered to demonstrate outside the building where the Greek Cabinet was meeting. In the week that followed there were disruptions of one sort or another almost daily: a strike at the Bank of Greece; pickets outside the Ministry of Labour. A strike broke out involving workers of the Athens municipality, the Ministry of Finance and the banks; next, some 600 civil servants gathered in Syntagma Square by the Monument to the Unknown Soldier. There were complete stoppages of tram, bank and postal services.

By the last week of February the city administration was in disarray: on 22 February municipal services stopped work; two days later a massive demonstration of workers, civil servants and students threatened to storm the Ministry of Labour and other government offices round Monastiraki Square, and the Greek police fired on the crowd. On the same day there were stoppages by the staff of several hospitals, protesting at inadequate food rations. When a student died of gunshot wounds he had received during the demonstration on the 24th, university students demanded that lessons be suspended. Finally, on the 28th, some 3,500 people gathered in Omonia Square with placards attacking the Nazi New Order, while in the adjacent church of Agios Constantinos – so Italian sources reported – the service ended in shouts of 'Long live Greece!' and 'Long live the Red Army!' Mass in another church in Kypseli was disrupted when several disabled veterans began to make speeches against civil mobilisation.[60]

The whole tenor of these protests was slowly changing. Though economic demands still predominated, the authorities were not fooled. According to an Italian report: 'Such demonstrations, however much attributed to the necessity of obtaining economic improvements in favour of civil servants and workers, have clearly allowed their real anti-Axis basis to emerge.'[61] The large demonstration on the 28th had followed a call by EAM for a general strike, and if the result fell some way short of its target, it nevertheless reflected the growing confidence of the population.[62]

Crudely printed pamphlets and newspapers from an enormous variety of clandestine outfits circulated from hand to hand, promising that 'the hour of liberty is at hand', and alerting the population to the Logothetopoulos government's plans for civil mobilisation. General Pièche reported on 24 February:

> The Greek situation is continuously worsening. Enemy propaganda . . . is developing with great intensity, assuming a tone of extreme violence and making itself available in all possible ways from endless radio broadcasts to graffiti, from the preaching of the most tendentious voices to the circulation of anti-Axis pamphlets and fliers, communist and nationalist, exciting the people to revolt. . . . Intense propaganda continues to be scrawled on walls against the civil mobilisation, against the arrest of hostages undertaken by the occupation authorities, against the Axis in general, and against the Greek government itself, which is accused of excessive docility against the occupier and held to be principally responsible for the catastrophic food situation of the country.[63]

*

In this increasingly excited atmosphere, one event seemed to crystallise the new mood. On 27 February Greece's most revered poet, Kostas Palamas, died at home. Laid out on a sofa in his library, his body was dressed in black and covered in almond blossom. A stream of visitors passed through the house and entered the candle-lit room to pay their respects. 'He was . . . even smaller than we remembered him,' recorded Theotokas. 'You had the impression that you saw laid out before you half a century of Greek life.'[64]

Well over eighty, the slight and gentle white-bearded poet had been out of the public eye for some time. Three decades earlier he had published his monumental historical epics of national liberation in which he likened the young Venizelos to a Nietzschean hero, who would lead Greece into a Byzantine imperial revival. After Greece's Disaster in Asia Minor his grand rhetoric fell out of favour. In the more uncertain mood of the interwar years he had sat at home, fashioning a new style – melancholy, intimate, reticent and nostalgic.

His funeral, however, marked the resurgence of an increasingly defiant spirit of nationalism. The memorial service began at 11 o'clock the next day. Although there had been no public announcement apart from a notice pinned to the window of Eleftheroudakis's bookshop, an enormous crowd gathered at the cemetery to pay their respects. Inside the chapel of Ayion Theodoron, Archbishop Damaskinos made a short, patriotic speech of farewell. Then it was the turn of the poet Sikelianos, who despite an illness of his own had insisted on paying public homage to his master. Looking pale, almost possessed, he rose to deliver the encomium he had composed for the occasion.

'Listening to Sikelianos declaiming, full of emotion, with his thunderous voice, with his well-known rhetorical and vigorous air, in that moment which was surely the pinnacle of his life, I felt for a moment that I was no longer walking on the earth! It seems incredible, but it was true. The declamation of Sikelianos – a truly revolutionary paean – was a unique experience for me.' Kostas Kazantzis's reaction was shared by many of the other listeners.[65] Even the guards seemed overwhelmed by the magnitude of the occasion. Totally disregarding the presence of Prime Minister Logothetopoulos and the Axis dignitaries, Sikelianos had launched into a call for a national awakening:

'Echo, you trumpets,' he began. 'Thundering bells, shake the country bodily from end to end!' With a defiant call for *eleftheria* (freedom), he led the procession out of the church into the graveyard, and urged the mourners to throw flowers on to Palamas's

19. Palamas's funeral: Having delivered his fiery and defiant oration, Angelos Sikelianos, flanked by the actress Marika Kotopouli and the writer Ilias Venezis, pays his last respects at the graveside. Athens, 28 February 1943.

coffin. The energy of his speech excited the onlookers. As Axis dignitaries waited their turn to throw flowers into the grave, and gave Fascist and Nazi salutes, the crowd began singing the national anthem, and shouted 'Long live Greece!' and 'Long live Freedom!' As Anna Sikelianou, his wife, later demanded: 'Who had gathered together that crowd, who gave them the courage to ignore the German guards and sing the national anthem in their faces that day? Who else but the dead poet himself and the living one.'[66]

*

Just one week after Palamas's funeral, the Germans' attempt to implement their civil mobilisation programme brought matters to a head, and revealed, for perhaps the very first time, that popular pressure could prevail against the Axis authorities. On 5 March EAM organised a massive demonstration against the mobilisation plans. It was a bitterly cold day and snow fell at intervals. But despite the weather, people gathered in the centre of Athens, and by around 11 a.m. the crowd numbered 7,000 or more, including civil

20. Contemporary woodcut of an EAM rally against the proposed mobilisation of the civilian population. Note the EAM graffiti on the wall and the crippled war veteran at the head of the procession.

servants, workers and other members of the public, with wounded soldiers and students prominent at their head. Walking down the icy streets, they carried banners with messages such as 'Down with the civil mobilisation!', 'Death to Logothetopoulos!' and 'Death to Pangalos!' On Panepistimiou Street, just by the Ministry of Labour, they clashed with a group of police, who panicked and fired at them, killing five and wounding about fifty. The crowd then scattered. In the Exarchia district there was a brief street battle between demonstrators and police. A crowd stormed the town hall, hoping to burn the electoral rolls so that they could not be used for the mobilisation scheme.[67]

Although eventually the police succeeded in restoring order, shops and businesses remained closed for the day – according to Pièche, turning the demonstrations into a 'real general strike'. German sources reckoned that 65 per cent of the government's employees and almost all the students had obeyed EAM's call. Forewarned, the Logothetopoulos government had already decided to shut all ministries for five days.

The following day there were no Greek papers – most had closed in sympathy with the demonstrators – apart from a special official bulletin with an 'important announcement' from the Prime Minister. He began by attributing the disturbances to 'the communist organisation EAM which has unfortunately subverted many civil servants and students'. But the momentous concession was there: he guaranteed that there would be no civil mobilisation and that Greeks working for the occupation authorities would not be sent to work outside the country.[68]

Although the demonstrators had won their greatest victory to date against the Axis, it was widely suspected that mobilisation had only been shelved, not abandoned. Throughout March and April demonstrations and work stoppages continued sporadically. The authorities tried to quell protests by arresting strike leaders and carrying out mass executions – a policy which dampened anti-Axis activity but did not manage to suppress it entirely. When Italian troops marched down the centre of Athens, Greek onlookers responded by singing the national anthem; and on the 25 March holiday, for all the precautions taken by the Italian authorities, the streets were filled with crowds: people waved the Greek flag, and shouted patriotic slogans. The use of force created martyrs, and it became common to see piles of flowers lying in the streets, placed over patches of dried blood where people had been shot.

To the Axis it was obvious that the Greek government was floundering. On 6 April Prime Minister Logothetopoulos was replaced by the Germans' favoured candidate, Ioannis Rallis, a prewar royalist politician. They hoped Rallis would be able to win some backing from traditional political circles and perhaps succeed in controlling the disturbances by forming an anti-communist front against EAM and the resistance. Rallis reshuffled his Cabinet and began planning the formation of his own security force, soon to emerge as the Security Battalions. More resilient and politically experienced than his predecessors, Rallis was the first quisling Premier in whom the Germans had any faith, and over the year and a half that he was in office he would have considerable success in driving a wedge between nationalist and communist elements in the resistance.

But in the early summer of 1943, this still lay some way in the future. As winter receded the political temperature rose, and from the enormous success of strikes called late in June we can see how far EAM's influence now extended through the capital. Neubacher's efforts to control inflation had broken down. Strikes went on even after Rallis promised a 50 per cent rise in wages, for the strikers were now also demanding grants for clothing, and the provision of food rations for their families as well as themselves. Then the Axis authorities announced that one hundred hostages had been shot for the sabotage of a train carrying Greeks to the Larissa concentration camp, together with another 27 for the sinking of an Italian ship in Piraeus harbour. The Greek public was outraged, particularly when the rumour spread that the train disaster had been accidental.

EAM circulated instructions to shopkeepers to close their premises and called for the whole population to turn out on the streets on 25 June. According to Italian intelligence, numerous organisations obeyed EAM's call, and even sent their representatives to a strike co-ordination committee. On the 25th, bank clerks and civil servants walked out of their offices to join the demonstrators. Even the police were on strike, supposedly over pay, but in fact to avoid a confrontation with the crowds. 'At 9 o'clock the church bells were rung, and the crowd . . . gathered at . . . the ancient church at the west end of Hermes St,' one marcher recounted afterwards.

Many of the demonstrators were furnished with black flags and banners like church banners, in mourning for those executed, which they had secreted in their clothing and unfolded as the procession began to march. Before they had gone far the procession was attacked by a small force of Italian motor-cyclists, with the butts of their rifles. Several people were felled, but the procession, consisting of many thousands of people, rolled on unchecked and reached the Old Palace, where shouts were raised of 'Down with the Fascists!' 'Down with traitors!' 'Down with the Nazis!' etc., and finally, outside the windows of the Old Palace, shouts for Rallis to protest at the executions, and if he could not stop them to resign and let the Axis govern by themselves.[69]

The Italians estimated that 100,000 protesters had taken part and feared that 'the spirit of the population has grown decisively against the occupation regime'.[70] Certainly, the events of that summer revealed the power EAM had acquired by organising those sections of society most ready to take part in actively opposing the authorities, and by exploiting the economic and nationalist grievances and the growing sense of sheer outrage which so much of the population felt.

EAM had made enormous progress since the postal workers' strike in April 1942. Many elements of resistance had been visible then – the protests on national holidays, the student demonstrations in the corridors of the university, unrest among the civil servants. But they had been isolated and uncoordinated episodes, vulnerable to pressure from the authorities. Helped by the favourable turn in the international situation, by the authorities' inept handling of public dissent, and finally by their largely unchallenged construction of EAM itself, the leaders of the National Liberation Front had brought into being a new type of political organisation.

CHAPTER TWELVE

Freedom or Death!

We know little about the activities of armed men in the Greek countryside before the formation of ELAS in 1942. Small mobile patrols of Greek gendarmes – four to ten men strong – were employed to keep order in the provinces, and to combat the 'delinquency and brigandage' which was reportedly on the increase; the fact that such tasks were entrusted to the Greeks themselves suggests that the Axis authorities were not yet seriously alarmed. The total strength of these patrols amounted only to 1,500 men. Large bands of opponents were obviously not anticipated. The gendarmerie were facing the sort of criminal activity that was bound to increase at a time when the state apparatus was in disarray and numerous homeless, displaced, unemployed armed men were on the roads. From reports submitted at this time to the Italian *carabinieri*, we find the Trikkala mobile patrol, for example, recording the capture of a couple of sheep stealers; another two men were arrested for robbing a village miller.[71]

Many of these incidents involved demobbed soldiers. Staff officers and politicians had been able to rationalise the need for the armistice with the Germans, since they knew how well they had been outflanked, but for many front-line troops news of the surrender had come as a bombshell after their triumphs against the Italians. Feelings of disgust and fierce anger lingered on for long afterwards. 'I told them,' recalled one Greek lieutenant, 'that the *archigoi* [leaders] betrayed us, that it is impossible for us not to win, and that we will go on fighting.'[72] Such convictions now propelled the discontented heroes from the front in various directions. Taking on the enemy directly at this stage appealed to few. But with the abundance of weapons, and the shortage of food, especially up in the mountain villages, an increase in violent crime was predictable.

There was, after all, much bitterness among those farming families who were going hungry through the winter because their menfolk had been called up during the sowing season. Mill-owners grinding the village flour, isolated shepherds and anyone wealthy or foolish enough to be driving a car – like the unfortunate Dimitri Psaromialos who was robbed at gunpoint on a mountain road of three drums of olive oil and seven boxes of currants – were high-risk targets for poor, out-of-work young conscripts, who felt abandoned by their officers and who were also under an obligation to obtain food for their dependants.

Millers of course presented an easy and tempting target, especially during winter when food was scarce. In February 1942, one was assaulted and tied up in the village of Deleri, while some way away a small gang armed with revolvers seized sacks of flour at the Avraam mill outside Trikkala. Priests were almost as likely to be attacked, for their relatively comfortable lifestyle attracted envy – 'A priest is like a storeroom,' ran the proverb. 'He needs filling' – and they suffered more than their fair share of kidnappings. In April 1942, for example, five men kidnapped a priest's son after the holy man refused to give them food. Fifteen villagers were caught trying to rob an isolated monastery near Karditsa.[73]

For over a year such violence was directed almost entirely at fellow-Greeks, overlapping with the traditional patterns of sheep stealing and petty rural crime. General Geloso felt fairly confident in the summer of 1942 that 'the blows inflicted by our troops, the combining of tactical manoeuvres with searches in mountain areas – that promising retreat of bandits – and the energetic and constant presence of the Greek gendarmerie have repressed and contained the phenomenon [of brigandage] within limits much lower than expected and not notably higher than normal.'[74]

But such optimism was premature, for in 1942 the Athens government's efforts to gain control of the new harvest produced a sharp increase in tension in the rural areas. Repeating the pattern of the previous year, farmers clashed with official purchasing agents. In mid-August occurred the first serious gun-battle between gendarmes and a band of about twenty 'brigands' near Almyra. It lasted five hours and left one gendarme dead and two wounded. As the grain ripened, such gun battles became more frequent. The government set up a new Security Commission with powers to deport individuals deemed a threat to public order. To curb the increase in 'brigandage' Tsolakoglu even instructed prefects to execute malefactors and burn their houses. On 25 August came news that the Italians had shot seven men from the village of Stylida who had attacked a lorry in Italian service and burned it.[75]

The authorities' constant description of their opponents as 'brigands' is worth examining. Brigands there certainly were in the mountains of central Greece, and wartime presented them with exciting new opportunities. Sheep stealing was on the rise in

1942, and many villagers were shot and sometimes killed trying to defend their animals or crops. One group of twenty-five robbers stole maize from a village and forced the inhabitants to hand over 203,000 drachmas from the proceeds of their harvest. Another band of 'evildoers' surrounded the village of Sykourion, murdering three shepherds, looting the house of a fourth and taking his flock.

But some groups were acting in a rather uncharacteristic way for brigands. They raided government warehouses and handed out the wheat to local people. Government officials warned villagers not to accept such gifts, threatening to cut off future supplies if they did not listen. One band disarmed three gendarmes near Karditsa and burned the local tax registry. Tax rolls and the records of farmers' debts at local branches of the Agricultural Bank were often the first targets of these 'social bandits'. In the Patras region, the local inspector of finances complained to Athens that 'because of the appearance of bands of *andartes* the collection of taxes [on agricultural products] has become impossible, since the bands seize any civil servant proceeding to the collection of taxes and after ill-treating him, destroy his papers and tax figures and threaten him with death.'[76]

From the summer of 1942 the perpetrators of such offences were no longer invariably termed 'brigands' and were increasingly identified in press reports and public announcements as *andartes* (guerrillas).[77] Stefanos Papayiannis, for example, hardly fitted the profile of the typical cattle stealer. He had commanded an anti-aircraft battery in Salonika in the spring of 1941, and following the collapse of the front, he made his way westwards to Epiros before joining ELAS in 1942. No more a 'brigand' was Kostas Tassopoulos. When he returned home from Albania, he told his fellow-villagers not to hand over their guns to the Italians, and to hide their mules and horses. His area – he boasted proudly after the war – 'was the only one not to surrender a single animal or gun to the enemy'. Whether true or not, such a claim encapsulated the intense national pride that led men like him into the *andartiko*. Naturally, his activities soon had the Italians on his trail, and he was one of the first to join ELAS in his district.[78]

The best-known of the early *andarte* bands was led by a KKE member, Aris Velouchiotis, who was one of the founders of ELAS. The well-educated Velouchiotis was a sadistically violent man, but he was no brigand. A strict disciplinarian, he marched his men into the mountain villages, holding up the Greek flag and singing the national anthem. They would disarm the terrified local gendarmes, make patriotic speeches in the square and enlist recruits. In his soft but compelling voice, Aris would tell his audience how the *andartes*

21.   Aris Velouchiotis (*nom de guerre* of Thanasis Klaras) (1905–45). Trained as an agronomist and a member of the KKE from the age of nineteen. One of the founders of ELAS, renowned and reviled in equal measure, and deeply suspicious of the British. He died in controversial circumstances after the war, surrounded by Government forces near the village of Mesounda.

fitted into Greece's long struggle for national liberation, and offered the villagers the chance to emulate the heroes of 1821 by taking up arms to fight for independence. As even the gendarmerie in central Greece admitted: 'A revolutionary spirit began to spread through these regions, and many nationally minded men rushed to join the *andartes*.'[79]

Sometimes, to be sure, the *andarte* and the brigand overlapped, and we learn of 'roving bands of ill-disciplined troops' who were not interested in attacking the enemy when they could intimidate farmers instead; 'only their rather tenuous connection with EAM prevents these groups being regarded as bandits'. Karalivanos and his men were a case in point: these ruffians preyed on villagers, demanding food and stealing sheep, supposedly to help feed the British mission. With his grimy Evzone dress, red fez, black beard and tommy-gun, Karalivanos must have been an intimidating presence. One night he and his men raided a village and seized two Greek gendarmes who were collecting potatoes for the Italian garrison some hours' march away. The two men were beaten up, stripped of their uniforms and sent back in their underclothes. Of course, this episode simply emphasized Karalivanos's power, and made the villagers terrified of Italian reprisals. EAM organisers tried hard to curb such activities. They issued orders in Thessaly and elsewhere that property, fields and crops were not to be damaged. ELAS leaders like Aris took stern measures to wipe out such lawlessness.[80]

'Karäiskakis', another old-fashioned brigand, had started off proclaiming his loyalty to ELAS. Operating with his three sons and a band of followers in the heart of traditional brigand country in Roumeli, he acted just like the klephts of the last century – stealing sheep, terrorising their owners and treating the mountain villages as his personal fiefdom. Such behaviour outraged local EAM administrators and brought the *andartiko* into disrepute. Eventually other ELAS units were brought in: they arrested his men, requisitioned his livestock and ordered him back to his village in disgrace. There could be no clearer illustration of how far the insurgency in the mountains had moved beyond the understanding and values of the traditional brigand entrepreneur.[81]

The Andartes

A motley crew, many *andartes* fell short of the Hague Regulations' stipulation that insurgents covered by the rules of war should wear

127

22. A group of ELAS *andartes*.

a clearly recognisable uniform. Their apparel included the battle
gear of at least three different nations – Greek, Italian and German
(the latter two of course prize plunder), gendarmerie uniforms,
suits and farming clothes among the rank and file, even the occasional fustanella harking back to the days of the Macedonian
struggle. Their weapons were also mixed: Kostopoulos's band was
armed with an Italian mortar, several machine-guns including an
American 'Thompson', and an assortment of grenades – Italian,
French First World War stock, and various others.[82]

With time, some distinctive features did evolve: the thick woollen
cloak, which Greek shepherds had long found useful both for
keeping off the cold and for bedding; the bandolier, or shoulder-
belt, and above all, the bushy, forbidding moustaches and beard of
the genuine *andarte*. One member of Karalivanos's five-man band in
October 1942 wore a 'grimy black Evzone uniform . . . 3 bandoliers
full of ammunition, one round his waist and one over each of his
shoulders. He carried a rifle at the ready. Several knives with
beautifully engraved handles, protruding from various parts of his
waist, completed his equipment.' Another associate of this band,
'Barba Niko', a man in his mid-fifties who sported a big walrus

moustache and had acquired an impenetrable form of English after living some years in the United States, was armed with 'an ancient musket and a rusty revolver', and clothed in threadbare civilian garb; his toes poked out of one of his shoes.[83]

Sometimes guerrillas were billeted in friendly villages, where they arranged matters in advance with local contacts and posted sentries to keep watch. More frequently they pitched camp in the open, using outlying barns, shepherds' and hunters' cabins, or even earth-dwellings which were little more than damp holes in the ground they dug themselves. They rediscovered the traditional *limeria*, or lairs, which the klephts and brigands of earlier generations had used. In the mountain forests they sheltered from the autumn rains under shelters built out of fir branches, lying on bracken floors. Between 25 and 200 men would cluster together at night round carefully placed fires.

How well the *andarte* ate depended upon the resources of the region. In Epiros food was scarce; in Thessaly, more plentiful. Myers records that he was looked after well in the mountain village of Stromni: the villagers brought him and his men brown bread and potatoes, delicious local apples, walnuts and other nuts. Meat they obtained by slaughtering sheep from local flocks, recompensing their owners with gold sovereigns. Other bands, less well financed than Myers's, took sheep without paying.[84] Maize bread, pulses and occasional portions of fish or meat were the staples of this diet as they were for most manual workers in Greece at the time. Walnuts, honey and arbutus berries were other common items. Overall, they provided sufficient nutrition to keep the *andartes* alive and surprisingly healthy.[85]

The ease with which food could be obtained from farmers coloured the guerrillas' relationship with villages under their control. Where food was relatively abundant, as for example in western Macedonia, relations between farmers and ELAS were better than in regions where food was scarcer, or where rival bands fought over the crops, or where the occupation authorities were prepared to hit back.

The *andartes* of course implemented their own food procurement policies: when they lacked funds they based this upon a flat 10–20 per cent requisition rate from all farmers of wheat, beans and livestock. They fixed purchase prices for wheat and cheese, and set out the rules for the compulsory contribution of cereals.[86] Mules and women from the mountain villages were used to carry grain up from the plains after the harvest. When grain stocks were exhausted in poor regions such as Epiros and Roumeli, EAM banned the export of grain from Thessaly, which normally had a substantial

23.   A group of *andartes*, together with a British Liaison Officer, sing while they wait for their
supper to cook.

surplus, and arranged for peasants from Epiros to make the five-
day journey there to buy maize.[87]

In some ways the rule of EAM/ELAS was like a mirror image of
the official state administration, and in both cases there was tension
between the fiscal guidelines issued from the centre and the way
they were interpreted by forceful agents at the local level.[88] But the
goodwill of the farming population was even more important to
the *andartes* than to the Athens government, for without their food,
and all the other services they provided, the *andartiko* was doomed
to collapse.

Yet Italian and German reprisals made association with the guerrillas dangerous and costly. It was, for example, reported that after
an ambush in the Sarantaporon Pass, occupation troops burned 29
out of 62 villages in the Elassona area. Since the guerrillas rarely
alerted villagers in advance of their plans, the latter were often
caught by surprise. Nor did Axis troops always check carefully that
the villages they selected for retaliation were in the vicinity of
the initial attack. With the expansion of the *andartiko* the task of
securing food became increasingly difficult, both because of the
risks involved in providing it, and because the number of mouths

to be fed was growing all the time, while the farming base was shrinking. A Swedish Red Cross delegate summed up the problem in 1943:

> The tendency during the summer was that the *Andartes* were extending their control over more and more areas in the north of Greece and the Peloponnese, particularly in the mountains. Both the Italians and the Germans had already been taking steps to meet all opposition on any considerable scale by burning down villages which they considered to be guerrilla centres. The inhabitants of these villages were sometimes put to death and sometimes taken as hostages. Those who managed to escape fled to the mountains and joined the *Andartes*. As their numbers increased, they were compelled to turn to new areas to obtain food from peasants. But every village which supplied the *Andartes* with food was burned down as soon as the occupying forces became aware of the fact. Thus the *Andartes'* movement was continually spreading from one part of the country to another. Farming became difficult or impossible, and the result was that in considerable areas the harvest was virtually a total failure.[89]

By the spring of 1943, British agents sent to support the resistance had become worried about alienating the villagers. They emphasised that the widespread belief that liberation was imminent kept morale high, and warned that if this belief was disappointed, there might be direct repercussions for the *andartes*. To minimise reprisals they also urged giving small-scale sabotage attacks priority over larger, more ambitious engagements. A similar constraint seems to have been felt by guerrilla leaders too. On one typical occasion they rejected certain operations on the grounds that 'villages will be burned' which 'supply 20 per cent of our wheat and potatoes'.[90]

For the villagers, feeding a band of *andartes* invited reprisals not only by the Italians or Germans, but often also by other bands, located nearby and prepared to destroy their rivals by the simplest and least dangerous method – burning the homes and looting the stores of their suppliers. The grubby, heavily armed and bearded men entering the village and looking for food must have aroused fear and uncertainty. Yet what could the villager do? Some peasants are reported to have slaughtered their mules to stop them being requisitioned by the guerrillas; but most farmers took such a drastic step very reluctantly.[91] A few richer peasants shut up their homes and moved down to the towns, but this was not possible for the majority. So rooted were most villagers to their fields, that they would build shacks, or find caves to live in when their own homes

131

were burned down, rather than move away. For them, as one young village schoolboy later put it: 'There was no question of refusing to provide food for the partisans; you do not argue when you are faced with men with guns.'[92]

Under the thumb of the *andartes*, it must have seemed to many villagers that one form of state had replaced another in the struggle for control of the food supply. In Thessaly EAM/ELAS was reportedly collecting taxes which had formerly been levied by the government, and distributing part of the proceeds for 'the needs of those who are suffering unduly'. At the same time, the guerrillas put pressure on villagers to ignore the decrees of the Tsolakoglu regime. In the summer of 1943, for example, prompted by reports that certain communes were still sending food and cattle to the occupation authorities, they commanded that 'in future no article or food of any kind be sent to the enemy'. Villagers were to reject any orders they received for such deliveries. They were instructed 'to apply immediately to the nearest section of armed bands or organisations which will take measures to attack the enemy and protect the village'. Since the likely effects of such an attack were, of course, further reprisals at the villagers' expense, the decree generously concluded: 'In the event of persons fearing reprisals from enemy sections, they may depart with their belongings to the nearest town.'[93]

*

The Italians had responded to the growth of EAM/ELAS by arresting large numbers of suspects. In the autumn of 1942, when informants gave them an idea of the extent of the resistance organisation, they seized over 50 members of EAM in Larissa, and over 200 in Lamia. Informants rarely provide reliable information, and many of those detained had nothing to do with EAM: they had been spotted drinking at the same *kafeneion* as a known EAM member, or – as in one case – they were simply lodgers in the house of a suspect. Not all of these innocent prisoners were subsequently released. By creating an atmosphere of alarm, the arrests forced many people who were at that stage uninvolved in subversive activity to think about taking 'the road to the Mountain' for their own safety.

One group whose members began to feel especially vulnerable in the towns was the officer corps. Ex-officers had continued to receive a monthly support payment from the government and this had provided an incentive for them not to leave their homes. But in mid-1942 the Italians began to suspect many of anti-Axis activity, and started transporting them to camps across the Adriatic – a hazardous crossing which some did not complete. A steady trickle of officers now went underground, providing the military leadership which the first armed bands had lacked. They included many Venizelists, who had been removed from active service when the King returned to power in 1935, and who now saw in the resistance their chance to fight for their country once more. As attacks on Italian troops increased, over the winter of 1942–43, other officers were seized as hostages and executed in reprisal killings. The trickle now turned into a stream. One unfortunate Italian captured by *andartes* in early January 1943 found that the band of 100–150 men was led entirely by former officers, among them a major, three captains and several lieutenants. Similarly, one of the first active groups in the Peloponnese was formed by a fifty-year-old army officer, Dimitri Michos, who had been imprisoned by the Italians until early 1943.[94]

The swift expansion of the *andartiko* loosened the government's grip on the country. Attacks on key road and rail points slowed down postal deliveries and prevented the prompt payment of public servants in outlying districts. 'Most of the civil servants in districts controlled by Greek guerrillas,' wrote two Greek administrators, who escaped to the Middle East in May 1943, 'have either been deposed or replaced by guerrillas or abandoned their posts through fear of Greek guerrillas and the reprisals of the Italians. There is complete chaos in the towns which are temporarily occupied by the Greek guerrillas – they replace the civil authorities by their own nominees in the towns, but as soon as they depart, the old authorities take over again. The inhabitants thus become divided; there is strife and friction and the administration literally gets dissolved.' In August 1942 the Tsolakoglu regime published a decree providing pensions for the families of murdered civil servants. This was small comfort for them, but a disquieting indication of their prospects.[95]

In fact, even before the *andartiko* unfolded, EAM had eaten away the power of the state from within, taking over regions by co-opting local civil servants. One of Tsolakoglu's protégés, Theodoros Sarantis, installed as prefect of Trikkala in late 1942, began passing on information to EAM about Italian preparations for an anti-guerrilla offensive in the spring of 1943. Sarantis's subsequent career – contact man between Zervas and the Germans in 1943–44, then a senior intelligence officer in the postwar Greek army – amply indicated his lack of sympathy with EAM's ideals, but it also demonstrated his ability to recognise where power lay at any given moment. In towns like Trikkala, far from Athens, power was slipping out of the hands of the Axis.

No public official was more conscious of the impotence of the government he was supposed to serve than the provincial gendarme. As early as the autumn of 1941, gendarmerie stations in Macedonia were being singled out for attack. In the village of Spilaios one police officer resisted and opened fire. But this demanded courage, stubbornness, or belief in a cause fewer and fewer adhered to; sometimes it must have seemed easier as well as more patriotic to back down.[96]

One month after ELAS unified a number of isolated bands in the Thessaly hills in September 1942, the first group of some fourteen gendarmes made their way from the village of Karyes, near Elassona, to join them. Many followed and by October Italian officials were alarmed at the extent of desertion in areas threatened by the guerrillas. In January 1943 the station at Polyneriou was stripped of its arms by *andartes*, assisted by some of the officers. Next month, the entire unit at Siatista, led by their commander, Thomas Venetsanopoulos, enrolled in ELAS and played a vital role in the 'Battle of Fardykampou' which was one of the earliest humiliations that the *andartes* inflicted on the Italians. As the *andartiko* gathered pace, senior gendarmerie officials resisted Italian efforts to form their men into small anti-guerrilla squads, insisting that it was out of the question to ask Greek officials to fire on other 'patriotic' Greeks![97]

The gendarmes' defection was vitally important for the development of the resistance in the countryside. It brought arms and ammunition as well as men, weakening the existing security apparatus and causing the Italians to lose confidence in the gendarmes who remained at their post. Italian sources noted that on the night of 28 February 1943, 'around 300 bandits, evidently not hindered, if not actually favoured by the local gendarmerie, liberated 140 prisoners who were held in the Greek civil prisons in Jannina'. They observed that the activity of the bands was directed towards 'the suppression of elements favourable and sympathetic towards us', putting their own candidates in positions of authority, seizing government stocks of local produce, disarming some members of the gendarmerie and capturing others. The assault on provincial jails continued: 40 freed from Levadia on 6 March, 32 from Kalabaka on the 11th. On 7 April it was reported that 'rebels dressed as gendarmes' entered the Sotiria sanatorium in Athens itself and engineered the escape of 52 communists! These raids disheartened the gendarmes who still resisted the blandishments of the bands, swelled the numbers of those enrolling as *andartes* themselves, and fuelled stories and rumours of the *andartiko* throughout Greece.[98] The Italians responded by closing down gendarmerie outposts in the more remote areas. The *andartiko* had grown beyond the point where Geloso's policing methods would work; unable to rely on small detachments of Greek gendarmes, the Italians were forced back on to their own military resources.[99]

*

Attacks on Axis personnel were rare in the initial stages of the *andartiko*, but from September 1942 they became more frequent. British intelligence documented the destruction of a train in the vale of Tempe, the capture of 300 Italians in the Lamia area, and many smaller acts of sabotage in the period before the destruction of the Gorgopotamos viaduct late in November.[100]

From December onwards, resistance operations became more ambitious. There was no lull in armed clashes in the countryside over the winter. The important chrome mines at Domokos in northern Greece were attacked and chrome stocks plundered; then, during a three-day battle near Agrafa the Italians were reported to have lost 150 men. One indication of the deteriorating outlook was that the Germans faced great difficulties in finding a contractor to continue work on the important Katerina-Elassona road.[101]

Clashes with the Italians were beginning to involve surprisingly large forces of guerrillas. On 11 February an Italian detachment of two companies was attacked near Kalabaka by 'a band some 800 strong'; it lost 75 men the first day, and 137 were taken prisoner the next. The guerrillas released them but kept their weapons. Near Amfikleia, a band of several hundred men derailed a German train, attacked the carriages and set them on fire. A squadron which had gone to repair some telephone lines near Trikkala came under fire and was captured. Motor convoys became a favourite target and when lorries containing 600 Italians were surrounded by ELAS guerrillas near Siatista, not even air support was sufficient to rescue them.[102]

By March and April the *andartes* were launching direct attacks on Italian guard-posts and barracks. A large band attacked the barracks at Thermon, though they were eventually beaten off. But at Farsala a group of forty *carabinieri* were taken prisoner, and at Tsangarada a small Guardia di Finanza detachment surrendered after a three-hour fight.[103] On 16 April, an Italian source noted that 'control throughout the north-east, centre and south-west of Greece remains very precarious, not to say nonexistent'.[104]

From several towns in central Greece the Italians withdrew completely, and the BBC hailed the guerrillas' achievement in establishing 'free cities' in occupied Europe. A British SOE agent was in Karditsa in the last week of March; later he wrote that 'driving

24. German soldiers pose by the ruins of a sabotaged viaduct at Isari in the Peloponnese.

through its streets it was difficult to believe that I was in a town in enemy-occupied country. The shops were open; the streets and cafes were full . . . I had almost to pinch myself to make sure that the scene was real and that I was not dreaming about a peace-time holiday abroad.' The local EAM HQ even found him an old Austin for the drive to Smokovo, some fifteen miles away.[105]

In May 1943 ELAS captured the town of Grevena, together with the Italian garrison there; the following month, they ambushed a German convoy in the Sarantoporon pass, and forced the Italians to pull out of the town of Metsovon, which straddled the vital mountain road between the Adriatic and Aegean seas. By this point, the *andartiko* covered most of mainland Greece. From the mountainous areas of Thessaly, Roumeli and southern Macedonia, it now extended to the west coast, where large bands under local leaders such as Zervas and Houtas threatened Italian garrisons in Arta, Ioannina and Agrinion; and to the Boeotian hills, which overlooked the northern fringes of Athens itself. Wandering up on Mount Parnes above the capital over Easter, hikers from the Athens Travellers' Club were amazed to stumble upon a camp of *andartes*, some in army uniform, some in civilian dress, some even wearing the traditional fustanella.[106]

It was, of course, no easy matter to find out the overall size of the *andarte* forces. No one was really in a position to provide a reliable assessment, least of all the guerrilla leaders themselves, for whom it was always tempting to inflate the figures. Rough estimates suggest that there were about 17,000 *andartes* in the field in May 1943, the vast majority of whom were affiliated to ELAS. During the late spring and summer months numbers increased very rapidly, and by July there may have been as many as 30,000. This development meant that the *andartes* were not just a military threat to the Axis; they would also help to decide Greece's future following the Liberation which almost everyone, after Stalingrad, believed to be only a matter of time.[107]

CHAPTER THIRTEEN

Politics of the Andartiko

On the night of 25 November 1942 an enormous explosion in a quiet valley in central Greece tore apart the Gorgopotamos viaduct, which carried the railway line connecting Athens with the north. Two complete spans plunged into a deep ravine, and a steel pier was demolished: the railway to Athens was put out of action for several weeks. This operation, the most dramatic carried out to date by the *andartes*, was planned and led by British soldiers.

They were members of SOE – the Special Operations Executive which Churchill had created to 'set Europe ablaze' – and they had parachuted into central Greece almost two months earlier. Their mission, code-named Harling, was led by Brigadier Edmund Myers, a career soldier. His instructions had been to blow up the Gorgopotamos in order to disrupt the flow of supplies to Axis troops in North Africa. The mission over, he and his men were to be taken out of Greece again. But things worked out very differently: the British Military Mission was to stay in Greece for the rest of the war, playing a highly controversial role in resistance politics. Not only were there tensions between the British and the Greeks, but there were also strains – often of equal intensity and bitterness – among the various branches of the British policy-making apparatus, most notably between SOE and the Foreign Office. Myers's own career would later be affected when he clashed with the Foreign Office over British policy towards the *andartes*.

After his arrival in Greece, Myers had quickly learned about the divisions within the resistance. Aris Velouchiotis, the ELAS *kapetan* to whom he first turned for help, was a KKE member and deeply suspicious of the British. He only agreed to join forces with Myers once the British began to look elsewhere for help. Kept waiting by Aris, Myers had already sent his second-in-command, a young Oxford graduate called Chris Woodhouse, on a long trek through the mountains to make contact with another rather shady resistance leader called Napoleon Zervas.

Before turning himself into an avuncular bearded klephtic hero,

25. Napoleon Zervas (1891–1957), the republican army officer who became leader of EDES in Epiros (north-western Greece). After the war he founded the right-wing National Party and served briefly as Minister of Public Order in 1947 until allegations that he had reached a wartime understanding with the Germans obliged him to resign. He served again as Minister of Public Works in 1950–51.

Zervas had been a Venizelist army officer whose ties to republican die-hards such as General Plastiras, the former dictator Pangalos and Colonel Dertilis stretched back to the 1920s. He had commanded Pangalos's personal guard during his brief period of rule in 1925, and had been active in the numerous coups and conspiracies of interwar Greek politics. Like many republicans he combined a hatred of the monarchy with an equally intense hatred of communism. When EDES was founded as a republican resistance organisation in the autumn of 1941, the ambitious Zervas found his niche. Many of its republican backers saw it as a vehicle to attack the King rather than the Axis. Its vague programme of constitutional reform made no mention of armed resistance, and it is unlikely that Zervas felt deeply bound by its commitment to fight for democratic socialism. In fact Zervas was slow to show much enthusiasm for any sort of fighting at all. In the spring of 1942 he had actually received 24,000 gold sovereigns from the British to take to the hills; but he only departed that summer after exasperated SOE agents threatened to denounce him to the Axis.

EDES (the National Republican Greek League) embodied many of the characteristics of what might be called the 'traditional resistance' – its reliance on the charismatic personality of the *archigos* rather than on ideology, its ties to different factions in the old political world, and its skilful manipulation of foreign backers – in this case both British *and* German. EDES was also notorious for its lack of administrative cohesion. SOE commented on Zervas's 'disregard of even elementary organisation' and noted that 'he hopes for the best but employs a crowd of useless officers, because it would disturb the peace to fire them. . . . As an organiser his value is NIL.' Likened by one British agent to a 'bland and easy-going company director', Zervas relied for his support in the hills on the prewar village committees, whose members were often friends or relatives of prominent officers under his command. Houtas, Konstantinides and Zervas himself all depended upon their extensive family connections in north-west Greece. Major Bathgate, the SOE operative assigned to Zervas in 1943, likened him to the 'chairman of a provincial tramway company which is boosted and kept going but always has hanging over it the shadow of radical changes to buses in the dim future. In the meantime, the chairman isn't doing too badly for himself, and if the future isn't too rosy, he himself is well-provided for.' Overweight and a terrible hypochondriac, Zervas nevertheless managed to exercise his considerable charm over a succession of British officers.[108]

After Zervas left Athens in 1942, the EDES committee there was torn apart by fierce infighting, with some members accusing others of collaborating with the Germans. Later on, Zervas himself would be forced to make a public break with his former associates. But as EDES's centre of gravity shifted from the capital to the hills, it very quickly turned into a vehicle for his personal power, with the organisation's policy commitments subordinated to this end. 'Faith in the leader. All for the leader. All from the leader', was how his political adviser Pyromaglou later summed up his philosophy. In his dreams, Zervas saw himself called on to lead Greece back to greatness.[109]

When Woodhouse arrived with news of the Harling mission, Zervas quickly realised the value of close collaboration with the British for his small outfit, which was vastly outnumbered by EAM/ELAS. British support became his lifeline. Hoping to satisfy Whitehall and reassure the British of his political reliability (in particular the Foreign Office, which was uneasy at supporting a known republican), he made an extraordinary volte-face on 9 March 1943, when, following a suggestion by Woodhouse, he repudiated EDES's earlier republicanism and sent a personal message of greetings and loyalty to the exiled King George. This was to jettison the one policy commitment which united his rather ramshackle organisation; Zervas, however, went even further. Contrary to British expectations he also denounced EAM/ELAS as a communist organisation.[110]

Although Whitehall rather complacently reckoned that he was 'an instrument in our hand', Zervas was very much his own man: through his vigorous attack against EAM/ELAS he had fired the opening salvoes in an anti-communist crusade which was intended to reduce ELAS's attractiveness to London. He followed it up by warning against 'the dark forces of Communism backed by Russia'. Recent research has demonstrated the benefits he derived: from British air-drops in the first five months of 1943 he gained roughly twice the weight of arms and ammunition which ELAS received. The imbalance in terms of financial assistance was greater still. Yet ELAS was at least five or six times larger than EDES in this period, and responsible for virtually all attacks on the Axis.[111]

The problem, therefore, for the British was that military and political considerations were pulling them in different directions. ELAS obviously had the greatest capacity to inflict damage on the Axis; but politically, supporting it seemed fraught with long-term dangers. It was impossible to imagine ELAS ever proving 'an instrument in our hand'; on the contrary, the powerful communist role within it excited British fears of losing Greece and the East Mediterranean to the Soviet Union. With time, such considerations came to play an important part in shaping British policy towards the resistance, and EDES came to be regarded as a potential counter-weight to the Left. Not even well-founded suspicions that from late 1943 Zervas had established a *modus vivendi* with General Hubert Lanz, in command of the Wehrmacht's 22 Army Corps in Epiros, would significantly alter British estimates of his usefulness in the long term.

With an Allied landing in southern Europe planned for the summer of 1943, however, resistance activity in Greece assumed a strategic importance, and Myers was instructed to prepare for a full-scale guerrilla attack on Axis positions. As this was impossible without the support of ELAS, Foreign Office anti-communism had temporarily to be subordinated to the requirements of British military chiefs. When the Foreign Office urged that Britain pursue an unequivocally pro-monarchist policy, they were overruled by Churchill himself, who accepted that limited aid should continue to be provided to ELAS. Foreign Office tactics now shifted to splitting EAM/ELAS by weaning its non-communist rank and file away into other British-sponsored groups with less alarming political objectives.[112]

Given the mistrust and ill-feeling between the British and EDES on one hand, and EAM/ELAS on the other, it was not an easy matter to get the various resistance groups to co-operate as Myers had been instructed to do. The British were outraged by reports that ELAS was forcibly dissolving rival bands. ELAS, on the other hand, took a dim view of the efforts of some British liaison officers to undermine its leadership of the resistance movement. Each side assumed that the other intended to position itself so as to dominate the post-Liberation scene. Both were correct.

And yet, despite this mutual mistrust, Myers did successfully negotiate an important agreement in May 1943 by which EAM/ELAS put themselves under the operational command of General Wilson, the senior Allied commander in the Middle East, as a force of the United Nations. The so-called National Bands Agreement was limited to military affairs, for EAM would accept no subordination in political matters. It thus fell some way short of a genuine unification of Greek resistance forces under British auspices. But it still represented a considerable achievement on Myers's part, and a Joint General Headquarters was set up by guerrilla leaders. Delegates from ELAS, EDES and EKKA (National and Social Liberation: a minor resistance group active in southern Roumeli) managed to agree on a common pricing policy for food supplies and requisitions; EAM's system of local government was also adopted by the other organisations, and they even agreed to set up joint garrisons in areas such as Arta where EDES and ELAS units overlapped. Most importantly, although EAM/ELAS did not sign the agreement formally until 4 July, they co-operated fully with Allied Headquarters Middle East from June, in time to ensure the success of a vital piece of strategic deception – Operation Animals.[113]

CHAPTER FOURTEEN

The End of Italian Rule

From the time the tide of war in North Africa began to turn, Axis military planners tried to guess where the Allied blow in southern Europe would fall. The British did their best to fool them. Only recently have we learned the full extent of the strategic deception which the Allies arranged in the first half of 1943: this ranged from the well-known Operation Mincemeat, involving 'the man who never was', to a notional '12th Army' poised to threaten the Balkans from Egypt, alongside a multitude of dummy troop displays, radio deceptions and currency forgeries.[114]

These stratagems were intended to provide cover for the Allied invasion of Sicily, and a crucial part was played by Operation Animals, the campaign of guerrilla activity which Myers and the Military Mission had been retained in Greece to promote. As the Allies knew, Hitler was virtually convinced that Greece was the Allies' intended target, for the Führer believed that Churchill wanted to wipe out memories of the Dardanelles fiasco with a successful Balkan campaign. In addition, German staff planners emphasised the importance of Balkan raw materials – chrome, bauxite, antimony and Romanian oil – to the Nazi war effort. By his Directive no. 27 of 28 December, 1942, Hitler defined the 'South-East' as an operational theatre of war, and nominated Lieutenant-General Alexander Löhr, in Salonika, as Oberbefehlshaber Südost.[115]

During the first half of 1943 the Wehrmacht Supreme Command organised an immense defensive build-up in Greece. The forces at Löhr's disposal at the start of the year were enlarged: the brand-new 11th Luftwaffe Field Division was deployed near the Corinth Canal; 117 Jaeger Division was sent south from Yugoslavia as fast as the single-track rail line would permit. Later, these troops were reinforced by 104 Jaeger Division, and by two first-rate units: 1st Panzer Division, a tank division deployed in the Peloponnese by June, and 1st Mountain Division, which reached its quarters in Jannina, in north-west Greece during July. This represented a considerable strategic investment for an army which was scattered across the vast expanse of Fortress Europe. The era of Italian 'predominance' in Greece was nearing its end.[116]

*

Of the 93,000 Italian troops on mainland Greece, 12,000 were ill with malaria. Another 70,000 manned the islands. General Geloso had been promised 24,000 men as reinforcements by Rome, but fewer than 2,000 arrived. 'All my troops,' Geloso wrote to General Vittorio Ambrosio in Rome, 'have *armamento antiquato*, lack almost any anti-tank or anti-air guns, or armoured transport.' They had no coastal artillery or bombers. Rome evidently regarded Greece as a sideshow. An influx of German reinforcements, Geloso warned, would cause overall control to pass out of Italian hands – as had happened in Egypt – 'even in an area which has been defined as and *is* our *spazio vitale*'. Yet Wehrmacht support seemed necessary if Greece was to be held. According to a memorandum drawn up for Mussolini by the head of the *carabinieri*, the general view among the Italian troops in the spring of 1943 was that an enemy landing in Greece 'could not be resisted'.[117]

The Italian army's disastrous performance in Albania had hit morale. From his headquarters in Athens, General Geloso did what he could to improve matters. 'Discipline,' he instructed the troops at the start of the occupation, 'should be *sostanziale, salda, sana*. A martial look and correctness are its outward expression.' But Geloso faced problems which ran much deeper than matters of appearance. He complained of his men's 'peace-time mentality'. Even when assaulted by Greeks, they hesitated to draw their arms. He was appalled to encounter an infantry regiment in the middle of Athens walking 'all over the road in disorder'.[118] One of his directives ended with a desperate reminder: 'Always keep in mind that the army is made for war and that war is a very serious thing' ('La guerra è una cosa seria')![119]

Many conscripts evidently felt differently. 'Soldiers frequently get drunk and curse the war in front of anyone who feels like listening to them,' reported escapees from Greece in October 1941. 'Porco Mussolini,' summed up the attitude in the ranks. 'Down with Mussolini, down with Hitler, down with the War,' shouted soldiers reeling out of a taverna in March 1943.[120] Others marching through the centre of Athens on a hot day ignored their officers' frantic orders, fell out, and sat on their packs in the middle of the road for twenty minutes.[121]

There was no love lost between the Axis forces, and German and Italian soldiers were often seen brawling in the street. 'That's the bloody end!' shouted one German sergeant arrested by the *carabinieri* after a scrap at the Chez-Nous bar, where a *Kameradschaftsabend* had got out of hand. 'Now we allow ourselves to be thrown out by these types. Who won the war anyway?' In the Athens suburb of Psychiko there was a shoot-out when an Italian patrol found some Germans refusing to observe the blackout: in the cross-fire, both Italians and Germans died.[122]

If the Italians thought the Germans were 'barbarians', the Germans disapproved of the way the Italians mixed war and sex. Salacious tales of Latin love-making circulated through the Wehrmacht. A German businessman in Athens wrote down the story of an unnamed Italian general who was reputedly 'well-known for having instructed the hotel management to provide an ample supply of young women ("every evening another one, to present herself in the room punctually at the appointed time")'.[123] In the Wehrmacht itself, soldiers were repeatedly warned to steer clear of contacts with Greek women outside the official brothels. Not only did Greek women pose a threat to security, physical health and racial purity; to direct feelings towards them that were more properly kept for German women was thought to threaten the soldier's will to act with the necessary harshness towards his enemy. In German eyes, therefore, the Italians' unwarlike attitude to women was directly connected to their feeble response to the burgeoning Greek resistance.

Certainly the Italians in Greece were a good deal more moderate in their treatment of the Greek population than their Axis partners. The burning of villages was chiefly the work of a small number of notorious field commanders, rather than general policy set in Athens. Geloso insisted in 1942 that reprisals were to be conducted with 'extreme foresight' and care: 'Firmness and inexhaustible energy against the guilty . . . must not degenerate into a blind brutality which is out of harmony with traditions of Roman justice in the Italian Army, harmful to our prestige, contrary to our very interests.' The spread of the *andartiko* did not alter his outlook.[124]

German diplomats and generals wanted the Italians to take tougher counter-measures. Löhr's HQ argued that Italian measures were 'as good as useless', showing the need for a 'systematic and thorough campaign against the bandits'. During the summit meeting between the two Axis leaders at Salzburg in April 1943, Foreign Minister Ribbentrop warned an Italian diplomat that 'brutal action would have to be taken if the Greeks got above themselves. He was of the opinion that . . . the Greeks should be shown in an iron manner who was master in the country'.[125] Field Marshal Keitel gave General Ambrosio similar advice: 'OKW's great plea was for the commander of the 11th Army to issue urgent instructions to crush this emerging banditry *mit brutalsten Mitteln* [most brutally]. In German experience, for instance in Norway,' Keitel continued, 'it helped to adopt such a ruthless approach from the start. And should a village be burned down without justification, that does no harm either – the word of a fast and tough strike is passed around, and helps too.'[126]

The Italians were unconvinced. In June 1943 Altenburg reported to Berlin that the Italians had reacted to German demands for 'sharp' measures with 'a hesitant attitude', refusing to act toughly despite his own 'most energetic' efforts to persuade them. Geloso and his successor Vecchiarelli clashed with their Axis colleagues over anti-guerrilla policy. Geloso castigated the Germans' use of hostages, who 'were taken at random, even sometimes from among those favourable to us, or from those who had never shown signs of hostility. . . . We did not take hostages; the system does not enter into our laws of war.' He regarded it as 'an odious procedure'.[127]

Such views helped to persuade the Germans of the Italians' unreliability. As OKW sent Wehrmacht reinforcements down into Greece to take up defensive positions along the coast, it also prepared to act in a more sinister direction – against the Italians themselves. In May, when the Axis forces in North Africa finally surrendered, the chances of a separate Italian peace bid hardened into virtual certainty. Berlin was well informed of the defeatist mood in Rome. On 20 May Hitler ordered plans to be drawn up for a German takeover in the Balkans. Originally code-named Konstantine, this operation was revised after the Allies landed in Sicily in June. Hitler remained convinced that a second blow would fall in the Aegean, and sent Rommel to Salonika. Five days before he arrived, a small German liaison staff travelled to Athens to work alongside, and unofficially to watch, the staff of the Italian 11th Army.

At the end of July these preparations were amply justified when Mussolini was unexpectedly toppled in a palace coup in Rome by Marshal Badoglio, a figure whose commitment to the Axis was, at best, lukewarm. In Athens the atmosphere was electric: four massive German tanks rolled into position on Amerikis Street, with their gun barrels pointed straight at the Italian HQ.[128] Rommel flew back to see the Führer, and General Löhr secretly ordered all the German units in the Balkans to be ready to disarm the Italian forces there in the event of an Italian withdrawal from the war. The code-word for this operation was Axis.

*

Mussolini's swift downfall astonished the Italian troops in Greece. However, only a handful of Fascist supporters seemed dismayed; the rest waited to see what the Badoglio regime would bring, hoping that their war could be ended quickly without further fighting. On Zante we learn that 'the soldier saw . . . the end of the war, his return home, and passed the day in eager anticipation. By now the men were exhausted.' On the islands of Fourni and Ikarya in the Aegean, where a friendly understanding existed between Italian detachments and the local inhabitants, the Italians 'made no secret of their intention of surrendering at the first opportunity and had their white flags ready'. On Samos, all Fascist emblems disappeared within a few hours of the coup. According to Raymond Courvoisier, a Swiss Red Cross delegate visiting the island: 'The commanding General was chiefly concerned to know where he would be sent after surrender and looked forward to meeting M. Courvoisier again in Kenya.'[129]

Signs of defeatism among the Italians in Greece had been obvious for some time. British liaison officers with the Greek resistance received many requests from demoralised military commanders during the summer. The commander of the Casale Division, General Mangani, made approaches through the mayor of Agrinion; General Delabona, commanding the 26 Army Corps in Epiros, had sought surrender terms via the Bishop of Jannina.[130]

Then, on the evening of 8 September, came the news that Italy had indeed surrendered. This was the first the troops had heard of the negotiations that had been proceeding secretly for several weeks between Badoglio and the Allies. Where no Germans were present, Italian soldiers and Greek civilians celebrated the war's end in riotous fashion. Ermoupolis was covered in flags – Greek, Italian, English, American – and people gathered and made speeches in the main square. On the small island of Simi the news was greeted with shouts of 'Irini, irini' [peace, peace], and villagers came down from the hills into the port to celebrate.[131]

As soon as news of the armistice became known, Italian troops sold guns, hand grenades and other equipment to resistance contacts. 'Once disarmed,' an Italian eyewitness recorded, 'the units – abandoned to their own devices by most of their officers – no longer felt bound by discipline. Officers and men began selling materiel, food and so on to the Greeks.' Athens on the morning of 10 September was like an 'endless market festival' as the Italians stripped their units of equipment and sold it on the streets – weapons, motorbikes, bicycles, blankets and boots, furniture from offices and messes, typewriters, even the occasional car.[132]

The Germans, however, were not caught napping. General Löhr had predicted almost a month earlier that an Italian armistice was 'only a matter of time'.[133] Now staff officers in Salonika and Athens reacted swiftly. At 6.45 in the evening of 8 September, the Italian

General Vecchiarelli called in General von Gyldenfeldt, of the liaison staff in Athens. Pledging that his troops would not take up arms against the Germans, he sought confirmation from the Germans that they would not use force against Italian troops. Gyldenfeldt made no reply but simply passed on the Italian request to Löhr at Army Group E. Löhr's answer was uncompromising. He instructed Gyldenfeldt that if the Italians refused either to fight as part of Army Group E, or to surrender unconditionally to the Germans, Axis should come into effect.

The German ultimatum had no basis in international law, since Italy and Germany were not at war, and an outraged Vecchiarelli lost no time in pointing this out. But General Gyldenfeldt ignored his objections: 'A totally unambiguous answer must be demanded. If there were a rejection of a continuation of the fight then the German Army must, for its own security, be certain that Italian weapons would never be turned on the Germans, i.e. they must be surrendered to the German Army.'[134]

As Vecchiarelli still held out, insisting on being permitted to return with his troops to Italy, some of Gyldenfeldt's colleagues became alarmed at the prospect of the heavy fighting ahead. They decided not to implement Axis at once; instead they turned the screws gradually. First they persuaded the Italians to surrender their heavy weapons and machine-guns. Then a few days later they insisted on taking possession of small arms as well. Their former allies were in no position to resist. It was, for example, reported from 1st Brandenburg Regiment that Italian soldiers, though 'only partially' obeying the commands of their own officers, were 'behaving in a disciplined and orderly way towards German officers'.[135]

In much of Greece, this patient if unscrupulous diplomacy was rewarded and Italian troops were disarmed under German supervision. Despite being outnumbered, the Germans managed to impose their will over their former allies; as Field Marshal von Weichs put it in a congratulory telegram: 'The martial spirit has triumphed over the majority.'[136] When the Italians were offered a choice between continuing to fight under German command or being evacuated by train from Greece, few took the necessary oath of allegiance to Mussolini's puppet Salò government, or to Hitler; the great majority, under the impression (which the Germans studiously avoided correcting) that they would be repatriated to Italy, were herded on to trains heading northwards to Yugoslavia and POW camps in the north.[137]

Away from the mainland, however, several Italian garrisons did resist German efforts to disarm them. On Rhodes there was heavy fighting for two days before the 7,000 men of Sturmdivision Rhodos regained control and took 40,000 Italians prisoner. Serious clashes also took place in the Ionian islands, where Italian units insisted on fighting, and even armed small groups of Greeks who were willing to join them against the Germans. Zante was soon pacified, but on Cefalonia – where 'the most complete anarchy reigned . . . during the days of negotiations between the two commands' – Italian forces beat off a sea and air assault by the 1st Mountain Division for almost a week before surrendering on 24 September; Corfu fell two days later.

German punishment was swift and staggeringly ruthless. Some 155 officers and 4,750 men captured on Cefalonia were executed by firing squad after the fighting had finished. An unknown number of Italian officers were shot on Corfu too. Many bodies were dumped at sea, and some were later washed back up on nearby beaches. A highly respected German military historian has recently described these events as amounting to 'one of the most unbelievable war crimes of German soldiers in World War Two'. At least 500 more Italian prisoners-of-war drowned when the ship which was ferrying them to the mainland capsized.[138]

*

Despite the Duce's ignominious fall from power, some Italians remained loyal to Fascism. For them Badoglio's defection had actually freed the movement from the conservative influence of the army and the court. Against a background of general fatigue with the war, these quixotic enthusiasts tried to rescue Italy from the taint of failure and stayed true to the Axis.[139]

On Crete a certain Major Fernando Cassini heard that his commanding officer, General Carta, had fled underground. Cassini immediately set up a body he called the Legione Italiana di Creta 'Giulio Cesaro', to salvage Italy's honour from the 'villains, subversives and Jews who are triumphing today'. General Carta, he wrote to Mussolini later, had been 'the typical expression of those military chiefs who have led us to disaster.' Good Fascist that he was, Major Cassini worked to regain the trust of the Germans, and desperately, but unsuccessfully, sought backing and encouragement from Mussolini, after the Duce was newly installed by the Germans in the Republic of Salò.

Units of Fascist Blackshirts continued to fight alongside German troops. Their commander on Rhodes, Captain Mario Porta, railed against the 'pestiferous incubation of the Badoglio Government' and called for renewed action: '"Only with blood can the shame poured over the Italian people be washed away." Only with sacrifice will we conquer a just peace to assure ourselves a future of tranquil labour and civil progress.' Backing him, General Kleemann wanted the Blackshirts to become 'the nucleus of a Fascist army which, unaffected by all the vicissitudes of the War, will stand in unbreakable loyalty and comradeship of arms by our side'.[140]

But Kleemann and Porta were to be disappointed, for there were probably fewer than 10,000 Blackshirts fighting alongside the Germans by 1944. German soldiers laughed at them, picked fights, and even, in moments of drunken high spirits, lobbed grenades in their direction; there was not much sign of 'comradeship of arms'. Not surprisingly, many Blackshirts looked for the first chance to desert to the Allies.[141]

In the most implausible gesture of all, some Salò loyalists even tried to restore Fascist party cells in Athens and Salonika. But hampered by lack of funds, German obstruction, and the unconcern of Mussolini himself, their project was doomed from the start. A valedictory report from the Ionian islands summed up the fate of Fascism's fantasy of a new Roman empire in Greece:

> The politico-administrative system installed in the Ionian islands had guaranteed the full annexation of these territories to Italy. Every sector had been treated: organs of justice, schools, the organisation of workers, industry and commerce corresponded perfectly to our aims. The Party, together with the Civil Consul, had penetrated by its action into the deepest nuclei of the collectivity. . . . In Zante and the other islands we published newspapers through whose columns the masses learned about the programmes of the Italian Government. Workers' canteens were set up; maternity clinics founded, to combat the disappearance of tradition and to help the worse-off. Agricultural initiatives with new, rational ideas for cultivation. . . .
>
> This was the overall great civil mission in the Ionian islands, and its results. The life of these islands now gave grounds for hope, and our mission seemed in its final phase. This land, where till recently disorder reigned, now securely approached a new life of prosperity and justice. All this work has been destroyed by the 'sad period' of the war.[142]

In fact, the vast majority of the Italians who opted to stay in Greece were uncommitted to the Axis, no matter what oaths they might have sworn. According to a 1944 report for the Fascist Party, most administrators in Rhodes, the one remaining centre of Italian influence, were not active party members: 'For five months they have continued to hold their positions like utter attentistes, hoping to see the arrival of English ships.' A German intelligence officer who visited Corfu in April 1944 reported that 'there remain on the island some 1,500 to 2,000 Italians who have found accommodation as workers with the farmers and traders. They are for the most part war-weary and not anxious to return to Italy; nor are they in any way willing to be on the side of Germany.'[143]

The real significance of the Italian collapse was that it contributed men, arms and psychological encouragement to the armed resistance to German rule. Across the country, large stocks of weapons and supplies fell into the hands of the *andartes*, while many Greeks took to the hills in the belief that the war itself would be over by the end of the year. In central Greece, an entire division, the Pinerolo, went over to the guerrillas under the supervision of British liaison officers. Several thousand ragged Italian conscripts were quartered in the Vlach villages above Metsovo. According to a British War Office estimate from April 1944, there were about 10,000 Italians up in the hills.[144] Italian soldiers who agreed to enlist in German units also deserted to the guerrillas. On 26 September, for example, twenty-three unarmed Italians serving with German forces in the Peloponnese deserted to the 'bandits'; several days later, guerrillas attacked an Italian mule column near Aegion on the north coast, causing all but one member of the Italian escort to desert. The War Diary of Army Group South Greece records that 3,000 to 4,000 Italians were 'disarmed' by guerrillas near Delphi. With thousands of disaffected soldiers at large in the countryside, public order deteriorated still further. Now that the Axis partnership had crumbled, it would be up to the Germans to hold Greece on their own.[145]

PART THREE

The Logic of Violence and Terror: 1943-44

*The enemy has thrown into bandit warfare fanatic, communist –
trained fighters who will not stop at any act of violence. The stake
here is more than to be or not to be. This fight has nothing to do
with a soldier's chivalry nor with the decisions of the Geneva
Conventions. If this fight against the bands, in the East as well as
in the Balkans is not carried out with the most brutal means, the
forces at our disposal may in the near future not last out to master
this plague.*

*The troops are therefore authorised and ordered in this struggle
to take any measures without restriction even against women and
children if these are necessary for success. [Humanitarian]
considerations of any kind are a crime against the German
nation. . . .*

Orders issued by Field Marshal Keitel
(following instructions from Hitler), 16 December 1942

CHAPTER FIFTEEN

The Logic of Violence

With the Italians disarmed, the Third Reich was now in sole charge in Greece, and the Wehrmacht's campaign against the *andartes* became the central issue of Axis occupation policy. Lieutenant-General Alexander Löhr, the commander of Army Group E, adopted a far more aggressive approach than Geloso had done. Löhr himself – a short, dapper, taciturn man – was a most unusual figure for a senior Wehrmacht commander: not only was his background in the Luftwaffe, rather than in the army, and in the Austrian rather than German service at that; but he was actually Russian Orthodox by birth, thanks to his mother, spoke Russian, and had a sophisticated understanding of the complexities of Balkan history. He had travelled widely, and was certainly not a slavish admirer of the Führer. None of this, however, prevented him from adhering to the strict and ultimately self-defeating guidelines for anti-guerrilla warfare which the German military had evolved under the influence of National Socialism. Most of Löhr's troops came into Greece from the brutal environment of the Eastern Front and Yugoslavia. Drawing on the experience they had acquired there, Wehrmacht and Waffen-SS units now began a systematic attempt to wipe out the *andartes*.[1]

For the first time Greece became the arena for a sustained anti-guerrilla campaign, suffering the sort of destruction that had already devastated parts of Bosnia, Serbia and the Ukraine. When Liberation came, late in 1944, over a thousand villages had been razed. One million Greeks had seen their homes looted and burned down, their crops damaged and their churches despoiled. More than 20,000 civilians had been killed or wounded, shot, hanged or beaten by Wehrmacht troops.[2]

As a counter-insurgency strategy, the policy of large-scale operations, hostage-taking and reprisals clearly failed, for by the time the Wehrmacht retreated northwards the resistance was as strong as ever. As a reflection of the values of National Socialism, however, the Wehrmacht's anti-guerrilla policy offers many insights into the

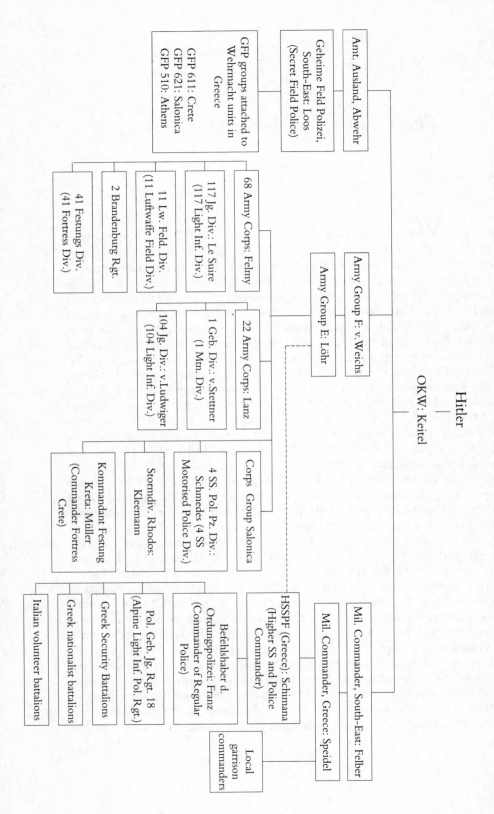

Wehrmacht Command Structure, early 1944

ideological foundations of Hitler's New Order, for the Wehrmacht no less than the SS were what one German historian has called 'the troops of the [Nazi] *Weltanschauung*'.[3]

Seeing the Enemy

Entering Greece in the spring of 1943, officers of 117 Jaeger Division were given detailed instructions for helping their men through a 'total war' in which they needed 'guidance, answers and a clear message': 'It is especially necessary to stiffen [the soldier's] resolve to fight and to encourage the soldierly virtues. The education of a resistance to crisis, toughness and *eine gewisse Brutalität* (a certain brutality) is absolutely necessary.'[4] But what were the 'soldierly virtues' and was 'brutality' among them? What were the criteria for guilt and innocence in a guerrilla war, and how was the enemy to be identified?

German soldiers had grappled with such intractable questions from the time of the Franco-Prussian War onwards. Then, as in Belgium in 1914, the harshness of their response – the uncompromising and systematic use of reprisals and a sweeping appeal to military necessity – had shocked many observers. Now an established body of military doctrine concerning guerrilla war was transposed into a new context and put at the service of a regime which interpreted resistance – like everything else – in racial terms. According to the troops' instructions, all civilians were to be regarded as potential enemies. 'Any contact with the Greeks is forbidden. Any Greek, even when he gets on with a German, wants something from him. For each favour he wants something in return. German good-will towards the Greeks is always misplaced. "Better shoot once too often than once too seldom."' For soldiers who had been offered no specialist training in how to tackle the tangled problems of guerrilla warfare, such sweeping instructions had at least the merit of simplicity and clarity.[5]

As the resistance spread, some familiar racial stereotypes were beginning to overlay the quite powerful philhellenism of Nazi ideology. German army officers were no less ardent admirers of ancient Greece than the Reich's archaeologists, architects and other professionals, and from Field Marshal Brauchitsch downwards many of them visited the classical sites as dutiful 'war tourists'. But this sort of vague classicism was accompanied by considerable ambivalence towards Pericles' modern descendants. Historians speculated about the malign effects of Phoenician, and hence Semitic blood,

26. Wartime philhellenes: soldiers visit the Acropolis.

upon classical Greek stock. Fallmerayer's thesis that racial continuity with the ancients had been interrupted by the seventh-century Slavic invasions found adherents in the Third Reich. Though the Greeks stood well above the Serbs in the Nazi racial hierarchy, Hitler's initial admiration for the brave performance of the Greek army in April 1941 wore off under the pressure of sabotage attacks on occupation forces. 'The Germans harbored no hatred against the Greeks,' wrote General Hubert Lanz. 'On the contrary, they admired the great past and lofty culture of Hellas. But how would they react to guerrilla warfare?'[6]

During 1943 the answer to Lanz's question emerged as visions of the 'lofty culture of Hellas' gave way to the nightmarish sterotype of the 'Balkan fanatic'. This bloodthirsty creature already obsessed those Germans fighting the partisans and Chetniks in occupied Yugoslavia. Many senior Wehrmacht officers in the region – Löhr himself, for example – were Austrians who had served in the Habsburg army during the First World War and still felt the old imperial prejudices against Balkan peoples. Such attitudes were strengthened by the ideological onslaught against communist partisans which the Nazi regime mounted throughout Eastern Europe after the invasion of the Soviet Union.[7] As the *andartiko* developed in Greece, the 'Balkan' stereotype came into play there too: 'bandits' were supposedly endemic in the region; they had no conception of military honour, and they were drawn from a primitive population which 'under the influence of fanatical leaders, can be incited to a warfare so pitiless and inhuman as to be scarcely conceivable'. The racial connection between ancient Greece and 'this land of neo-Greeks' was openly doubted.[8]

Such opinions were fostered at the highest levels. Recalling the *Vernichtungskrieg* (war of annihilation) on the Eastern Front, Löhr reminded his officers that 'this is a fight to the death, without a halfway house'. Criticising those who harboured residual sympathies for the *andartes*, he warned that 'ideas of a "peaceloving people's heroism" etc. are misguided. Precious German blood is at stake.' Hitler himself issued orders to drop words like 'franc-tireur' (*Freischärler*) and 'partisan' for the more unequivocal term 'bandits' when referring to the guerrillas.[9]

Reinforcing their fears of local insurgents, the rank and file heard horrifying stories of how the guerrillas mutilated captured German soldiers: these Balkan primitives and communist fanatics were, of course, ignorant of civilised behaviour. Erhard Glitz, an officer stationed south of Thebes, described one occasion when 'a tribunal of [guerrilla] judges showed the soldiers a selection of knives and let them choose the one with which they preferred to be stabbed to death. With the bandits cheering raucously they were, one by one, stabbed between throat and chest from above by means of the notorious "Schaecht" thrust. . . . Those who did not die immediately were kicked and clubbed and then left lying.'[10]

Glitz had not witnessed these horrors himself; he admits that he had only heard about them from another soldier, though he insisted that they had happened just as he had described. Yet certain motifs in his story – the perversion of justice, the inhumanity of the 'bandits', and the incongruous anti-Semitic allusions – drew upon standard Nazi propaganda about racial inferiors and 'anti-social' groups. The reference to the so-called '"Schaecht" thrust' was a common anti-Semitic accusation against Jewish cattle traders in the Third Reich which had little to do with *andartes* in Greece.

Glitz was not the only one living with such nightmares, and actual contact with the guerrillas sometimes brought unexpected reassurance. Lieutenant Ludwig Günter, to take one example, who was captured by the guerrillas in August 1944, was astonished at the good treatment he received. Hermann Franz, head of German paramilitary police troops in Greece, confirms that those of his men who were captured by ELAS were not ill-treated, apart from being stripped of their boots (a scarce item in the mountains). Of course the *andartes* did kill captured Germans, but there is no evidence that they delighted in this any more than their opponents did: shortage of food was usually their motive, not sadism.[11]

Another stereotype drummed into the troops was that of the guerrilla as criminal. Gunther Kleykamp, a staff officer in Athens, claimed for instance that the *andartes* included 'numerous rootless characters who would not have found a position under normal living conditions'. From the Peloponnese, 117 Jaeger Division reported in December 1943 that 'the bands are recruiting . . . chiefly from gangsters from the large cities'. Such bizarre pseudo-analyses employed the characteristic vocabulary of policing from the prewar Reich in a new context. Here too supposedly objective intelligence was shaped and coloured by the observer's own expectations.[12]

The Wehrmacht, in other words, was certainly not the 'untarnished shield' beloved of an earlier generation of historians, and soldiers did not remain immune to the influence of Nazi values. What they saw, they saw through the eyes of men who had grown up with certain ideological and, particularly, racialist beliefs. What is true is that the majority did not see themselves as fanatics or extremists. On the contrary – and this phenomenon was certainly not confined to the German army – they usually identified their opponents as the fanatics, and by portraying themselves as the restorers of order, were able to justify a regime of extraordinary brutality to their own satisfaction.

Regarding the guerrillas as inhuman, criminal or racial inferiors undoubtedly helped to erode the troops' moral and legal inhibitions against the use of 'harsh and ruthless measures'. The German soldier was warned that he would need to be 'even craftier and more ruthless' than his opponent, and ready to use 'all means' in the fight against a 'brutal, underhand and crafty enemy'. And he would, by implication, have justice on his side since the *Banditen* were not identified as members of an oppressed national group fighting for their freedom, but as subhuman criminals who refused to recognise the legitimate authority in their country. They were not 'worthy opponents', but subversive elements. For many soldiers, therefore, the fight against the guerrillas came to be seen as a policing action rather than war. Thirty years later, a former machine-gunner, Walter V., would still talk about the time he had spent in Yugoslavia and Greece executing 'delinquents' and 'death-worthy criminals', when he really meant innocent civilians shot in reprisals. In these attitudes and images, as in so many other aspects of the German response to the *andartes*, we see a pattern of reactions which would become increasingly familiar in the postwar world from soldiers caught up against their will in 'dirty wars' from Algeria to Vietnam, Ireland and beyond.[13]

Information

At Army Group E headquarters outside Salonika it was the intelligence department (1c/AO) which collected material on the guerrillas. The chief analyst on Löhr's staff was Hans Wende, who had been a teacher at the German School in Athens before the war. Unlike most of his superiors, Wende had lived in Greece, knew its people well and genuinely understood the strength and passion of Greek nationalism. As head of the 'Greek Resistance Movement' section of the 1c department, subordinated to a certain Lieutenant Kurt Waldheim, he had access to information from field commanders, counter-intelligence agents and the local military police. Contacts with anti-communist circles in Athens provided further material. He wrote the first report on 'the bandit situation in Greece' in April 1943, at the request of General Winter, Löhr's chief of staff, and within several months was producing reports regularly.[14]

Obtaining the raw intelligence was not easy. As in Russia, agents (so-called V-men and women) were infiltrated into the resistance. In the Peloponnese, for example, soldiers were sent into the hills pretending to be deserters. But as the guerrillas grew more suspicious, they interrogated new arrivals carefully, and shot agents they unmasked. Later they stepped up security by issuing passwords and ID cards of their own.[15]

One agent who did return from the field submitted a report which bore eloquent testimony to the intelligence difficulties the *andartes* posed for the Wehrmacht. On 28 September 1943 he spent the night in the market-town of Tripolis. Early the next morning he hitched a lift on a truck to Megalopolis and then continued on foot along the winding road through increasingly broken country towards Karitena. As the town loomed on its hill ahead, he left the road and started to walk through the fields:

A shepherd who was looking after his sheep close by on a hill had apparently observed me, because 10 minutes later he came to keep me company. I asked him where the Andartes were. He pretended not to understand the word Andartes and also gave me no further information about them. In a little while, five civilians appeared who greeted me in a friendly way and conversed with me about trivial matters. We did not reach a real understanding.

Then, from a hill top close to the Megalopolis-Karitena road, we heard a tune played on a pipe, which was repeated on three more hill-tops. The civilians became very agitated and explained to me that I should hide in the bushes as German soldiers were coming. A short while later, 2 groups of riflemen did march through the hollow in the direction of Karitena. Half an hour later, three short whistles rang out, whereupon the civilians exclaimed that everything was all right again.

When it became completely dark, 4 other civilians appeared, each armed with a rifle. The four men invited me to follow them. After a few hours' march, I heard a solitary man singing in the distance. At this one of my companions gave three short whistles and we sat down.

Shortly a man appeared holding a lantern; he had a parcel under his arm. He also greeted me in a friendly fashion. There was half a loaf in the parcel, 3 hard boiled eggs, cheese and grapes. Then they invited me to eat heartily. We sat there for roughly 2–3 hours, then we continued on our way. The civilian who brought me the food came with us. Once again we travelled all over the countryside, and at dawn we arrived in a village, Karatula. A few hours later I saw 12 men standing around me. They were armed and in uniform.[16]

In this report the line between civilians and guerrillas has blurred almost to vanishing point. Was the shepherd working for the *andartes*; or had his approach simply been motivated by curiosity, and his subsequent silence by caution? Why were those groups of civilians wandering through the fields, idly, at a time when honest farmers were working? If they were not guerrillas, how did they understand the warning that German troops were approaching? Had they hid because they had guilty consciences, or because they simply feared that as civilian males they provided the customary target for the Wehrmacht? Not even the agent himself could offer an answer to these questions.

By November 1943, 68 Army Corps in southern Greece was finding it difficult to get information from undercover operatives. Wehrmacht spies were followed when they tried to return, and were sometimes murdered in broad daylight; despite increases in pay, the supply of recruits for such work was dwindling. On Crete, women suspected of co-operating with the German forces were roughed up, and their heads were shaved. The life of the V-man (and woman) became increasingly hazardous.[17]

Fortunately for the Germans, there were other ways of obtaining intelligence. Under the threat of reprisals if guerrillas operated in their neighbourhood, many villagers reluctantly agreed to alert the Germans to the presence of *andartes*. An early example of such behaviour was reported in Macedonia in the winter of 1941. Three days after Wehrmacht troops burned two villages in the Struma estuary and shot their menfolk in mass executions, the frightened inhabitants of nearby Efharpia handed over two other men to the authorities as suspected guerrillas. Elsewhere, worried farmers set up watch-groups armed with axes to prevent the entry of strangers and reported 'suspicious newcomers'. In 1944 two fishermen from the island of Ikarya spent six months in jail on Chios after their boat was blown off course and villagers from Pyrgi notified the local police of their presence.[18] Such behaviour was less in evidence away from the security of a permanent Wehrmacht garrison. But even in more remote areas villagers did prove a plentiful source of information, despite the threat of guerrilla revenge. One islander wrote sadly to a friend abroad that 'they had fifteen Germans in the village and some traitors who were friendly with them invited them home and communicated everything to them'.[19]

Villagers volunteered news from a variety of motives, however, and their personal grudges and quarrels inevitably distorted the information they offered. Agents were always a headache: they had their own lives to lead, and their controllers found it hard to keep watch over them. A detachment of 117 Jaeger Division revisited the village of Bozika, and found the house of one of their agents, Georgios Benekos, burnt down; searching through the ruins they also found two cartridges, possible indications of a struggle. Villagers said that Benekos, who had been helping the Wehrmacht in anti-guerrilla investigations in Attica a fortnight earlier, had been arrested by partisans, put in chains and taken away. But as the officer who reported the news observed, 'it is possible that this operation was just a ploy'. In the absence of Benekos himself, no one could be sure whose side he was really on. One remedy for the Germans was to send spies, posing as guerrillas, to make contact with unreliable informants to check on the latter's loyalty to the Axis cause. An undercover British officer travelling by mule in the Peloponnese was mistaken for one of these: when he greeted a peasant working in a field in fractured Greek, the man responded with a wary, 'Ja Ja Jawohl', and turned away.[20]

To add to the confusion, there were the customary feuds between rival intelligence organisations. Regular army intelligence (1c) usually co-operated in the field with the Abwehr (AO: counter-intelligence), and with the rather shadowy Secret Field Police (GFP). But sometimes 1c/AO and the GFP ran separate networks of agents. Then there was the SS, which worked independently, and whose different branches also got in one another's way. Such intense competition created a seller's market. A Greek source noted that Germans swallowed 'whatever the Greek agents tell them'. So who was using whom? GFP 621 in Salonika relied on informers like Liana, a dancer, and Panayiotis P., a smuggler and casino manager – both of whom were 'more interested in making money than in providing information', according to a reliable source.[21]

A spectacular fiasco in Corfu during the spring of 1944 illustrated the perils of such arrangements. Agents sent out by the Abwehr office in Tirana began to report the existence of large spy networks, linked to an active resistance movement on the island. 'This led to the deployment of vast numbers of agents, GFP squads and radio monitoring units who brought neither system nor success to their work, whether in cooperation or rivalry,' ran the post-mortem. Eventually a senior intelligence operative was sent from the Secret Field Police unit in Jannina to clear up the confusion. 'It was soon discovered that there was no question of there being an enemy intelligence-gathering centre on the island or any organised resistance movement. In consequence the unnecessarily expanded counter-intelligence network was dismantled and the 1c office closed down.' The agents in Wehrmacht pay, a couple of enterprising Albanian doctors, had simply been feeding the Abwehr rumours they had picked up in the streets of Corfu town, while using their spare moments for a spot of lucrative black-marketeering. They were well known round the island, and made no attempt to hide their intelligence connections. Good contacts with the security services were invaluable to black-marketeers and, as in this case, the two activities were frequently paired.[22]

*

A minor GFP investigation into the so-called 'Pietro Band' on Rhodes late in 1943 allows us to reconstruct the difficulties the Germans faced in cutting through the fog of rumours, ignorance and uncertainty, while suggesting at the same time how far their own preconceptions shaped their inquiries into the resistance. This was an investigation which started a few weeks after the Italian troops on Rhodes had surrendered to the Wehrmacht, and the island was slowly being brought under German control. The atmosphere was still tense and the German garrison uncertain of the size of the task ahead of it, when one day snipers shot at a solitary German soldier in the hills of central Rhodes; a patrol was sent out and a group of nine Italian deserters was arrested without much effort.[23]

The scared young conscripts were willing enough to talk, but raised as many questions as they answered. Who, for example, had formed the 'band' and recruited them? Twenty-three-year-old Giuseppe Sterantino had only the vaguest idea. Following the Italian collapse, he had been wandering from village to village, with no fixed plans, when he met another soldier called Georgio on the road to the village of Arcangelo:

> He asked me where I'd been and where I was going, if I was hungry and what I planned to do. I said that I hadn't been with a unit for a long time; I'd been always on the move and was pretty hungry. Now I just wanted to find a place in a camp. He invited me to come into the hills with him, where there were other comrades and something to eat. I said: 'That's the main thing, there's something to eat – I'm coming with you.'

The German investigators homed in on the figure of this mysterious recruiter, but neither Giuseppe Sterantino nor any of the others knew who he was. All twenty-year-old Enea De Michiel knew was that 'Georgio' used to go down daily to the village of Arcangelo to buy tomatoes, olives and melons. Chamico Quirico too had gone into the hills after he met two Italian soldiers in the fields in Arcangelo who promised him food.

Sterantino, De Michiel and the others had even less to say about the leader of the 'band', a man they knew simply as 'Pietro'. One said that he had originally heard that 'Pietro' was English, but found when he met him that he looked Italian, and insisted on being addressed as 'Capo' or 'Commandante'. De Michiel described him as: '1.68–1.70 metres tall, slim, with black hair combed back, a tanned face. He speaks pure Italian, with no trace of dialect.' But he then went on: 'Opinions about Pietro varied. Some maintained he was English, others that he was a Greek. I asked the 5–6 men who were with Pietro before us, whether he was from here. They told me that P. first came to the island after the hostilities. Some of us guessed he came by parachute, others thought he was brought by boat. We could never make out what his mission was.'

So the men's ignorance covered not only the identity of their leader, but even the purpose of his activities. They were no clearer about the number of men he commanded. Mario Vergari mentioned a story that there were 400 men in the mountains, so heavily armed they even had a cannon! Another talked of a second band Pietro had established elsewhere on the island. De Michiel was more cautious: 'I know nothing about other bands. I have only heard rumours that there are bands nearby on the island.' In their own group there seem to have been no more than fifteen poorly armed men, trying for the most part simply to keep out of harm's way.

When the GFP investigators started questioning the prisoners about the 'network' of Greek civilians whom they believed had supported the 'band', the confusion multiplied. Mario Vergari claimed that a certain Simeon Agius, a fisherman from the village of Arcangelo, had told him that he supplied Pietro with food: 'S. also told me that in a short time they would be masters of the island.' However, Vergari himself was under a cloud: the Germans suspected him of having something to do with an arms cache that had been discovered in a barn where he used to stable his horse. Was he now trying to ingratiate himself with them? There were similar complications regarding another man who had denounced Agius. This was one of his fellow-villagers, Stefano Crusallo, who owned the local taverna. Crusallo told the Germans that he had seen two Italians at Agius's house who he was sure were 'band members'. But not only had Crusallo himself been brought in as a suspect; he and Agius had a long-standing quarrel over a debt which Agius had failed to repay.

When questioned, Agius claimed that he had nothing to do with any 'band'; he had to travel to sell his fish (which he caught with the aid of some dynamite his nephew had filched from Italian airforce stores). Yet who could be sure that his travels were not a cover for his resistance work? A thirty-eight-year-old woman called Zambika Lambrianou, who shared a house with her mother, admitted letting Italian soldiers sleep there at Agius's request: 'Altogether there were three occasions when Italian soldiers stayed in my house; they would come around in the evening, when I got in from the fields.' Another villager reported seeing an Italian staying with Simeon's brother: 'He said that he was picking olives with Agius and doing other jobs.' The chief suspects in the village, the Agius brothers and the Copellos family, who owned a nearby mill, disclaimed all knowledge of 'Pietro' and his 'band'. The curtest response came from seventeen-year-old Sava Copellos: 'I know nothing about a bandit organisation and know no one called Pietro. What I am accused of bears no relation to the facts.'

Food had been the real recruiter for the young, illiterate conscripts of the 'Pietro Band'; in all probability, they had wanted nothing more than to sit out the war in the hills. Nevertheless, the GFP felt confident that they had uncovered the existence of a 'band' operating against the Wehrmacht. Sterantino, De Michiel and six other soldiers were executed by firing squad. So were the Agius brothers, Sava Copellos (described in the files as a 'permanent attendant to the bandit leader' and 'recruiter for the band') and Zambika Lambrianou (described as a 'ringleader').

Komeno
317 villagers shot
16th August 1943

① **Operation 'Augustus'**
August 1943

② **(Panther–Tiger–Puma–Hubertus)**
A series of operations
October–November 1943

Kalavryta
casualties include 511 male inhabitants
of Kalavryta
December 1943

Athens
200 hostages shot on
1st May 1944 in reprisal
for guerrilla attack on
Gen. Krech near Molaos

Klisura
215 villagers shot
5th May 1944

Distomon
c. 300 villagers shot
10th May 1944

Khalkis
100 hostages shot
17th May 1944

④ **Operation 'Steinadler'**
July 1944

⑤ **Operation 'Kreuzotter'**
August 1944

③ **Operation 'Maigewitter'**
April 1944

The German Anti-Guerrilla Campaign, 1943–44

27. Lieutenant Glitz interrogates a shepherd during an anti-guerrilla operation in the hills of the northern Peloponnese, 14 December 1943.

In his summing up, the senior GFP investigator warned his superiors that the 'Pietro Band' might be part of a much larger and more threatening network, which would be broken up only through extensive surveillance, 'necessary in order to identify the headquarters of such bands and eliminate them through a major operation'. Revealing the real motive behind some of the executions, he went on: 'Tough sentences in this case will deter the civilian population from giving their active support in the future, and provide a shocking precedent. This sort of small rebel band may seem harmless at first sight; but when it is better understood how wide the circles are in which such an organisation operates . . . then one realises how dangerous such a movement is.' In future, such threats to public order would be met, in the words of the commandant of Sturmdivision Rhodos, with 'energetic and merciless assaults'.[24]

Tactics

Since 1945 the world has become familiar with guerrilla warfare. In Malaya, Algeria and Vietnam regular armies found themselves obliged to develop what have become known as techniques of counter-insurgency. By bitter experience we have learned that partisan warfare has political as well as military dimensions, and that soldiers alone can often achieve relatively little in the absence of some sort of a political dialogue. These lessons were not available to the Wehrmacht. Its officers had received no training in the problems of guerrilla warfare, while the ideology of the regime they were fighting for encouraged the view that military force alone would suffice to overcome the opposition. In Greece, the results can only be regarded as a catastrophic failure: hostage-taking, reprisals and a doctrine of collective civilian responsibility for guerrilla actions caused immense suffering and physical destruction, but did not succeed in wiping out the resistance.

*

The Wehrmacht's initial attempts to root out the guerrillas involved sending small detachments of troops in company strength into the hills. These excursions were unsuccessful and dangerous. The *andartes* usually retreated before German units into the mountains. Shortages of maps, interpreters and even drinking water made pursuit into the arid and pathless interior difficult for troops unused to the burning heat and harsh terrain. Frustrated field commanders, newly arrived in the country, were soon calling for the wholesale deportation of the local male population, a suggestion which was turned down by their superiors, chiefly on logistical grounds.[25]

The construction of strings of so-called 'strongpoints' along key roads, a technique borrowed from the Eastern Front, also failed to achieve the desired results. Rather than guaranteeing German control in their vicinity, these concrete blockhouses, surrounded by barbed wire and mines, became symbols of the occupiers' vulnerability, and were subjected to frequent attacks at night from resistance forces. Efforts to 'clear' roads by sending detachments either side of the main highway resulted in a large number of burnt villages but did not end guerrilla attacks. Colonel Salminger, of 1st Mountain Division, led one such bloody 'combing' operation down the twisting road through the mountains south of Jannina at the end of July; two months later he was ambushed on that same road and died in the wreckage of his car.[26]

German staff officers began to plan a 'more systematic' approach to anti-guerrilla operations in Greece even before the Italians left the scene. The liaison group in Athens held talks with their Italian colleagues in early August, and persuaded them to abandon their reliance on small and sporadic raids in favour of larger operations with more precise strategic objectives. Reporting to Salonika, General Gyldenfeldt spoke of getting the Italians 'to do some work'. 'The hitherto rather unsystematic Italian war against the bands will be controlled,' he went on.[27]

Operation Axis diverted German attention temporarily in other directions, but from the autumn of 1943 full-scale *Säuberungen* (mopping-up operations) were carried out. In the north-west of the country, 22 Army Corps co-ordinated several operations – Panther, Leopard and Puma – against ELAS units stationed near the Jannina–Metsovo road. In October German troops attacked from the north and from the west, pushing the guerrillas back deep into the Pindos, and capturing large amounts of munitions and stores. On 26 October, Army Group E reported on the 'complete success' which Panther had achieved in scarcely one week; it predicted that traffic would be able to move freely along the Metsovo road again, and that the rail link from Trikkala might also be reopened. Two weeks later the picture looked still more promising: the 'bands' on the Pindos had been 'shattered' and split up, forced to flee in different directions, whilst further operations to the south, in the Karpenisi area, had also stamped out active resistance.[28]

Impressive casualties seemed to have been inflicted upon ELAS. It had lost much valuable materiel, and many of the mountain villages that provided shelter and food for its men had been burned

28. General Lanz (seated, left) confers with General von Stettner and staff officers of 1st Mountain Division during a major operation against the *andartes* near Igoumenitsa in the summer of 1944.

down. The town of Kalabaka, at the eastern end of the Metsovo road, was gutted; a local observer reported that in that area German troops had killed several hundred people and made thousands homeless. 22 Army Corps itself reckoned that it had killed hundreds of 'enemy' during Panther alone, though it made no distinction between civilian and guerrilla casualties.[29]

A Waffen-SS unit which had also fought during Panther concluded that 'following the losses sustained by the bandits in men, weapons and materiel, and also the burning down of all villages in the region of the pacified area from which shooting was observed, the bands have suffered severe damage'. But the report went on: 'Still, it is possible that after most of the regiment is withdrawn, new bandit groups will slip into the whole area.' Other units also doubted whether these 'large operations' (*Grossunternehmen*) would have a lasting effect.[30]

Later, General Hubert Lanz, who commanded the troops in Panther, admitted that such doubts had been justified. Keeping the newly won Metsovo road clear required frequent engineering work: tunnels had been blocked, open stretches mined. Night attacks slowed down traffic. Burnt-out vehicles lay in the ditches by the roadside. 'Unfortunately,' Lanz wrote, 'the terrain was altogether too inviting for guerrilla warfare. High mountain ranges followed the road on both sides. On the long, partially wooded slopes were villages and many isolated farm buildings. The partisans and those who assisted them lurked everywhere.'[31]

Similarly in southern Greece, at the end of 1943, 68 Army Corps admitted its disappointment at the results of three months of 'large operations'. They lacked enough men to throw a tight ring around *andarte* forces; when they tried, gaps appeared in the circle and the guerrillas slipped through them. Movements of large concentrations of German troops could not be kept secret, so that the guerrillas had time to adjust to German plans. Even specialist mountain troops deployed in battalion strength failed to make much impact; their morale suffered, and in some cases they proved vulnerable to the *andartes'* own counter-attacks.[32]

During 1944 Wehrmacht planners came to believe that they had too few troops to eliminate the guerrilla movement, and began to turn in other directions. Army Group E, after initial reluctance, approved the idea of forming Greek volunteer units. The Security Battalions became increasingly important in southern Greece, taking over garrison duties in towns in the Peloponnese, and participating in anti-guerrilla operations. During the winter of 1943–44 four new Evzone battalions were formed to help in central Greece. Anti-communist irregulars of mixed reliability also took part in Wehrmacht operations in Macedonia. In the last few months of the occupation the Wehrmacht and the SS seem jointly to have hit on the idea of setting up 'counter-terror' units – death squads, in plain English – to combat the resistance by indiscriminate slaughter of civilians. In both expedients – the creation of reliable local auxiliaries, and the use of death squads – the Germans were blazing a path which others would follow when the war was over.[33]

Yet the fundamental strategic problem remained unresolved. ELAS recovered from the shock of the first large sweeps, and grew in influence. The deteriorating situation in the south led Army Group E to declare the Peloponnese a war zone in the spring of 1944. For all their misgivings, the planners at Army Group E continued to co-ordinate large-scale sweeps of the mountains against ELAS. The most plausible alternative strategy, deploying troops down in the plains to guard the harvest and starve the guerrillas out, was suggested by some intelligence officers, but not taken seriously by planners.[34] It was almost certainly too defensive a policy for an army whose philosophy and basic inclinations lay in assault.

Reprisals

In the absence of a coherent military strategy for countering the guerrillas, the Wehrmacht relied heavily on policies and standing orders which targeted civilians in rural areas. One of the basic assumptions behind German occupation policy was that 'terror had to be answered with terror' to force the population to withdraw its support from the insurgents. Although reprisals are often the instinctive response of isolated, frightened and trigger-happy troops in the field, the concept of retribution occupied a special place in German tactical thought. For the Wehrmacht it was a fundamental principle of military justice, fixed within the broad framework of social attitudes in the Third Reich, and demanded with all the authority of his office by the Führer himself. In other words, the Wehrmacht's reprisal policy in Greece, as throughout Eastern Europe, reflected the character of a regime with what was by historical standards an uninhibited and even in some respects a positive attitude towards violence and terror.

In April 1941 Field Marshal von Weichs issued orders which set the tone for anti-guerrilla policy in the Balkans. He instructed German troops in Yugoslavia that they were to shoot male civilians in any area of armed resistance, even in the absence of specific evidence against them. Guilt was to be assumed, unless innocence could be proven.[35]

When Crete was taken in late May, similar policies were introduced. Outraged by the part the islanders had played in resisting the invasion and attacking German paratroopers, General Kurt Student, commander of the XI Air Corps, ordered 'Revenge Operations', and explained to his troops what these were in terms that left no room for ambiguity: '1) Shootings; 2) Forced Levies; 3) Burning down villages; 4) Extermination (*Ausrottung*) of the male population of the entire region'. What these instructions led to was captured on film by Franz-Peter Weixler, who photographed an *ad hoc* firing party shooting the men of Kondomari in cold blood in the olive groves outside their village on 2 June. In Student's words: 'All operations are to be carried out with great speed, leaving aside all formalities and certainly dispensing with special courts. . . . These are not meant for beasts and murderers.' Greek sources estimate that 2,000 civilians were shot on Crete at this time. This figure is probably exaggerated; but we do know that the village of Kandanos was razed to the ground as a warning, and that large numbers of villagers were summarily shot not only in Kondomari but also in Alikianos and elsewhere.[36]

The commander of 12th Army, Field Marshal List, confirmed

29a. The mass execution at Kondomari on 2 June 1941, in the aftermath of the invasion of Crete: following the discovery of the corpse of one of their comrades, men of the 7th Parachute Division round up the able-bodied male villagers of Kondomari.

the draconian guidelines for mainland Greece that September. Following his instructions, soldiers of 164 Infantry Division burned down the villages of Ano and Kato Kerzilion in Macedonia, and shot several hundred men in mass executions, because guerrillas were reported to have rested there. Neither Student nor List, it is worth noting, could be described as a committed Nazi. List in particular was a cultivated and religious individual, linked to Greece by family ties. Yet neither man hesitated to enforce the most brutal policies against any manifestations of armed resistance.[37]

Following the invasion of the Soviet Union, anti-partisan doctrine developed rapidly, under the watchful gaze of both Himmler and Hitler himself. The growth of partisan activity during 1942 in occupied Soviet territory could only be answered, according to Hitler, by intensifying German terror tactics. 'Whatever succeeds is

174

29b. Having separated the women, children and elderly, they form a shooting squad and take aim at the men in the olive grove.

29c. An officer finishes off the wounded men by firing at point-blank range.

correct,' he insisted. In December 1942, following the Führer's remarks on the subject, OKW issued new guidelines which guaranteed the troops judicial immunity whilst they 'exterminated this plague'. They were to use 'any means, even against women and children, provided they are conducive to success'. It is in the way it reflected a policy laid down at the highest political levels that German military brutality differs from, say, the American experience in Vietnam, or the French in Algeria. An appreciation of the real power Hitler possessed in the so-called *Führerstaat* is absolutely essential for an understanding of the nature of Wehrmacht policy in the Second World War.[38]

Because 1st Mountain Division, and most other troops in Greece after the summer of 1943, came from the Eastern Front, or from Yugoslavia, they approached their task in Greece in accordance with what had become customary in these other areas. In August 1943, for example, detachments of the 1st Mountain Division received the following guidelines for one of their first operations in Epiros: 'All armed men are basically to be shot on the spot. Villages from where shots have been fired, or where armed men have been encountered, are to be destroyed, and the male population of these villages to be shot. Elsewhere all men capable of bearing arms (16–60 years old) are to be rounded up and sent to Jannina.'[39]

These instructions provoked the opposition of Italian commanders, at a time when they still retained some power. General Vecchiarelli emphasised: 'I am not in agreement with the aim of the action and issue the strict order, that the combat-worthy male population . . . will not be taken away.' He suggested a much more discriminating policy 'directed towards seizing the weapons and ammunition from the bandits, wiping out the bandits themselves and their stores, arresting actual suspicious elements and those who are firmly believed to be so, or those who act in a way which is hostile to the Axis'.[40]

A month later Vecchiarelli was in German captivity, and the Wehrmacht could conduct its anti-guerrilla policies without worrying about Italian sensitivities. Still, Vecchiarelli's objections did raise important issues concerning the treatment of the civilian population. Was it not possible to pursue a policy that distinguished, in the manner he seemed to be suggesting, between guerrillas and civilians? Might reprisals not be counter-productive?

German commanders were inclined to doubt both points. In the first place, some guerrillas were not wearing uniforms, and could thus slip in and out of civilian life. Hence, as we saw, German troops were told to regard all civilians as potential enemies. Second, the guerrillas relied upon the civilian population for food, shelter

and information. As in so many other guerrilla conflicts, the occupying forces came to regard the entire civilian population as 'a
responsible community'. 'You are the people who feed the *andartes*.
You are the ones to be blamed,' shouted one soldier as he beat an
old villager near the town of Karpenisi.[41]

Where the Wehrmacht differed from many other regular armies
pitted against an 'invisible' enemy was in the degree to which
reprisals were used systematically as a way of intimidating the
population. Again, this was a policy dictated from the uppermost
echelons of the military hierarchy. On 14 July 1943, for example,
General Löhr instructed 1 Panzer Division to take the 'most severe
measures' against any signs of hostility, warning that commanders
who failed 'out of negligence or softness' would face disciplinary
measures. It was the duty of 'every German soldier to break any
active resistance of the population by force of arms, immediately
and relentlessly' or face being brought before a court martial. Löhr
reminded his subordinates that such measures should not be indiscriminate. Yet he went on to point out that the 'friendly population'
in Greece was only a 'very small percentage' of the total. So 'it
must not happen that, for example, if German soldiers were shot at
in a village, nothing is done because the perpetrator was not clearly
determined. In such cases reprisal measures have to be effected by
the immediate arrest and shooting, or better still by the public
hanging, of influential personalities of the village.'[42]

Wehrmacht troops seized doctors, teachers, priests and other
'influential personalities' from the villages and kept them in camps
as hostages. They justified the hostage policy by claiming that these
individuals were the 'troublemakers' who whipped up the peasants
to revolt. Over time people in such exposed professions left, if they
could, for the mountains or the cities – by 1944 Athens was full of
doctors who had fled from the countryside – and the Germans
simply arrested any able-bodied men they found.

Near the beginning of the occupation OKW had issued precise
quotas for reprisals: 50 to 100 hostages were to be shot for any
attack on, or death of a German soldier; 10 if a German was
wounded, and so on. In practice such horrific guidelines often
proved unworkable because it was impossible to arrest enough
hostages.[43] General Lanz, in command of 22 Army Corps, was less
convinced of their utility than his subordinate General von Stettner,
who commanded 1 Mountain Division. In fact, the two men clashed
on several occasions over this issue. Speidel and Felmy, based in
Athens, were less aggressive in carrying out reprisals than the
irascible General Le Suire in the Peloponnese. Actual reprisal quotas
therefore varied considerably. The death of Colonel Salminger in

north-west Greece at the beginning of October resulted in the killing of fourteen hostages in a nearby town, as well as tens of civilians shot at random by troops in the area where he had been killed; but the death of General Krech and three aides at Molaos in the Peloponnese the following April led 68 Army Corps to recommend the shooting of 200 'communists' in Athens, another 100 'bandit suspects', as well as 'all the men whom the troops encounter in villages on the Molaos–Sparta road'.[44]

Meanwhile, the quota system came to be regarded as quite normal by the German troops. '15 to 20 Greeks had to be shot as a deterrent (*als Abschreckung*),' a soldier who served in Thrace would matter-of-factly recall. A typical entry from the war diary of Army Group South was: 'Levadeia: as reprisal measures for one murdered German soldier, 10 Greeks hanged.' 68 Army Corps reported on 29 November 1943: 'As reprisal for band attack on Tripolis–Sparta road, 100 hostages shot at the place of attack.' And on 6 December: 'For attack on railroad stronghold east of Tripolis, 50 hostages were hanged.' From September 1943 until the end of the occupation, such items appeared daily in military bulletins and reports. Bodies were hung from trees lining country roads, or strung up on make-shift gallows in town squares; in Arta one summer morning, twelve men were marched out from detention and hanged in public after it was discovered that guerrillas had cut down twelve telephone poles on a road leading out of the town.[45]

As an instrument of terror, the reprisals certainly worked. But their effect on guerrilla activity was less clear-cut. From Jannina, 22 Army Corps reported that Zervas and EDES had approached the local commander for an armistice. Villagers were now afraid to help the guerrillas, and readier to provide information to the Germans. Caught between the Germans and ELAS, Zervas had realised his position was extremely perilous, and opened a secret channel of communication to General Hubert Lanz in Jannina.[46]

Lanz's success with Zervas, however, was not repeated outside Epiros with leaders of ELAS. When villagers on Mount Pilion, for example, asked the local ELAS *kapetan* to cease attacking the Germans, in order to save their villages, they were told that ELAS would continue to fight so long as the Germans continued to establish garrisons in the rural areas. In general, villages came over to the German side where the proximity of Wehrmacht garrisons or the facts of geography made it sensible to do so. Elsewhere, reprisals might cause anger at the guerrillas, for having brought such suffering on the civilian population, but it was just as likely that anger would be directed against the Germans too, and, more importantly, that the destruction they had caused and fear of their unpredictable vengeance would actually drive able-bodied villagers to join the *andartes*.[47]

That reprisals were often counter-productive was spotted by many intelligence officers who warned that the guerrillas provoked them deliberately in order to turn the villagers against the Germans. At Army Group E headquarters, Hans Wende tried to make his superiors see that the killing of hostages simply created martyrs and inflamed nationalist sentiment. Reprisals were a spur not a deterrent to insurgency, he reported after a trip to Athens. A similar message was conveyed from the rural areas which had been subjected to *Sühnemassnahmen* (atonement actions). Reprisals might appear to the Germans to contain a retributive rationality, but to the Greek villagers at the receiving end they often came like a bolt out of the blue.[48]

*

One massacre in particular – the mass shooting of over 500 men from the town of Kalavryta – turned the reprisal policy into a highly controversial political issue. At the end of October 1943, guerrillas in the northern Peloponnese had abducted and killed 78 soldiers of Le Suire's 117 Jaeger Division. This occurred at a time when the notoriously anti-Greek Le Suire felt the region under his command was slipping from his control; the guerrillas were forming 'a state within a state' in the Peloponnese despite his extensive operations against them over the past few months.[49] In retaliation for his men's abduction, he embarked on a brutal series of reprisal raids in the mountains around Kalavryta and by the middle of December his troops had burned 25 villages and shot 696 Greeks, including the entire male population of Kalavryta itself, where his informants claimed the abducted Wehrmacht soldiers had been taken.[50]

News of the killings quickly reached Athens, where Prime Minister Rallis and Special Envoy Neubacher expressed their anger and shock. Neubacher, who was trying to build up an anti-communist front in Greece, forced the Wehrmacht to agree that reprisals should take his 'new political objectives' into account. Löhr's chief of staff, General Winter, commented wryly that 'it is unfortunately not possible to cut the head off everybody. When people proceed with an atonement action, they should go for the truly guilty and for hostages, rather than razing places that have nothing to do with it to the ground. That only increases the bands.' Winter added that reprisal quotas were now to be regarded as maxima rather than minima; only 'bandit helpers' and known 'communists' were to be targeted.[51]

In Corinth the local Wehrmacht territorial commander had been disputing the value of reprisal actions with Le Suire for several months. He observed pointedly on 31 December that 'since the atonement action [at Kalavryta] was carried out, the number of attacks and acts of sabotage has in no way diminished'. For a time, even General Le Suire was prepared to confess that 'we are on the wrong track' and to accept the need for greater precision in identifying guerrilla targets.[52] But Le Suire's change of heart did not last long. By May 1944 he had reverted to his old views: anti-guerrilla actions must offer 'terror for terror' so that the civilian population would end up 'fearing us more than the bands'. On 16 May his authority in fact increased when the Peloponnese was turned into a 'battle zone', allowing him to declare martial law throughout the region.[53]

Le Suire's reversion to a hard line would not have been possible if the political objections of Prime Minister Rallis and Neubacher had carried the day. But Neubacher's efforts to build support for the New Order within Greece were secondary in Wehrmacht eyes to the immediate need to secure the Peloponnese against the threat of an enemy landing. Löhr and Army Group E were swayed only briefly by their complaints, and the reprisal policy in practice remained unchanged.

The lack of any real change in attitudes was highlighted in the most gruesome way by further massacres in the spring of 1944 – at Klisura in Macedonia and at Distomo, near Delphi. On these occasions the soldiers ran amok, killing women and children as well as men. Neubacher angrily pointed out that the Klisura atrocity contravened the standing orders on reprisals, which had supposedly been modified after Kalavryta. But his protests had little impact, even after the same unit attacked Distomo the following month. The view from Army Group E was summed up by Colonel Warn-storff, the senior intelligence officer on Löhr's staff, in the margin of a report on Greek public opinion in April 1944. Despite a lucid presentation of the arguments against the *Sühnemassnahmen*, Warn-storff noted briefly that 'there is no other solution'.[54]

For all the widespread doubts about their utility, reprisals remained a characteristic response to guerrilla attack for the duration of the occupation. Eventually some commanders even abandoned the charade of searching for 'communists' or 'bandit suspects'. In August 1944, for instance, instructions were issued to the troops on Crete, calling for 'vigorous action by our Division in order to force our will upon the Greek population, and in order to prove that we can assert our power on the whole island. To this end discretion can no longer be observed towards innocent men, women and children.' By this point, the categories of guilt and innocence had ceased to be pertinent. Their efficacy questioned, reprisals were stripped of their dubious legality as well.[55]

The Impact of Operations upon the Greeks

According to General Winter, Löhr's chief of staff, success in the operations against the 'bandits' was to be measured in terms of the numbers of dead, prisoners and booty rather than territory wrested back from their control. Troops ended reports of anti-guerrilla actions with so-called 'booty-lists'. On 13 November 1943, for example, 22 Army Corps reported the final results of Operation Hubertus to Army Group E. Enemy losses after sweeps through the Pindos mountains were estimated at 165 dead, around 200 wounded and 61 prisoners against 8 Wehrmacht dead and 14 wounded. Under the heading 'booty', the report listed: '55 rifles, 3 machine pistols, 3 pistols, 1 flare pistol, 24 hand grenades, around 2,000 rounds, including 1 belt, dum-dum bullets and fuse (40 metres), 75 kg. dynamite', and many other items. The 'booty-list' submitted by 7th SS-Polizei Panzer Grenadier Regiment at the end of Operation Panther contained no less than fifty-five items, including '10 sacks of meal, 1 sack of maize meal, 171 sacks of pulses, 14 hundredweight of barley, 1 sack noodles . . . 121 bales of tobacco, 45 mules and donkeys, 18 pigs, 42 piglets, 331 sheep and 50 goats'.[56]

These reports hint at how one-sided the troops' engagements with the 'bandits' were. As in occupied Russia, Wehrmacht casualties were very much lower than those inflicted on the guerrillas. In October 1943, for instance, 22 Army Corps claimed 755 'enemy dead' against own losses of 19; the following month there were over 700 'enemy dead' against 21 German losses. These figures reflected the 'success' of two major offensives against ELAS strongholds in the Pindos mountains. Later operations produced a similar tally: 339 'band losses' against 8 Wehrmacht dead at the end of Operation Maigewitter in April 1944; 298 against 23 after Operation Kreuzotter. 'Band losses' were invariably disproportionate to the quantity of guns and ammunition captured.[57]

Even if the figures for enemy losses were inflated by ambitious field commanders – and the evidence, it should be noted, often suggests the reverse – the struggle between a primitively trained and equipped irregular force and a well-disciplined, highly armed modern army was evidently not an equal one. Some senior Wehrmacht officers realised this, and worried what would happen when their soldiers had to fight a genuinely powerful opponent. Com-

30. A ruined village near Athens, 1944.

plaining at his men's tendency to exaggerate the 'tough battles' they had supposedly fought against the *andartes*, one German commander in Macedonia pointed caustically to their own losses – 'usually small, frequently almost none'. The main reason why the disproportion between Wehrmacht and enemy losses was so great was that it was civilians who were bearing the brunt of their attacks.[58]

*

'STEFANI FINNI AM 19.10.43 VORMITTAG 10 UHR'. A German soldier left this grim message written in Gothic letters on a half-fallen wall. Stefani, of course, was not the only village to be obliterated, though it was one of the closest to Athens.[59] Using flamethrowers, incendiary grenades, or occasionally just petrol, German troops methodically burned down entire villages. By July

182

1944, according to a report of the Greek government in exile, 879 villages had been totally destroyed, 460 in part. 'Are there other countries in Europe which have undergone – in relative terms – such devastation?' a relief worker asked herself in January 1944, after a tour of the north-west.[60]

The government in Athens could offer little help to the victims. In the stricken region of southern Macedonia the peasants were 'unable to find any state authority or service . . . to which they can address themselves with confidence'. Indeed, few people were in a more desperate plight by the middle of 1943 than the civil servants in market-towns like Kalabaka and Grevena. Their salaries lagged so far behind inflation that they and their families were soon reduced to poverty. To fend for themselves, they sold off all their possessions. Their homes lacked any furniture; some civil servants even sold their gold teeth. Athens might have been on another continent so far as they were concerned. 'The occupying powers have been indulging in a sadistic orgy of ruin and destruction for the past two and a half years,' noted one report in January 1944. 'The State has been dissolved, administrative services have been dislocated and whole districts such as Macedonia, Thrace and Crete have almost no communication with the central administration.' 'The state services,' Vasmazides wrote, 'give an impression of complete disorganisation.'[61]

The greatest devastation was in central and northern Greece, on either side of the Pindos massif. In the year to March 1944 85,000 people were reckoned to have been affected by military raids in western Macedonia alone. Punitive expeditions against the guerrillas led to more than sixty villages being burned down in the hills around the town of Servia: the region was turned into a 'dead zone' of ruined property and rotting harvests: 'In these areas not even one-tenth of the prewar area is cultivated.' The effects on peasant life were catastrophic: livestock were taken away by the troops, and hundreds of men were shot or imprisoned. Many families moved away; only a few stayed on, living in wretched conditions: 'They have no blankets, clothes or shoes and are exposed to the fury of rain and wind.' Most peasants were afraid to approach their fields lest they be killed; in some cases, villagers were actually forbidden by the Germans to sow or reap their crops. Between 2 and 16 July 1944 another round of German anti-guerrilla operations near Grevena resulted in fifty-one villages being looted or burned, affecting over half the population of the area.[62]

There was similar destruction on the other side of the Pindos mountains, in Epiros. During the *Säuberungsunternehmen* the 'terrified population' rushed into the hills, taking only what they could

31. This family were living in the open after their mountain village had been burned down. They had little to eat apart from potatoes. Northern Greece, 1944.

carry. They lived through the winter in caves, or thatched straw *kalyves*; some became vagrants, looking for shelter in more fortunate communities.[63] Perhaps there was some exaggeration in the Red Cross report that 40 per cent of the rural population had 'had . . . their homes burned or looted and are in immediate danger of extinction'. But food was so scarce by the spring of 1944 – a difficult period of the year at the best of times – that near Arta farmers were selling stalks of maize, which they had always previously given away free. By the side of roads used regularly by the Germans, the fields lay deserted, clogged with water and weeds.[64]

Anti-guerrilla operations continued right up to the Axis withdrawal. In August 1944, during the last major *Säuberungsunternehmen*, Karpenisi was devastated by Waffen-SS troops. At the nearby village of Agios Georgios they burned down every house, polluted the wells with the corpses of dead mules, and destroyed the crops in the fields. The villagers who had fled in time returned in a state of shock; some were unable to find words for what had happened, others 'describe these things as if they were occurrences in a wild, unreal dream'. Karpenisi itself, a small market-town in the mountains of central Greece, had become 'nothing but a mass of rubble'. An American doctor who visited it with the *andartes* several days after the Germans had left described the ruins:

> The highway on which we arrive comes to an abrupt halt before an enormous rock pile that was once a fine three storey building. On our left are the remains of the hospital completely demolished and the largest church only partially so. A few people aimlessly climb over the wreckage, others are probing through the debris in the hope that something of value may have been left, and above us a woman arranges pieces of battered furniture in a room unconcernedly, as if she didn't know the entire face of the building had fallen, leaving her living room minus one wall and totally exposed to the public view.[65]

Fear of random arrest or execution by German troops disrupted the working routine of men in the provinces, and more or less forced many to join the *andartes*. 'The town of Arta has remained utterly empty; males between 14 and 60 years old have abandoned it. For provisions it is in a desperate state: there are no male workers,' ran one report. In many villages men under the age of sixty were an unusual sight, and so when Axis troops burned down the villagers' homes, it was the women, children and the elderly who were most directly affected and left to fend for themselves. As a result, the normal web of family relationships came under strain, to be replaced in many places by strange, new patterns of behaviour.[66]

*

'What,' speculated a relief worker, 'will be the psychological effect on the children of this atmosphere of fear and mistrust?' From the scanty evidence that survives we can try tentatively to offer an answer. Barefoot and bare-headed, shaven against lice, many village children were left parentless and banded together in gangs, looking for shelter and working for anyone who would find them food. To the scruffy urchins kicking their heels under the eyes of an ELAS guard in the summer of 1944, there had been little to choose between the Germans in the city, who had promised them bread if they brought them back information about the guerrillas, and the *andartes* themselves, who had caught, imprisoned and fed them. The war meant nothing to them apart from a world of destruction which they had to survive. Without schooling, family, and often any other kind of discipline, they had been forced to turn quickly into tough little vagabonds.[67]

Some small boys, their fathers and elder brothers absent, took upon themselves the duty of looking after their female relatives. As one later recollected: 'In that time I grew very quickly, and a great change occurred within me. The frightened and unsure little boy became a responsible man. A man who knew his duties. I stopped being afraid of the dark. . . . To the great love I felt for my mother was added the desire to protect her.'[68]

Often, of course, there were no men, or even boys, around and young girls suddenly had to fend for themselves. Nausikaa L., from a village outside Kalamata, saw her father killed by the Germans in July 1944, her mother and one sister thrown into jail, and her home burned to the ground. In danger from local right-wing gunmen who regarded her whole family as Leftists, she was forced to flee from the village she knew with her other sister: the two girls eventually found their way to Athens. Not surprisingly, she developed a passionate sense of commitment to the cause – 'our struggle', in her words – with which her father and family had been identified. Writing as a young woman after the war to a friend, she told him that 'since 1943 . . . even though I was a child then, with what strength I had I did what I could.' As she herself stressed in 1955: 'since 1944 till today we have not had a proper home'.[69]

Thousands of girls joined the resistance – defying rural conventions for the first time, and ignoring or persuading their parents – and became politically active. From this point of view, the destructive character of German rule had revolutionary consequences. They made speeches in church, and organised food supplies to the *andartes*; some would eventually even fight. Diamanto Gritzona, a teenager when the Germans arrived, recalled later how her parents 'didn't want me to "be organised". They feared the Germans, they feared what people would say. . . . If I remained in the Organisation I wouldn't be a "good girl" any longer.' But eventually she persuaded them, and was soon active with other girls in her village, carrying food and clothes to *andartes* in the hills. By shattering the moral foundations of rural life, the German raids had permitted an unprecedented challenge to parental authority.[70]

Children quickly came to regard war as a normal part of life. Theotokas recorded with horrified astonishment that some boys were playing football a few yards from where the corpses of executed resistance fighters dangled from trees. Pavlos Simha, recalling his childhood as a Jewish boy in hiding in Athens, has described his fondness for war games of every conceivable sort – forming an 'army' with his friends, building mock fortifications, constructing their own weapons or even an imitation aeroplane. 'Our imagination ran wild,' he writes, 'but our warlike passion was justified, as we had grown up in the middle of a war.' Neither the

32. Children in the ruins of a house following the burning down of the village of Mikro Chorio, central Greece, 1943.

Germans, the Battalionists, nor even ELAS *andartes* frightened them very much: 'One might say that we had grown familiar with the war and with battles. I don't remember that we were alarmed by the situation.' What went for a small boy, living without his father, in hiding under an assumed name in a strange city (his family had fled from the northern city of Cavalla) no doubt also corresponded to the experience of many less articulate children in rural areas, whose memories and experiences have not been recorded.[71]

Children's bodies were at least as vulnerable as their minds. Wartime photos capture the distended stomachs, stick-like limbs and great dark eyes of starving five-year-olds from the mountain villages: 'Those whom the marshes have left standing have been hit by dysentery, those who have escaped dysentery are finished off by

187

the cold, under cow-sheds with scanty shelter at altitudes where men lived only during the summer, and where, if there is no snow, there is rain, and if not rain, a dampness and wind which passes through their thin bones, leaving them tubercular skeletons.' As many were dressed only in rags, it is not surprising that tuber-culosis took a heavy toll of children in the mountain areas, while malaria spread from the valleys upwards into the hills. In Epiros, where food was particularly short in the spring of 1944, many children were anaemic and showed signs of enteritis. Shaving their heads offered little protection against lice in the absence of soap. Their bellies were swollen from the lack of food, and malnutrition made them apathetic and, in severe cases, temporarily blind.[72]

For their part, village women too were subjected to terrifyingly harsh physiological and psychological strains. The absence of their husbands, brothers and sons left them vulnerable and was a con-stant source of anxiety, not least as they often had no way of knowing whether their menfolk were alive or dead. German and quisling Greek troops sometimes attacked and raped women sus-pected of having relatives in the resistance. A young American doctor serving with the *andartes* recorded one case of puerperal fever which cast a sad light on the terrors of daily life in the mountains: he tells how a pregnant woman miscarried after being scared by reports of Germans nearby. As other villagers stood by helplessly, she screamed hysterically that she had been raped by numerous men. Premature births became more common, brought on by anxiety and fear. Total war of this intensity inflicted deep psy-chological wounds on many of its victims. Often these took time to emerge, and generally the people concerned were unlikely to receive the attention of a psychiatrist. Frantz Fanon's studies of the mental scars inflicted on his patients by the Algerian war of in-dependence point to an aspect of total war which has till now been virtually ignored by historians of this period.[73]

It was, after all, tempting for outsiders to assume that the rural population bore its misfortunes with stoical or fatalistic patience. Allied liaison officers liked praising the powers of endurance of the 'simple peasant'. But physical toughness did not preclude psycho-logical vulnerability, and sometimes it was difficult to distinguish stoicism from apathy and withdrawal. Told that her house had just been burned down, one village woman from Evvia shrugged her shoulders: 'It doesn't matter so much now,' she said. 'It's warm and we can live in the open.' Only many years later perhaps would the full cost of such experiences become apparent. We learn, for example, of Anna Kosmidou, from the village of K. in western Macedonia, who died at a respectable age in May 1981 – to all

33. Women mourning. Epiros, 1944.

outward appearances another of those tough elderly peasant women dressed in black one sees selling their produce in any local market in Greece. In her case, however, those signs of mourning hid horrifying memories, for on 23 April 1944 German troops had suddenly raided her village, killing five of her children and many of her friends. She survived, after being left for dead, but was thereafter haunted by her memories: every night until her death, according to her daughter, she had nightmares in which she relived the events of that day.[74]

CHAPTER SIXTEEN

Anatomy of a Massacre: 16 August 1943

The Language of Brutality

In the summer of 1943 Lieutenant Kurt Waldheim – a young Austrian wounded on the Eastern Front and transferred out of front-line duty – was serving in the planning office of the German general staff in Athens. His superior officer remembered him as 'somewhat servile' but a hard worker. Troop reports from subordinate units arrived each day on Waldheim's desk; he would read through them, note their implications for the overall strategic situation and then summarise them in his own daily reports to Army Group E HQ in Salonika. These reports were written in a special language of their own, and Waldheim had become proficient in it.

On 12 August, for example, Waldheim received that day's report from 1st Mountain Division HQ in Jannina. It included the following brief item of information: 'Kuklesi (17 [km.] north of Filippias) burnt down. Ammunition went off. 10 suspicious civilians shot.' Waldheim was not to know that the original troop report, which 1st Mountain Division HQ had received from the field, had talked bluntly of '10 civilians shot dead'. But Waldheim was evidently unhappy at *any* explicit mention of civilian casualties, suspicious or otherwise. In his own report, sent off the following day to Army Group E HQ in Salonika, he changed the reference to the victims once again. Now it read: 'Kuklesi (17 km. north of Filippias) burnt to the ground. Ammunition went off. 10 bandit suspects (*Banden-verdächtige*) shot.'[75] Thanks to Lieutenant Waldheim and staff officers of 1st Mountain Division, the civilians shot by Wehrmacht troops had been transformed into 'bandits'.

German troop reports, like the whole official vocabulary of the Third Reich – what the philologist Victor Klemperer ironically labelled the 'LTI' (Lingua Tertii Imperii) – were rich in such euphemisms. The expression 'shot in flight', for example, would immediately have been understood by all Wehrmacht personnel ('In reprisal for the attack recently perpetrated in the Larissa area, 2 villages burnt down, 65 suspects shot in flight'; or from Crete: 'Operation Vianos: . . . 280 Greeks so far shot in flight'); the reference to ammunition exploding in 'suspicious' villages was frequently employed as a cover for the destruction of villages where in fact no evidence of guerrilla activity had been found.[76]

If we knew why the Third Reich had evolved such a convoluted and highly euphemistic language, we would have advanced far down the road to a better understanding of the nature of that regime. No doubt the sort of vocabulary described above had been developed as a convenient psychological screen to shield the staff officers who made policy – men like Waldheim and his superiors – from the brutal and increasingly criminal reality of their orders. In this respect, the German anti-partisan war was clearly a precursor of other, better-known conflicts in the postwar period, and shared with them the bureaucratic structures and managerial attitudes of modern industrial warfare. But euphemism also helped resolve the ultimate paradox which lay at the heart of Nazi ideology, between the regime's self-image as a guarantor of legality, and its desire to wipe out any opposition through untrammelled violence. Crude and appalling brutality – the cold-blooded murder of civilians far from the battlefield – could be dressed up in the vocabulary of the LTI as a measure of military justice and public security. One specific example should make this clear.

The Massacre at Komeno

Today the village of Komeno attracts few visitors. Quiet and out of the way, it is situated on the marshy flatlands of the Arachthos estuary, in western Greece. Its inhabitants make a living by farming, growing oranges, and fishing. From the flat roof of the *kafeneion*, one looks over the dark orange groves that surround the village: the bay is to the south; the town of Arta lies across the fields a few miles to the north, and further off to the east the steep sides of the Pindos mountain range are visible on the horizon.

In the middle of the main square, some yards from the *kafeneion*, there is a surprisingly imposing marble monument. Cut into its sides are the names of the 317 villagers who died during a Wehrmacht raid in August 1943. In terms of age, they range from one-year-old Alexandra Kritsima to seventy-five-year-old Anastasia Kosta; they include seventy-four children under ten, and twenty entire families. The troops responsible for this atrocity were highly trained regular soldiers from one of the elite divisions of the Wehrmacht.[77]

*

For two years, Komeno had enjoyed a peaceful war. The village children attended school in Arta while their parents worked in the fields. Mooring their caiques at the river mouth, black-marketeers from the Ionian islands stopped to barter food with local farmers. The Italian commandant in Arta had stationed a customs officer in the village, and he soon reached an amicable understanding with the traders. Early in 1943 *andartes* appeared on the scene to requisition foodstuffs from the shopkeepers and farmers. This does not appear to have worried the Italians, who took no action against them. As for the villagers, there was nothing they could do. On 12 August 1943 a small group of *andartes* visited Komeno. They propped their rifles against the tree in the centre of the square, and began collecting food as usual.

But new protagonists now appeared. Catching everyone by surprise, a two-man Wehrmacht reconnaissance team drove into the village. As soon as the Germans saw the guerrillas and their weapons, they turned round and drove back the way they had come. Behind them they left some very frightened villagers, who had not seen any Wehrmacht troops in the region since the end of the Albanian campaign more than two years earlier. That night they slept out in the fields, fearing a reprisal attack, even though no soldiers had been killed. Next day they sent a delegation to the Italian commander in Arta to explain what had happened and to ask if it would be safe to return home. The fifteenth of August was the Feast of the Assumption, and they hoped to be able to celebrate; the Italian officer assured the village president that Komeno would come to no harm. Preparations went ahead, and the night of the 15th saw the usual festivities, songs and dancing.

*

But the reconnaissance unit had already reported sighting guerrillas at Komeno to 1st Mountain Division HQ in Jannina. So far, the Division's efforts to wipe out the *andartes* in north-western Greece had been unsuccessful; now, after informing Athens, it decided to proceed in a few days' time with a special, exemplary 'surprise operation' against Komeno. The task was assigned to the 98th Regiment, which had spent the last fortnight pushing southwards through the mountains towards Arta. The troops had not been in Greece long, and many were already feeling the effects of the heat

34. Colonel Josef Salminger, commanding officer of 98 Mountain Infantry Regiment, inspects his men in the course of anti-guerrilla operations in the mountains of Epiros: autumn, 1943.

and the mosquitoes. On the evening of 15 August, 12 Company, camped in a valley just north of the town of Arta, were called from their tents. Their wiry and much-decorated young regimental commander, Colonel Josef Salminger – a self-made man who liked to boast that he had turned the 98th into a 'regiment for Hitler' – delivered a typically short, blunt speech to the conscripts: German soldiers, he told them, had been killed – it was time for tough measures against the partisans. The following morning they were going to wipe out a guerrilla lair.[78]

*

Young Dimitri Apostolis was a keen hunter, and this saved his life. He rose before dawn on the morning of 16 August and was already some way beyond the village when he heard the low rumble of motors approaching from the direction of Arta. From his vantage-point in the fields, he cautiously tried to see what was happening. Meanwhile, thirteen-year-old Alexandros Mallios was woken by his father, who had also heard the trucks. His father had been up all night, because he and most of the Mallios family were celebrating the marriage of one of his daughters. He told the young Alexandros to take their sheep and goats out of the village so that the Germans would not get them. 'I went outside and could see flares being set off in the sky,' Alexandros Mallios recalled forty-five years later. 'I ran out towards the fields and met a friend running in the same direction. . . . He had come from the village square and said: "The Germans – they're shooting and killing everyone." The sound of gunfire was very loud.'[79]

*

About one hundred men from 12 Company had set off in lorries for Komeno before daybreak. At 5 a.m. they stopped just outside the village, and the canteen staff handed out coffee. Then the company commander, Lieutenant Röser, a former Hitler Youth leader now in his mid-twenties, gathered the troops and issued his orders. One phrase remained in his men's minds years later: they were to go into the village 'and leave nothing standing'. The assault troops carried machine-guns and grenades, the rest were equipped with rifles. The village was encircled, and then two flares were fired, to give the signal for the attack to begin.[80]

If the soldiers had expected the guerrillas to fire back, they must have been surprised. There was no return of fire and 12 Company would report no casualties as a result of the attack. In fact, there were no guerrillas in the village, and those spotted requisitioning on the 12th had been outsiders. The houses stormed by the first wave of assault troops were occupied by sleeping families. As people awoke and tried to run away, the soldiers manning the guard-posts on the outskirts of the village began shooting at them. Women and children were among the victims. Most of the paths through the fields were raked by machine-gunfire. Alexandros Mallios and one of his sisters were almost hit as they ran away; they fell flat, and managed to crawl into the thick canes that grew by the river bank. The only escape route the Germans had overlooked lay across the river. Several hundred villagers managed to swim to the other side, and in this way almost half Komeno's population survived.

Standing by the lorries, the canteen staff heard the crackle of gunfire and the screams of the inhabitants, and watched as the village houses burst into flames. The dark cloud of smoke that rose into the sky could be seen from the villages of the Tzoumerka, miles away on the slopes of the Pindos mountains. Towards noon, Lieutenant Röser hurried back up the road, and proudly urged his battalion commander to come and see 'how his men had done'. The soldiers themselves, however, had mixed feelings. 'We sat in the shade of the orange trees out of the sun and awaited the return of the lorries. After the shooting it was very quiet. Most of the comrades were very depressed. Almost none agreed with the action,' recalled one.[81]

The scene in Komeno was nightmarish. Six hours of total destruction were followed by an eerie silence, punctuated only by the crackle of burning timbers. A nineteen-year-old conscript later recalled that 'it had become very hot in the meantime. Everything was quiet. I went into the village with some other comrades. Bodies lay everywhere. Some were still not dead. They moved and groaned. Two or three junior officers went slowly through the village and gave the dying "mercy shots".' The men of the *Aufräumtrupp* (literally, the Collection or Clear-Up Unit) collected the 'booty', including cows and other animals, and began loading them into the lorries. While several soldiers helped themselves to whatever they could find, including carpets, jewellery and other valuables, others were too depressed to bother. Karl D. recalled: 'After the massacre, one comrade had taken some hens' eggs, which he had found in a stable. I said to this comrade, I can't understand you, I've lost my appetite.'[82]

Röser ordered some soldiers to set fire to the few houses that had remained intact. Then at 1 p.m. the troops withdrew from the village. The canteen staff distributed the midday rations – rice pudding and stewed fruit – cleared up and drove back to the camp. The rest of the men followed an hour or so later. 'When we left for our camp on the lorries,' one remembered later, 'all the houses in the village were in flames.'[83]

Even the churchyard had not been spared: Röser himself had shot the village priest as he came out to meet him in the first minutes of the assault. Hiding behind the churchyard wall, Alexandros Mallios watched the Germans leave, taking the villagers' livestock with them: 'I was probably the first person to enter the village when the Germans left. All the houses that I passed were burnt. I heard the crackling of the corn burning and thought at first the Germans were still shooting. I did not realise at first what it was. I took another path through the village, but everywhere I looked the houses had been burnt. I saw no one alive. There were many bodies in the street; men, women and children, and most of the bodies appeared to be burnt. I saw one old woman, who had apparently burnt to death in a sitting position. The houses were burning as I walked through.' He went on to his own house and on the road outside he found the bodies of his own family, lying on the ground. 'I did not go into my house, because I fainted at this point. When I regained consciousness I was by the river, and someone was bathing the blood off me.'

35. Alexandros Mallios stands by the river across which he escaped with his sister in 1943: Komeno, 1988.

The Bureaucratic Response

Within the Wehrmacht there were two sorts of response to the Komeno massacre.

The first was bureaucratic, impersonal and highly regulated – a series of reports and briefings – which began almost immediately with the *Mittagsmeldungen*, or noon reports, for 16 August. This was 98th Regiment's description of events in Komeno, radioed back to Jannina at 14.45 hrs:

> G.J.R.98:   This morning during the encirclement of Komeno,
> 14.45hrs   which was carried out on three sides, 12 Co. came
>   under very heavy gunfire from all the houses. There-
>   upon fire was opened by the Co. with all weapons,
>   the place was stormed and burned down. It appears
>   that during this battle some of the bandits managed
>   to escape to the south-east. 150 civilians are estimated
>   to have died in this battle. The houses were stormed
>   with hand-grenades and for the most part were set
>   on fire as a result. All the cattle as well as wool

were taken away as booty. Booty-report follows separately. In the burning of the houses large amounts of
ammunition went up in smoke and hidden weapons
are also likely to have burned with them.[84]

The language of this communiqué implied a judicious, scientific
and reliable view of events. Yet the report was riddled with inac-
curacies and straight fictions: the death toll was more than double
that cited; there had been no shooting at the troops from the village
at all.

The evening report repeated the same description, but added the
details of the captured booty, listed as: 'Booty: Roughly 150 dead
civilians, 16 head of cattle, 1 lorryload of wool-sacks, 5 Italian
carbines, 1 Italian machine-pistol.'[85] And when the 1st Mountain
Division passed the news on to their superiors in Athens, it was
summarised as follows:

Results of Clean-up operation (*Säuberungsunternehmen*) Komeno:

150 enemy dead, some head of cattle, hand weapons of Italian
origin. Explosion of large quantity of munitions during burning
down of the village.

Result of this action confirms once again the opinion and report
of this Division that a strong guerrilla centre is located on the east
bank of the Gulf of Arta, including strong, active bandit groups.[86]

As news of the massacre moved up each link in the command
chain, its character was being transformed. All hints of uncertainty
or imprecision were gradually eliminated. The original report had
invented a clash where none had taken place, but it had also indicated
that civilians had died. By the time news of the operation reached
Athens, these had become 'enemy dead', and the entire operation
was being cited as an illustration of certain strategic theses of the
divisional staff in Jannina.[87]

In Athens, the conscientious Lieutenant Waldheim entered the
information the following day in his unit's War Diary: '17 August:
Increasing enemy air raid activity against the Western Greek coast
and Ionian islands. In the area of 1st Mountain Division, the town
of Komeno (north of the Gulf of Arta) is taken against heavy
enemy resistance. Enemy losses.' In accordance with his duties, he
also informed Army Group E in his day report that there had been
'heavy enemy resistance against the *Säuberungsunternehmen*', and that
the 'enemy losses' had totalled 150. In view of the way such 'know-

ledge' was generated, we should not be surprised to find that an intelligence assessment from early September mentioned Komeno as one of only two engagements when guerrillas took on German troops in battle![88]

Finally, of course, it is important to note just how selective and short-lived the 'knowledge' acquired in such ways could be. In April 1988 the former intelligence officer of 1st Mountain Division, a retired lawyer called Kurt R., was interviewed in Hamburg. Part of the exchange ran as follows:

Do you remember an operation or a surprise attack against the bands or their supporters near the Gulf of Arta, in the village of Komeno?

[Answer]: No idea. Was that really the 1st Mountain Division? Wasn't it the neighbouring division?

North of the Gulf?

I don't know. We must check. . . .

Komeno.

I don't know it. Never heard of it.[89]

The Soldiers' Response

But the troops in the field could not be cushioned from reality in quite the same way as staff officers like Kurt R. or Kurt Waldheim. Questioned in 1970 about what had happened twenty-seven years earlier, a former member of 12 Company, a self-described 'little man', confessed he remembered the whole operation clearly: 'the outcome wound me up so much that even today I am not free of the terrible memories . . . I have never talked about these executions with anyone, not even my wife, although the whole business continues to affect me.' Colonel Salminger, his subordinates, and above all the ordinary conscript were implicated in the *Säuberungen* too deeply to be able to enjoy the staff officers' ambiguous sort of ignorance. How, then, did they react?[90]

Historians have identified the Wehrmacht's junior officers as the section of the army which believed most whole-heartedly in the violent ideology of the Nazi regime.[91] The attitudes of Colonel Salminger appear to bear this out: he boasted that the 98th Regiment which he commanded was *ein Hitlerisches Regiment* – a Hitlerite regiment – and his own bravery and impetuous nature coexisted with a frightening harshness and brutality. Lieutenant Röser, who commanded 12 Company, was another aggressive young officer. He was a former Hitler Youth leader, who passed on the orders to kill everyone in Komeno with enthusiasm, and participated in the killing himself. His nickname among his men was the 'Nero of the 12/98', and he appears to have had no qualms or misgivings about the massacre.[92]

Other officers, however, were more reserved. The battalion commander, von K., stayed out of the village, sitting by the roadside, until Lieutenant Röser came back to show him the outcome. The sight that greeted him included 'bodies of women and children lying in the street everywhere, people lying shot in the houses and doorways'. Von K., a doctor by training, went white and told Röser that 'the Herr Oberleutnant will have nothing more to do with the war. I want nothing to do with this.' Another officer, Lieutenant D. – a teacher by profession – 'was utterly drained'. According to one member of 12 Company, 'he was terribly pale and told me that he felt sick and that such an operation was unworthy of a German soldier'.[93]

The reactions of the conscript soldiers were equally troubled. On the lorries that drove them back to Filippias, they argued about what they had done. Many of them seemed depressed and shocked. Karl D. recalled that 'within 12 Company there was much discussion of this action. Soon all the soldiers knew about it. Few thought it right. I myself was so affected by these cruelties that I did not regain my mental balance for weeks.' During the shooting one NCO is reported as having thrown down his cap at Röser's feet and shouted: 'Herr Oberleutnant, just remember, that's the last time I take part in something like that. That was a *Schweinerei* (disgrace) which had nothing to do with fighting a war.' According to Franz T., 'the argument was so heated that I might almost describe it as a mutiny'. Summing up the experience of the previous few months, a chaplain from 1st Mountain Division wrote with extraordinary frankness in October 1943 that 'the mass killing of women and children during operations against the bands is producing a difficult inner burden on the conscience of many men'.[94]

Yet it must also be said that many of the soldiers did not dissent in this way. Some felt that they'd had to act against people who would otherwise have shot them, and described their victims as 'just riff-raff'. At least twelve to fifteen men had been willing to volunteer for the operation before Röser decided to use the whole of 12 Company. Against their comrades who insisted that it had been 'a *Schweinerei* to shoot defenceless civilians', some argued that 'they were all a potential enemy, if they supported the partisans against us soldiers'.[95]

Even the dissenters – and in the initial aftermath of the massacre they may actually have been in a majority – were not prepared to press their point very far. Their misgivings had certainly not prevented the killings taking place. The troops' disquiet over Komeno stemmed chiefly from their feeling that, as one of them put it, it had been a 'plunder raid' (*Raubzug*) rather than 'a pure retaliation action' (*eine reine Vergeltungsaktion*). There was never any real chance of a 'mutiny' and the principles of the reprisal policy continued to be accepted: 'In the end,' admitted Otto G. 'we lacked the courage to desert. Not a single man deserted.' In the words of August S., 'We fell back on the conclusion . . . that we had just obeyed orders.' Subsequent operations by 98th Regiment showed that provided commanders stuck to the normal procedures for reprisals – avoiding the indiscriminate killing of women and children in particular – the troops would obey orders with few misgivings.[96]

For a very different attitude to the whole idea of reprisals we must turn to a man like Herr G., who served in another unit in Greece. A decade later he recalled: 'When we heard about punitive expeditions against the old men and children in the surrounding villages, where the entire male population was shot in front of the women, who had been driven together with riflebutts, an enormous bitterness overwhelmed us at the thought that we too would have to take part in such operations.'[97]

G., however, was a most untypical soldier. Before the war, he had been thrown into Buchenwald for his involvement in an outlawed socialist group. He was taken out to serve in one of the so-called 999 battalions, made up of political prisoners and criminals, which were rushed into Greece in 1943. He was relatively old – thirty-eight, when the men of 12 Company were on average twenty to twenty-one – and this may have contributed to his independence of mind. During their posting in the Peloponnese, he and several friends who were also disgusted at the brutality of Wehrmacht policy actually deserted to join the guerrillas. But such 999ers formed a striking contrast with the vast majority of the men serving in the Wehrmacht in Greece. Although there were in the ranks men of very different religious outlooks – from Catholics to committed atheists – and of different origins – including Austrians, Silesian Poles, Caucasian Tartars, Bosnian Muslims, and others – the Wehrmacht as a whole remained a remarkably cohesive force to the very end, enforcing the draconian policies of its leadership with only minor qualms.[98]

CHAPTER SEVENTEEN

'The Loveliest Time': The Behaviour and Values of the German Soldier

Maintaining morale was not something the German army took for granted. Officers tried to forecast the sort of problems that might arise among their men, and made a conscious effort to establish a rapport between themselves and the conscripts. When, for example, in April 1943 the territorial commander in Greece briefed the officers of newly arrived troops, he reminded them that 'total war brings many questions before the soldiers – wife, family, job, money matters. The soldier will not be able to deal with these all by himself.'[99] Field commanders were given instructions covering not only the material welfare but even the 'spiritual-political guidance' of the troops. It was the combination of persistent concern and control which made the Wehrmacht itself such a powerful organisation, and its troops such a contrast with the disaffected Italians.

Welfare

To the ordinary soldier Greece was, above all, an escape from the freezing cold of the Eastern Front. New recruits counted a posting to the 'South-East' as a blessing, old campaigners saw it as a respite from certain death. In the 4th SS Polizei Panzer Grenadier Division, which fought in various guises across Europe, 'the general view was that after France, Greece was the loveliest time for the men of the Division'. Fritz Bergmayr recalled that 'after the hard defensive battles round Volchov and the Ladoga Sea in the summer of 1943, the news reached the Panzer-Jaeger Section of SS.Pol.Div. that most of the Section was to be posted to Greece. We felt a warm sense of endless spring and sunshine.'[100]

Before the war, most soldiers had probably never left the Reich. As they travelled vast distances for the first time, they found loneliness was often at hand. 'Left St. Die on February 12, 1944,' one

36. 'The loveliest time': German soldiers pose for a souvenir photograph in front of the Parthenon, 1941.

wrote, 'and went via Strasbourg, Offenbach, Munich, Augsburg, Vienna, Belgrade, Budapest, Bucharest and Salonica to Athens.' 'At present I am on a lonely signal post, previously occupied by Italian sailors,' a marine wrote home. 'The guard is from noon to noon, that is 24 hours. . . . The signal post is situated directly on the wide sea. You can imagine, the wind blows sharply, but nevertheless the temperature never gets below 10 centigrade.' Receiving the increasingly gloomy news from the Reich, soldiers felt guilty that 'the enemy gets ever closer to the borders of the Reich while we ourselves are a couple of thousand kilometres from home'.[101]

Service as an immobile occupation force, rather than on the front, brought travails of its own. Army brothels were often in far-off towns, turning sex into a distant memory for young conscripts manning isolated outposts; alcohol was a partial and unsatisfactory solace. 'It would not be quite so bad if there was some fun in the village,' one soldier wrote home from his island lookout. 'But it is quite as dull there as up here between the bare walls of the rocky mountain . . . up here there is nothing but wine. As time goes on you get used to it, but for the summer I'm still pessimistic . . .

202

the heat is supposed to be 45–55 centigrade. In addition to that, mosquitoes. Let us hope we shall be spared from malaria.'[102]

This was a common plea among the ranks in Greece, where mosquitoes were known as the 'second enemy' and a serious cause of casualties: malaria immobilised far more men than the *andartes* did. The film *Feind Malaria* (Enemy Malaria) was shown regularly to the troops, and their camp-beds and windows were draped with netting. German field doctors collaborated with Greek administrators to try to control the disease; in Dachau, the sinister Professor Claus Schilling was encouraged by Himmler to inject inmates with malarial strains in order to find an effective vaccine for the troops. Meanwhile, one company stationed near Elassona reported that 80 per cent of its men had gone down with malaria at least once. Some 25 per cent of 22 Army Corps was afflicted. In a specialist police mountain regiment which arrived in Greece after serving in Finland, the numbers of sick men rose rapidly from 30 to 400.[103]

Not surprisingly, when the staff of Sturmdivision Rhodos organised a competition for the best description of the soldier's experience of life on the island, the winner was a poem entitled 'Atebrin', after the prized anti-malaria pills which were distributed to the troops:

> Der Landser, der gewesen
> im Land der Balkanesen,
> der kennt sie auch – ich wette! –
> die Atebrin-Tablette.
>
> Wenn die Zikaden schrillen
> reicht man die gelben Pillen.
> Von Rhodos bis Semlin:
> Triumph der Medizin! . . .
>
> Wo Fiebermücken zwicken,
> muss Atebrin erquicken.
> Drum, Meckerer sei stille!
> Nimm lieber noch 'ne Pille!
>
> [That old foot-soldier
> Who's walked the Balkans over
> Also knows – I bet –
> The Atebrin Tablet.
>
> When the cicadas shrill
> He grabs the yellow pill.

From Rhodes to Semlin:
The triumph of medicine!

When the fever moves
Atebrin smoothes.
Stop moaning, stay still!
Just find another pill!][104]

*

But Atebrin's psychological equivalents were less easily identified –
to counter the debilitating impact of anxiety, homesickness and
war-weariness on the troops. The commander of 164 Infantry Division, for example, alerted his junior officers to the men's tendency
to dwell upon their personal difficulties rather than on the general
problems created by the war. Seeing matters from a 'personal
standpoint' could lead to an 'inner crisis'. The officers' task was to
'overcome the crisis-points in the spirit and attitude of the troops'.[105]

In planning for the soldiers' leisure time, divisional personnel
stressed the importance of organised entertainment as a cure for
loneliness. 'Comrade evenings' provided a sense of community
among the men where they were able to discuss their personal
problems together and openly instead of brooding about them in
private. Films were shown over a wide area, despite formidable
logistical difficulties. In the autumn of 1941, for example, eight
were shown monthly to the men of 164 Infantry Division, dispersed among small garrisons throughout northern Greece; even on
the islands in the East Aegean films were shown weekly. Propaganda units arranged tours of German theatre troupes as well
as the Kraft durch Freundschaft's own review, 'Liebe, Gluck und
Sonnenschein' (Love, Happiness and Sunshine). The diary of a
soldier in the Waffen-SS shows that he saw sometimes as many as
two or three shows a week during 1944. In July, shortly before a
major anti-guerrilla operation in central Greece, Kurt L. saw nine
films (including *Feind Malaria*), and enjoyed a cabaret show, a
concert and a *Kameradschaftsabend*.[106]

At the same time, the troops were encouraged to make their own
entertainment. The choleric Fritz Schmedes, who commanded the
4th SS Polizei Panzer Grenadier Division in Greece, was so fond of
music that he organised a small regimental orchestra, which greeted
him on his birthday on 17 October 1943 with a performance in
the main square in Larissa, and later gave concerts in Athens. At
the Hubertusheim in Jannina, men of the 1st Mountain Division
formed their own 'Edelweisskapelle', made up of the usual mixture
of saxophones, drums, trumpet, accordion and violin; evenings and

37.   Troops make their own entertainment: a donkey race among members of a coastal battery unit: Peloponnese, August, 1943.

days off would be spent carousing and singing folk-songs from home.[107]

164 Infantry Division organised its own sports days with games of handball, cross-country running and football. Prizes were offered for the best contributions in singing, handicrafts, photography, painting, marching songs and literature. The judges were told to look for 'brevity, a confident tone, no sentimentality'. As for the photographs, they were to display 'no personal but rather entirely soldierly feelings; painterly vision; good technical execution'.[108]

Books and magazines were supplied to the troops from a variety of sources, including the Nazi Party itself and OKW. Alongside the inevitable political texts by party ideologues like Goebbels and Rosenberg, there were popular novels and adventure stories. In addition, educational courses were laid on to train the men for the post-war world. Driving lessons were popular, as were classes in electrical engineering and mechanics. Divisional commanders insisted that career officers needed to keep their men's very different preoccupations in mind: 'The longer the war lasts, the more the civilian occupations of the men must be assisted. The . . . education of the soldier in his chosen fields must continue, so that he is convinced of his absolute worth *vis-à-vis* the civilians at home. Each unit commander should take pride in ensuring as many of his men as possible attend training courses.'[109]

News was provided for the soldiers through newspapers and periodicals which were specially printed for the Balkan theatre. In the islands, where feelings of isolation and homesickness were strongest, local propaganda services often produced their own editions. The soldiers on Rhodes, for example, were able to read *Wacht auf Rhodos* from October 1943 onwards, when it appeared with an initial print-run of 2,000 copies. *Wacht auf Rhodos* offered political and military news summaries, as well as lighter entertainment. The four-page Saturday edition contained pieces on the history of Rhodes and the Aegean islands for the benefit of the soldier-tourist.[110]

Such papers were sensitive to the soldiers' demands; they solicited articles from them, and underlined the historical importance of their contribution to the war effort. On 13 December 1943, for example, Gunner Hanhelmuth Bubat had the satisfaction of seeing a piece he had written appear in print. It was called 'Baptism by Fire', and had won first prize in a competition for the best description of the fighting with the Italians on Rhodes just three months earlier. A vivid if moralistic piece, it ends with a rather unoriginal rhetorical flourish:

> Life has worth when one lives correctly, and the more difficult life is, the more richly endowed it is. We do not live any longer for ourselves; we live and fight for them who came before us, for those who will come after.
>
> We live for a great idea, for the Reich, for the historical Ideal of our *Volk*. The greatness of our *Volk* is the Mastery of the Reich, our eternal task. Knowledge of this will carry us with longing on the path to great goals. That was what we were thinking in the bunker, while enemy grenades exploded about us, the grenades of the traitors.[111]

*

Such a crudely ideological appeal to the spirit of racial self-sacrifice cannot but raise in our minds the question of the role played by Nazi propaganda in the German army. Of its influence there can be little doubt: few scholars today hold the once-fashionable view that the army remained impervious to Nazi dogma. But the degree of that influence, and the forms it took, are hotly debated.

As though to imply that the army's basic distaste for politics *had* remained largely intact, some historians have focused on the figure of the NSFO – the National Socialist Guidance Officer, a sort of Nazi commissar who made his appearance at the end of 1943, after complaints from party sources that army training methods were playing down ideology. Generally, the NSFO was much disliked, shunned and even feared when he arrived at his new posting. This obnoxious figure criticised divisional chaplains, reported men for defeatist talk, and checked incoming book deliveries for ideologically unacceptable material.[112]

Yet if his influence on the ideological education of the troops was ultimately slight, it was not because the army was a bastion of anti-Nazi traditions which successfully quarantined the ideologues. The reason was quite the reverse: the Wehrmacht was disseminating much of Goebbels's message through books and films well before the NSFO appeared on the scene. When we examine the indoctrination of the troops from 1941 onwards, it becomes evident that many divisional commanders did not need an NSFO to shepherd them along the path of ideological correctness. The demands of military discipline and the officers' own values, as well as the ideological extremism which became particularly visible in the Wehrmacht after the invasion of the Soviet Union, led them to emphasise central themes of Nazi rhetoric without outside prompting.[113]

For the commander of 164 Infantry Division, for example, it was obvious that the war was a struggle for the existence of the *Volk*, so that the soldiers had a duty to preserve the racial purity of the race by avoiding sexual contact with Greek women. He underlined that 'the education of the soldier into a determined and aggressive fighter is inconceivable without a living National-Socialist training', and insisted on the need to give the troops the basic elements of the 'National Socialist *Weltanschauung*'. These views dated from November 1941, long before the NSFO had been dreamed up. General Le Suire of 117 Jaeger Division demanded obedience to the will of 'our Führer', and expressly forbade the slightest criticism of Hitler. In 1st Mountain Division, both Colonel Salminger and General von Stettner were unquestioning supporters of the Führer, while Standartenführer Schümers of the Waffen-SS was another who needed no NSFO.[114]

Some field commanders, it is true, were more ambivalent about the regime. General Lanz, in charge of 22 Army Corps, and Lieutenant-General Löhr himself, at Army Group E in Salonika, were cases in point. When Lanz's doctor shot himself after the failure of the 20 July plot to kill Hitler, Lanz read the funeral oration, and is supposed to have slept with a revolver under his pillow in anticipation of a visit from the Gestapo. Löhr's staff prided themselves on their anti-Nazi credentials, and chased out new arrivals who took a more credulous attitude towards the Party. Yet the practical consequences of such 'anti-Nazi' views were negligible. Often based on social snobbery as much as objections of moral principle, they were confined to a tiny circle of confidants in staff circles who were as fearful as everyone else of the Gestapo watchdogs from Prinz-Albrecht-Strasse.

The Role of the Officer

Nazis and anti-Nazis alike agreed that the key to military cohesion was the junior officer. Enormous responsibility rested upon his shoulders; he was, in the words of General Winter, the 'master of life and death for all soldiers in his area'. Troop morale, another General emphasised, depended on 'the spiritual guidance (*geistige Führung*) of the men by their company commander.'[115] He should meet regularly with his men and listen to their problems, discussing current political and military matters with them and generally encouraging a convivial atmosphere.[116]

Contact with the company commander, and supervision by him, was the most direct way of checking that sense of isolation among the men which was felt to be so dangerous for morale. When several 999ers deserted to the *andartes*, General Le Suire suggested that one factor that had contributed to their flight had been neglect by their officers and their consequent 'sense of loneliness'. 'Don't leave the soldier alone,' was typical advice. Because the Wehrmacht was even more reluctant than Allied armies to admit psychological explanations for problems of morale, the responsibility of the company commander was even greater than that of his British or American counterpart.[117]

On the one hand, the officer was supposed to dominate his men. It was suggested that they be told that their mail was being opened; officers were also advised to keep an eye on their men's diaries. Thus the company commander was, in part at least, a constant guard over their thoughts and feelings; he was to aim at ensuring their 'transparency' and to guard against any signs of withdrawal or secrecy, for these were sure indications of emotional turmoil, 'crisis' and defeatism. Their discussions, like their characters, were to be 'open and sincere'. What worried officers were soldiers like those 999ers, who were described as 'impenetrable, crafty and unpredictable'.[118]

But the officer was supposed to gain support for the regime and its aims as well as plain obedience. From 164 Infantry Division came a reminder that 'the company commander is not only the military leader, he is above all . . . the political representative of the Führer himself'. He was responsible for '[the soldiers'] attitude towards the National Socialist state and the life-struggle of our *Volk*'. His duties demanded, beyond discussions and instruction, the personal demonstration of what it meant to be a soldier. 'His own behaviour will boost or puncture the morale of his men. The saying applies especially here: "As the rider, so the horse."' Another pithy phrase to be instilled in the minds of the men was, 'If the Chief does it, it's right.'[119]

Furthermore, a successful company commander was one who made his men realise that he had their interests at heart; they must come to feel that their welfare was important to him. By his example, he had to demonstrate that selflessness which was demanded of all the troops. We read of officers who were 'loved' by their men, a sentiment which had little importance in other armies, where the emphasis on psychological relations between ranks was less pronounced. A character assessment of Fritz Lautenbach, the twenty-six-year-old Waffen-SS company commander who was responsible for the Distomo massacre, described him as someone who 'for all his verve and enthusiasm never forgot his responsibility or concern for his men'. He was 'vigorous and cheerful' and his 'blameless soldierly bearing' won him the 'love' of his subordinates and fellow-officers. By contrast, his junior officer, twenty-four-year-old Georg Weichenrieder, was said to be unsuited for a position as company commander because he had been 'swayed by many personal interests'. He appeared to be 'outgoing and honest', but in fact he had turned out to have an 'impenetrable and fickle' character. He lacked maturity and suffered from 'a deficient sense of responsibility'.[120]

Even in death, the officer could be used to exemplify the virtues of the German soldier. After Colonel Salminger was killed in a guerrilla ambush in north-west Greece, General Lanz reminded his men that he had been 'a battalion and regimental commander hardened in a hundred battles in West and East, whose exemplary brave and eager leadership (*Führerpersönlichkeit*) will live on in the hearts of his *Gebirgsjäger* and in the annals of his regiment for all time'.[121] In June 1943 General Le Suire notified his men of the death of a certain Lieutenant Esterbauer in a guerrilla ambush near Kozani. He distributed the text of a letter which Esterbauer had supposedly written to his wife as he lay dying. She should not grieve, Esterbauer had counselled her; rather she should be 'proud, that your husband gave his life for his Führer and Germany, for a goal which is truly worth giving up one's life for. Bring up our Heide-Marie to be a true German, as our Führer desires.' And Le Suire urged his men that 'this manly and upright entry into the last fight, the oath of faith in Germany and its Führer, must become an everlasting duty and a solemn vow for us in the 117th Jaeger Division. The attitude of this officer and his men are an example to us in our work and struggle.'[122]

Violence and Discipline

Moving through the unfamiliar olive groves and exposed mountain slopes on dirt roads or the ancient donkey tracks which could disappear one minute into the ground and reappear some distance away, weighed down by packs in the unbearable heat, the soldiers felt acutely vulnerable. 'Suspiciousness, alertness and watchfulness' were their watchwords. Reporting back to base after one reprisal expedition, a unit of 117 Jaeger Division observed that the villages they passed through had been deserted by most of their inhabitants. They knew why, too – they had fled 'out of fear of seizure as hostages'. Those left behind they described as trying 'to prove that they had nothing to do with the bands by exaggerated and submissive politeness, and by proclaiming their sympathy'.[123]

Colonel Salminger used similar language in the summer of 1943. He interpreted natural civilian responses to the appearance of German troops as signs of their 'treachery' and 'deceit'. To divisional headquarters, he mentioned that the seizure of hostages had produced an immediate change of behaviour throughout the area: 'Today all the villages are without their menfolk, and I have the unmistakable feeling that there is some treachery here.' He was struck by the way that farmers encountered in the fields raised their hands and 'adopted a safe, harmless pose'. His view was that the *andartes'* leadership had ordered their men 'to disguise themselves as peaceful farmers during the current operations.'[124]

Surprisingly few soldiers were actually killed by the *andartes* (1st Mountain Division, for example, lost fewer than one hundred in Greece in the last six months of 1943); many would eventually leave Greece without ever having seen a guerrilla, but all sensed their presence.[125] Despite Greece's apparent peacefulness, soldiers felt confused by this new type of warfare, and longed for the simplicities of the front, where the enemy was known and visible. Standartenführer Schümers, described as 'an outstanding Front officer' in a confidential assessment, was one such man; his subordinate Werner Schlätel observed that: 'he hated partisan warfare. . . . He wanted an enemy in front of him, not like here in Greece, where a man could be shot at from behind, where the roads were mined.'[126]

If an officer's men were attacked, he was obliged under standing orders to retaliate with a punitive raid. Because, as we have seen, officers were threatened with proceedings if they failed to react with the 'necessary severity', it was not easy for a company or battalion commander to ignore orders from the divisional staff to carry out a reprisal. When one battalion commander rang back to query Standartenführer Schümers's orders to kill women hostages near Siatista, he simply provoked a violent tirade. 'They're not women, they're female sharpshooters,' Schümers screamed down the phone. His order was carried out. Another time, a local commander managed to get General Le Suire to reduce the numbers of hostages to be hanged for an attack on a railway guard from one hundred to fifty. More than this could not usually be gained, unless officers took the risk of simply ignoring divisional instructions.[127]

In such a context, it was not clear what would constitute an 'excessive' use of force. After all, General Felmy for one had warned his troops that 'in the war against the bands, weakness is as bad as excessively tough operations'. Though most of the troops did not object to the idea of punitive expeditions and reprisal policies in themselves, what did arouse some misgivings were, first, attacks against women and children, and second, reports that German soldiers had been 'cruel' and 'malicious', or in other words, sadistic, in carrying out reprisals. For both cases seemed to run contrary to the 'soldierly values' which the men had been brought up to believe in, and both seemed to set them on the same level as the 'bandits' themselves. However, the sweeping authority which was delegated to junior officers, and the sympathy shown them by their seniors, made it extremely rare for even these forms of 'excess' to be investigated.[128]

A case in point was that of the vicious Lieutenant Hans P., who commanded a company of 117 Jaeger Division near Argos in the Peloponnese. No action was ever taken against Lieutenant P., despite behaviour towards non-combatants which verged on sheer sadism. With a group of younger men from his unit, Lieutenant P. indulged in 'radical' measures against the villagers of Merbaka, where he was stationed. One day, for example, he had a young Greek civilian male aged between twenty and thirty brought before him. According to Private Alois W., 'I happened to be around and so I was an eyewitness when P. said to an officer, "Look, this is what you do. Give him a kick on the backside [upon which P. kicked the Greek, who was not tied up, in the rear so that he ran off] and now shoot him, so that he's shot in flight."' The officer did so. In this village, Lieutenant P. was indeed 'master of life and death' and there were apparently no limits to his power.[129]

A rare instance where an atrocity *was* investigated shows that so long as the commanding officer argued that he had been acting in accordance with the interests of his men, it was not likely that action would be taken against him. In June 1944, in one of the worst atrocities of the entire war, a Waffen-SS unit on patrol against the guerrillas entered the village of Distomo and ran amok, massacring several hundred people in their homes. A Red Cross team which arrived from Athens a couple of days later even found bodies dangling from the trees that lined the road into the village.

The only reason that an investigation took place was that a GFP (Geheime Feldpolizei – Secret Field Police) agent, Georg Koch, had accompanied the troops that day, and submitted a report which contradicted the official troop report made by company commander SS-Hauptsturmführer Fritz Lautenbach. Lautenbach claimed that his men had been fired upon 'with mortars, machine-guns and rifles from the direction of Distomo'. Koch revealed that this was untrue: the troops had actually been attacked in an ambush several miles outside the village; it was only after the 'bandits' retreated success- fully into the hills that 2 Company turned round, drove back into Distomo and killed everyone they could find. When Special Envoy Neubacher took up the matter, concerned at its impact on friendly circles in the Greek administration, a military investigation could not be avoided.[130]

At the inquiry, the youthful Hauptsturmführer Lautenbach ad- mitted that he had gone beyond standing orders. However, he pleaded that 'mindful of those killed and wounded in my company I consciously made the decision to follow the spirit rather than the letter of the orders governing reprisals. I was aware that my orders could be construed as formal insubordination, but expected that they would be retrospectively approved on soldierly and humane principles.' Lautenbach argued that the guerrilla attack on his men would have been impossible without the knowledge of local civi- lians. Their presence working in the fields nearby was designed to lure the troops into an ambush, and proved 'their previously planned and rehearsed co-operation with the bands. . . . My mea- sures also had the purpose of possibly preventing further losses which could be expected.'

The military tribunal does not seem to have called any Greek witnesses. Had it done so, it would have received a dramatically different view of the day's events. Nitsa N., who lived in the middle of Distomo, looked out of the window when she heard the Germans return. The first thing she saw was a soldier in the street

38a. (*top*)   Distomo, 1944: Lautenbach's men watch the village burn.

38b. (*left*)   Distomo, 1945: Survivors of the massacre the previous year.

shooting wildly. Then others burst into her house, looting it and killing her family in front of her. In postwar affidavits, other survivors testified to rape and plundering by the troops. Sofia D. had been riding back from the fields with her father and her brother when they saw smoke rising above the village. Fearing that the Germans were taking men hostage, their father told them to go on, while he took a safer route across country. As they continued down the road, German lorries approached, a soldier shot at her brother, and a second shot and wounded her. Luckily both children escaped by feigning death, though their horses were killed. As these testimonies demonstrated, the men of Lautenbach's company had simply fired at anyone they saw.[131]

The tribunal listening to Lautenbach probably did not need Greek witnesses to uncover the truth, but still found in his favour. 'Military necessity' had fully justified his use of arms; indeed, 'non-use of arms would have led to proceedings for the negligent release of prisoners'. If the villagers had claimed that there were no guerrillas in the vicinity when in fact there were, this proved their guilt. Lautenbach's breach of standing orders was condoned because he had been motivated, not by 'negligence or ignorance' but by a sense of responsibility towards his men. The findings continued: 'In such a striking case of civilian membership of the bands as occurred at Distomo, the Company commander believed he had to set an example, by which the occupying power would prove with all due severity that it knows how to counter even the most underhand and lowest form of so-called "warfare".' Regimental commander Schümers simply requested permission to punish Lautenbach himself through disciplinary proceedings. His Wehrmacht superiors tacitly allowed the matter to drop.

There were several peculiar features about the individuals involved at Distomo. Not every division in the Wehrmacht resembled the 4th SS Polizei Panzer Grenadier Division with its lethal combination of poorly trained, under-age Volksdeutsch recruits and politically committed officers. Few company commanders had begun their military career like Lautenbach, in the elite SS Leibstandarte Adolf Hitler. Few senior commanding officers had participated in the vicious fighting in Silesia with the Freikorps after the First World War, like Brigadeführer-und-General Major der Waffen-SS Fritz Schmedes. And there can have been few less attractive characters than Lautenbach's regimental commander, the thirty-nine-year-old Standartenführer Schümers, whose natural aggression had not been quietened by the head injuries he had suffered on the Eastern Front, who was commended for his dedication in conveying the essence of National Socialist thought to his subordinates, and who even his defenders admitted was prone to 'extremely draconian' measures.[132]

But Schümers's men did not operate in a vacuum, and they had been under the operational command of Army Group E. The investigation into the Distomo massacre revealed as much about Wehrmacht attitudes as about Waffen-SS behaviour. Even if such atrocities were not welcomed by senior commanders, they were prepared to condone them, and to do so on terms which made some future repetition likely. Perhaps Lautenbach's men lacked the discipline of elite army units. But the massacre at Komeno had already shown what the latter were capable of.

'Scenes from the Wild West'

Some senior officers did worry about the effects of continued reprisals on the discipline of their men. Anti-partisan directives sought to distinguish between *Vergeltungsaktionen* and 'unjustified murder' which 'of course is forbidden'. Lanz made efforts to ensure that civilians were properly treated. General Felmy warned that 'infringements by the troops' such as individual plundering and acts of cruelty had to be prevented since 'troop excesses have a lasting impact on discipline and inner attitudes and weaken the troops for future operations against worthy opponents'.[133]

Service away from the front, in areas like Greece, had apparently led to an increase in crime among the troops, at the expense both of fellow-soldiers and of the civilian population. When the men of 1st Mountain Division left the Caucasus, after nearly two years on the Eastern Front, and journeyed to the Balkans, their discipline deteriorated, and thieving and plundering increased. Paid in virtually worthless drachmas, soldiers were tempted to earn a little extra – as soldiers often are – by stealing from defenceless and 'inferior' civilians, and by selling army materials on the black market, where an extensive network of dealers and agents existed.[134]

Their fear of being caught must have been greatly eased by the knowledge that the military police were understaffed and overstretched – roughly thirty men policing over 12,000 in the case of 1st Mountain Division. As a result the Feldgendarmerie could not possibly pursue all crimes with the same zeal. They reserved their energies for the most serious – thefts of Wehrmacht property, or of the property of fellow-soldiers – and devoted little time to investigating crimes against civilians. Of the seventy-five cases pursued by the military police in 1st Mountain Division in May and June 1943, twenty-two involved the theft of army property, another eight were 'theft from comrades', and only three involved plundering from Greek civilians; these last were punished with sentences of just six weeks, compared with months, or even years, for the other charges. Despite the warnings of their superiors, it was clear to the troops where the disciplinary priorities of the Wehrmacht lay.[135]

The enormous power which members of the Wehrmacht possessed *vis-à-vis* the Greek population inevitably strained the bounds of military discipline. Sometimes the outcome could be almost benign, as when three members of a 999 unit stationed in the Rhodes countryside gave permission to local farmers to harvest their crops, and even pointed out to them where mines had been laid, in return for some milk, eggs and fruit. But such cases lay at one end of a moral spectrum; at the other was Private Walter Bernhardt, who swindled money from a Greek family by pretending that he would arrange for the release of a jailed relative; or still worse, Petty Officer Herbert Petschinski on Chios, who arrested a Greek during a raid without any cause, and released him only upon the payment of a large quantity of olive oil.[136]

In many respects, of course, these men were simply behaving as soldiers anywhere will. Most armies have their disciplinary problems, especially when acting as an occupation force. Stationed on guard duty in one place for long periods of time, the German troops had a better chance of forming relationships with the civilian population than they had had at the front. Boredom, alcohol and sexual frustration were often too strong for the army's racially motivated apartheid. The islands in particular seem to have been the classic location for crimes of passion. When Captain Erich Schiele, on Kleemann's staff on Rhodes, was charged with beating up a Greek girl in broad daylight, it turned out that he had been having an affair with her, driving 60 kilometres each day in his car to see her. He had forbidden her to meet with other soldiers; she had ignored his prohibition. When arrested, he rounded on a fellow-officer, accusing him of corruption and involvement in a prostitution racket. Sexual involvement with a Greek woman seems in this case to have had disastrous effects on feelings of 'comradeship'.[137]

Other characteristic crimes of occupation included theft, burglaries and random assaults. On the island of Leros, for example, three 999ers forced their way into some houses and stole money, lingerie, clocks and jewellery. Two soldiers in Patras robbed a Greek of 1.4 million drachmas in gold, and a platinum ring; a woman was raped by a soldier, who ran off with her wrist-watch; in Argos, seven Luftwaffe men robbed a Greek of 200,000 drachmas, beat him up and threatened to shoot him when he complained.[138]

In the cities, tavernas and hotels were a common target for criminal attacks. It could take proprietors some time to realise that their raiders had an eye to more than 'official' business. When two German soldiers burst into a taverna in the middle of Athens, they announced that they were searching the premises for weapons and fugitive Italians. But during their search they forced the owner to hand over the keys to his safe and helped themselves to over 4 million drachmas. Half an hour later on the same day, 2 January 1944, another taverna in Mavromichalis Street was also robbed.[139]

This sort of incident, however, has taken us beyond what might be regarded as the 'normal' behaviour of occupation forces, and shows how the climate of violence and fear created by official Axis operations had opened up possibilities for private gain. The SS's terror system provided further opportunities of this sort by allowing enterprising if unscrupulous individual soldiers to take advantage of the popular fear of the 'Gestapo' – as most Greeks termed the different branches of the secret police. Two soldiers, for example, claiming to be Gestapo agents were actually caught robbing a Greek member of a pro-German volunteer battalion. Since bona fide security police were also notoriously susceptible to bribery, it was difficult for Greek victims to tell them apart from impostors. A certain Corporal Humme, who stayed behind in the capital instead of joining his artillery regiment in the Peloponnese, started off making money by collecting 'fines' from Athenians for 'violations' of blackout regulations. Claiming to be from the Gestapo, he and an accomplice carried out residential searches at gunpoint, and took away stockings, soap, cigarettes and other valuable items. For greater authenticity, the two of them confiscated their victims' ID papers, and ordered them to report to their local command post. Eventually Humme was arrested, and found also to be implicated in a far more serious offence – the theft of army truck tyres – for which he was sentenced to death.[140]

In the countryside some Wehrmacht troops did not bother with this sort of disguise. Sixteen unidentified soldiers drove up to the village of Melandrina one day and looted it thoroughly. They left with large quantities of oil, sheep, goats, maize, china and money. This raid took place at a time when the whole of the north Peloponnese was being scoured in anti-guerrilla operations: how could the villagers be sure that this was not another 'mopping-up' operation, indeed one in which they had escaped lightly? No one was killed, though a village woman who protested was beaten up.[141]

In nearby Corinth, the local territorial commander was horrified by the Melandrina affair and appalled at the wholesale deterioration in military discipline that it indicated. He warned Athens bluntly of the consequences of the soldiers' 'gangster methods'. If anti-guerrilla tactics had failed to dampen insurgency in the Peloponnese, he wrote, they had caused troop discipline to deteriorate to the point where the soldiers' behaviour was reminiscent of 'scenes from the Wild West'. The soldiers were completely ignoring his strict prohibition on taking the law into their own hands; their assaults on the security and property of the civilian population had reached such proportions that 'they must be described simply as robbers'.[142]

The head of the Corinth Feldkommandantur was worried about the political implications of the troops' misbehaviour, for lawlessness on this scale alienated the Greek population and undercut his attempts to build up an anti-communist, pro-German constituency among the Greeks to share the burden of confronting the *andartes*. We shall explore this political dimension a little later. Here it is important to stress what his report tells us, not about policy, but about the routine conduct of German soldiers. The effort of the military authorities to preserve a distinction between two forms of violence – between an acceptable, disciplined use of force for the sake of the common good and public order on the one hand; and on the other, a reprehensible, wild violence which aimed at private gain – had broken down. No doubt all occupation regimes face difficulties of this sort, but not perhaps in such an extreme form. A regime which glorified violence and dehumanised its opponents to the extent that the Nazis did found it difficult to control the uses of military violence, particularly in a country like Greece, where its soldiers were isolated, bored, frightened and powerful. As a result, the German military ideal of an attitude towards the civilian population which combined collective sternness with individual self-control papered over a brutal reality. For the Greeks, the daily threat of an apparently random and undiscriminating violence became central to their experience of the occupation.

CHAPTER EIGHTEEN

The SS and the Terror System

No sooner had German troops entered Greece in 1941 than the Gestapo started rounding up 'enemies of the Reich'. Lists of political opponents in various countries had been prepared over several years at the Reich Security Head Office (RSHA – Reichssicherheitshauptamt) in Berlin. In Athens Sturmbannführer-und-Kriminalrat Geissler set to work tracking down the figures named in his 'Search-book'. But by arresting senior Greek civil servants and even searching the homes of foreign diplomats, Geissler soon annoyed those German officials who were trying to win over Greek opinion, especially as he himself usually had no idea what his victims were supposed to have done. Eventually he was hauled over the coals by Altenburg, the Foreign Office's chief envoy in Greece, and made to leave Athens.[143]

For the next two years, SS activities in Greece remained on a small scale. Himmler paid a brief visit to Athens in May 1941, chiefly – it seems – to see the Acropolis. Offices were established in Athens and Salonika as outposts of the SiPo/SD (*Sicherheitspolizei/Sicherheitsdienst*), the combined state secret police and SS intelligence service which was run from the Reich Security Head Office in Berlin. The Gestapo officials who headed them found themselves on the margins of the occupation bureaucracy. They followed the ins and outs of Greek politics, and remained well informed about developments within the Greek Communist Party, but were prevented from playing a more active role by the 'predominance' of the Italians. Among the German services, the SS lagged far behind the Wehrmacht and the Foreign Office in its ability to influence affairs in Greece. Even in intelligence matters the SiPo/SD was dwarfed by the Wehrmacht's vast Abwehr (military counter-intelligence) organisation in Athens.[144]

For two years, summary courts martial were run by the Wehrmacht without any interference from the SiPo/SD. Ioannis Sontis, a Greek lawyer trained in Heidelberg, defended several hundred Greeks accused of sabotage, theft and communist activities

before German military judges. At Nuremberg after the war, he
testified that court procedures were adhered to during these trials,
although the Secret Field Police (GFP), and military intelligence (1c)
officers sometimes took little notice when verdicts of innocence
were handed down, and simply quashed the proceedings. What is
revealing in this context is that Sontis was unaware of the existence
of the SiPo/SD *Dienststelle* in Athens before 1943, so little impact
did it make on his activities.

After the Italian collapse that autumn, however, the swift expansion of the SS transformed judicial practice. The court martial of
the military commander for Greece virtually stopped functioning
and became, in Sontis's words, 'a shop without customers'. SS
practices, he said, put earlier judicial crimes in the shade: 'The
SS, of course, had no court martial. Their tortures were a daily
occurrence, and the people were not shot on the basis of a legal
verdict.' He added: 'They were not shot singly, but *en masse*. 40,
100, 25, 30 etc., there were so many cases that I cannot remember
them.' There were, in fact, SS courts; but these regarded the rule of
the law – in the words of Higher SS-and-Police Führer (Höherer
SS–und Polizeiführer: HSSPF) Walter Schimana – as 'an administrative means for higher political considerations'.[145]

It is no coincidence that any semblance of legal process vanished
as the SS's power grew: from September 1943, Greece experienced

39. The SS in Greece: (*previous page left*) Jürgen Stroop, HSSPF/Greece, August–October 1943. (*previous page right*) Walter Schimana, HSSPF/Greece, October 1943–October 1944. (*top right*) Hans Dörhage, head of the SiPo/SD in Athens, 1941–42. (*bottom left*) Walter Blume, head of the SiPo/SD in Greece, 1943–44. (*bottom right*) Paul Radomski, commandant of the Haidari camp, 1943–44.

the development that had already taken place under the Nazis elsewhere in Europe: the absorption of whatever remained of earlier juridical norms into a system of terror. Fresh from the killing fields of the East came men like the stocky, violent Sturmbannführer Paul Radomski, the Viennese Franz Kleedorfer, who boasted of having personally killed 2,000 people in Russia, and SS-Standartenführer

Dr Walter Blume, who had commanded Sonderkommando 7a in the Vilna area and shot hundreds of civilians in accordance with the Führer's *Judenvernichtungsbefehl* (Order to Annihilate the Jews). The man Himmler picked to carry out the expansion of his service in Greece was a rising star in the SS and apparently well suited for the task: SS-und-Polizeiführer Jürgen Stroop, the destroyer of the Warsaw Ghetto.

The Expansion of the SS

In May 1943 Stroop's men had overcome the last heroic vestiges of Jewish resistance in Warsaw, and then razed the ghetto to the ground. Two months later, on hearing of Mussolini's downfall, Himmler summoned him to Berlin and informed him of his new posting as Höherer SS-und Polizeiführer (HSSPF) in Greece. At the end of August he flew to Belgrade, where he held talks with the experienced SS police chief there, before proceeding to Athens.[146]

The Italians' sudden collapse that summer created a power vacuum which different German agencies rushed to fill. From its HQ in Salonika, the army organised a new command structure in southern and central Greece. At the same time, Hermann Neubacher, successfully bidding for supreme political responsibility, managed to get Hitler, who admired his abilities, to upgrade his appointment in August to 'Special Representative of the Foreign Office for the South-East'. By September the two Austrians, Neubacher and Löhr, were clearly in overall command in Greece, sharing without too much fuss the political and military aspects of occupation policy. Both were Austrians, both were secretly pessimistic about the war, and both appreciated the need to build up support within Greece among local anti-communists so long as German forces remained there.

In this situation, Jürgen Stroop's own position was unclear. The new HSSPF had rather limited powers, despite his grandiose title; he was chiefly supposed to symbolise the prominence of the SS and to remain in close touch with Himmler. His executive functions lay in the sphere of policing and anti-partisan operations. In a country like Greece, where the Wehrmacht and Foreign Office were both well established, co-operation with other parts of the occupation bureaucracy was unavoidable. Indeed, formally, the HSSPF took orders from Wehrmacht commanders and was assigned most of his troops by them.[147]

But the brutal and boastful Stroop was not known for his diplomatic finesse. Evidently he saw his new posting as a chance for glory, and so he ignored the bureaucratic niceties in his haste to assert himself on a grand scale. His first act on arriving in Athens was to call in Prime Minister Rallis and his Interior Minister: in future, he told them, they would be answerable to him, and were not to communicate with General Löhr in Salonika without his permission. He then made what his successor later termed a 'bloodthirsty' broadcast on Radio Athens, which included a long and vicious diatribe against the Jews. He tried to assert his jurisdiction over the entire anti-guerrilla campaign in Greece, and also ordered the compulsory registration of all Jews in southern Greece.[148]

After barely a month in Athens, Stroop had succeeded in antag-onising his more powerful colleagues. Not only had he challenged Löhr's right to conduct anti-guerrilla operations; he had also im-plicitly attacked Neubacher's handling of Greek politics. Neubacher, in particular, was a dangerous enemy. From his early days in the Austrian Nazi movement, through his time working for I.G. Farben and his period as mayor of post-Anschluss Vienna, the suave and charming Austrian had acquired an enviable circle of friends and admirers. These included such fellow-Austrians as Hitler himself, and Himmler's deputy, Ernst Kaltenbrunner, who was actually Stroop's boss in Berlin. (So closely did the Wehrmacht and Kaltenbrunner work with Neubacher that at one stage they pro-posed him to Hitler as Foreign Minister.)[149] Neither Kaltenbrunner nor Neubacher wanted a clumsy extremist like Stroop treating the Greeks as he had treated the Poles. Neubacher dropped a hint to his old friend about Stroop's lack of political finesse, and the result was that on 4 October, after barely a month in his new post, Stroop received the unwelcome news from Kaltenbrunner's department that he was being sent back to the Reich: 'You will be sorry to have to leave Greece so soon!' commiserated his informant.[150]

On that same day, hundreds of miles to the north in Posen, Heinrich Himmler was making a shocking and revealing speech. In the course of a long address to his assembled Gruppenführers, he discussed the psychological burdens that had been imposed on the SS by the need to exterminate the Jews and carry out the Final Solution. This was one of the very few occasions when Himmler spoke openly about the Final Solution. Tacked on to the end of his address, among the details of anti-partisan operations and personnel matters, was an insignificant item: Stroop was being transferred from Greece, and replaced by an anti-partisan specialist, Walter Schimana. Schimana was in the audience, and had already been informed by Himmler of his new posting.[151]

The new HSSPF turned out to be very different to Stroop –

slower, stolid and notably lacking in ambition or initiative – and there is more than a suspicion that he had been selected for just these qualities. To US interrogators after the war he seemed 'a pleasant-mannered little man who does not give the impression of being a tough SS leader'. A Nazi veteran, formerly a gendarmerie commander in Vienna, and a personal friend of both Kaltenbrunner and Neubacher, his war had so far been undistinguished.[152] As he settled into a luxurious villa overlooking the royal gardens in the centre of Athens, long-time members of the German community in the city viewed him with a mixture of distaste and amusement. He surrounded himself, one wrote, with young, blond secretaries and stressed his informal style with his underlings just as the old Nazi hands liked to do, childishly proud of his uniform and his new responsibilities. As no doubt Neubacher had intended, the new HSSPF ignored politics for other tasks, such as overseeing the formation of new Greek police formations, building up paramilitary auxiliary units and working alongside Wehrmacht commanders in operations against the partisans. Meanwhile, in the light of Stroop's unsubtle power bid, Hitler reaffirmed Neubacher's responsibility for political affairs in the Balkans.[153]

The real force behind the SS in Greece was not the lightweight Schimana but his deputy for security affairs, SS-Standartenführer Dr Walter Blume, the new commander of the SiPo/SD. A quiet and rather sinister bureaucrat, the coolly ambitious Blume took charge of the small Athens *Dienststelle*, and soon turned it into the hub of a nationwide terror apparatus. He began to chart his own course, bypassing the HSSPF (who probably preferred not to know what Blume was doing in any event), and taking orders direct from the Gestapo HQ in Berlin. This was characteristic of the structure of the SS throughout occupied Europe, for one often finds the HSSPF acting merely as a figurehead, and the security police beneath him actually determining policy in conjunction with the Gestapo.[154]

Blume's Athens headquarters grew from fewer than a dozen officials in October 1943 to over forty a few months later, controlling a vast network of agents. Other SS personnel were assigned to newly created SD outposts (*Aussenstelle*) around the country. Their brief stretched from criminal matters like black-marketeering to political policing tasks concerning the partisans, liaison with the Waffen-SS and the Greek police, and surveillance of the Jewish community.[155]

In December Blume flew back to Berlin to demand more staff, asking in some annoyance if he was expected to do all the work himself. But he was not entirely dissatisfied with his men. That Christmas, as a token of appreciation, he gave each of his staff a present of some clothes. They could guess their provenance, for none of the recipients was ignorant of the deportation of the Jews of Salonika, or of the mass shootings of civilian hostages which were taking place throughout Greece almost daily. Recently Blume's security police had acquired the right to confiscate property belonging to Athenian Jews who had gone into hiding: his men's Christmas presents had cost him little.[156]

Political policing is invariably a highly competitive field and nowhere was this truer than in the Nazi empire. Blume's chief rival in Greece was the wily Roman Loos, who headed the vast Secret Field Police apparatus in the Balkans. (Loos's skill in avoiding the limelight helped him re-enter the Austrian police force after the war and work in its Interpol liaison branch until his retirement in 1962). The GFP remains a rather shadowy organisation – loosely assigned to the Wehrmacht, many of its operatives were in fact members of the SS. The bitter struggle between Blume and Loos mirrored the tension between the two intelligence arms generally throughout occupied Europe. However, the competitive element in their relations can easily be exaggerated, for it largely reflected the personal and institutional ambitions of a few men high up in the Nazi hierarchy. At lower levels, and in the mundane business of policing the occupied territories, the SiPo/SD often worked comfortably with the GFP and the regular armed forces. The GFP usually took the lead in rural areas, where there was a heavy Wehrmacht presence, whilst the SD were based in the cities where they controlled Greek and German police units.[157]

Army intelligence officers routinely handed captured foreign commandos over to the SD; against the *andartes* too there was some overlap between the Athens SD's anti-partisan section and the military. Wehrmacht commanders were told that the SD would provide 'communists' to shoot, when the troops failed to find enough actual suspects. SD outposts became collection and delivery points for civilian hostages rounded up in lightning sweeps known colloquially as 'bloccos'. What happened in Lamia early on St George's Day, 1944, was typical of such operations: part of the town was suddenly blocked off by soldiers, and all inhabitants above fourteen years old were ordered to stand in the main square with their hands raised. SD officials checked their papers and on the advice of a hooded Greek collaborator, many people were thrown into prison. One week later thirty-five of them were taken to Levadia and shot there. Others were killed later in further reprisals.[158]

These round-ups caught guilty and innocent alike. When Blume's headquarters in Athens ordered a shooting it specified only the number of victims, not their names, for SS justice had virtually dispensed with the notion of individual guilt. 'I consulted my colleagues who had a list of names, from which we picked the correct number of persons to be shot,' recalled the former SD commander in Lamia. 'The number was usually between five and fifty – not large.' For many city-dwellers, the so-called 'bloccos' became the equivalent of reprisals for the rural population – the chief source of that unpredictable fear and insecurity which the occupation authorities aimed to sow in the minds of the civilian population. 'What I felt most of the time,' one teenager recalled later, 'was the sense of terror; not, of course, that I had actually done anything, but then were those they arrested really guilty either?'[159]

*

If there was one place in Greece where the use of terror was refined and exploited to the full it was in the SS-run camp at Haidari, several kilometres outside Athens. In part a transit camp where Italian soldiers, Jews and others were held before they were sent north out of the country, Haidari also housed prisoners awaiting interrogation at SS headquarters, as well as hundreds of hostages who were selected for mass executions. It was from Haidari, for example, that at dawn on 1 May 1944 200 hostages were taken to be shot at the firing range at Kaisariani. Though there were other camps and prisons around the country, none acquired Haidari's reputation. Nor was this accidental; from the time it was set up in September 1943, its reputation itself became an essential element of the terror system. As one Greek writer explained: 'Haidari was founded more for the benefit of those outside than the inmates. . . . It was to become widely feared, synonymous with death, and thus to enter the imagination of our vulnerable people.' Officials of the Greek War Crimes Office noted that the Germans themselves spread stories about what was happening inside Haidari as widely as possible.[160]

The camp lay on a rocky hillside off the Elefsis road, just beyond the Byzantine church at Daphni. Originally built as an army barracks, it had never been finished and lacked proper accommodation and sanitation. There were no beds and just a few threadbare blankets. Water had to be brought from Athens, and petrol shortages sometimes prevented the truck from making its deliveries. Because the drains were not emptied regularly, prisoners relieved themselves in the corridors and stairways. Food rations consisted of bread, beans and water. Prisoners were covered in lice, and those who fell ill could not expect medical attention since the only doctor in the camp lacked medicines to dispense. Only rarely were sick patients given permission to miss morning roll-call.

The prison guards punished any infringement of the camp's numerous regulations with beatings and whippings, or by unleashing their dogs. Sometimes they inflicted punishments *en masse* for no obvious reason: once, guards threw all the prisoners' belongings out of the windows, confiscated valuable items and burned the rest. As one former inmate recalled: 'It was all part of the degradation of camp life, every cruel detail, every humiliation was thought out and was there.'[161]

This was due, in no small measure, to its commandant, Sturmbannführer Paul Radomski, who had brought the murderous values of the Eastern Front to Greece. Radomski had not been in Greece long when, on 26 October 1943, a certain Constantine Vatikiotis and his wife were arrested by the SS in their central Athens apartment and sent via the Averoff prison with a batch of other inmates to Haidari. In a postwar statement, Vatikiotis describes how Radomski introduced himself to them by shooting one of the new arrivals – a Jewish army officer – on the spot:

> Upon arriving at Haidari, during the afternoon roll-call, the Governor called the interpreter and handed him a paper; he then ordered the unhappy prisoner, who stood next to me, to advance towards him. After lashing the prisoner's face with a whip, he turned to the interpreter and told him to read aloud the written order.
>
> The interpreter read as follows: 'The Governor of Haidari, Major Radomski, will personally execute before you the prisoner named Levy, for attempting to escape on the day of his arrest. Beware! The same fate awaits you in such a case.'
>
> A shudder of horror went through us all. The terrible Governor then proceeded to carry out his threat. He drew his revolver and fired at the unhappy man, who crumpled to the earth in a bloody heap. His German assassin then calmly ordered us to remove him. But, before we had had time to lift the man, the Governor fell upon us and began to lash at us with his whip. Then, tearing his victim out of our hands, he fired at him once more and ordered us to remove the man's shoes. They were new, and consequently, a good prize.[162]

The purpose of such actions, as a team of Greek psychologists pointed out after the war, was not to punish those responsible for offences, nor to prevent further crimes. The aims of the terror system – throughout occupied Europe – were more far-reaching: to extinguish the will and the imagination of the subject population. Hence, the conditions in the camp and the behaviour of the guards were designed to put the inmates in constant fear of their lives.[163]

Few prisoners lasted in Haidari for long. Many were brought in following one of the road-blocks in Athens, and were transported to Germany as forced labourers. Others were sent back to the SS building in Merlin Street for interrogation, and either died there, or collapsed as a result of their injuries when they returned to Haidari. Some went mad, their nerves frayed by loneliness, boredom and fear of execution: they either killed themselves, or were killed by the guards. All inmates were liable to be shot as hostages, and the names of those selected were usually called out at morning roll-call. But sometimes an extra roll-call took place, and sometimes the authorities pretended that those whose names had been called out were to be released. Old hands learned that prisoners taken to Block 15 were destined for execution, while others, who passed through Block 21, still had some chance of survival as they were to be used as human shields in the steel cages that the Germans fixed to the front of their trains to prevent them being blown up by the *andartes*. Vatikiotis reckoned that about 2,000 prisoners, including 25 women, were executed as hostages while he was at Haidari. He himself worked for several months in a storeroom, packing items raided from Greek homes and sorting out the clothes of the men who had been shot.

When he was released it was with as little explanation as when he had been arrested. In his entire time at Haidari he was never once interrogated about his supposed crimes. Justice in the terror system operated purely demonstratively, for effect: in Haidari, as during the 'bloccos', the question of individual guilt or innocence had become all but irrelevant.[164]

Men of the SS

The guards at Haidari were brutal and sadistic. Soldiers who manned the trucks that drove prisoners into the camp gleefully pointed out the skull and crossbones above the main gate. Officers used whips and set their Alsatians on the inmates; they swore and shouted at them incessantly and devised tortures to humiliate them. They were particularly cruel to prisoners who had been selected for execution as hostages. On one occasion, according to Vatikiotis, they spent the night with a group of one hundred inmates who were to be shot the next day, jeering at them with the words 'Morgen kaputt!' Then they beat their victims as they harried them on to the trucks that would take them to the firing squad.

Most of these guards were middle-aged Volksdeutsche, family

men in their mid-twenties or early thirties, who had been recruited belatedly into the Waffen-SS in Hungary and Romania. Neither they – nor by 1944 the SS generally – could be said to represent any sort of Aryan elite. When Himmler's bureaucrats belatedly thought to check on their credentials, it transpired that few of them had brought their green passes of racial authentication. The official from Blume's bureau who went round making enquiries heard time and again that they had 'left it at home'. Instead they showed him documents which had been issued by their local German Volk Association in some small town in central Europe, a much less reliable guide to racial purity in the eyes of the RSHA.[165]

Such men were anything but enthusiasts for the Third Reich. They felt little commitment to the Nazi *Weltanschauung*, and knew that they would occupy no central place in the *Volksgemeinschaft*, the racial community, that Hitler promised. It may be that the racial marginality of these men and their suspicion that Germans from the 'Old Reich' looked down upon them fuelled their brutality towards camp inmates. But to reduce the guards' behaviour to an expression of their own personal humiliations ignores the fact that the organisation they served was deliberately designed to make them act as they did. The decisive role was played by their superiors, and these were almost always Reich Germans.[166] Radomski, for example, had nothing to learn from Hungarian Volksdeutsch where brutality was concerned. It would be fairer to say that the camp commander set the tone for his men.

The stocky, uneducated Radomski had a violent past stretching back many years: fatherless from a young age, he had been one of the 'first Hamburg SS men', fighting Leftists on the streets alongside Himmler's future deputy Reinhard Heydrich – or so he claimed. He had served a prison sentence during the Weimar Republic for his part in the murder of a left-wing opponent, and was an early recruit into the SS, with an exceptionally low SS membership number. With such a background he was well qualified for the killing fields of the East, where he served at a POW camp in Stettin and then, on Heydrich's personal orders, as an SD commander in Kiev, before travelling south. In 1942, shortly before taking up the Kiev post, he was described in glowing terms by his superiors as 'always ready for action, energetic and made of iron'.

This judgement, however, was to be radically revised, for in Greece Radomski's penchant for violence eventually ran so far out of control that it led to his dismissal. The reason, needless to say, had nothing to do with his treatment of the inmates. On 17 February 1944, after drunken birthday carousing with several other officers, he lost all self-control, and in a moment of rage threatened to shoot his own adjutant for mislaying his room keys. 'You'll not see your family again, I'm going to shoot you!', he screamed at the man as other officers stood by.[167]

Having committed the serious error of mistreating a fellow-SS man, Radomski was suspended from duty and brought before an SS tribunal, which rather belatedly now assessed him as a 'very primitive man, without any education or suitability for leadership'. The judge, SS-Sturmbannführer Wehser, described him unequivocally as 'primitive in all his thoughts and feelings'. Radomski's ill-treatment of the prisoners in Haidari had no bearing on the tribunal's deliberations. For the crime of mistreating a subordinate he was sentenced to six months' imprisonment. However, the six months he had served for a political killing in 1932 were put to his credit, and allowed to cancel out his current sentence. He was simply demoted and placed under a three-year alcohol ban, before being assigned by Eichmann's office to Riga, where his trail peters out. At Haidari he was replaced as commandant by an Austrian officer called Lieutenant Fischer, who appears to have soon become equally feared and hated by the inmates.[168]

*

Radomski's constant violence, drunkenness and insensate rages certainly bear out the image of the typical SS man brought away by the inmates of Haidari and other concentration camps. But to focus on the sadists and mass killers is to misunderstand the dynamics of the terror system. This, after all, was run by senior SD officials who sat in their offices, proud of their professionalism, their education and their bureaucratic expertise – qualities they combined with a fervent belief in the chilling values of the Nazi state.

To a large extent, the SS in the occupied territories was simply following the prewar policing methods of the Third Reich; many in the SiPo/SD apparatus in Greece were civil servants first and Nazi supporters second, who had successfully exploited the career opportunities offered by the Nazi seizure of power and the expansion of political policing in the 1930s. Kriminalrat Hans Dörhage, for example, the first head of the Athens SiPo/SD, had enjoyed a secure but uneventful career in the Weimar police until his Nazi sympathies propelled him upwards through the ranks of the Gestapo after 1933.[169] Most of his colleagues only joined the SS long after they had embarked on careers in the secret police. At the same time, though, even if they were slow to join the Nazis, many held extreme right-wing views. Dörhage and several other SD officers in Greece had fought in nationalist militias in the early 1920s before their police careers began.[170]

In thirty-eight-year-old Dr Walter Blume, the last head of the SiPo/SD in Greece, this combination of professionalism and strong support for Nazi ideals reached its apogee. Blume's father had been a teacher, and he himself had a doctorate in law. Unlike his colleagues in Greece, he had travelled widely as a young man. In the spring of 1933, when the Nazis took power, Blume, who was then just twenty-six, won his spurs by acting as political inspector of the police in Dortmund, his home town. In other words, he participated in the initial Nazification of the police force, and not unnaturally began working in the Gestapo as soon as it was set up on a national basis. By the end of the 1930s the young chain-smoking lawyer with the 'strong, brutal face' was a high-flying SS bureaucrat at the RSHA in Berlin.[171]

At the start of the invasion of Russia he was ordered to the Eastern Front as commander of Sonderkommando 7a, one of the SS killing squads which operated in the rear areas. He had been personally informed by Heydrich, Himmler's deputy, that he and the ninety-one men he commanded had a single task – to carry out what he would later describe as the *Judenvernichtungsbefehl*, the order to exterminate the Jews. Heydrich made it clear to him that this was on Hitler's orders. Several of the Einsatzgruppen, which were responsible for the deaths of hundreds of thousands of people, were led by men like Blume – highly educated lawyers, academics and economists. Sonderkommando 7a was not the most efficient of these squads, and Blume stayed in command for only one and a half months. In that time, however, it drove through White Russia and killed almost a thousand civilians, most of them Jews. Blume himself shot an unspecified number of victims at point-blank range with his revolver. He appears to have been recalled to Berlin because of his reluctance to shoot women and children, and this led to him acquiring a reputation among his fellow-SS officers for being 'weak and bureaucratic'. By the time he arrived in Greece he had first-hand experience of how far SS men were expected to go in the war against partisans, communists and Jews.[172]

For all his experiences with Sonderkommando 7a, Blume was devoted to Hitler; it would hardly be an exaggeration to say he worshipped him. Even after the war he regarded the Führer as a man who 'had a great mission for the German people'.[173] In Athens his men termed him a 'dogged bloodhound' – a ruthless, unimaginative but highly efficient administrator, who would go to any lengths to carry out his orders. Yet he was not a sadist like some of the men he commanded, nor does he appear to have derived pleasure from the physical act of killing. According to one of his junior officers who served under him in Athens, the blue-eyed, blond-haired Blume made 'an extremely correct and serious impression. I know of absolutely no lack of correctness on his part.'[174]

Blume's 'Chaos Thesis'

Only at the very end of the occupation did the dour commander of the SiPo/SD lose his grip, and here it was perhaps a case of the logic of the terror system defeating itself. Blume's fall from grace came over the issue of how the Germans should withdraw from Greece: should they follow a scorched-earth policy and leave the country in turmoil, or try to negotiate with the Allies for as smooth a departure as possible? Blume, needless to say, favoured the first course, but on a scale that beggars the imagination. Influenced perhaps by earlier SS policy in Poland, in the summer of 1944 he began to talk about the so-called 'Chaos Thesis': not only should the departing Germans blow up factories, docks and other installations; they should also arrest and execute the entire political leadership of Greece – leaving the country in a state of total anarchy.

By this point, with an Allied landing only months away, those Greek politicians serving the Axis were increasingly tense, suspicious and uncertain of themselves. The Rallis government was close to collapse. Rallis himself quarrelled violently with his own Vice-Premier, who had accused him of watching Greece slide into civil war. On 31 July he also lost his temper with the newly appointed Minister for National Defence, forcing him to leave a cabinet meeting amid a hail of curses. The Axis authorities were wondering whether to oust him, but while some planned to form a government of royalists – on the grounds that this was traditionally the most pro-German faction in Greek politics – others were thinking of turning to a core of hardline anti-communist republicans, loyal to General Pangalos.[175]

In this nervous and unstable atmosphere the extremism of the 'Chaos Thesis' led to a serious rift between Blume and the Foreign Office. Formerly, the powerful figure of Hermann Neubacher had supported Blume in his work; Neubacher had even urged the SS in Berlin to expand his anti-communist activities. In return, Blume had apparently been sensitive to Neubacher's diplomatic goals in Greece. However, some people had long suspected that the 'strongly bureaucratic' Blume was 'not elastic enough' for Greece, and events were to confirm these fears.[176]

The 'Chaos Thesis' evolved against the backdrop of the anti-communist sweeps of the Athens suburbs, which at Blume's behest were taking place regularly in the spring and summer of 1944. These incredibly brutal operations did nothing to quell the resistance, and indeed street fighting in Athens intensified. Now, in addition to protesting at the politically harmful impact of anti-partisan operations in rural areas, Neubacher became more and more opposed to such random sweeps. In July he protested at Blume's plans to seize the entire able-bodied male population of certain quarters of Athens for labour in Germany: such actions, according to Neubacher, would inevitably lead the population to flee to the guerrillas; he preferred the more discriminating and difficult task of trying to track down the communist leadership. But to Neubacher's dismay, the round-ups continued, and when he visited Athens in August after an absence of several months he was shocked at how far public order had deteriorated.[177]

Worse still, Blume now planned to imprison any Greek politician suspected of having links with the exile government. To Neubacher, this seemed doubly idiotic. First, he hoped to make use of such contacts in pursuit of his plans to gain Allied co-operation in a joint campaign against the Soviet Union and EAM/ELAS: 'Today we are the sole obstacle in Greece to the revolutionary success of Soviet policy against British interests in the Mediterreanean,' he noted at this time. Second, as he put it quite accurately: 'all Greek politicians, with a few exceptions, are to be suspected of direct or indirect contact with the exile government'. For Neubacher, the question of their feelings towards the British was irrelevant so long as their fear of EAM/ELAS led them to work alongside the Germans. Blume's clumsy tactics would alienate Anglophile moderates, strengthen the Left and complicate the Germans' eventual withdrawal from Greece.[178]

Blume simply ignored Neubacher's objections, however, and at the end of July a number of the most prominent Greek politicians were imprisoned in Haidari. Those the SD arrested included the elderly Liberal Sofoulis, and even Archbishop Damaskinos was put under house arrest. When German diplomats protested, Blume replied that the politicians would be released only if there was no new evidence against them of anti-Axis activity. He added – and he may have been right – that he was simply carrying out his instructions from Gestapo HQ in Berlin. But Neubacher's representative commented in alarm that 'we should concentrate on fighting against real communists, rather than using terror operations like imprisonment, deportation and even the liquidation of bourgeois, nationalist figures'. As time ran out, and rumours reached his office that executions were imminent, Neubacher was forced to abandon his effort to reason with Blume; instead, he simply reasserted his prerogative in all political matters. Writing from Belgrade on 4 September, the Reich Special Plenipotentiary for the South-East sent a stiff and unambiguous message to Athens: 'Blume knows he must coordinate his operations absolutely with the military authorities and my office. I prohibit terror- and "chaos" operations against the anti-communist front.' He closed by reminding Blume that he had Hitler's backing.[179]

What finally brought Blume to a halt and led to the abandonment of the 'Chaos Thesis' was – in addition to Neubacher's unwavering opposition – the Wehrmacht's decision to declare the whole of Greece a 'combat zone' in September 1944. After being told to release the politicians held in Haidari, Blume was eventually ordered to leave Greece by Neubacher's friend Kaltenbrunner, and security duties were transferred back from the SD to the military. The Gestapo were reined in, and the military and the diplomats reasserted themselves. On 7 September a meeting in Athens chaired by General Löhr agreed to scrap the 'so-called political Chaos Thesis'. This, according to one of the diplomats involved, had referred to 'the view that for the period after our eventual withdrawal we should create political chaos through the removal of broad layers of the leadership'. Greece's shaken politicians returned home to recover. At the very end of the occupation, the worst excesses of the terror system had been curbed, but only because more realistic men than Blume – inside and outside the SS – had recognised that a German defeat was now inevitable.[180]

CHAPTER NINETEEN

Greek Jewry and the Final Solution

In 1943 and 1944 tiny teams of SS 'specialists' succeeded in sending tens of thousands of Greek Jews to the death camps. They could not have managed this enormous task by themselves. The Wehrmacht and the Foreign Office assisted them, and in some cases anticipated their wishes or carried out their own anti-Semitic initiatives. Scholars who view the Third Reich's war machine as beset by bureaucratic rivalries, anarchy and infighting underestimate the extent to which different German agencies did manage to work together on issues of ideological importance. While the Italians and the Greeks were disgusted by Nazi racial policy against the Jews, and even tried to oppose it, the SS, the Wehrmacht and the Foreign Office – with a few noteworthy exceptions – appear to have shared a broadly similar outlook, and worked alongside one another with chilling efficiency.[181]

*

German diplomats in Greece were passing information about the Jewish communities there back to the SS in Berlin at least as early as 1938. When the war broke out, the regime's 'Jewish experts' had a fairly clear picture of the size and character of Greek Jewry. They knew, for example, that the community overall numbered between 70,000 and 80,000, and that the population itself was mixed. On the one hand, there were small communities of highly assimilated Romaniot Jews, whose first language was Greek, living in the Ionian islands, Athens and central Greece. These were among the most ancient Jewish settlements in Europe, dating back to before Byzantine times. Overshadowing them numerically and politically were later arrivals, the Sephardic Jews, who had settled in northern Greece after their expulsion from Spain in 1492 and still spoke a strain of medieval Spanish known as Ladino. Under Ottoman rule the port of Salonika had become virtually a Jewish city. Even after its absorption into the Greek state in 1912, it remained one of the leading centres of European Jewry.[182]

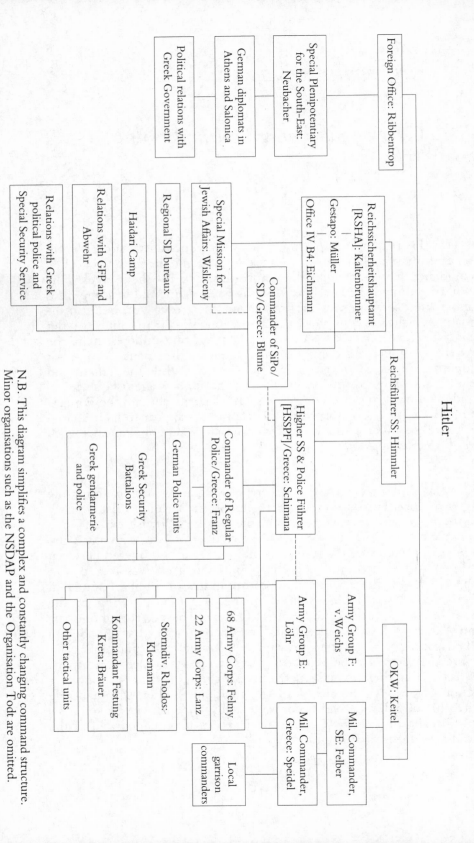

German Authorities in Greece, late 1943

N.B. This diagram simplifies a complex and constantly changing command structure. Minor organisations such as the NSDAP and the Organisation Todt are omitted.

40. Pre-war Jewish life: Members of the cast of a Purim play taken in Chalkis, 1928.

The information obtained by the Foreign Office was put to use as soon as the occupation began. In 1940 Hitler instructed the regime's chief ideologue, Alfred Rosenberg, to seize 'all scientific and archival materials of the ideological foe' for a new institute to be established in Frankfurt to educate the German people about the Jews. First Rosenberg plundered the cultural treasures of French Jewry; then came the turn of Greece. On 23 April 1941 Rosenberg informed Bormann, Hitler's private secretary, that his team was already in the Balkans, enjoying the full support of the army and the SD. In Greece, local military commanders issued orders to their troops instructing them to assist the so-called Rosenberg Sonderkommandos. Between May and November a unit of more than thirty officers and German academics scoured the country, visiting no less than forty-nine synagogues, clubs, associations, schools, banks, newspapers, bookshops and hospitals as well as over sixty individual homes. Archives, synagogue ornaments, manuscripts, incunabula and priceless collections of rabbinical judgments were taken. Two years later, the director of Rosenberg's new 'Library for Exploration

237

of the Jewish Question' boasted proudly that among his 500,000 volumes was a collection of 10,000 books and manuscripts from Greece. 'In the New Order of European Organisation,' he predicted, *the* library for the Jewish Question, not only for Europe but for the world, will arise in Frankfurt.'[183]

However, the Rosenberg raids were the first and last unified Nazi operations carried out against Jews throughout the whole of Greece. After the country was split up among the Axis powers, the fate of Jewish communities in different regions diverged sharply. Once the Italians took over most of the mainland in June, all further persecution of the Jews there ceased, and the Italian authorities successfully resisted German attempts to introduce anti-Semitic measures. The Germans were forced to go ahead with preparations for the Final Solution in the regions they controlled, and this meant, in the first place, Salonika – known proudly to its Jewish inhabitants as the 'Mother of Israel'.

Salonika, 1941–43

In the first weeks of the occupation in Salonika, the Germans closed down Jewish newspapers, and encouraged local anti-semites to paste anti-Jewish notices on cafés, tavernas and shops. The SS resurrected an anti-Semitic republican political movement called EEE (National Union of Greece) which Metaxas had dissolved in the 1930s. Jewish families were turned out of their homes to make way for German lodgers. Some properties were actually expropriated, and rabbis were publicly humiliated, while the Rosenberg Kommando ransacked the community's treasures. In the months that followed, a number of Jews were arrested, and several were shot as 'communists'. For over a year, however, nothing occurred to give any indication of what was to follow.[184]

The first public action against the Jews *en masse*, after a long period of anti-Semitic campaigns in the local press, did not take place until July 1942, when the Wehrmacht commander of northern Greece, General von Krenzski, announced that he had decided to mobilise the city's Jewish population for civilian labour, and ordered the male Jews of the town to gather in Eleftheria (Freedom) Square on 11 July to register. Whether this was actually von Krenzski's idea or a move suggested by the local SD remains unclear.[185]

At dawn on the appointed day, the men went to receive their work cards. It turned out that they were to be deliberately humiliated. Crowds gathered to watch the spectacle. Surrounded by armed

41. Jewish men are publicly humiliated and forced to do physical drills by German soldiers during the forced registration in Salonika, 11 July 1942.

soldiers, almost 10,000 men were kept standing in the sun for hours. They were forbidden to wear hats – forcing them to contravene religious custom (it was a Saturday) – and some eventually collapsed in the heat. German soldiers kicked and beat them or doused them in cold water. Some were forced to do physical exercises until they were exhausted. Military personnel snapped photos of the scene while Greek civilians watched from their balconies. Actors and actresses visiting the city with the army's theatrical agency, 'Strength through Joy', applauded the entertainment the army had laid on.[186]

At the end of the day the men were released. They were deeply shocked, and many had suffered physical injury. But they had just begun to recover when they were ordered to report for work on the roads and airfields that were being constructed in Macedonia for the Wehrmacht. Rations were pitiful – 100 grams of bread and some cabbage soup – and many of the workers contracted dysentery. Swollen feet, sunstroke and malaria were common ailments. Not even frequent beatings could force men to work productively in such conditions. When the community elders decided to try to buy their way out of the mobilisation decree, they found a ready response from the German army. By October, after several weeks of bargaining, a deal was struck: 7,000 Jewish workers were released upon payment of a massive sum, which was only raised as a result of contributions from Jewish communities outside the city.[187]

Any relief, however, that Salonika's Jews felt as their menfolk

239

came home was to be short-lived. In December the Germans began to demolish the great Jewish cemetery which lay on the eastern side of the city, and used the ancient tombstones for roads and fortifications. Families frantically searched for the remains of their dead relatives, and tried in vain to halt the destruction. But within several weeks, wrote an eyewitness, 'the vast necropolis, scattered with fragments of stone and rubbish, resembled a city that had been bombed, or destroyed by a volcanic eruption'.[188]

*

Throughout the last months of 1942, the Germans had been trying with a signal lack of success to persuade the Italian authorities in Athens to consider deporting the Jews from their zone. As it became obvious that the Italians were unwilling to agree, SS-Sturmbannführer Adolf Eichmann decided not to wait any longer to make the German zone 'free of Jews'. He sent an aide on a preliminary visit to Salonika and selected one of his most trusted 'experts', Dieter Wisliceny, to take charge of the whole operation. The deportation of the 50,000 Jews of Salonika, he told Wisliceny, was to be completed within six to eight weeks.

Wisliceny had worked together with Eichmann for many years and was on close terms with him. During 1942 Eichmann had sent him to organise the deportation of Slovak Jewry to Auschwitz, and to smooth over any diplomatic problems with the Slovak authorities. Slovak Jews were among the first to be gassed at Auschwitz, and it is possible that at first Wisliceny was ignorant of the precise fate that awaited his victims. In June of that year, however, he had visited Eichmann in Berlin; for the first time – according to his postwar confession – he now learned of an order 'which directed the annihilation of all Jews'. To his interrogators at Nuremberg in 1946, he described how Eichmann went to his safe and took out an order from Himmler which indicated that 'the Führer had ordered the final solution of the Jewish question'. Eichmann then explained to Wisliceny that 'the planned biological annihilation of the Jewish race in the Eastern Territories was disguised by the concept and wording "final solution".' 'It was perfectly clear to me,' Wisliceny admitted at Nuremberg, 'that this order spelled death to millions of people.' By the time he went to Salonika, Wisliceny was fully aware of the fate that awaited his victims.[189]

'The thick-set Wisliceny,' wrote the rather gentle Errikos Sevillias, who saw him in action and suffered at his hands, 'at first glance appeared to be a polite school teacher or a clerk, especially when he wore civilian clothes. When he became angry, however, he acted cruelly and even kicked. The SS, with its rich experience, had no pity or humanity. For years they had been doing the same work, and a peculiar expression was printed on their faces.'[190]

Together with his colleague, the sadistic Alois Brunner, Wisliceny arrived in Salonika in early February 1943. There he contacted Dr Max Merten, the head of the city's military administration. What was the division of responsibility between the SS team, led by Wisliceny and Brunner, and the Wehrmacht, represented by Merten? Even today the issue is far from clear. Without a doubt, the impetus for the deportations came from the SS: if many of the orders were actually signed by Merten, they were drawn up by Eichmann's representatives. But the Wehrmacht in Salonika was not simply the SS's reluctant accomplice. In an effort to prepare the ground for the SS, none other than *Generaloberst* Löhr had tried in December 1942 to persuade his Italian opposite number, General Carlo Geloso, to permit the Jews to be deported from the Italian zone. And we have already seen that orders for the labour mobilisation that July had come from General von Krenzski himself. Few people would now sympathise with his argument that he had been motivated not by 'some sort of hatred for the Jews' but – on strategic grounds – 'by the very poor roads of northern Greece'. Like von Krenzski, Merten too turned out to be attentive to ways in which the deportation of tens of thousands of Jews could be turned to the advantage of the German authorities. His assistance was essential for the success of Wisliceny's mission, and Wisliceny himself commented later that 'the action in Salonika never could have taken place without the close participation of the military administration'.[191]

Wisliceny and Brunner moved ahead very rapidly. Shortly after their arrival the German-controlled press launched another violent attack on the Jewish community. At the same time the Jews were instructed via their rabbis to abandon certain quarters in the centre of the city. At least 6,000 families were affected: the keys to their apartments were handed over to the German authorities, and they were forced to find new lodgings. Several large ghettos were constructed for their confinement. From 15 February the Jews were subjected to a special curfew, whilst ten days later they were ordered to wear the yellow star, inscribed 'Jude' and 'Evraios' in German and Greek. Conversations with non-Jews were forbidden. The whole battery of Nazi anti-Semitic legislation was being brought to bear on the community to isolate it from the rest of the city.

On 25 February the Italian consul Zamboni learned that 'within the next few days measures will be taken against the Jews which are much more severe than those already taken'. Two days later Merten told him privately that the ghettos would house the Jews only temporarily, before they were transported to Poland. The front

42. A rare shot of Jews being deported, place unknown.

page of *Apoyevmatini*, a German-controlled Greek paper, carried an editorial on 27 February entitled simply – 'Get Rid of Them!'[192]

In early March Wisliceny notified Chief Rabbi Koretz that Eichmann wanted the entire community to be deported. Koretz was deeply shaken, and begged Wisliceny to use his influence to halt the process. He suggested instead using the Jews as labourers within Greece for this was the period when the Germans were finding it difficult to enforce their civil mobilisation decree among the rest of the Greek population. But not for the first time ideological considerations were put before economic rationality. Koretz's pleas failed to sway Eichmann, who instructed his officials to proceed with the deportations. Once a German police unit arrived from Belgrade, the train transports to the north began. The German consul in Salonika, who had been monitoring local Jewry since before the war, informed Berlin on 15 March that the first transport of 2,600 people had already left the city.[193]

Koretz now made one last desperate effort to halt the deportations. Despite having been warned by Wisliceny and Brunner not to contact any Greek politicians, he managed to see Ioannis Rallis, who visited Salonika in early April shortly after becoming Prime

Minister. As he was ushered in to meet Rallis, the rabbi's nerves gave way and he broke down in tears. He begged the Prime Minister to intervene with the German authorities 'so that the community which had existed for two thousand years in Salonika would not be liquidated'. Rallis told Koretz that he was in no position to help. As a result of this meeting, Koretz was interrogated by a furious Wisliceny, and placed under house arrest. The Greek government expressed its unease to the Germans, but was unable to stop the deportations.[194]

*

Itzchak Nehamas was a thirty-three-year-old Jewish businessman whose experiences mirrored the fate of his community. After fighting as a medical orderly in the Greek army in Albania, he returned home in 1941. In July 1942 he was among the men forced to stand in Freedom Square, and was beaten severely. By the spring of 1943 he had survived a spell working as a labourer for the Germans, and an outbreak of typhus in his apartment building. But at 6 o'clock one morning in April, shortly after quarantine restrictions had been lifted, he was visited by an SS officer who ordered him and his wife to report to the Baron Hirsch camp in half an hour. Nehamas immediately rang the local Greek police commander and sought his help, but after a brief discussion with the Germans, the police officer told him that they would have to go.[195]

When they arrived in the Hirsch camp they found it in uproar. Adjacent streets were crowded with newcomers clutching their belongings in sacks – they had been forbidden to carry cases. Greek and German police shouted out orders and beat people indiscriminately. Inside, the camp was dirty and disorganised. Normally, the Hirsch district housed 2,000 people or so; now it contained 8,000 to 10,000, herded together in range of the machine-guns placed opposite the main gate. The inmates were mocked by soldiers, policemen and Jewish camp guards alike. After a night under the floodlights, Nehamas and his wife were ordered to an office where they were made to change all their gold and other currencies for zlotys. Officials told them that they were being sent to Poland to form a Jewish state. They were given receipts, and told to cash them when they arrived. (Their money in fact went into an account at the National Bank of Greece which was placed at the disposal of Merten's office.)

They were marched to the siding, and crammed into a freight car together with seventy-six other people. Nehamas does not mention whether anybody died during the journey. In the crowded, fetid, insanitary conditions deaths inevitably occurred. But he says that of the seventy-eight people in his wagon, only ten survived the war. His wife was killed in Auschwitz; so were his parents, who had been deported two weeks before him, and his brother.

The majority of Salonika's Jews were deported between 15 March 1943 and the beginning of June, although the last transport left in early August. Almost all were destined for Auschwitz. The records of Auschwitz-Birkenau show that 48,974 Jews arrived there from northern Greece; of these, 37,386 were immediately gassed. Hardly any of the remainder returned home. According to Michael Molho, fewer than 2,000 Jews lived in Salonika in 1947.[196]

*

What then did people know about the fate of the Jews? The German-run Greek press on 9 November 1942 had actually headlined Hitler's claim that 'international Judaism will disappear from Europe'. Few people can have taken the Führer at his word. But in the ranks of the Wehrmacht and the German police units serving in northern Greece were men who had been involved in shooting Jews and gypsies in Serbia in 1941–42. Some of them may have known about the use of gas-vans to kill Jews in Serbia. And suspicion about German intentions had arisen more widely.[197]

In two written protests that Greek political leaders sent in March 1943 the signatories raised the fear that the Jews were destined for 'extermination'.[198] In Berlin, similar fears were highlighted in a remarkable conversation between a senior Foreign Office official and a Spanish diplomat. Discussing the vexed question of the return of Spanish Jews from Salonika, the Spaniard remarked that while his country could accept that Jews with Spanish citizenship might have to be removed from Salonika on 'security grounds', it could not stand by and see 'Spanish citizens being liquidated in Polish camps'. Legationsrat and SS-Obersturmführer Eberhard von Thadden must have been taken aback at such plain speaking. 'I answered,' he noted in a subsequent memorandum, 'that one could not talk about "liquidation", even if enemy atrocity-propaganda was making much of such goings-on.' Concerned at mounting international unease, the Foreign Office alerted officials in Greece in July that when the Spanish Jews were deported to the transit camp of Bergen-Belsen they should not be treated in the 'customary way', to avoid 'any opportunity for atrocity propaganda'.[199]

Meanwhile, the Italians were under no illusions about the dangers facing the Jews and did what they could to help. Aware of their opposition to the deportations, hundreds of Jews fled to the Italian zone, with the courageous assistance of Italian diplomats and soldiers. The Germans had closed down all the other consulates in

Salonika in November 1942, so Zamboni, the Italian consul, found himself in a position of unique importance. De Maricourt, the French chargé d'affaires in Athens, appealed to the Vichy government for backing to protect French nationals in a similar fashion. On 6 April he sought authority 'to save at the eleventh hour from an atrocious deportation our Israelite subjects from Salonica (about a dozen families), including several ex-veterans and invalids from the Great War'. But he received no answer from Vichy, which was already co-operating with the Gestapo in France, and he was unable to do anything for his co-nationals.[200]

In Salonika itself, the brutal behaviour of the Germans during the deportations alarmed observers. A well-informed Italian onlooker thought it cast 'a sinister shadow on the events of this war'. With time, suspicion increased. The Italians gave the Germans a list of people whom they wanted returned from Poland: these included eighty-three-year-old Mazaltov Massarano ('Star number: 27878'), Sunhula Saadi, who was eighty-five, and sixty-four-year-old Isaaco Errera, who was blind and lame. The inclusion of such elderly people in the deportations showed up the duplicity behind the Germans' official excuse that they were carrying out the operation on grounds of military security. By late 1943 virtually nothing had been heard from Poland; a Jewish escapee from Salonika left Greece in December convinced that the Germans planned to exterminate the deportees. After all, those deported included blind and maimed war victims, former inmates of lunatic asylums, and even people over ninety years old. In his opinion, 'some of the stories current about mass killings are undoubtedly true'. Another Greek Jew, who managed to escape from Athens to Istanbul in August 1943, told a friend there that Salonika's Jews had been deported 'to the slaughter-house'.[201]

The Greek train drivers who drove some of the transports as far as Belgrade also saw enough to alarm them. The novelist Giorgios Ioannou, who witnessed the deportations as a schoolboy in Salonika, remembered his father returning home distraught after one of these journeys:

Late one night we heard sobbing in the kitchen. My father had returned. . . . He was depressed and exhausted, but more than anything else, miserable. He asked to see my young brother, who was then 3 or 4. We woke him up and carried him into the kitchen. He had been asked to drive a train with Jews right into Serbia and had seen terrible things with his own eyes. The Jews had already begun to die. The Germans stopped the train at a quiet spot – they had their plan. From inside, the Jews shouted and beat the wooden sides. Packed in as they were, they could not breathe, and they had no water. The Germans, guns in hand, began opening the wagons, not however for the benefit of the Jews, but to steal their hidden jewellery, watches and coins. There was much crying. From one wagon they threw out a young boy dead, and laid him – without of course burying him – in the ditch alongside the tracks. It seems he looked like my brother. As my father looked out from the engine, they threw him a handful of watches.[202]

'This Stupendous Problem'

Jewish houses, apartments, shops and factories were not left abandoned for long. Under German pressure the community's elders had drawn up a register of almost 2,000 commercial premises, and even before the first train left Salonika, German administrators began disposing of the property. On 7 March Dr Merten contacted the Governor-General for Macedonia, Vasilis Simonides, and instructed him to set up an office to find Greek 'custodians' for Jewish businesses.[203] Simonides handed the task over to Elias Douros, the director of the city's branch of the National Mortgage Bank.[204]

Firing could be heard most nights on the streets of the deserted Jewish quarters as vacant properties were looted under the eyes of the police. Douros complained bitterly of a 'complete collapse of law and order'. Policemen were taking bribes to stand aside while shops were ransacked. German soldiers were also helping themselves. When Douros's staff started valuing the properties and their contents, they too pilfered goods. In the end, only one-third of the 1,898 premises on Douros's list were ever inventoried.

Applications from would-be 'caretakers' of the properties were considered by a special committee, which met in the spacious hall of the Chamber of Commerce. Its members included the president of the Chamber himself, bankers, and civil servants charged with looking after refugee interests.[205] But Merten and the SD kept a close eye on their recommendations and often attended the committee's sessions. They put forward the names of their own nominees, and expected these to be accepted. The way was open for corruption on a vast scale. Greek refugees in genuine hardship were ignored, whilst the relatives of committee members or collaborators profited. A Secret Field Police contact, Nikolaos K., related to one of the city's leading businessmen, was assigned a Jewish haberdashery at 44 Egnatias Street; George Poulos, who ran anti-communist squads for the SD, took over the jewellery business formerly owned by Isaac and Chaim Boton on Mitropoleos Street, and immediately sold off the contents. The city's most notorious anti-Semite, Laskaris Papanaum, who had offered his services to virtually every German bureau in Salonika, was awarded two tanneries for his pains. Douros's office protested at this favour to 'a bad Greek' – 'the beast of Salonika' – but Merten tried to appease them by explaining that he was obliged to co-operate 'even with these scoundrels'.[206]

By the summer, tensions between Douros and his German supervisors were running high. Douros resented the constant interference of the military administration and the SD: out of 300 new contracts, around 250 had been made at the command of the German authorities. For their part, the Germans were irritated whenever Douros reminded them that legally the new occupants were only in temporary possession of their premises, and had no right to sell off the contents. Relations deteriorated so far that German officials threatened Douros's staff with imprisonment. On 28 July Douros himself was arrested by one of Merten's subordinates who drunkenly waved a gun in his face. Merten was apologetic, but Douros had been warned. Shortly after, he submitted his resignation; it was not accepted.[207]

Though the official Service for the Disposal of Jewish Property remained in existence through the war, it was little more than an empty shell. The real power lay with Max Merten and the local Wehrmacht administration. Long after the Jews had been deported, and Wisliceny's SS unit had left Salonika, Merten's office was still 'distributing' Jewish properties. Transactions were smoothed by payment of the appropriate fee – 100 million drachmas, for example, in the case of A.G. Nathan's furniture shop – payable in monthly instalments to a bank account specified by Merten himself. The abandoned properties had been turned into a gigantic financial racket, enriching collaborators and Germans alike.[208]

Taking advantage of his contacts with the Abwehr, a casino owner called Nikolaides bought up the Hirsch camp on the cheap, demolished its buildings and sold off the land to contractors. The same thing happened elsewhere in the city: synagogues, community offices and libraries, which might have housed thousands of the refugees from Thrace, were levelled. New 'owners' of abandoned Jewish property knocked down walls and dug into the foundations looking for jewels and valuables which they were convinced were hidden there. No wonder that a Greek civil servant, reporting on conditions in Salonika to the Ministry of the Interior in Athens in October 1943, found the treatment of Jewish property alarming and scandalous. The housing shortage in the city, he noted, remained acute, though it should have been alleviated by the apartments the Jews had vacated. Most of these, however, had become uninhabitable following the plundering of their wall and floor materials. Many houses had been levelled, and their materials sold off to contractors. 'My personal impressions of the general treatment of this stupendous problem are sorrowful,' he wrote.[209]

The Germans themselves used a synagogue to stable their horses, and blew up others. By Liberation only one out of more than thirty synagogues in the city remained relatively undamaged. Following the demolition of the cemetery, Jewish tombstones were used for building. 'People still walk on gravestones in streets and courtyards,' wrote a visitor to Greece in April 1945. It is sad to record that almost fifty years later this remains true. In modern Thessaloniki, Ottoman Jewish tablets can still be seen set into walls; on the pavement Hebrew inscriptions are trodden underfoot. In the courtyard of Agios Dimitrios, one of the finest Byzantine churches in the Balkans, boys kick their footballs against an untended pile of marble tombstones.[210]

Few houses survive which bear any trace of their former Jewish owners. But on Tsimiski Street, in the city centre, Molho's bookshop still testifies to the cultural importance of the Jewish community in Greek life. And then there is the small *fin-de-siècle* villa, originally the home of a bourgeois Jewish family, which is sandwiched between postwar blocks of flats in a residential suburb on the way out to the airport. The empty house with its courtyard and abandoned garden is almost invisible behind the iron fencing and barbed wire that surround it. The busy life of the city goes on outside. There is nothing to indicate that it was here, in Via Belisario, that Dieter Wisliceny stayed for several fateful months fifty years ago.

In the Italian Zone, 1943–44

The Italians were completely opposed to the German policy towards the Jews. Both General Geloso and plenipotentiary Ghigi rebuffed their German colleagues' suggestions that they should adopt similar measures in the Italian zone to those adopted in the north. Zamboni, the Italian consul in Salonika, seems to have had their support for his efforts to help as many Jews as possible flee southwards. Although Germans attributed this behaviour to self-interest and corruption by Jewish money, at heart the Italians were simply more humane towards the Jews than their Axis partners. Their differences involved a clash of cultures as much as a divergence of interests.[211]

Estimated Numbers of Jews Deported from Greece, 1943–44
Source: M. Gilbert, *Atlas of the Holocaust* (London, 1982)

So long as Italy remained in control of the southern zone, the Jewish communities there were safe, frustrating the SS as well as German Foreign Ministry officials who wanted 'to commence measures in the Italian-occupied area without delay'.[212] But after September 1943, when the Germans took over the entire country, Italian protection disappeared. Almost at once, Eichmann began to prepare for further deportations. Jürgen Stroop arrived in Athens as HSSPF, and Walter Blume was sent as commander of the SiPo/SD. Wisliceny had barely returned to Bratislava from Salonika when on 20 September he and three other SD 'specialists in the Jewish question' were transferred to Athens to set up a department for Jewish affairs under Blume. Impatient with the delays the Italians had caused, Eichmann gave Wisliceny strict instructions that he wanted all the Jews in Athens and the rest of Greece to be rounded up and sent to Auschwitz immediately. But events did not move as smoothly as Eichmann hoped.[213]

As soon as Wisliceny arrived in Athens he summoned Elias Barzilai, the Grand Rabbi of Athens, and gave him three days to provide addresses and other information about the Jewish community. Barzilai, of course, knew about the deportations from Salonika. Moreover, he had received the disturbing information from the Red Cross in Geneva that there was no trace of the deportees, and so he was under no illusions about the nature of the game Wisliceny was playing.[214]

What exactly happened next remains something of a mystery. All we know for sure is that over that weekend, between 23 and 25 September, the Grand Rabbi was spirited out of Athens by EAM/ELAS. He claimed later that it had been his idea to flee 'like Moses' in order to warn his congregation. But according to other accounts, his abduction was set up with EAM/ELAS by Jewish activists, who notified Barzilai and succeeded in quieting his fears about what the Germans might do to the rest of the community if he fled. EAM's Kostas Vidalis organised an escape plan. On the Sunday morning several unknown men, whom the disconcerted Rabbi at first took for German agents, called at his home and told him to pack quickly. Hidden in a mail truck, Barzilai, his wife and daughter were driven out of Athens and into the hills of central Greece, where they survived the war with ELAS.[215]

This extraordinary ruse totally disrupted Eichmann's plans and saved the lives of hundreds if not thousands of Jews. Following their Rabbi's disappearance, many in Athens fled into the mountains, went into hiding in the city or prepared to escape. On 3 October the frustrated Stroop issued a decree ordering all Jews to register within five days on pain of being shot, and thereafter to report every other day to the main communal offices. When many Jews refused to register on time, the Germans prolonged the registration period to 17 October. But of an estimated 8,000 Jews in Athens, only 1,200 ever registered.[216]

The extension of the Final Solution into the former Italian zone raised several other problems for the SS. The Jews were not conveniently located in one place, as they had been in Salonika; they lived in numerous small communities, including some on the islands. Politically, too, the Greek authorities were prepared to intervene quite forcefully on behalf of the Greek-speaking Romaniot Jews, and on 7 October Prime Minister Rallis sent Altenburg a long memorandum indicating his displeasure at the prospect of future deportations. On top of these local considerations, German diplomats were absorbing the implications of the recent fiasco in Denmark, where Eichmann's insistence on going ahead with deportations in the face of strong Danish objections, and in the absence of a powerful German police presence, had led to many Danish Jews fleeing abroad, and had jeopardised relations with the Danish authorities.[217]

It was against this background that the German Foreign Office recommended proceeding cautiously in Greece. At first the Gestapo disagreed, arguing that 'the RSHA had learned a lot from the Copenhagen experience'. But Neubacher persuaded Kaltenbrunner, who headed the RSHA, that there was no point in going ahead at that time with the deportation of the few Jews who had registered. In Athens the newly arrived HSSPF Walter Schimana agreed. According to Wisliceny: 'Schimana had no personal interest in a strong action in the Jewish question. [He] told me repeatedly that he had no understanding of Himmler's attitude on the Jewish question.' Eichmann was furious, while the local SD under Walter Blume contented themselves through the winter by laying claim to any property belonging to Jews who had failed to register. They broke into flats and houses and ransacked their contents.[218]

*

Eichmann was clearly annoyed that Wisliceny had done so little since October. Whether or not this inactivity was because his formerly loyal lieutenant had begun to have doubts of his own – as he was to claim later – is difficult to say. In any event, Eichmann recalled him abruptly in January 1944 and told him that he was transferring him to another post – as commandant of Theresienstadt – where he would be able to give his 'philanthropic sentiments' free rein.[219]

Eichmann had decided to go ahead with further deportations at all costs and as fast as possible. In late February, Hauptsturmführer

Toni Burger was instructed to take over from Wisliceny, and to organise the deportation of the various communities that had so far escaped. It was a complex logistical task that would test to the full the co-operation between the SS and the Wehrmacht.

In Athens the end came suddenly. On the morning of Friday, 23 March 1944 Burger went to the synagogue in Melidoni Street to attend the usual registration. This time, however, he instructed his interpreter, Constantin Rekanati, to tell the assembled men that owing to their Anglophile sentiments they were going to be deported to Germany to work, and would only be allowed to return at the end of the war. As they absorbed the shocking news, the synagogue doors were suddenly slammed shut by SS men armed with sub-machine-guns. Twenty young Jewish men were given armbands, ordered to round up the women and children and bring them to the Centre. In view of the fact that so many Jews had gone underground by this time, it must be assumed that many of those who had continued to register did so not because they were unaware of what the future held but because personal reasons made flight impossible. In fact, some people came to the synagogue of their own accord when they heard the news, so as to avoid being separated from relatives. Others were brought in from hiding by the Greek police and SD agents.

By noon, between 700 and 1,000 people were being held at gunpoint inside the synagogue. The doors were opened again in the early afternoon, and as the people inside emerged into the sunlight they saw soldiers with machine-guns lining the streets, and crowds of onlookers watching from either end. They were pushed into waiting trucks and driven the 5 kilometres out to the Haidari camp. About ten days later, watched by members of Department IVB 4 (the Gestapo unit for Jewish affairs), they were herded on to a train bound for Auschwitz. When it arrived there, after a harrowing journey, in the second week of April 1944, Dr Josef Mengele was at the ramp to meet them; he selected 320 men and 328 women for his own 'research'. The others were immediately gassed and burned in the crematoria.[220]

*

The Athens deportations were timed to link up with similar round-ups in other towns on the Greek mainland. In Jannina where there was an ancient Jewish community, life had continued virtually undisturbed during the winter of 1943–44. Although news of the deportations from Salonika had reached them, many Jews were convinced that they had escaped the worst.

But before dawn on 25 March, a bitterly cold day, troops surrounded the Jewish quarter of Jannina down by the lake. At 5 a.m. the heads of the community were told that in three hours every family must be at the designated meeting place, with no more than 50 kilograms of luggage. Failure to turn up was punishable by death. The Wehrmacht supplied eighty lorries to transport the 1,700 Jews out of the town, and the operation went off smoothly under the eyes of the GFP patrols who policed it. Ninety-five per cent of the Jewish population of Jannina was driven over the icy Metsovon Pass, which had been blocked by snow only two days earlier. They were taken to a concentration camp at Larissa, where they met the train coming north from Athens on its way to Auschwitz.[221]

At this time the SD bureau in Athens was occupied with the task of rounding up the Jews in the capital. Its own permanent staff in the provinces was tiny. In Jannina, therefore, the SD relied on the co-operation of the Wehrmacht. The SS official called Major Havranek who was put in charge depended on the Wehrmacht for trucks; the GFP policed the operation. The Waffen-SS units who provided drivers and guards also came under Wehrmacht command. With the final extension of the *Judenverfolgung* (persecution of the Jews) to the islands of Corfu, the Dodecanese and Crete, such co-operation would extend to the German navy as well.

*

In Corfu, Stroop's registration order was still in force in April, and men reported once a week to the local police station. Yet, once again, the community as a whole felt little sense of threat for the end of the war seemed in sight. The Allies were already across the Ionian Sea in Bari, and people felt that their daily humiliations at German hands would turn out to be the worst they had to suffer. What else could explain why they had been untouched when the Jews of Jannina had been deported?[222]

Behind the scenes, however, a most unusual dispute was taking place. Preparations had been afoot as soon as the Jannina deportations were concluded to move on to Corfu, and on 25 April Wehrmacht intelligence reported no military or political objections to the planned deportation of the island's Jews. But at this point the territorial commander, Oberst Emil Jaeger, made a quite re-markable intervention, insisting that the deportation would cause unrest among the Greek population. Unfortunately his courageous stand failed to win support at higher levels in the Wehrmacht. 22 Army Corps HQ at Jannina, under whose authority Corfu fell, confined itself simply to requesting the SD to take care of 'the Jewish question.'[223]

Jaeger tried again to stop the deportations even after an SD officer from Jannina informed him that Himmler had ordered them to proceed. Jaeger replied that there was no way to transport the Jews off the island; moreover, the Italians left on the island represented a greater threat to German security than the Jews, 'against whom incidentally there have never been any complaints'. He raised other problems: the Greek population was showing solidarity with the Jews; a Red Cross ship currently delivering food in the harbour would witness the deportations and fuel 'atrocity propaganda'. Most remarkably of all, Jaeger warned that the proposed operation would lead to 'a loss of ethical prestige in the eyes of the population'. Another historian has justly noted this virtually unique written reference by a German military commander to moral considerations in the context of the persecution of the Jews.[224]

From Athens SD, however, Burger had anticipated Jaeger's objections and already demanded that the navy make shipping available. At the end of May he visited Corfu himself, and persuaded the local shipping official to permit him to use three concrete lighters that happened to be in the harbour. Then he inspected the Old Fort, where the Jews were to be assembled prior to deportation. In early June his colleague Linnemann and the interpreter Rekanati also flew out from Athens.[225]

On 8 June orders were passed from family to family that the following morning they were to assemble by the Old Fort, a former prison. Some people fled into the hills, but most were reluctant to leave their relatives. Next morning, they gathered in front of the fortress. German officers called out each family in turn, and ordered them to hand over their house-keys and jewellery; then they were locked inside the fort. For several days they were detained in primitive conditions, sleeping on floors without a blanket. As shipping became available, they were embarked at the harbour immediately below the fort. It took a day and a half for them to arrive at the island of Lefkada, where a makeshift detention centre had been constructed out of barbed wire in the town square.[226]

On the day the first transport arrived there, a horrifying incident occurred. A Greek priest approached the detainees and offered one man a cigarette. Seeing this, Burger – who had accompanied the group to the island – leapt up and ran towards the compound, pistol in hand. Beside himself with anger, he shot the prisoner on the spot and would have shot the priest too, had he not been restrained by Greek police. They came up and demanded the name of the dead man. Burger pushed them away. 'Toni, you weren't in order there,' chided a fellow German officer. Burger simply pointed to the dead man and observed: 'That one is the luckiest of all these Jews.'[227]

*

Despite German warnings, the townspeople of Lefkada continued to show their sympathy for the detainees. Several days later, when twenty-nine-year-old Armandos Aaron and his family reached the island on the third transport, the local population tried to feed them by pushing bread and vegetables through the barbed wire.

At Patras, where the ships finally docked, an episode took place which saved Aaron's life, and illustrated how difficult it was to predict who might try to escape, and who would choose to remain close to their families. It began when Aaron bumped into a former schoolfriend in the crowd that had gathered on the quay to watch the Jews' arrival. The friend was surprised to see Aaron looking so dirty, and told him to wait while he fetched some food. During the time he was gone, German soldiers and Greek police moved in to cordon off the area, and in the confusion Aaron found himself on the wrong side. He did not know what to do: if he disappeared, his family might be punished; but if he stepped forward he might be shot for failing to keep up with the rest of the party. At this point a stranger approached him and offered help, took Aaron to his house and washed and fed him.

When the Germans found he was missing they hunted with their dogs through the streets by the harbour. Aaron wanted to return to his family. But his saviour, a man called George Mitsialis, pointed out that going back might endanger his own life for sheltering a Jew. Aaron realised he had no choice: he spent that night in the house, and the next day walked out of Patras into the mountains, hoping to make his way to Athens to rejoin his family there. Instead he met partisans from ELAS, and spent the rest of the war with them. In this way, he alone out of his family survived and returned to Corfu.

Another chance for escape presented itself to twenty-three-year-old Perla Soussi, who had arrived in Patras together with her family several days before Aaron, on the first transport from Corfu. Security in the town was extremely lax: the Jews were housed in old school buildings and guarded by Greek collaborators, who showed little enthusiasm for their task. One of them took Perla Soussi, her sister and a friend into the town to buy shoes and then offered to let them escape, saying he would tell his superiors they had slipped away when his back was turned. But they were too scared to follow his advice; they did not know where to go, and had no money, so they went back.

Thus Perla Soussi returned to her family, and like the other Jews from Corfu passed through Haidari prison, where she stayed for a week, before travelling by train in packed, stinking cattle trucks from Athens to Auschwitz. 'My two sisters and I returned to Corfu,' she has recounted. 'But my brother, mother and father did not. Of the 2,000 Jews who left Corfu, approximately 120 returned.'[228]

In June 1944, following the deportations from Corfu, the tiny, ancient communities of Crete were wiped out, after the ship carrying them to Athens was sunk, probably by a British torpedo. And the following month, on the eve of Liberation, the communities on Rhodes and the other Dodecanese islands were evacuated in IVB 4's last mission, detained at the Haidari camp, and then deported to Auschwitz, where they arrived on 16 August. Almost a year and a half had elapsed since the arrival of the first death transport from Greece.[229]

*

Few countries in Europe lost a higher proportion of their Jewish population in the Final Solution than Greece. Possibly as many as 90 per cent of Greek Jews were killed, although precise figures are difficult to find, since there are no exact details either of how many Jews were in Greece when the deportations started or of how many escaped or survived the camps. At the outbreak of the war there were between 70,000 and 80,000 Jews in Greece, of whom over 50,000 lived in the city of Salonika. Fewer than 10,000 survived, and some of the oldest Jewish communities in Europe perished as a result.

The pioneering and scrupulous researches of Danuta Czech have cast some light on the question of the numbers of those who were killed in Auschwitz, the final destination for almost all the deportees from Greece. On the basis of surviving camp documentation, she estimates that more than 54,533 Jews arrived in Auschwitz from Greece. In her view, the estimates of Wisliceny and Höss, the Auschwitz camp commandant, that 60–65,000 Jews were brought from Greece, may well be accurate.

As for the numbers that survived, Höss himself told Eichmann in July 1944 that 'the Greek Jews were of such poor quality that they all had to be eliminated'. Asked during his interrogation at Nuremberg why he was so certain that the Greek Jews had mostly been killed, Wisliceny replied: 'When one knew Eichmann and Höss personally, it is not difficult to reach such a conviction.'[230]

We do know that no more than 12,757 men and women were admitted to the work camp at Auschwitz-Birkenau – the rest of the arrivals were immediately gassed. But most of those who were not killed at once died in the camp later. Many were weak and sick. Some were subjected to atrocious experiments at the hands of the 'human anthropologist' Josef Mengele and Professor Carl Clauberg. Others suffered compulsory sterilisation and castration. A report from Birkenau Women's Camp in August 1943 gives the names of 498 women who were sent to the gas chambers; 438 of these were clearly Greek. Some of the younger men were made to work in the groups that burned corpses, before themselves being gassed in July 1944 by SS guards. By 2 September 1944, it is likely that only 2,469 Greek Jews were still alive in Auschwitz. Some of these were still alive on 17 January 1945, when they set off on foot with other inmates on the march into the Reich; those too ill to go were liberated on 27 January by Soviet troops.[231]

*

Although with hindsight we can see that the mass murder of the Jews was the central feature of Hitler's systematic racial restructuring of Europe, this was not at all clear at the time inside Greece. Coming from a society where racialist philosophies had little appeal, people found the Germans' inhuman behaviour completely bewildering. Auschwitz inmate Errikos Sevillias – 'an ordinary person born in Athens in the good old days of 1901' – wrote after his return from the camps: 'An inexplicable and unexpected great adventure befell me. It seized me like a tornado . . . lifting me high and then throwing me down, again it lifted me high and again threw me to the earth.' Orthodox Greeks shared this incomprehension. In the words of the novelist Giorgos Ioannou, the chronicler of Salonika's misfortunes: 'The Germans suddenly introduced into what today seems the almost idyllic atmosphere of our unsuspecting, dusty Balkan culture all the abysmal medieval passions and idiocies of Gothic Europe.'[232]

Anti-Semitism as the Germans understood it had no place in Greece. Most Greek Jews had no doubts that whatever the familiar petty prejudices and hostilities they might sometimes encounter, Greece was their home. Jewish men had fought in the Greek army in Albania, and many older ones had fought during the First World War as well. One of the most moving affirmations of their identification with their Orthodox compatriots comes in a note in Greek which was discovered in 1980 at the site of one of the crematoria in Birkenau. Written by an unnamed Jewish man, anxious to record his experiences for the world outside the camp, the scrap of paper was addressed 'to my beloved friends, Dimitrios Athanasios Stefanides, Ilias Cohen, Georgios Gounaris and all my *parea* [gang], Smaru

43. Errikos Sevillias (1901–74) walking in central Athens in 1946 with his wife Rachel and daughter Lisa. Sevillias had been sent to Auschwitz in April 1944. His brothers-in-law were killed following the unsuccessful revolt by crematorium workers in October. He was liberated by the Red Army in May 1945 and returned to Greece in August. His wife and daughter had survived in hiding.

Eframidou of Athens and other friends I will always remember, and finally to my beloved fatherland GREECE whose faithful citizen I have always been.'[233]

By and large, Orthodox Greeks reciprocated such sentiments. As the commander of the Sonderkommando Rosenberg had already found in 1941, 'for the average Greek there is no Jewish question. He doesn't see the political danger of world Jewry.' Only in Salonika did an anti-Semitic movement exist, stimulated by economic rivalries dating back generations and by the linguistic gulf which separated the Ladino-speaking Jews from the Greeks; even there, however, local anti-Semitism did not play a large part in the process of deportation. The vulnerability of the Jews in the Macedonian capital owed less to the indifference or hostility of fellow-Greeks than to the fact that they were the first to be persecuted. Flight was difficult from Salonika because the mountains were far away, and resistance was still in its early stages. While some Orthodox Greeks enriched themselves at the expense of the Jewish community, many others hid Jewish children, or helped young men join the resistance.[234]

In Athens German efforts to whip up an anti-Semitic movement were entirely unsuccessful. The largely Greek-speaking Jewish community there was small and highly integrated into Greek life. After the registration decree, the Jews found support from all quarters of the population, from EAM/ELAS to the official authorities. Rallis's philosemitic Education Minister, Nikolaos Louvaris, addressed an appeal to the Germans to cease their persecution of 'the Jews of Old Greece'. Archbishop Damaskinos ordered priests to tell their congregations that the Jews were to be helped. The Greek police often ignored instructions to turn Jews in hiding over to the Germans.[235]

Despite the threat of imprisonment, many non-Jews hid Jewish friends in their apartments, or helped them to escape. Alfredos Cohen, a lawyer from Athens, recorded the spontaneous support of neighbours and friends:

> I will never forget the terror which seized us one night while I was hiding my large family in one of the houses, when it was announced that the Germans had published an order declaring that all the Jews who were caught in hiding would be shot, and the people who were hiding them would be sent to the concentration camp.
>
> Then one of us said that it was not right for us to stay in that house and endanger the lives and peace of aged people and even women. The answer was: 'No, you must stay. Indeed my son, why should our lives be more precious than yours?'[236]

A similar attitude led people to offer hospitality to Jewish children, a phenomenon which reached such proportions that the Germans were forced to issue public warnings against it. The registry book of the 'Esther' orphanage in Athens for 1945–46 shows that these warnings were ineffective. Many Jewish children survived after their parents were deported. One Jewish six-year-old was cared for by an Orthodox family in Salonika in 1943, remaining with them even after they too were arrested and sent to Germany. When they all returned at the end of the war, he could no longer remember his real Jewish parents.[237]

Overall, Orthodox Greeks showed a remarkable generosity of spirit towards the Jews which bears comparison with that of any other group in Europe. In central Greece, in particular, non-Jews helped hundreds of Jews to hide or escape. Following Barzilai's flight to the mountains, the rabbis of Volos and Larissa also went underground. Largely as a result, less than half the Jews in Athens, Volos, Trikkala and Larissa were seized. On the island of Zante, the mayor, Loukas Carrer, and Metropolitan Chrysostomos refused to

44. Jewish orphans who have survived the war protected by non-Jewish families prepare to leave Greece for Palestine. These children have no reliable information about the fate of their parents: Piraeus, 1945.

hand over Zante's 257 Jews to the Gestapo, and hid them instead in the villages.

Though the fugitives received support from many quarters, the outstanding role was played by EAM/ELAS, whose underground organisation was the most extensive in the country. Thanks to EAM, hundreds of Jews survived the war. About 650 of them served in the resistance, in combat units or as interpreters. They were highly valued on account of their training and high level of literacy. Many had served as officers in the Greek army in Albania.[238]

While some Jews headed for the hills, others managed to escape from Greece altogether by travelling to the coast at Evvia, from where caiques took them to Turkey. Help did not always come without a price. One Jewish family from Athens was searched by *andartes* fifteen minutes before their boat was due to sail, and asked to hand over three-quarters of their gold coins and most of their luggage. Other Jews in hiding had to pay their landlords a deposit in case they were suddenly discovered and deported.[239] In general, however, they were rarely denounced, despite the rewards offered by the SS. And although some thieving by ELAS members took place, more noteworthy was the remarkably sympathetic attitude their organisation showed towards the refugees.

The Greeks' overwhelming disapproval of German policy towards the Jews meant that the Greek state and its forces could not be relied upon to support Eichmann's men. As a result, the 'Jewish experts' in Blume's SD headquarters were obliged to seek the help of the German army. Only in Athens was an operation carried out by the SS alone: elsewhere the deportations could not have been successful without the assistance of the Wehrmacht. Colonel Jaeger on Corfu offered an example of stubborn resistance to Eichmann's men, but he was exceptional. The Final Solution in Greece provides a powerful argument against drawing too sharp a distinction so far as the attitudes of the occupation bureaucracy are concerned between the SS, the regular army and, for that matter, the Foreign Office. Despite their differences, they worked together to maintain the authority of the Reich over its enemies – real and imagined.

PART FOUR

A Society at War: 1943–44

Society had become divided into two ideologically hostile camps, and each side viewed the other with suspicion. As for ending this state of affairs, no guarantee could be given that would be trusted, no oath sworn that people would fear to break; everyone had come to the conclusion that it was hopeless to expect a permanent settlement and so, instead of being able to feel confident in others, they devoted their energies to providing against being injured themselves.

Thucydides, *The Peloponnesian War*, trans. R. Warner
(London, 1975), 3: 85

CHAPTER TWENTY

People's Democracy in Free Greece

The Wehrmacht's extensive anti-guerrilla sweeps failed to prevent EAM/ELAS tightening its hold over a vast, mountainous area which stretched from the Gulf of Corinth to the Yugoslav border, and from the western slopes of the Pindos to Greece's eastern coastline. By the middle of 1944 even much of the Peloponnese had become a 'state within a state', according to General Le Suire. The Germans were increasingly confined to the towns and the main roads between them, and only left the security of their garrisons in armed convoys. J.M. Stevens, a British SOE officer, went so far as to say that 'Greece today forms two separate countries, occupied and unoccupied.' Passes were necessary for strangers entering guerrilla-controlled areas, though the precise boundaries with Axis-held territory were indeterminate and shifting, marked by blackened houses and burnt fields.[1]

Inside 'Free Greece' EAM/ELAS held sway, with rival bands and organisations like EDES challenging its authority only in a few peripheral areas. It organised economic activity, reshaped the judicial and educational system, and introduced social reforms for women. EAM officials handled relief for the victims of Axis raids and for guerrillas' dependants; they brought in a new system of local self-government, and even held national elections in March 1944. The experience of 'Free Greece', in other words, involved something reaching far beyond provisional military control by the guerrillas; EAM/ELAS wanted to bring into being a new type of local and national administration.

To work out what sort of political project this involved is no easy task, for the Cold War has distorted our understanding of wartime radicalism. While some writers have depicted EAM forcing Marx on the Greek peasant, others, on the Left, replied by praising EAM's daring search for a democratic solution to the country's social and economic ills. Both schools of thought have tended to see EAM as a monolithic organisation, and by failing to explore the environment within which it operated, both have ultimately

45.   A mule train in the mountains of 'Free Greece'.

substituted political explanations of its activities and origins for
social ones.

For a less anachronistic sense of what EAM was doing, several
points need to be made at the outset about the sort of society that
existed in wartime Greece. In the first place, this was a world of
rumours, confusion, fear and ignorance in which the state and
society had disintegrated at a national level, and opinions and stories
circulated locally. *Andartes* in Volos in the spring of 1944 had no
idea about what was happening fifty miles away, and 'listened to
what sailors had to say about Piraeus and about life in Athens . . . as
if they were hearing about a distant country'. Radios were scarce,
telephone connections were unreliable, and runners could take days
to reach their destinations. Even a powerful organisation like EAM
could scarcely act in a unified way, or ensure that instructions from
the centre were obeyed at the periphery, and the mountains and the
pressures of wartime tested its cohesion to the full. 'From its incep-
tion the Greek resistance was marked by a lack of centralisation and
an unusual degree of local initiative. That quality was to prove
crucial, for it critically minimised the ability of the Communists to

266

organise it.' Gabriel Kolko's acute assessment of EAM/ELAS has sadly been ignored by most of the scholars who followed him.[2]

Secondly, to understand why so many people supported EAM, one must realise how far the Second World War had radicalised the population. 'It is clear,' wrote Justice Emil Sandstrom, head of the Greek Relief Commission, 'that hunger, scarcity of all the necessities of life, inflation, the difficulties arising from a state of occupation, terror, the life of privation in the mountains, guerrilla warfare and the collapse of Government authority – in fact, all the sufferings of the Greek population – had a strong radicalising influence on the masses.' A 'veritable social revolution' caused by inflation and food shortage led to 'the veering towards the Left of elements of the public who, before the war, were among the most conservative'.[3]

What was happening in Greece was little different in this respect from what was happening in, say, Yugoslavia, China or the Philippines at the same time. Here too, Kolko offers some highly pertinent observations in the context of the war as a whole:

> Psychologically and intellectually, the experience of war unleashed a seemingly unlimited skepticism among the masses towards the legitimacy and pretensions of the prewar constituted orders. . . . Politics no longer remained an abstract avocation for ambitious men or literate intelligentsia; for millions it became a means for their eventual deliverance from the causes and consequences of a world gone mad with destruction and terror. To an unprecedented extent, countless people throughout the world lost their fear to act, and they learned to do so in innumerable ways that gravely threatened the existing order.[4]

Behind the growth of mass resistance in Greece lay the fact that the prewar party leaders had lost 'a great deal of prestige'. Young people in particular now wanted to 'show our elders what this country is capable of. It must not be the *tsifliki* [the estate] of this or that Party boss or Deputy,' wrote one nationalist youth paper. 'The youth of our country,' noted one Greek observer, 'almost in its entirety . . . has aligned itself with the Leftists, and the enemy occupation has accustomed them [*sic*] to express their ideas fearlessly, and to uphold them by any means.' This sweeping change in attitudes was so bound up with the effects of the occupation on day-to-day life that it was little understood outside Greece, either by the Greek *émigrés* in the Middle East or by the British.[5]

At the same time, however, the occupation brought that enormous political confusion which is typical of moments of dramatic upheaval. 'Everything that occurs here is ideological, but the ideology is fluid, undefined,' writes Kapuscinski. He is describing revolutionary Algeria, but he could easily have been talking about wartime Greece. 'Some new quality is being born, and it is not yet expressed in any doctrine: everyone understands it in his own way.' Even Greek royalists acknowledged the need for some form of socialism after the war, and on the Right, the Populist Party bizarrely committed itself in 1943 to a future 'monarchical socialist democracy', although what this meant was quite unclear. Similarly, an anti-EAM faction in Patras came out with a slogan which ran: 'Greece–Freedom–Social Justice'. Like 'socialism', the concept of 'social justice' had become ubiquitous, but it was rarely defined or spelled out.[6]

The place where this sort of ideological confusion had the most serious implications was inside EAM itself. How free should 'Free Greece' be? What sort of democracy was implied in the slogan 'People's Democracy'? Far from being a communist monolith, EAM was riven by internal disagreements over such basic questions. Social democrat intellectuals hesitated before the choice which they felt confronted them – 'whether to sacrifice democracy to socialism or socialism to democracy'. Communist activists were split between the revolutionaries who wanted to seize power when the Germans left and the moderates, who eventually prevailed, who favoured co-operating with the other parties and the British.[7]

The Greek Communist Party (KKE), which played the leading role in EAM, was even schizophrenic about its own rapid wartime expansion. General Secretary Siantos warned of the 'serious dangers' the Party faced through the flood of new applications from rural areas, while party ideologues remained trapped in the grip of sterile sectarian formulas which did not equip them to understand the very new conditions created by the war. Far from having a clear aim of what to do with the power it had acquired through EAM – still less a coherent plan to seize power – the Greek Communist Party remained uncertain and hesitant. These uncertainties deepened in 1943, when the dissolution of the Comintern left the Greeks without a clear line from Moscow, and deepened still further, it seems, in the summer of 1944, when Stalin sent a military mission to tell the KKE to face geopolitical realities and co-operate with the British.[8]

Resistance radicalism, in short, was not a unified and fully formed political force; it was fragmented, inchoate and often paradoxical in character, the natural expression in many ways of the political and geographical features of wartime Greece itself. If EAM/ELAS was genuinely popular, it could also act extremely repressively. Its orders were issued in high, 'pure' Greek – just like those of any bourgeois ministry – while its social reforms, which now appear years ahead of their time, were the work of highly educated intellectuals, journalists and activists who frequently found themselves trying to convince suspicious, or simply uncomprehending, villagers to change their ways. Yet ordinary people who were not interested in theory, or in political programmes, felt that EAM, and even the KKE, were 'theirs . . . close to them . . . speaking their language'. To see why they might have felt this we should begin in the villages, those reservoirs of food, shelter, information and recruits without which EAM/ELAS could not have survived.[9]

Organising Free Greece

Before the war, the poor, mountainous province of Evrytania in central Greece had suffered like much of the country from the indifference of the politicians in Athens. The land reform had left many local estates untouched. Villages still remained several hours' walk from the nearest road, hospital or law courts. While prominent politicians from the area sat in the capital, obsessed with the constitutional issue, the region seemed condemned to backwardness and neglect.

In 1935 a regionalist movement sprang up in Evrytania which aimed at replacing 'old partyism' (*palaiokommatismo*), with a progressive local popular front. At the same time, enterprising citizens in the hill village of Karoplesi, fed up with having to make the long journey down to the town of Karpenisi whenever they had legal business to attend to, founded a so-called 'Conciliation Committee' to provide local justice. Meeting in the schoolhouse once a month, the committee was staffed by two farmers and two shepherds elected by the villagers, the president of the village, the schoolmaster of the village and the priest. Between them, they adjudicated on cases concerning damaged crops and trees, water rights and other petty disputes. Though they left other matters for the professional lawyers in the towns, their very existence irked the latter, particularly once other villages copied Karoplesi's example.

After 1936 the Metaxas dictatorship put an end to such local initiatives. Metaxas banned a proposed regional conference, which was to have debated the social and economic difficulties facing Evrytania. The 'Conciliation Committees' were also forcibly dissolved, and villagers once more faced the arduous journey and heavy costs of official justice. What the dictatorship could not do, however, was abolish the memory of what the villagers had achieved. From 1941 the occupation, and the collapse of Athens' authority over the provinces, created a power vacuum which local initiatives again began to fill.

Georgoulas Beikos was the energetic and enterprising son of a farmer from the hill village of Kleitsos. He had attended the prestigious Gymnasium at Karpenisi in the early 1930s. In 1936, at the age of seventeen, he became involved in regional politics, and also joined the KKE. Together with some high-school friends he founded a paper called *Voice of Evrytania*, before being forced underground and persecuted by the Metaxas dictatorship. The dictatorship was deeply unpopular among the rural population because of its legislation curbing the grazing of goats. By protesting against such policies, Beikos and other activists gained substantial local support from farmers with little interest in communism or the Party.

After fighting the Italians in Albania, Beikos returned to Evrytania and started to take an active part again in local affairs. Even before reviving the *Voice of Evrytania* in 1943 (Beikos claims it was the first paper published in Free Greece), he had helped set up a village committee in Kleitsos in August 1941 to tackle the shortage of flour. With supplies unavailable locally, the twenty-two-year-old Beikos managed to obtain food for the village from the far-off town of Karditsa. This success won him great local esteem, and so when he received the call from Athens to spread the word about EAM, he was able to recruit many of the influential older men in the locality who would have had nothing to do with a young communist before the war. By 1943 Beikos and his friends had become the driving force behind the new self-government institutions of the resistance in central Greece.[10]

*

On 11 October 1942 Aris Velouchiotis and his guerrillas made an unexpected appearance in the nearby village of Fourna. To the villagers' disbelief, they shut down the local gendarmerie (one gendarme joined Aris's men, the other two left for their homes), burned its archives and announced the suspension of the local court. The state whose apparatus Aris had attacked had existed in name only for some time. Now it was utterly destroyed. Aris, however, had given little thought to what should replace it; neither had his nominal but distant superiors at EAM's headquarters in Athens.

Learning about what had happened in Fourna, the twenty-three-year-old Beikos invited Aris to visit him, and the next day Aris's band made its entrance into the village of Kleitsos to an enthusiastic reception. The inhabitants immediately chose a new village council, a food committee and school committee, and also – on Aris's insistence – a church committee to ensure that the local priest was properly paid. Among the members of these new bodies were many old faces from the past, for, as Beikos remarks, in such difficult times the villagers put their trust in men who had prior administrative experience, even under Metaxas.

Gradually, the new village committees were drawn into contentious issues such as the need for local land reform, protection of the communal forests, grazing rights and the distribution of food stocks. As EAM consolidated its power over the region, Beikos and his fellow activists realised that a more systematic approach to the management of village affairs was needed. The question of land reform became especially pressing after some villagers, urged on by a band of *andartes*, began squatting on an estate belonging to a pro-EAM notable. An EAM land policy became a matter of urgency.[11]

On 4 December 1942 Beikos met secretly in the forests near Karpenisi with other regional members of the KKE to draw up a code for village self-government and 'People's Justice'. On land reform they took a moderate position, deciding that the large estates would not be expropriated, since that would drive the wealthier elements out of EAM. The Kleitsos model for administration was adopted in other villages. The regional tier of local government was also reformed, and village courts to settle local disputes were set up. These new arrangements were known as the Poseidon Code. Shortly afterwards, the chief *kapetan* of Thessaly, a lawyer from Karditsa known by his *nom de guerre* of 'Nikitas' (The Victor), introduced the code into western Thessaly. The Phthiotis–Phokis–Evrytania EAM committee issued a circular in early 1943 ordering similar measures to be introduced throughout central Greece. In fact this was already happening on a wide scale across the country, with many local variations, as villages responded to the need to establish some form of legally constituted local authority. By 1944 new committees had been formed in most villages in Free Greece, and a regime of local 'self-government' was institutionalised.[12]

*

Based on Karoplesi's prewar 'Conciliation Committee', one of EAM's most popular reforms concerned the law courts. Before the war villagers had to travel to the district court to settle disputes, making litigation expensive and time-consuming. Lawyers conversed in high Greek, *katharevousa*, which was like a foreign language to the peasant. 'People's justice' by contrast took place in the village on a weekly basis, and proceedings were public, free and

46. Meeting of a People's Court, 1944.

conducted in demotic. Lawyers were rarely engaged; plaintiff and
defendant presented their own cases and introduced witnesses before
a tribunal whose members were appointed by election in the
community.[13]

Village justice was 'in some ways something very democratic, in
some other ways as weak as human nature is weak', according to an
observer. Written law was regarded as no more important than
local tradition in providing a guide to settlements. Sentences were
often based on the views and attitudes of the local population.
Often cases did not come to court: the local EAM *ypefthinos* (representative) established the 'general feeling' in the village and sentenced the accused accordingly. Sheep stealing quickly died out
after several notable culprits were shot. One had his head shaved
and was paraded through the village where he had offended, with a
sheep's entrails wrapped round his neck. In general, the new system

of justice seems to have proved popular in the villages. In areas like Mesolonghi, where the old 'bourgeois' courts continued to operate, peasants abandoned them for the People's Courts.[14]

Because few participants in the village courts could read or write, hardly any descriptions of their proceedings have been preserved. ('What were the village courts like?' I asked an elderly *kafeneion* owner in the Peloponnese recently. 'Just a few illiterates playing games,' he responded.) Fortunately, a young American doctor with the *andartes* kept a detailed account of a session he attended. It took place one Sunday afternoon in the schoolhouse: this was the usual time and place. The five judges were two of the older men of the village, the EAM *ypefthinos*, a twenty-year-old boy representing the village youth, and the court's president, Costa Zarmakoupis, 'a middle aged man of fine clean-cut appearance'. The priest took the position of court reporter as he was one of the few men able to write well enough. Most other people who attended were illiterate. The judges sat in front of a small table which contained a bible and the priest's papers; behind them were a blackboard, a map of Greece and an anatomy chart left behind after classes had finished.

On the afternoon of 19 March 1944 this court heard a number of cases. A grain merchant had brought a suit against four village notables, including the *ypefthinos*, over the matter of some unpaid horse feed. Evidently EAM officials were not so powerful that other villagers feared taking them to court. Another case involved men and boys who had failed to help ELAS transport munitions from Epiros to another area. Normally during ELAS's civilian 'mobilisations' the church bell was rung, and all the villagers gathered in the square to help carry the guns and ammunition to the next village. Often women and girls did most of the work. The men regarded it as degrading to help, and in this case their reluctance had prompted EAM to bring some of them to court.[15]

In this village, at least, women remained social inferiors. EAM/ELAS wanted men to work alongside them in carrying arms and supplies because the organisation could hardly afford to allow male labour to remain idle. But no women made an appearance in the 'People's Court'. They remained shut away at home, and their husbands, fathers or other male relatives represented them in court, and could be prosecuted for failing to do so. Official EAM guidelines for the 'People's Courts' did not discriminate between the sexes in this way. The villagers, however, did not allow their traditions to be swept aside, and kept women out of public affairs as far as possible.[16]

*

This was the theory behind the village system of self-government: members of the governing council and the specialist committees were to be elected at meetings of the village general assembly; all citizens – male and female – over seventeen had the right to vote there, and voting was by secret ballot. Although the local EAM group would put forward its own candidates, other candidates were also allowed to stand. The municipal council was to meet monthly, and a general assembly of all the villagers was to be held every three months.[17]

To illustrate what the village committees actually did we can look at Argalasti, a large village on the southern slopes of Mount Pelion and one of the few places where wartime administrative records have survived. There the old Governing Council of the village was dissolved after news of Italy's withdrawal from the war and a new People's Committee was set up. It is unclear whether the ten members were actually elected by the villagers; in practice, elections were often dispensed with. The new committee met four times in the first six days, and then more regularly on a weekly basis.[18]

One of its first actions was to order local olive growers and traders to declare the quantity of olives and oil they possessed. It also set the prices at which firewood could be sold in the village. To help manual labourers, it ordered all householders or employers who required workers to apply to the local work centre for hands. It forbade private work contracts and set wage rates. Olive trees on communal land were harvested by workers under the committee's supervision 'so as to avoid their exploitation by crafty and well-off people'. Argalasti had been hit by a wave of petty crime during the famine of the first year, as poor villagers stole foodstuffs and olive oil from the stores of richer farmers. Now measures were taken to ensure that unemployed workers and children were regularly fed. On 6 December 1943 the committee decreed that every shepherd and butcher should hand over some meat for public consumption at Christmas; they would be repaid partly in cash, and partly in olive oil.[19]

While the committee redistributed goods within the village, it tried to guard against outside calls on its scanty resources. It monitored the movement of goods in and out of the area, and a tax was levied on produce leaving the village. When a wealthy farmer asked for permission to transport 500 okes of oil to Volos 'for family needs and barter', he was refused: no more than five okes, the committee informed him, could be sent untaxed. It also rejected a request from the village president of Trikeri, some miles away, to allow his starving villagers – fishermen who could not practise their

47.   Meeting of a village council in Epiros, 1944.

livelihood – access to woodland owned by Argalasti. And it rejected
a plea from another neighbouring village for financial support for
the medical centre there, saying that Argalasti's own medical centre
required all the assistance it could provide.

One thing the committee could not refuse were direct requests
from EAM/ELAS. To help village families who had members
fighting in the resistance, it gave money to the local branch of
EAM's welfare section. On 19 December 1943 the committee's
chairman raised the question of the share of the harvest tax which
should be given to ELAS. The village would need a substantial
percentage, he agreed, for its own needs. But the remainder should
be made available 'to cover the requirements of our holy struggle'.
He suggested giving ELAS at least 60 per cent of the crops collected
by village officials. The rest of the committee backed their chairman, declaring their support for EAM's policies of fighting for
'People's Democracy'. Less than two weeks later, evidently after
further pressure from regional EAM/ELAS officials, the People's

Committee of Argalasti agreed to hand over all the remaining money at its disposal 'for the needs of the struggle'.

*

The official minutes from Argalasti hint at the powerful conflict of interests which the local administrators faced between concern for the welfare of the village itself and obedience to the higher leadership of EAM/ELAS. EAM's national organisation might well have been more extensive than any of its resistance rivals, yet many of its members felt that they belonged first and foremost to their village or hamlet. For all its importance, such a conflict of loyalties was rarely discussed openly, either at the time or later. But it did provide the subject-matter for a boisterous wartime comedy by Georgios Kotzioulas, the youthful director of an EAM troupe of travelling players. In his *O Ypefthinos* (The 'Responsible'), Kotzioulas depicted country life under EAM's rule in a way that diverged from the normal propaganda line, exposing the sometimes sharp divisions between the traditional expectations of rural society and the reforming zeal of EAM officials.

The hero, thirty-five-year-old Panos, the EAM *ypefthinos* of 'a large village in Epiros, during the period of slavery', is torn between the complaints of the villagers and those of his superiors. His mother cannot understand her son's hectic activity. He earns no salary, and has no time to think about finding a wife. 'Tell me, Sotiris,' she asks her brother as the play starts, 'what's got into Panos?' 'Don't worry,' Sotiris assures her. 'He's not suffering from anything. He's just become "ideological".'[20]

Panos makes his entrance wearing woollen gloves and carrying an umbrella as if to show he is already one step removed from his parents' rural life. Back from his studies in Athens to run the village, he is forced to listen all day to the villagers' complaints about the *andartes* who have been billeted there. To his fellow-villagers, he is simply acquiescing in the plunder of their crops and property. Then, with the appearance of the *perifereiakos* – his superior, the regional officer – Panos comes under criticism from a different quarter.

The *perifereiakos* has come to inspect the administration in Panos's village. Soon Panos's complaints come tumbling out: 'We are killing ourselves with work, and no one gives us credit: memoranda, meetings, phone calls, instructions about everything, shouts, arguments, that is our daily drama here in the villages.' But his superior takes a strict view of his duties. Are the villagers complaining at having to give food, lodging and wood to the guerrillas, or having to carry their belongings?: 'They must be enlightened properly about the purposes of the struggle.' Are they reluctant to come to the village? Then, 'they are subconscious reactionaries'. Worse still, Panos tells him: 'We call them for labour service and they don't show up. We call again, and they plead ill-health. One mentions his bunions, the other remembers the pleurisy he suffered from twelve years ago. Some don't even let their women come. And they blame me for everything – I am the root of all evil.' 'Perhaps they are stirred up by remnants of the reactionary element?' asks the visitor, but Panos assures him that there are none in the village. The villagers are simply 'a little backward'.

The Ideology of the People's Democracy

Just like the Russian revolutionaries recently described by Richard Stites, Greek resistance activists wanted to inspire people to action with their utopian social visions and revolutionary dreams.[21] Through Kotzioulas's plays shines the bright future for which EAM/ELAS was fighting. After Liberation, says Kotzioulas, village life will be transformed: 'In the future we will all be one, villagers and town-dwellers, rich and poor,' declaims the EAM *ypefthinos* to his doubtful father in *O Prodotis* (The Traitor). 'If it is the will of the All Mighty', his father mutters. But his son corrects him: 'It is our will, the People's.' There was no room for apathy or religious fatalism in Free Greece; Kotzioulas, like EAM in general, was preaching a new style of politics founded upon what one might call a morality of mobilisation. 'What have *you* done for the struggle today, patriot?' ran one of the commonest resistance slogans in the villages of Kotzioulas's native Epiros.

In another play – commissioned by the *andartes* to encourage more recruits to come forward – the ghost of Karaïskakis, a hero of the 1821 War of Independence, returns to rouse the villagers, and prophesies a time when 'our soil is not trodden under the boot of the tyrants with the black flag, dark as their souls. . . . The burned houses, the ruined villages will slowly be rebuilt and a new life will begin for all. The villager whom the rich have always kicked around will get his turn to sit on the golden throne.' This was the sort of message guaranteed to raise a cheer in the mountains.[22]

But other parts of Kotzioulas's image of the future were less predictable. In the remarkable *Ta Pathi ton Evraion* (The Sufferings of the Jews), Haim, the son of a rich merchant, and Moises, his former employee, meet on equal terms in the hills. Moises, who has joined the *andartes*, tells Haim to rid himself of his 'prewar mentality'. In the mountains there is no room for selfishness, or

48. 'Halt! What have you done for the struggle today, patriot?' Resistance graffiti at the entrance to a burned village in Epiros, 1944.

thoughts of individual profit: 'Here everything is shared. We live like brothers.' Haim is worried at the thought of living alongside Christians; but Moises reminds him: 'Now we must change our way of life, change our habits.' The Jews need not think any longer about emigrating to Palestine; the *andartes* will build a new society in Greece.[23]

Ta Pathi ton Evraion must have startled the villagers who heard it, with its insistently secular tone. And the sound of the new Jerusalem to be built in EAM's Greece appealed even less to some when they learned what this would mean for relations between the sexes. In *O Prodotis* (The Traitor), old Barba Zikos resists the idea of emancipating women. His son Stavros, the local EAM representative, insists that unless women take part in 'the struggle', society will not move forward: 'The woman should not be the slave of the man. We must agree on that, father.' 'I can accept everything except that,' Barba Zikos replies. He is unhappy at the thought of girls taking part in public meetings: 'You should ask their parents.' Stavros is uncompromising: 'Some of them have thick skulls, so

278

what should we ask them! Even so, we do try to enlighten them as far as we can.' His father is shocked: 'So from now on, you mean to say that the father has no control over his child?' 'Who told you that?' demands Stavros. 'Some numbskull reactionaries, probably. . . . It isn't correct. We are not trying to dissolve the family but to make it stronger, to put it on firmer foundations.' Barba Zikos's misgivings were fully justified, however, for both women and the younger generation were targets of EAM's reformist programme.[24]

In the villages, especially, women's lives were unenviable. They were, as one shocked American liaison officer remarked, 'regarded as little better than animals and treated about the same'. They were also often very poorly educated: the older women in one mountain village were left speechless by the electric lights brought by an Allied mission, and tried to blow them out. Resistance propaganda preached the need to improve their lot. Pamphlets were circulated on topics such as 'The Girl And Her Demands'. 'In today's struggle for liberty the mass participation of the modern girl is especially impressive,' claimed one resistance broadsheet. 'In city demonstrations we see her a pioneer, a fighter, courageous and defying death; first in the line of battle the country girl defends her bread, her crops; but we see her even as an *andartissa*, wearing the crossed belt of the andartes, and fighting like a tigress.' This modern girl was fighting, according to the author, for a double victory: 'from the foreign yoke, and from the bias and superstition of our country'.[25]

Women were given the vote for the first time in Greece's history, and their help was enlisted in numerous ways. Many entered the resistance through their involvement in welfare work, running food kitchens in towns and villages. Others joined the *andartes*, in fighting formations, or in more traditional female roles, as nurses and washerwomen. Among them were outstanding figures like twenty-two-year-old Maria who headed the provisioning service in the Evvia village of Setta. Like many women Maria was dressed entirely in black: her brother had been executed, her mother had died of hunger during the famine, and her father was in prison for resistance activity.

Almost as suspect to the ordinary male villager as the emancipation of women must have been EAM's appeal to the young. Resistance was often portrayed as a chance for Greek youth to put right the mistakes of their elders. Through the national youth organisation EPON, EAM mobilised teenagers in the villages and cities. They, and their younger siblings, the *Aetopoula*, or Little Eagles, carried out many useful tasks under the noses of the Axis

49. A woman delegate speaks at a meeting of the EAM welfare organisation EA.

authorities. They took part in demonstrations, helped transport supplies and carried messages, organised relief work and laid on cultural events. Many EPONites enlisted, or were 'volunteered' for the ELAS reserve militia, and some then advanced into fighting units based far from their homes.[26]

EPON itself eventually emerged as a shadow national organisation to EAM. Like EAM, it organised regional conferences which hundreds of youthful delegates attended. Illustrated broadsheets and pamphlets, written in demotic, were printed for use in villages in Free Greece. EPONites produced plays and puppet shows, replacing older themes with 'new works drawn from the flames of the National Liberation Struggle'. Almost a thousand village cultural groups were sponsored across Greece, in addition to the travelling theatre troupes like Koutzioulas's. Reflecting the high value EAM attached to education, EPON members still attending school were told that their activity in EPON should not distract them from their lessons, nor lead them to question their teachers' authority. On the contrary, they should try to prove themselves fine students as well as conscientious political activists.[27]

Given its progressivist slant, it is not surprising that EAM attracted many outstanding educationalists, among them Rosa

280

50. The Little Eagles: children with wooden rifles are drilled in the village of Zitsa in 1944.

Imvriotis, a pioneer of female emancipation and the first woman principal of a high school in Greece. Ascetic and dedicated, a bitter opponent of the old Metaxas dictatorship, she embodied the idea of resistance as a process of internal reform and improvement. During the last year of the occupation, after travelling widely through Free Greece, she established a primitive teacher training college in a mountain village. She and a group of university professors and high-school teachers ran courses, mostly without books, for students from Thessaly, who were then sent out to teaching positions in the region. 'A school in every village', was Imvriotis's motto. Sadly, the Civil War would lead her to be written off as a dangerous radical: Greece was not to see such an impressive and dedicated effort to improve rural schooling for another thirty years. For many women – whether political exiles like Sofia Vlachou, who never returned to Greece and died in Romania, or those who like Imvriotis lived through the Civil War and the conservatism of the 1950s – the years when they had been active in the resistance would remain a disturbing and poignant memory of a time when the conventions of Greek life had been challenged and they had briefly tasted freedom and power.[28]

ΤΑ ΑΕΤΟΠΟΥΛΑ

Ἀναγνωστικὀ γ΄ κ δ΄ τάξης

ΕΚΔΟΣΗ Π.Ε.Ε.Α.
1944

51. The Little Eagles: title-page of a children's school book issued by the resistance for use in Free Greece.

*

Many of EAM's leading reformers were university graduates and intellectuals; most saw the countryside through a city-dweller's eyes. A senior figure like Petros Roussos, a member of the KKE central committee, had no real knowledge of the mountains, and apart from an occasional day's hiking, had never gone 'into the hills' before the war. Now, however, 'the notion of the Mountain acquired a different meaning and other dimensions in our imagination. A different atmosphere, other emotions awaited us,' he wrote. Scores like him were leaving Athens to run Free Greece and quickly became almost intoxicated by the experience. But country people were cautious. They had learned not to take issue openly with powerful visitors – 'We have been tyrannised over for so long that now, whoever comes, we say to him "Welcome",' an old Slavophone farmer told a British officer – but they were suspicious of innovation, remembering, in the words of the proverb, that 'Satan takes learned heads for a ride.' So it is not easy to gauge how the villagers actually reacted to EAM's dramatic social innovations.[29]

The records of an EAM inspector who visited Thessaly offer

282

some clues. He found – perhaps not surprisingly – incomprehension and some outright resistance to the new ways. In the town of Nivoliani, for example, the local council's efforts to increase revenues by taxing shepherds had foundered on the shepherds' refusal to pay: the council ended up contracting a loan, with the harvest as surety, from a local moneylender. At nearby Kapnista, EAM's instructions concerning the maize had been widely ignored. The inhabitants of Koukourava did not, reported the inspector with regret, 'understand clearly the meaning of the principle of self-administration'. In Voulgarini the various village committees had become bitter rivals, each criticising the work of the others. They did not keep written records of their meetings – a common problem – and failed to meet regularly. At Neromyloi even the local council members were baffled by the idea of self-administration. They did not understand the purpose of the general assembly, and most left it before it had finished its business. In general, they did not attend unless they had some personal issue to discuss.[30]

Effective indoctrination required people to listen, but as a small cog in the resistance propaganda machine, the playwright Kotzioulas found that even free entry to his plays was not always enough to attract an audience. Some villagers did come along, attracted by the novelty of the entertainment; but others stayed away for the same reason: 'Many followed our shows . . . *andartes* and civilians, men and women,' he reported to his ELAS commander, 'though most of the villagers, being illiterate and untravelled had never seen a show before in their lives, and were not in a position to work out beforehand what we were up to. Most of them anyway were busy with farming tasks which they could not leave, and others, with that suspicion so characteristic of the agricultural element, avoided taking part in a gathering when they were unsure what it would mean for them.' Kotzioulas decided that his plays would work only if they took into account the 'poor capabilities of his public', while the well-known Athenian head of another theatre troupe, Vasilis Rotas, quickly found himself embroiled in a fierce debate over the excessive demands some critics argued his plays made upon their peasant listeners.[31]

The most enthusiastic supporters of the travelling players turned out to be the *andartes* themselves, children, and young women. Many boys and girls embraced the resistance out of excitement, the chance to travel, and not least as an escape from their household chores and shepherding duties. For just the same reasons, the elders of farming families were wary of an organisation which threatened their own parental authority, left them with more work and fewer crops, and reduced their economic independence. There are many accounts of villagers' reluctance to let their children, especially their daughters, join ELAS. For villagers with seed to sow and fields to water, resistance was chiefly just another burden and drain on their time. Often they wanted nothing more than to be left alone, and it took a visit from German troops, burning and looting, to make them change their minds and look more tolerantly upon EAM's vision of social co-operation.

Enthusiasm, Freedom and Coercion

We need, then, to be careful about taking EAM propaganda at face value. Much more research is required before we can establish with any confidence in what sections of society EAM's most loyal constituencies were to be found. But it would be equally misguided to approach the question of the nature of EAM's political support in the manner of a political scientist investigating a parliamentary party, assessing degrees of commitment, separating the waverers from the committed voters; this, after all, was a movement emerging during a protracted and ferocious military and ideological conflict. Popular support had a quite different and much more urgent meaning here, for without it the movement was doomed to collapse. Let us examine EAM propaganda from another, and perhaps more pertinent, angle – as an instrument for acquiring and hanging on to power. How was enthusiasm generated – and opposition contained?

It was not just what EAM activists were saying, it was additionally, and perhaps primarily, the manner in which they said it that ensured EAM's success. The emphasis on *organisation* – conveyed through the form of innumerable and to all apparent intents and purposes often redundant committees, councils, meetings and conferences – allowed activists to feel that they were not isolated. The power of 'the Organisation' was made visible, encouraging them to persevere with what was highly dangerous work, while simultaneously of course impressing and alarming potential opponents.

In like fashion, the institutions of self-government need to be judged not only in terms of their administrative efficiency but also as mechanisms through which EAM extended and consolidated its own power. The schools and nurseries set up by idealistic reformers served, in addition to teaching illiterate country children how to write, to build up support for the resistance. Whether or not many peasants were able to read the hundreds of pamphlets, posters and broadsheets generated by the underground is a moot point; yet it is clear that the press, like the educational initiatives, formed part of a vast apparatus for generating enthusiasm and respect. People felt great pride in supporting a movement which was capable of such innovations. The endless speeches made by EAM activists on almost every conceivable occasion served a similar purpose, representing for the inhabitants of Free Greece a quite new style of political practice.

In these various ways EAM was showing people that politics was no longer the preserve of a specific elite of Athenians and local notables. It offered the promise – indeed the demand – of an all-inclusive pattern of mass activism. The first-person plural became the characteristic voice of songs, speeches and posters. 'We are the Little Eagles,' ran one children's song. 'With freedom in our hearts/ Blessed children of Greece and offspring of the People.' Teenagers and adults were singing songs like this too. As one resistance playwright noted: 'The youth of the villages had become accustomed within the struggle to speak before the people, to express themselves without the "usual formalities". At assemblies, conferences and meetings they always spoke.' Milovan Djilas comments that perhaps the single most important resource available to wartime revolutionary movements was popular enthusiasm; like the Yugoslav partisans, EAM realised that enthusiasm could be produced, and indeed *had* to be if it was to endure.[32]

This insight, of course, came naturally to communist activists. For them, popular support would come, not so much through propaganda – a word which hardly conveys the sense of passionate intensity and involvement they wanted to put across – but through the construction of a new revolutionary morality and the force of their own personal example. Ironically perhaps, the party cadre fulfilled a role in EAM not dissimilar to that of the company commander in the Wehrmacht. The activist was reminded of the need to be a 'People's leader', 'a national hero' capable of inspiring similar heroism in the rank and file. Commitment and enthusiasm for 'the Struggle' were regarded as contagious: a 'patriotic enthusiasm' would earn the loyalty, devotion and comradeship of others.[33]

Greek culture offered fertile soil for such convictions. Idealised masculine virtues included *leventia* and *pallikaria*, two vibrant notions for which 'bravery' or 'courage' offer pallid and inadequate translations. A powerful sense of patriotism also stimulated people to support the resistance. We will look in more detail later at the complex of motives which drove ordinary individuals to 'take to the mountain' and fight; here it is enough to note that EAM was

52a.   Village farmers listen to a speech by EAM/ELAS activists.

evidently highly successful in attracting support. Popular enthusiasm for the cause was undoubtedly widespread and genuine.

But revolutionary enthusiasm and the pursuit of what amounted
to a new, wartime morality had its dark side too. We should never
forget that this conflict had become a war of ideological hatreds in
which, as Djilas noted, 'life itself was metamorphosized into an
idea, and all outsiders were consigned to hell'. We cannot, nor
should we, ignore the increasingly repressive reality of EAM rule in
many areas; if we follow Djilas's analysis through, it becomes clear
that enthusiasm and hatred were ultimately two sides of the same
coin of ideological polarisation.[34] Theatre troupes were presenting
their plays in mountain villages where ELAS firing squads were
executing prisoners. The coercive aspects of EAM's policies became
increasingly evident as the war went on, and helped by its end to
plunge parts of Greece into civil war.

*

EAM stressed the need for national unity. According to the underground press, this was already a reality in Free Greece. There the

286

52b.   An ELAS orator. Epiros, 1944.

people were boss – the *afendi* – in their own land. According to the manifesto *Two Years of Activity by EAM*, the 'wholehearted support' of the people had led to 'a general People's rule' in which hundreds of thousands of Greeks 'live and work in harmony, security and order, and fight with enthusiasm as pioneers for the freedom of the entire country'.[35]

Since EAM declared itself open to anyone willing to work for the 'Great Aim', it followed that opposition to its activities could arise only among those unable or reluctant to recognise what it stood for: 'Our goals are so clear and well-founded in reality and truth that they are only resisted by a notorious minority who oppose the interests of the People and put their own interests first.' This demand for unanimity soon led to the surveillance of a range of enemies, and even the eventual creation of a political police, OPLA, which started out in the autumn of 1943 as a security service for high-ranking resistance activists, but degenerated into a network of assassination squads, operating chiefly in Athens.[36]

ELAS itself acted as a police force in Free Greece, and tried offenders at so-called '*Andartes*' courts', where justice was often summary and execution swift. In the summer of 1944 an 'independent' police force was also established, the National Civil Guard. It was manned chiefly by politically reliable *andartes*, elderly recruits to ELAS and villagers from the ELAS reserve. The inhabitants of Free Greece were told how different this body would be from the prewar gendarmerie: the Guard would not be an arm of the central state, but the guardian and supporter of the People, securing their individual rights and the safety of the People's Democracy.[37]

Even in Free Greece, a few traditional nuisances continued to plague country life. Despite the draconian punishments meted out by People's Courts, some sheep stealers and brigands still followed their old ways. In January 1944, for example, the 'police detachment' of an ELAS unit in the Peloponnese arrested Panayiotis Karalis, a forty-five-year-old brigand, whose life of crime dated back at least ten years. In 1939 a large reward had been placed on his head. Now, five years later, it was an ELAS military court which sentenced Karalis to death.[38] Other offences arose as a result of the war. Following Glinos's harsh words about 'prostitute traitors' in his EAM pamphlet, *What is EAM and What does it Want?*, village girls were sentenced 'for unbefitting conduct'. To fall in love with an Italian soldier became an act of treachery. For this Louisa T., from Mazeika, was condemned like many others to public ridicule by having her hair cut off. Black-marketeers received heavy fines. Gendarmes were arrested for collaborating with the enemy.

With the rise of tensions within the resistance, however, the charge of treachery came to embrace a range of new political offences. 'Anyone who was not on their side was naturally to be considered an enemy,' noted an American observer. EAM's attacks were by no means confined to collaborators, or to the 'attentistes' who had delayed entering the resistance; they increasingly included anyone who was not fighting within EAM/ELAS. The claim that EAM/ELAS was not only the first but also the sole genuine resistance organisation led other resistance groups to be identified with the 'reaction'. One begins to detect a disturbingly Manichaean, Stalinist tone in EAM's propaganda. Against the newly awakened People a 'reactionary coalition' was working, composed of 'social nobodies and dregs, brigands, pimpish guardians of order, degenerates, incompetents and bankrupts'. Villagers around Pilion were warned to 'tighten up the ranks of your EAM and be prepared for your defence. Enemies are springing up all around you like poisonous mushrooms.' Often EAM's bark was worse than its bite, and the ferocity of resistance broadsheets was not always translated into action; nevertheless, enthusiastic members of 'the Organisation' did not need much prompting to do whatever was required to protect the People. A show of force was sometimes necessary for their own safety in the village, as the threat of retribution might be their best guarantee that they would not be denounced to the Germans by other villagers; and it was easy enough for existing village feuds and animosities to be settled in terms of the People's interests.[39]

In the summer of 1943 EDES members were often singled out when food and animals were requisitioned, and if they refused to leave EDES for EAM they frequently lost property before being threatened more directly. Officers were watched closely if they failed to enlist in EAM. Evangelos Beltzios, a twenty-four-year-old airforce pilot who had been released from the Larissa concentration camp in April 1943, was regarded as a 'reactionary' by the local EAM delegate on his return to his village, and placed under surveillance, simply because he had followed King George to Crete in 1941. At the beginning of September, after months of intimidation, he heard of an EDES unit being set up in Karditsa and promptly joined it. Two weeks later he was forced into hiding following an attempt on his life, and realised that his only safety lay in joining an armed unit of EDES. So even before fighting broke out between EAM and EDES in October 1943, EAM's policy of suppressing all political alternatives contributed to a tense atmosphere in the villages it controlled.[40]

Most supporters of EDES knew the risks involved if they fell into the wrong hands, but other victims of EAM's policing did

289

not always realise that 'objectively' they were working against the organisation. Verbal support for the British was enough to attract a warning; more active involvement could lead to death in regions where EAM rule was especially harsh, as for instance in the area around Delphi, where Aris Velouchiotis held sway, or in parts of the Peloponnese. By mid-1944, against a background of complaints about Churchill's monarchist sympathies, anti-British sentiment within EAM was powerful. George Stefos from Thebes was arrested on the grounds that: 'Although warned, you have continued to work for the English who are, broadly speaking, Gestapo agents.' A British liaison officer reported that a shepherd who had purchased some wheat for him had been charged with aiding the British and beaten to death.[41]

The Civil Guard meted out rough justice, often of a very brutal sort. Strangers were liable to be imprisoned if there were the slightest grounds for suspicion, particularly if they were city-dwellers. Political opponents could expect to meet a harsh end. The six collaborators tried before one People's Court in a Thessaly village were told they were being given a conditional discharge and sent home. In the event, they were ambushed on a mountain path and lynched by villagers in what was clearly a planned incident. 'They've killed them,' shouted one girl triumphantly running back into the village. 'They've killed them with beatings and stones!' Here was a typical case where ideological 'enthusiasm' had been whipped up for murderous ends. 'The people here have their own leaders, their own laws,' wrote one bemused and frightened young Athenian, who was also detained by EAM. 'It's a dictatorship . . . an absolute dictatorship of the countryside.'[42]

In Valtos, the so-called 'Robespierre', the communist head of the Civil Guard, terrorised local villagers. Frequent arrests by ELAS and the Civil Guard threw a large section of the population of Levadia into 'a continual state of anxiety' about EAM's ultimate goals. According to the captain of a Civil Guard detachment, the small minority of 'war criminals' who had collaborated with the Germans could be detected by their pro-British attitude, and by the fact that they were 'uneducated', If his victims were slow to learn, however, most of the population was not and by mid-1944 villagers were too afraid of ELAS to do anything against it.[43]

The intensity of the repression varied across the country. Worst affected were regions where there was or had been a real threat to EAM's monopoly of power. When Zervas decided in July 1943 to recruit in western Thessaly, he triggered off a wave of arrests, charges and killings by EAM/ELAS against his supporters. The presence of Colonel Psarros's EKKA group in central Greece made

EAM rule south of Karpenisi particularly harsh. EAM/ELAS were slow to seize control in the Peloponnese, and the strongly royalist tinge of opinion in many areas there forced EAM to struggle hard to prepare the villagers for People's Democracy. Areas where no rival appeared, such as Evvia and parts of central Greece, escaped such systematic persecution.[44]

'Revolutionary Elections'

In such a rigid vision of society, with its satanic opponents, 'spontaneous' enthusiasts and enlightened, disciplined and determined leadership, what room existed for the recognition of popular opinion? What indeed did 'popular opinion' actually mean in a country under enemy occupation? These questions leads us straight to the strange, underground 'national elections' of April 1944, which marked the culmination of EAM's ambitions to transform itself into an alternative state apparatus.

Early 1944 was a critical moment for the Greek resistance. During February and March, EAM/ELAS, the British and other resistance groups negotiated a truce, ending the internecine fighting which had continued since the previous October. At the same time, the credibility of the exile government sank to new depths as a result of King George's obstinate insistence on returning to Greece after Liberation. Inspired by Tito's example in Yugoslavia, EAM's leaders started to dream of forming their own government in the mountains.

During the winter of 1943–44 EAM had approached George Papandreou and other progressive figures from the prewar political scene, and invited them to head a provisional government in Free Greece. Papandreou rejected their overtures because he believed that the communists held an unbreakable stranglehold over EAM, and he did not wish to provide cosmetic cover for the KKE. But figures from the left wing of the old Liberal Party, and social democrats such as constitutional lawyer Alexandros Svolos were more receptive. Eventually they convinced themselves that their participation in the new organisation, by diluting the power of the KKE, would make a peaceful political transition at Liberation possible.[45]

On 10 March 1944 – while discussions with Svolos were still in progress – the EAM-sponsored Political Committee of National Liberation (PEEA) was sworn in as the supreme political authority in Free Greece. It was led by Colonel Bakirtzis – the so-called 'Red

53. The National Council: delegates from the Peloponnese pose in the school building at Koryschades where the Council sessions took place. The back wall is draped with allied flags under the motto 1821–1944. Along the side wall there are painted portraits of heroes of the War of 1821 and EAM slogans.

Colonel' – who had left Psarros's EKKA organisation in disgust at its monarchist and collaborationist direction. PEEA was dominated by communists: General Mantakas, secretary for Army Affairs, had secretly joined the Party, Bakirtzis was sympathetic, while the 'Old Man', Siantos, combined his duties as general secretary of the Party with a new post as PEEA secretary for Internal Affairs. But despite the KKE's predominance, PEEA's declaration of aims was strikingly moderate in tone.[46]

The main reason for this was that PEEA's composition was not yet complete, for EAM hoped to obtain greater non-communist support. Indeed, in April PEEA was reformed on a broader basis when the non-communist Professor Svolos became president, and Colonel Bakirtzis his deputy; two progressive Liberals and two university professors also acquired portfolios. However EAM – with its communist direction – was still the executive through which PEEA representatives worked, while as PEEA's secretary of Internal Affairs, KKE boss Siantos controlled Free Greece's administrative apparatus and the Civil Guard. Svolos and the other newcomers retained intellectual prestige but little real power, and they soon came to realise this.

PEEA had pledged to hold elections for a National Council, and EAM's apparatus was essential in organising these. Because the elections eventually coincided with momentous diplomatic developments in Cairo, and because information about the way they were conducted is so scanty, little attention has been paid to them. EAM claimed, however, that 1.5 million people took part – more than in the last free elections in 1936 – and hailed the results as a clear mark of popular support. One historian has seen the elections as 'the first opportunity the Greek people had during the occupation to express its views with votes'.[47] Whether or not these large claims are justified, the National Council episode is still worth a look for what it tells us about the paradoxes of wartime radicalism.

Even at the time, people were confused about the idea of holding elections under enemy occupation. KKE member Kostas Despotopoulos, the legal adviser to ELAS, was told by Siantos to prepare guidelines for forthcoming elections. 'You're joking,' he exclaimed. But another communist official, Porfyrogenis, put him on the right track: 'Do you think we invited you to draw up a decree, an electoral law like that we're used to? No, we'll have revolutionary elections, as we're under occupation. . . . We will not call the voters to the ballot-box, we will go ourselves to their offices and tell them: these are the candidates for Athens for the National Council. You want them? You like them? Sign.'[48]

Voting procedures bore little relation to peacetime practice. EAM teams delivered ballot papers and instructions to individual houses, and returned later to pick up the completed forms. The voter could change names on the list, but could hardly mount a campaign for alternative candidates. Thus, individuals selected by EAM were sure to win, even though the election was supposedly open to members of all parties.[49] In the provinces villagers were supposed to choose electors on the basis of the number of inhabitants in a given district: the electors would later vote on a representative for the National Council. For the first time in Greek history, women were – in theory – allowed to vote in elections. Voting was secret, and illiterate villagers were allowed to ask anybody to write down their choice for them. EAM committees ran the polling, and selected a list of candidates, though in principle anyone over the age of twenty-one was entitled to present themselves for election.[50]

EAM's candidates swept the board, of course, though not all EAM candidates belonged to the KKE. In Evvia, where elections were relatively open, Liberal and royalist candidates stood in several villages, though they were usually defeated by large margins. In Agios Georgios, which had only ten communists before the war, the two members elected were a non-communist EAM candidate, with 149 votes, and a communist EAM member with 137. In Setta, which housed an ELAS regiment, there were four candidates: the two belonging to EAM received over 200 votes each, while the Liberal collected five, and the royalist four. Each of the four EAM candidates in Karpenisi was elected with over 900 votes; only ten people dared to vote for a lawyer said by EAM to be an 'arch-reactionary'. One reason for this timidity was that in many cases the voter was expected to sign his or her ballot sheet, making a large vote in support of EAM almost meaningless; even refusing to return a ballot paper became an act of courage.[51]

Before 1936, too, elections had usually given the ruling party various underhand and coercive ways of attracting rural voters: in this respect at least, things were not much different during the war in 'Free Greece', and we should avoid idealising the National Council as a free expression of the popular will. It is true that the deputies to the Council, who made their way to its session at the village of Koryschades in May, represented a much broader cross-section of Greek society than had been found in prewar parliaments. The traditional stranglehold of lawyers and doctors had been broken: speakers in the extraordinary and undeniably moving Council sessions included women, farmers in their working breeches, workmen, artisans, priests and journalists. Their presence, however, was the product of deliberate, if well-intentioned, political engineering by EAM electoral committees. There are disquieting historical analogies with this extraordinary wartime episode to be found in the People's Democracies of Eastern Europe after the war. Such analogies would not be entirely just to EAM, since it was operating in wartime – with all the constraints that brought – and, more significantly, because it was not regarded as an instrument of Soviet oppression but, on the contrary, as an organisation fighting for national liberation. Even so, hindsight should not always be ignored, and the postwar evolution of, say, Tito's partisan movement into a one-party state should prevent excessive naivety about what EAM's organisers meant when they talked about 'revolutionary elections'. Rather than being the powerhouse of a 'bourgeois' democracy, the National Council symbolised EAM's overriding stress on social inclusiveness.[52]

In the end, even EAM turned out to have little use for its new creation. The Council itself became redundant after negotiations between PEEA delegates and the exile government in Cairo led to PEEA members entering George Papandreou's Government of National Unity under British auspices. It never met again after May, and was formally wound up in November. Rather than the foundation of a permanent new political system, as some of EAM's more radical activists had certainly hoped, the National Council turned out to have been a tool of EAM's leaders in their protracted negotiations with the politicians in Egypt.

As unsettling perhaps as this question of the true significance of the National Council was the ambiguity that hung over the key concept of People's Democracy (*Laokratia*) itself. Perhaps no other phrase was more often mentioned inside EAM, yet none was so obscure – enticing supporters, and exciting the worst suspicions of EAM's opponents. OSS agent Costas Couvaras asked a young *andarte* what *Laokratia* meant. Twenty-year-old Georgios said that he had joined the guerrillas to drive the occupiers out of Greece and to take his revenge on their Greek collaborators; he had not given the future much thought. He answered vaguely: 'It will be a type of government where the common people rule the country.' As Couvaras observed, the word *Laokratia* had 'a good ring to it', especially after the experience of the Metaxas dictatorship; its very vagueness added to its appeal in times when people had their eyes fixed on the present. 'No one can explain what People's Democracy means,' wrote Theotokas, 'nor even cares. People don't feel the need for an explanation. They like the sound of this word and the indefinite trend towards a "state of the People". The People rise up, the People will be the Boss, the evil-doers will stop treating the People unjustly – that is what people want.'[53]

*

What the 'People wanted' was not much clearer at the top of the movement, where the KKE leadership was split between revolutionaries and reformists. Following the news that PEEA delegates had committed EAM/ELAS to join the British-backed government in exile, the KKE Central Committee convened in the summer of 1944 for a crisis meeting in the mountain village of Petrilia. This was the moment when the choice between a peaceful or a violent road to revolution could no longer be postponed. Ioannides, the Party's second in command, insisted that there must be no rupture with the British: the KKE had to work together with the bourgeois parties and demonstrate its right to govern. However, his arguments were countered by the communist secretary of the EAM Central Committee, Thanasis Hadzis, who complained that the resistance was being betrayed. In a bitter speech which reflected the views of many EAM activists, Hadzis argued that they had already established 'another power' in Greece by creating EAM/ELAS: why then bow to the British and their clients? 'We cannot follow two paths,' he warned, 'We must make our choice.' But Hadzis's position was weakened as other party delegates made it clear that EAM would lose much support if the non-communist parties broke away from it, as they might were EAM to 'go it alone.' Even more decisively, no doubt, a Soviet mission arrived to steer the KKE back towards moderation, for following secret exploratory talks with the British over the carving up of Eastern Europe, Stalin was happy for Greece to come within a British sphere of influence.

The KKE leadership certainly did not know of these high-level deals and may have been confused by Stalin's unexpected moderation. There had been no clear lead from Moscow ever since the dissolution of Comintern in the spring of 1943, and for men used to obeying orders from above this must have been extremely disconcerting. As Woodhouse noted later, EAM's leadership was split between 'hawks' and 'doves', and the 'Old Man' Siantos was 'both in turn'. At this decisive juncture, desperately trying to hold the Party – and EAM – together, Siantos finally backed Ioannides and the policy of co-operation. But his arguments were uncertain and hesitant. 'It was difficult for anyone to derive clear conclusions as to the new line he proposed,' noted a depressed Hadzis. Ultimately, the KKE got the worst of both worlds: its half-hearted commitment to legalism frustrated many activists inside the Party without removing the suspicions of its bourgeois opponents.[54]

CHAPTER TWENTY-ONE

ELAS: the People's Liberation Army

EAM's military wing, ELAS, dwarfed the other guerrilla organisations. It was uniquely independent of Allied support and carried out the most attacks on Wehrmacht units. But of course it also threatened other Greeks, who were increasingly worried about the spectre of Bolshevism. It did not take long for ELAS to become the object of fantastic and often quite mythical accusations.

Lurid stories circulated in the terrified salons of upper middle-class Athens. According to conservative politician Dino Tsaldaris, for instance, Greece was under the grip of 'an organisation so barbarous and savage that its terrorists resort to the practice of killing people by biting'.[55] More predictably, perhaps, others warned that ELAS was 'not national or fighting for freedom, but an organisation with obscure aims entirely contrary to the idea of the Fatherland and popular liberties'. One infantry colonel was put in mind of the Terror during the French Revolution, when – according to him – 100,000 Jacobins, 'mostly ex-convicts and failures in life', persecuted 25 million Frenchmen.[56]

The wily and expert Zervas was playing the anti-communist card for all it was worth as early as the spring of 1943. The collaborationist press was slower, but by the beginning of 1944 it too was denouncing EAM/ELAS as the 'Bolsheviks of the Greek mountains'. Possessed by a 'Satanic spirit', 'gangs of bandits' were spreading havoc through the countryside. 'Criminals' and 'gang-sters' encouraged 'anti-social elements' in every village. Conservatives called for assistance in 'cleansing the countryside of anarchic elements'. The *andartes* were described with revealing snobbery as 'an army of shoe-makers and carters'.[57]

A wealthy landowner from Pyrgos told her son simply that she had become afraid of 'the Mountains'. Returning with understandable relief from captivity at ELAS's hands in Free Greece, a young Athenian felt that coming down from the hills and making his way to the coast near Corinth he was re-entering civilisation. 'And what civilisation!' he wrote later. 'Entering Aigion [a small coastal town] I could swear I was entering Europe.' To many urban bourgeois, ELAS seemed to be little less than the revenge of the long-neglected provinces on the *politeia* – the culture of the city. 'The mountain types,' noted a British officer, 'struck terror into the city-dwellers' hearts.' This 'ELAS-mindedness' played no small part in fuelling the civil war which followed Liberation, even infecting British officers like SOE's Donald Hamilton-Hill, whose description of the 'scruffy and evil-looking bandits' he met on Poros was quite characteristic – in its mixture of scaremongering horror and contempt – of many anti-communist accounts.[58] Even today ELAS remains a controversial and highly emotional subject in Greece. But was ELAS a communist-controlled army? If so, what did that mean? Who actually fought in ELAS, and for what reasons?

*

An ELAS central committee was set up as early as February 1942, yet the *andartiko* remained uncoordinated for much longer than that. It took another year for the first local groups and their *kapetans* to become aware of one another's existence, link up, and be brought under some central direction. The KKE's national leadership was cautious about supporting the guerrilla struggle. The 2nd Panhellenic Party Congress in December 1942 demonstrated that so far as the Communist Party was concerned, the cities remained a more promising venue than the hills for political agitation. This angered some party members like *kapetans* Aris Velouchiotis and Markos Vafiades, who had become involved with *andarte* bands.[59]

Partly to check the *kapetans'* autonomy, a general staff was created on 19 May 1943; but it was not until the summer that it began functioning effectively. Its three-man command – Sarafis (military commander), Aris (*kapetan*) and Tsimas (political adviser) – had been appointed at a meeting of the EAM-ELAS Central Committee in Athens. Sarafis's memoirs mention elliptically that 'it was pointed out that the struggle needed direction'. He does not say by whom. Aris and Tsimas, however, were both long-standing party members. Sarafis himself, a former Venizelist army officer who had taken to the hills with a republican band which ELAS units had dissolved, was by this stage sympathetic to the Party's aims, and may already have joined. Hence the new central command of ELAS gave the Party great influence over its future development.[60]

The movement was physically unified by concentrating all the *andarte* forces on the Pindos mountains in the late spring of 1943. Faced with an Italian offensive, *andarte* units in Macedonia and the hills of Eastern Thessaly were instructed to make the dangerous journey across the plains up into the safety of the Pindos. According to *Kapetan* Boukouvalas, this 'great movement' changed the mentality of the guerrillas. The *andarte* ceased to identify himself with his own village or mountain. Seeing himself as part of a larger force broke down his 'narrow localised attitude'.[61]

Throughout ELAS right down to the smallest group, each unit had its political adviser, usually a member of the Party. The *politikos* 'enlightened' the *andartes* about the nature of the struggle, and ensured that military commanders took political considerations into account. Thanasis Mitsopoulos, a schoolteacher (and a party member) was appointed *politikos* of his unit on Mount Paikos when he was twenty-three. The *andartes*, mostly youths from the surrounding villages, sat around under the trees, or stood and listened. Standing before them, book in hand, Mitsopoulos discussed Glinos's manifesto, *What is EAM and What does it Want?* Mario, an Italian deserter with socialist sympathies who had escaped from Salonika, delivered fiery revolutionary speeches in fractured Greek. He told the *andartes* about the death of Matteoti, and taught them songs like 'Bandiera Rossa'.[62]

In Mitsopoulos's unit there were also regular party meetings. At first these were held 'secretly', according to instructions from above: the party leadership was anxious not to substantiate rumours that ELAS was 'a communist army, which would have alienated the People, who were not yet aware of who the genuine patriots were'. In fact, the Party's role must have been an open secret: Mario, after all, was telling his listeners that 'communism will win'.[63]

In March 1944 the figure of the *politikos* was abandoned at lower echelons, and ELAS moved towards a two-man command structure. By this time, EAM had consolidated its grip on daily life in Free Greece, leaving ELAS to concentrate on military duties. But communist influence remained as strong as ever. The centralisation of ELAS suited the Party as well as the army officers it was trying to attract into ELAS. Both preferred a rigid system of command, with a strong central authority, to the decentralised small groups with which the resistance had begun. Both supported what one *andarte* proudly termed the 'armyfication' of the movement. Through his position as ELAS representative on the EAM Central Committee, Party Secretary Siantos wielded enormous power over ELAS itself, and it was quite customary for disputes between different officers within ELAS to be referred to him for settlement.[64]

However, the predominance of the Party did not necessarily mean that ELAS was committed to an eventual seizure of power

54. ELAS *kapetans* in Epiros, 1944.

once the Germans left. As in EAM, the most significant disputes over policy were occurring within the Party. Both Aris, the belligerent *kapetan*, and Andreas Tsimas, the sophisticated spokesman for a Tito-style partisan campaign, clashed with Party Secretary Siantos. By taking over from Tsimas, and sending Aris off to the Peloponnese, Siantos made it clear that his policy of legalism would prevail, and that ELAS would remain open to the possibility of working together with the British.

The Kapetans

This, like many party decisions, did not please the *kapetans*. Bold, charismatic and fiercely independent, these men were, or regarded themselves as, the founders of the first guerrilla bands: they had appreciated the possibilities of armed resistance earlier than anyone else; they knew what it required.

Aris Velouchiotis, the bearded 'God of War', was the outstanding figure among them. He was a troubled soul, for before the war he had publicly repented of his party activity in order to be released from prison, and many other party members regarded him with suspicion. But he was a charismatic leader of men; in the mountains songs about his exploits circulated widely and it was he who had been largely responsible for persuading party functionaries in Athens to take the *andartiko* seriously. In early 1943 they had allowed him to continue his activities, but sent Tsimas to keep an eye on him. Stocky and softly spoken, Aris and his special bodyguards, the 'Black-caps', were capable of terrifying brutality. 'Fear of the Lord is the beginning of Wisdom,' says the country proverb, and Aris had taken it to heart. His early pre-eminence in the *andartiko* in central Greece had been achieved through exemplary executions and the torture of traitors, informers, and others who crossed his path. Sarafis saw in Aris's brutality the traces of the many years' cruelty he had suffered as a party activist at the hands of the police before the war. Others saw only a frightening sadism.

Kapetan was basically a term of respect accorded by the cautious peasant to the leader of any armed gang that crossed his path. By no means every *kapetan* was politically active: 'Tsavelas' and 'Orestes' had been gendarmerie officers before the war. Karalivanos was a professional brigand. But many leading ELAS *kapetans* were indeed educated men with radical views. 'Akritas', a lawyer in his mid-thirties, was 'a revolutionary by nature'; 'Kissavos' and 'Lassanis' were teachers; 'Kikitsas' was a former bank employee. All of them seem to have regarded communist advisers with respect, if not actually to have become party members. The dashing 'Boukouvalas', who served in the cavalry in Albania and founded an ELAS cavalry unit, looked up to party functionary Karayeorgis: 'We listened to him like a god – such influence he had over us.' 'Diamantis', 'Nikitaras' and 'Markos' were already committed communists. 'Napoleon' and 'Mitsos' in the Peloponnese were younger men, trained as officer cadets, who gravitated towards the Party.[65]

But the *kapetans* were not the sort of men to lose sleep over the need for party discipline, and the leadership in Athens was often tempted to do away with them altogether. For their part, the *kapetans* felt the party apparatchiks were too timid for their own good, with little faith in the revolutionary potential of the *andartiko*. Markos Vafiades, who would later lead the Democratic Army during the Civil War, chafed at the indecision of his party superiors. He scorned their defensive tactical thinking and despised the way they had turned a mobile, aggressive guerrilla force into a sluggish imitation of a 'bourgeois' army.[66]

According to Markos, the Party in its desperate desire to attract regular army officers had clogged up ELAS with useless staff types and elderly military bureaucrats, who had no idea how to fight a guerrilla war. This was not, according to him, entirely the officers' fault. Given a different setting, they might have offered valuable technical and scientific advice to a 'mass, popular and revolutionary army . . . with a proletarian composition'.[67] *Kapetan* 'Boukouvalas' shared Markos's misgivings. Many career soldiers had failed to adjust to life in the mountains; often they were 'clearly incompetent'. Meanwhile, the Party was too timid about effective political indoctrination. In his judgement, 'the political direction in ELAS never presented itself adequately or strongly enough'.[68]

The *kapetans'* chief complaint was echoed by British and American officers, who also bemoaned the excessive bureaucracy of ELAS and wanted a looser structure to increase its military efficiency. Like the *kapetans*, but for very different reasons, they would have liked to see a less centralised organisation.

The *kapetans* have been eulogised by the French author Dominique Eudes, who sees them as the unsung heroes of the resistance. For Eudes they were the men who could have carried through a revolution in Greece if only the Party had heeded them. This seems unrealistic. The *kapetans* gave ELAS its dynamism; but they were not co-operative men and did not act or think as a group. For the most part they operated on a regional level, not a national one. By themselves they could never have provided the leadership for a nationally co-ordinated resistance movement. The only time they ever gathered together, in November 1944, was after the Germans had left, and on that occasion they reaffirmed their loyalty to ELAS headquarters and rejected the idea of a forcible seizure of power.[69]

The Officers

The army traditionally occupied a highly respected position in Greek society, and the Party knew that the presence of regular officers in ELAS would reassure potential recruits. However, the military, which had intervened so frequently in civilian politics before the war, showed more caution, particularly at higher echelons, about heading for the 'mountains' and the uncertainties of irregular warfare. The response was more positive from younger officers and cadets. But many were put off by ELAS's communist associations, and joined up with other smaller bands, or bided their time. The majority of the officers who went 'to the Mountain' ended up joining Zervas rather than the 'communists'.[70]

Those who entered ELAS came under pressure to join the Party and accept the advice of the *politikos*. Colonel Ferraios, commanding officer of the 5th Brigade, managed to relegate his political adviser 'Heraklis' to a marginal position. Yet Colonel Papathanasiou, chief of staff of the 13th Roumeli Division and an excellent professional officer, found that political control made effective military command impossible. Brigadier Kalabalikis – a 'short cheerful bespectacled man' and 'an able military commander' – had to share his command of the Macedonian divisions with Markos and with his *politikos*, Lassanis. He saw this as an insult to his professional qualifications, and certainly was not sympathetic to their hopes of founding a 'People's Revolutionary Army', nor to their tendency to order reprisals against 'reactionary' villages in their area. 'Kapetanie! you're taking all my units. What sort of General am I?' Kalabalikis expostulated on one occasion.[71]

Because the Party was anxious not to alienate Kalabalikis, Markos was eventually reprimanded. But this was most uncommon, and other officers were so disturbed by the political undercurrents that they tried to leave, despite having sworn allegiance to ELAS. An exceptional case was that of Colonel Dimaratos, a monarchist, who had made it clear when he joined ELAS that he was not interested in politics. When fighting with Zervas's EDES broke out, he was acting as military commander of Macedonia. Upon receiving orders to send units against Zervas, he and several other officers resisted, on the grounds that they had no desire to be involved in a civil war. Dimaratos was allowed to resign and to return to his village.[72] But when other officers tried to leave, especially for another resistance movement, they were treated as deserters and shot.

Those officers who did join ELAS were more likely to be republicans than royalists. Some of them had suffered personal hardship and even exile during the Metaxas dictatorship. ELAS's commander-in-chief, Sarafis, and General Grigoriadis were two of the most prominent republicans attracted into ELAS. The ideological transition for such men was often surprisingly smooth. Major Fotis Zisopoulos, who commanded an ELAS regiment on Mount Paikos, was so passionate a republican he had even baptised his daughter 'Republic' because she was born in the year (1924) it was declared. 'Grandpa' – as Zisopoulos was disrepectfully known by his men – soon became more radical in his political aims than his party adviser. A large number of former army NCOs and cadets even became party members.[73]

Their assimilation becomes more understandable when we bear in mind that officers whose main desire was to fight the Germans had good reason to join ELAS. 'Paparas', for example, unimpressed with what he saw of EDES's will to fight, chose ELAS on this basis. We have the disillusioned diary of a young EDES *andarte*, in which he freely expresses his disgust at the poor organisation, factionalism and inactivity of Zervas's bands. And there is similar evidence regarding Colonel Psarros and his EKKA outfit. Psarros was good company and personally courageous, but he 'could not command a band of 10 *andartes*, let alone a regiment,' wrote a disgusted OSS observer. For all the reservations about its military performance, expressed in particular by some hostile British liaison officers, there can be no doubt that ELAS, whether or not it was attacking as many enemy positions as it might have done, was certainly attacking far more than any other resistance movement.[74]

The politically charged atmosphere did not prevent the old officer corps gaining a position of some prominence in ELAS by Liberation. Sarafis reckons that there were some 800 regular officers, and about 1,500 republicans like him from the reserve list under arms: they easily outnumbered the thousand or so *kapetans*. Indeed, since some *kapetans* had actually been junior officers in the Albanian campaign, it starts to look as though officers from the prewar army were fairly well represented.[75]

This makes it easier to understand the complaints of a radical *kapetan* like Markos, a man with no formal military training, that ELAS had been taken over by the officer corps. It certainly had not, and many of these officers found the egalitarian atmosphere, the variable quality of their men and the harshness of life in the mountains difficult to get used to. But they did their best to turn ELAS into the sort of army they recognised. What is doubtful, of course, is whether this actually benefited ELAS from a military point of view. The verdict of John Mulgan, a young New Zealander with the Allied Military Mission, was scathing:

> The movement had outgrown itself and become militarily worthless. At some stage, Greek army officers, whose sense of dignity and grandeur outweighed their intelligence, had made a movement which should have been small, compact and irregular in design into a vast army. They spoke of divisions, regiments and battalions, first, second, and third bureaux. . . . They had nothing but contempt for the small, personally-led bands with which the movement had started. Their new army gave them a sense of dignity and status; the fact that it was of no military value didn't strike them.[76]

The Rank and File

Revolutionary armies are rural armies, and to understand them, we have to understand the land and the people who work it. The distinctive feature of the Greek countryside was its relatively egalitarian social structure, and the absence of either a landowning aristocracy or of poor, landless peasants. The typical Greek *choriatis* (villager) or *agrotis* (farmer) was a smallholder, with his own few strips of vines, wheat and potatoes. Though his crops did not usually bring in much, sometimes forcing him and his children to look for extra sources of income by emigrating, or working in the towns, he had a keen sense of independence and called no one *afendi* (boss). The young men from the mountains who formed the backbone of the movement had a still stronger sense of *filotimo* (honour); to the more polished Athenians who joined them, these shepherds and charcoal burners displayed 'a Corsican wildness, a grotesque egoism, a chivalrous pride'. They made up in natural argumentativeness and quick wit what they lacked in schooling. All of them had their own reasons for fighting. We do them no service by presenting them as cannon fodder for the Party. We must find out who they were and why they joined.[77]

*

The *andartiko* was a young man's war. Most ELAS fighters were aged between fifteen and twenty-five, male, stationed in units which were based near their home village. Data is scarce, but of 5,000 *andartes* from ELAS regiments in central Macedonia, 80 per cent were farmers or agricultural labourers and only 5 per cent were white-collar workers or professionals, such as teachers and doctors. Most of them were from the region.[78]

For many who went 'to the mountains', the Albanian campaign of 1940–41 had been a formative experience. Of 600 former ELAS fighters held in the Averoff prison in 1946, 220 had been wounded at the front, and more had fought there. Of 20 ex-ELAS men held in Amalias jail at the same time, all were veterans of the Albania campaign. The overall proportion of 1940–41 veterans in ELAS was initially perhaps as high as 50 per cent, though falling over time as more teenagers joined.[79]

The veterans of the Albanian 'epic' had hated the humiliation of having the Italians lord it over them. Dionysios Goumas, who had been an infantryman at the front, felt 'untamed fury' at seeing the *macaronades* strutting through the streets of Athens. He joined ELAS and was soon taking part in the rallies and street battles. Yannis P., who fought with a cavalry regiment in 1941, was later arrested by

55.   A young man's war: youthful *andartes* on the march in the mountains of Epiros, 1944.

the Italians 'for patriotic activities', tortured and interned. When he escaped in 1943 he joined ELAS. Kostas G., who had been seriously wounded in Albania, was arrested and tortured by the Italians after he returned home because he had not handed over his pistol. He got himself set free with a generous bribe of olive oil, and then joined a team of ELAS saboteurs in Messenia. After spending the whole war fighting in ELAS he suffered a fate that was to be sadly typical: he was arrested in July 1945 by right-wing government forces on a trumped-up charge, and was still languishing in prison seventeen years later.[80]

While some *andartes* were forced into the mountains by their defiant nationalism, others joined up voluntarily. Village boys often heard about the *andartiko* by word of mouth, or when their village was visited by one of the local bands. The *kapetan* would make his speech in the village square, and there would be singing and dancing. Swept up by the atmosphere, many volunteered on the spot. Some were swayed by the advice of patrons or respected local figures. Others joined up because of the lack of work, like twenty-

56. New recruits to ELAS pose under the Greek flag.

year-old Nikos Paraschakis, a cobbler by trade, who barely survived the first winter of the war, and then found a band in Thessaly with the help of his uncle.[81]

Recruits often joined together: a group of three or four from the same village would set off into the hills, looking for the *andartes'* lair. There are cases of brothers signing up, or a father and sons. An unusual case was that of Spyros Papastafidas, a gendarmerie officer with four boys. His eldest son Gianni, arrested by the Italians for helping English soldiers escape from Greece, broke out of jail, took to the hills and joined ELAS's 54th Regiment above Volos. His own position now jeopardised, Spyros fled too and became a recruiter for the 54th. Another son, Vasili, still at school in 1940, volunteered for ELAS after the Italians surrendered in 1943.[82]

Of those who joined at the period of greatest expansion, in the summer of 1943, a large number certainly believed that the war would be over in a matter of months. Mitsopoulos describes a group of men from one village who made a real nuisance of themselves after it became obvious that the Germans were staying for another winter. 'They said two or three months and everything

307

would be over,' they grumbled.[83] Eventually they became so un-popular that they were allowed to leave.

As time went on, new reasons for joining ELAS emerged. The large quantities of weapons ELAS captured from the Italians in September 1943 allowed it to recruit more widely. Anti-guerrilla operations, which swept the country from the second half of 1943, brought random shootings, mass arrests of hostages and reprisals, forcing young men – the highest-risk category – to flee to the bands for their own safety. Persecution by right-wing bands, armed by the Wehrmacht or the SS, had the same effect.[84]

ELAS, in its turn, urged gendarmes and members of collabor-ationist units to defect. It attacked its opponents where they were most vulnerable, through their families. In 1944 the approach of the Red Army, and EAM's entry into the Cairo government, gave new force to such demands. In some areas, by that summer, it took considerable stubbornness or courage *not* to join the *andartes*. Consider the very forceful warning, evidently not the first, an ELAS messenger left in late August 1944 for an unfortunate gen-darme in the isolated port of Karystos:

> Fellow-fighter,
> We've sent you many messages – to join the Civil Guard. Now we send you once more the chance to save yourself, THE LAST. Come this evening and present yourself in the village of Kalyvia, bringing your gun and other equipment. If you don't heed this last warning, you will be considered a traitor with all the consequences.
> Learn that Paris has fallen, Romania is suing for peace and the Germans . . . are scared. Also that National Unity was agreed in Cairo, so that EAMite Ministers enter the Government, so that not even from there is there any hope of salvation for traitors. . . . Again we invite you, in the name of the Greek fatherland, to save yourself.
> Freedom for the People – Death to Fascism,
> Heraklis.[85]

Obviously, it was not just ELAS's opponents who were forced to worry about their families. On top of the other hardships an *andarte* faced there was the anxiety about the suffering his activity would bring to friends and relatives. In most villages it was soon known which families were connected to EAM/ELAS. Female relatives of ELAS fighters were beaten and sometimes raped by Security Battalion men, and their homes were the first to be burned. ELAS guerrillas relied on village EAM representatives to give their dependants security. But they did not like to move too far from them in case they were needed.[86]

Relatives often paid a heavy price for an *andarte*'s activity. Dionysios Goumas lost four brothers to the Germans. One had been killed after a street chase. Three were arrested, tortured by the SS and shot in Haidari concentration camp; Goumas only discovered their fate after Liberation. Most of the men Winston Ehrgott worked with in an ELAS cavalry detachment 'had suffered either bereavement or other personal sorrow at Nazi hands'. Over a quarter of the detainees in the Averoff prison in 1946 – held for resistance activity – had had close relatives killed by the Germans or their agents.[87]

Some *andartes* thirsted for revenge: their relatives' blood 'pulled them along', and they enlisted in combat units or execution squads. Christos Jecchinis recalled taking part in an attack on a train in Thessaly when he followed a young *andarte* as he ran through the bombed wreckage, coming upon a German soldier, and knifing him to death with the words: '*This* is for my brother, you filthy bastard!' Personal grief overwhelmed men like Mitrany, a Jewish doctor from Salonika, who begged to be assigned to a combat unit so that he could avenge his father who had been deported. He got his way, and eventually died in a gun battle with German troops. The executioner for an ELAS band on Mount Kissavos was 'Clearchus, a thin gentle-looking man of wide interests'. Clearchus was a former civil servant from Athens. Although his wife and children had survived that first winter, he had been dreadfully affected by the sight of the people dying in the streets, and could not understand how other Greeks had allowed fellow-countrymen to starve. Revenge dominated his thoughts. He confided to a friend that it gave him 'a thrill of pleasure in hacking off the head of a fellow-Greek who had shared in the guilt of the Germans in starving Greeks to death'.[88]

However, grief did not only lead to such cruelty. For many *andartes*, the sorrows the war had brought them were what deepened their commitment to the 'Organisation' and the 'Holy Struggle', sustaining them in harsh living conditions, and giving them fortitude. Goumas, who fought under the name 'Manoli', described himself as 'a tireless, rather shy and very serious fighter'. Couvaras noticed a combination of 'fatalism combined with a lack of fear' in many *andartes* and remarked that 'people have a kind of inner pride when describing how a certain number of their family died fighting the enemy or quislings'. 'These men were hardened not only by battle but also by having been deprived of their youth, their families and normal existence,' writes Djilas of the Yugoslav partisans in terms which apply equally to their Greek counterparts.[89]

The Cause

Joining the resistance brought a second baptism: to protect his family, the first thing the new recruit did when he arrived on 'the mountain' was to choose a *nom de guerre*. And the names they chose offered the first clue to what they saw themselves fighting for.

A few, of course, acquired nicknames almost inevitably: 'Corakas' (the crow), was so called for his very dark moustache, and 'Pappous' (Grandpa) was a military officer in his mid-fifties. There was 'Sleepy' and 'Six-Fingers', and an Italian deserter called 'Rigoletto'. More often, however, the would-be *andarte* picked a name to stress his determination and ambition. *Kapetan* 'Nikitaras', a former lawyer and reserve army officer, and 'Nikiforos', the renowned young *kapetan* who operated around Mount Parnassos, both held out the promise of victory (*niki*). 'Lefteris' would bring freedom (*eleftheria*) to Greece, and 'Keravnos' would strike the enemy like a thunderbolt. The *kapetans* 'Kissavos' and Pilioritis' and even more humble *andartes* like 'Agrafiotis' and 'Paikos' boasted of the mountains which had become their home.

Classical heroes also played a prominent role: 'Heraklis' and 'Achilles' were both twenty when they helped blow up the Gorgopotamos viaduct; 'Clearchus', as we have seen, executed traitors in eastern Thessaly; 'Periklis' was a former employee of the Lamia Electricity Company who became a *kapetan* and later ended up in exile in Poland. 'Pelopidas' was one of the first party members to go into the resistance, and became well known for his '*pallikaria* [youthful bravery] and his *entimotita* [sense of honour]'. He was later killed in the Civil War; a wartime photo shows a medium-built man with a bushy black beard and dark eyes, tight-lipped, standing with his great coat open to show an old army uniform, Sam Browne belt, and his bandolier slung across his chest – the classic *andarte* pose. 'Odysseus' terrorised the villagers of Evros, while the more affable 'General Orestes' in Evia had been a civil servant in housing before becoming an officer in the ELAS 5th Brigade where he cut a striking figure in his 'Brooks quality flannel shirt, gabardine jodhpurs, good boots, sheepskin coat, fur cap and large handlebar moustache'.[90]

Alongside the legends of ancient Greece, great heroes of the 1821 War of Independence were resurrected. They included men like 'Ypsilantis', a classics teacher from Siatista, *kapetans* 'Botsaris',

'Androutsos' and 'Karaiskakis'. One immodest army NCO from the Peloponnese proudly called himself 'Kolokotronis' after the greatest Turk-slayer of them all. The heroes of 1821 were household names for generations of Greek schoolchildren, and when the young men of 1941 felt the 'thirst' to fight for the freedom of their country, not surprisingly they cast their minds back to the earlier liberation struggle. 'We are the boys of '21,' *andartes* told 'Paparas' when he joined ELAS. Zaroyianni writes that when the *andartiko* suddenly expanded in Thessaly in 1943, everyone thought of 'our ancestors' fights against the Turks'. 'The '21 lives again,' an ELAS officer told his men. 'Let it be now as it was then. Freedom is not given, it is taken!'[91]

Remarkably few names were drawn from later times. *Kapetan* 'Boukouvalas' named himself after one of the martyrs of the 1910 peasant uprising at Kileler. But Kileler was his family village, so his choice can also be seen as a typical example of local pride as well as a sign of agrarian radicalism. There were obvious ideological messages in names like 'Epanastatis' (revolutionary) and 'Oktovrianos', 'Spartakos', 'Josef' or 'Vladimiros'. But such names were not common, and it was clearly not the Bolshevik Revolution which provided the ideal for most *andartes* as they entered the 'struggle'.[92]

In the Peloponnese, a senior army officer in ELAS took a close look at a band of 220 guerrillas, many of whom were local boys he knew personally: he reckoned that no more than fifteen could have been described as communists, and said, 'I doubt whether some of those knew what communism is.'[93] A former *kafeneion* owner turned *andarte* from Salonika, asked by his instructor what EAM was fighting for, stood up straight and answered: 'The aim of EAM is to wipe out communism in Greece.' He was clearly one of those obtuse good-for-nothings who are an NCO's nightmare in any army. Yet *andartes* who *were* party members thought it odd when ELAS as a whole was labelled a communist organisation. In their minds, there was a clear distinction between the Party and ELAS itself. Boukouvalas agreed, and reckoned that the policy of political indoctrination had run into 'serious difficulties'.[94]

As important an influence on the largely illiterate rank and file as party propaganda were the strong oral traditions of popular Greek culture. Resistance songs often echoed the klephtic ballads with their tales of brigandage and Turkish villainy. Yet there were some intriguing differences, for the *kleftika* described a very different world from the resistance. They glorified the *pallikari* (young warrior), a heroic individualist who fought for himself and his immediate kin in a hostile, competitive world. The *andarte*, on the other hand, saw himself as part of a larger community, and traditional klephtic themes of revenge, prestige and treachery now acquired a global rather an individual significance. In the words of a popular wartime song: 'The People are always One.'[95]

Thus the accusation that the *andartes* were nothing more than old-fashioned brigands could not have been further from the truth, and real brigands in wartime Greece had difficulty adjusting to ELAS's values. At least two renowned professional sheep stealers – Dezis and 'Black Eagle' – were shot by ELAS, and others muttered about the good old days 'before Aris came to the mountain'.[96]

Unlike these individualists, the *andarte*, according to the resistance songs, was fighting for 'the People', 'the hungry, the barefoot and the poor', 'the honest ones' and 'the toiling working class'. Reflecting the values of the peasant smallholder, manual work was esteemed (which would have astonished the klephts) as was private property. People's Rule – ELAS's shadowy goal – was seen as ending *exploitation* by rich 'plutocrats' rather than property ownership itself. The *andartes*' songs made no mention of 'socialism' when describing People's Rule and offered no glorification of the urban, industrial proletariat.

In other words, the revolutionary aspirations of ELAS diverged both from the traditional values of 1821 *and* from communist doctrine. They reflected the rural character of the *andarte* movement, and built on peasant farmers' long-standing dislike of the Greek state and the political class in Athens. This is why the *andartes*' targets almost always included the tax registers of the local inspectorate, and the debt records at the nearest branch of the Agricultural Bank. In central Greece, ELAS's links with the co-operative and agrarian movements were strong, and as a result co-operative presidents often came in for rough treatment from ELAS's opponents.[97]

Yet the resistance challenged the limited horizons of the farmers as well. Villagers traditionally called their village *patrida* (fatherland), and termed people living in the next valley *xenoi* (strangers). Now they were encouraged to look further afield. Traditional values – such as *filotimo* – remained powerful, but now motivated fighters to act for the People rather than for themselves. A group of ELAS fighters bawled defiantly at the collaborationist troops who were attacking them: 'Back traitors, the time has arrived when the People will hang you!' Similarly, in a proclamation issued in June 1944, an ELAS officer called 'Epameinondas' spurred on his men – 'the children of the People' – in the following words: 'Once more together. The butcher with his knife, the grocer with his weights, the cafe owner with his chairs, the greengrocer with his scales, women and children with wood and stones; the ELASite, the unsleeping guard of his quarter with his pistol, his rifle, his automatic.'[98]

For virtually all *andartes* it went without saying that the People referred to were Greeks. Internationalist sentiment was very weak, and ELAS – whose very name played on the Greeks' word for their country ('Ellas') – was little drawn to ideals of Balkan brotherhood. Albanian partisans wore the red star on their cap to show solidarity with the Red Army; this was an extremely rare sight in Greece. Memoirs suggest that patriotism was perhaps the single most important reason why individuals joined ELAS, and many of them were certainly worried when it turned out that they were to act against an 'internal enemy' as well as the Germans.

Yet that same sense of proud self-reliance put Greece's traditional Anglophilia under strain. ELAS GHQ walked a tightrope by affirming its commitment to the Allies whilst criticising the British for their paltry support. Many *andartes* were more outspoken than their leadership and judged the British in the light of the 'age-old anti- "Frank" feelings of Greek peasants'. An old poultry farmer summed things up in 1943: 'If we are all united and decide things on our own without taking advice from foreigners, then we will achieve our aims; otherwise, if foreigners and those who fled abroad get involved, the vultures will get the better of us.' Echoes here of General Makriyiannis a century earlier urging his countrymen to 'put an end to dealings with foreigners and mind our own business'. Axis attacks on villages left the *andartes* blaming perfidious Albion: 'The unfaithful Allies have betrayed our people who are burned and slaughtered.' There were numerous variations on this theme. 'They promise us white elephants and rivers of milk,' complained 'Odysseus'. 'But nothing has ever materialised.'[99]

How, after all, could British gold match the physical sacrifices the *andartes* were making? Aris, who was deeply antagonistic towards the British, believed their offers of assistance were designed to put the resistance in their debt. It made his hackles rise: 'I made it clear to them that if these sovereigns meant that we were obligated [*sic*] to the British, I didn't want them, but would only accept them if they came as the gift of one ally to the other. We are poor and we give our blood; you are rich and you give your gold.'[100]

ELAS *andartes* disparaged the men who joined Zervas and caught the 'yellow fever'. 'Have your billions! Crows! Traitors!' jeered an ELAS proclamation. 'We have our spirit made of steel and the gold of the People's will!' Zervas, who was amply supplied with British gold sovereigns, was regarded with disdain even by guerrillas indifferent to broader ideological issues. So far as they were concerned, he had 'sold himself' to the British. Men like Papakonstantinou, whose fierce pride was responsible for pushing them into action in the first place, disliked such greed. One spirited *andartissa* helped both Zervas and ELAS, before deciding that she preferred to devote herself to those 'who did not talk of money the whole time'. Of course, many ELAS fighters were not indifferent to British sovereigns, and the organisation badly needed the funds. But it was much more suspicious than Zervas of what the price might be.[101]

Attitudes to religion confirmed how far traditional Greek values outweighed Marxist dogma within ELAS. When an ELAS officer called 'Kassandra' visited the town of Aigion in 1943, his first act was to call on the town's bishop to seek his blessing. The two men agreed that Orthodoxy and communism had many points in common, and the bishop asked 'Kassandra' to keep in mind the needs of the Church.

Among the many priests in the resistance was Father 'Anypomonos' (The Impatient One), a thirty-year-old abbot who fled when the Italians tried to arrest him in early 1943, and entered ELAS. Father 'Papakoumbouras' had ridden alongside Aris before being captured and killed by EDES. Probably the most notable church dignitary to back EAM was the very worldly Metropolitan Ioacheim of Kozani, who lost no opportunity to express his revolutionary views. His sermon in church on National Liberation Day 1944 to a crowd of ELAS dignitaries was typical. According to an American officer in the congregation, it was 'cheap simple propaganda which I would hardly have believed could have come from such a distinguished venerable looking old man'.[102]

In fact, it was not the communists but their idealistic social democrat allies who put forward the most radical proposals regarding state–Church relations in Greece. Not surprisingly, perhaps, these small 'parties' – which were basically groupings of educated Athens intellectuals – failed to gain a foothold in Free Greece. The communists were much too concerned about alienating the peasantry to go along with their dangerously atheistic ideas. Aris, for example, always emphasised the importance of the Church, as did many other *kapetans*. At resistance parades, large numbers of priests would take part. They were, after all, from the same social background as most of the *andartes*.

Overall, Basil Davidson's verdict on the Italian partisans is very much to the point here: 'the politics of armed resistance had become the politics of a radical democracy'. 'ELAS is clearly regarded as a revolutionary army in the social sense,' concluded an American officer who had been in the field for several months.[103] For most *andartes*, this was a revolution directed against any return to the prewar world of Metaxas and his dictatorship, and against any attempt to reintroduce the monarchy by force with the aid of the British. 'They pointedly remark that one type of dictatorship is as bad as another, whether the dictators speak German, Greek or English,' wrote Captain Ehrgott. 'The dictatorship is still intolerable and destroys the possibility of decent living.'[104]

In the *andartes'* eyes, then, ELAS stood not for Bolshevik rule but for the emancipation of the *chorio* (the village) from domination by the 'political world' of the capital, and they linked this to a language of independence which described the country's traditional elite as the lackeys of an international 'plutocracy' and demanded Greece's liberation from the shackles of 'British capital'. It was this sensitivity to the calls for social change which made ELAS such a politicised resistance movement, and which made it so threatening to the established political parties. Like many other radical guerrilla organisations of the war and immediate postwar years – the Huk in the Philippines, the partisans in Italy, the FLN in Algeria all offer striking parallels – ELAS was essentially fighting *not* for communism, but for what it called a dual war of liberation – for national liberation against an external oppressor, and for internal social reform.

Discipline, Morality, Justice

As members of a revolutionary army, the *andartes* had no time for the conventional forms of military hierarchy. They greeted each other proudly as 'Fellow-combatant'. Professional soldiers had trouble getting used to their ways. A British NCO who tried to stop his charges falling out of line before they had been given permission was reminded angrily by one that 'in ELAS every soldier has his rights!' They talked back to their superior officers, demanding explanations for orders, and wasting time to demonstrate their independence. What was the *andarte* fighting for if not freedom?[105]

The general level of training was very low, and little time was devoted to improving it. Enthusiasm and a desire to fight the Germans did not always compensate for these inadequacies. The assessment of one young American lieutenant who served alongside the *andartes* in southern Macedonia is worth quoting:

In all the areas that I travelled through . . . the Andartie [*sic*] as an individual was mainly the same. He either joined the organisation as a source of food and living, or he wanted to take a crack at the Hun. The past four months, many Andartes were drafted by

ELAS. He loved to sing and show off. He took little interest
in his equipment, although carrying his gun and ammunition
wherever he went. I have often inspected their rifles and never
yet seen one that was in a clean condition. . . . As a whole,
although the organisation claimed otherwise, he would steal or
lie when possible.[106]

Accusations of ill-discipline need to be examined carefully, especially as the *andartes* have to be judged by the standards of an
irregular force rather than of a professional army, as American and
British officers tended to do. Were the *andartes* little more than
glorified thieves? Many recruits had undoubtedly joined ELAS out
of hunger, and were easily tempted to seize what they could from
farmers and shopkeepers. Some evidently felt that the sacrifices
they were making entitled them to expect the support of any
civilian they encountered. And in certain areas, notably the Peloponnese, morale slumped in the second half of 1943 after it became
obvious that Liberation was still some way off, and discipline
deteriorated as *andartes* indulged in looting and brigandage. Many
andartes – we are told – 'want to go home to their families and are
heartily sick of the whole thing'. For them the *andartiko* had lost its
glamour, and tensions grew with the villagers, who regarded them
more and more as a burden.[107]

However, this is by no means the whole story, for ELAS's
revolutionary morality had a much sterner side as well. In central
Greece, in particular, Aris successfully stamped out petty thieving
and looting by executing men for such minor offences as stealing
chickens. The shock effect was dramatic, and in many ELAS units
individual *andartes* were deterred from misbehaving by the threat of
such draconian punishments. As a result, the ideals of extreme
personal restraint and austerity by which party members had lived
before the war spread through ELAS. Many guerrillas, despite
their unkempt appearance, unruly behaviour and not totally reliable
fighting qualities, *were* learning willy-nilly to conform to the code
of a new revolutionary morality.

Sensitive to allegations that they planned to destroy the family
and lead young women into sin, ELAS's leadership also laid
down very strict rules to protect women inside and outside the
organisation. Sexual relationships between male and female members of ELAS were prohibited. Aris was notorious for having
executed men in his unit who had assaulted village women, or who
had even made love to them *with* their consent. According to
kapetan 'Kavallaris', this regime of enforced deprivation left some
andartes impotent after Liberation.[108]

Costas Couvaras, a young Greek-American serving with OSS, tried making advances to an *andartissa* called 'Tempest'. He should have known better. Displaying the seriousness of purpose we have already commented on, she rebuffed him gently: 'This is no time for love, fellow-combatant. We have a great task ahead of us, and we cannot waver.' 'Tempest' had sacrificed a lot to join ELAS. She had been quietly married to a provincial chief of police, before quarrelling with him over her support for the resistance. Eventually she left him for the mountains, where she was first a nurse, and then part of a combat unit. When Couvaras met her, she had become 'a real fanatic', for whom the Marxist teachings she had heard 'brought a new religion to her heart'. Couvaras saw her behaviour as the sign of an 'extreme morality'. 'Tempest' never returned to her old life, and died fighting the British in Athens at the end of 1944.[109]

Sometimes their concern for the needs of the 'Struggle' led ELAS officers to handle the villagers roughly. 'Paparas' was infuriated when men in an unfamiliar village refused to obey his orders; he lost his temper and hit them. His superior told him later: 'It doesn't matter that you struck them; even if you'd killed one or two, you'd still have been justified.' The threat of violence was frequently being used for deliberate effect – in situations similar to those Cobb describes in the case of the French *armées révolutionnaires* in 1793 – by men who knew they had to 'strike terror' into the hearts of the peasants if their missions were to succeed.[110]

Often, though, a *kapetan*'s authority simply went to his head, and military necessity became a convenient pretext for the whims and vanities of men with power. *Kapetan* 'Nikitaras', a lawyer in peacetime, made himself 'the supreme court' in his region. He sat in session in a *kafeneion* and let the peasants bring their problems to him. The illiterate Nikos Zaralis – four pens prominently displayed peeping from his tunic pocket – was another *kapetan* who behaved like a petty despot, 'reviewing' his men in the various villages where they were stationed, and cracking his whip at the villagers who had to feed and house them. He tried to terrify them into producing feed for his horses by threatening to hang 'one or two'.[111]

Considerably more frightening in its implications than this rather arbitrary use of power was genuine revolutionary terror. Some ELAS *politikoi* started on about 'conspirators', 'traitors' and 'reactionaries' at the drop of a hat. They threatened to 'root them out to the tenth generation', wrote off whole villages as 'reactionary', and compiled lists of families against whom action was to be taken. ELAS units unleashed a reign of terror among the villages of western Macedonia, and in the mountains south-west of Delphi. In both areas, rival guerrilla bands existed, and in Macedonia some villages had been forced to accept arms from the Germans. After clashes between armed villagers and ELAS units, ELAS started burning 'reactionary' strongholds and the region descended rapidly into civil war.

The youthful *kapetan* 'Periklis' was a typical scourge of the bourgeoisie, easily carried away by the sound of his own rhetoric, and eager for a bloody reckoning with the 'enemies of the people'. Before the war he had worked as a clerk in a provincial electricity company. Now he made angry, passionate speeches against those who 'exploited the system . . . who drink the blood of working people like leeches'. He was against the *gravatoforoi* – those who wore ties – and against the *papionati* – the bow-tie brigade. Another *kapetan*, from Thebes this time, told an appalled British officer that 'there were certain . . . Fascist elements in the immediate vicinity which it was his intention to exterminate.'[112]

It would be quite mistaken to write off such utterances as mere rhetoric, for as the war went on there were unmistakable signs of ELAS's determination to wipe out any potential rivals. ELAS's execution of the royalist Lieutenant Drosopoulos in the Peloponnese and the killing of rival band-leader Colonel Psarros in Roumeli in the spring of 1944 were two examples from the last year of the occupation of its ruthless determination to monopolise armed resistance. Aris in particular has been identified with a hardline approach to possible resistance rivals or opponents, and it is certainly true that his seniority within ELAS, his links with the Party and his presence in the heartlands of Free Greece gave him enormous influence over ELAS policy. But perhaps the most chilling illustration of the revolutionary mentality at work within ELAS is the much less well-known story of *kapetan* 'Odysseus' and his reign of terror in the distant north-east of the country.

*

An alert and intelligent man, the uneducated 'Odysseus' was in many ways an impressive figure. He was a born leader, who needed little food or sleep. His admiring followers were mostly illiterate villagers, differing in political views but united by the suffering their families had endured at the hands of the occupation forces. At first, despite their ragged clothing and few arms, they succeeded in stamping out much of the black market activity in the Evros region. They pasted lists of food prices on walls and shop doors, and executed known profiteers. For a month or so in 1943 'Odysseus' and his *andartes* gained enormous popularity.[113]

He boasted that his men were prepared to sacrifice everything for

57. Two of Aris's bodyguards, identifiable by their black caps, 1944.

Greece's liberation from 'the claws of Hitlerofascism'. They had, he insisted, killed only 'traitors and stoolpigeons', 'men who aimed to sell out the country, for which *we* struggle a deal more than anyone else'. Gradually, however, a more vicious note crept into his rhetoric, as he talked about executing the 'pseudodemocrats' – the 'scum who want ill for the People'.[114]

Early in 1944, things turned very sour. 'Odysseus' had ELAS's local political adviser, Major Stathatos, arrested and brought before a People's Court. Found guilty of treason, Stathatos and several other men were beaten to death, and their heads were cut off and exhibited by the side of a nearby highway. A special mounted 'Death Battalion' was sent out with the names of informers to be killed. Arguments broke out among the members of the battalion over some of the names on the list, but 'Telemachus', their commander, cut them short: 'This is a revolution,' he told them, 'And things have to be done – even if a few innocents are killed, it won't matter in the long run.' There surely was the authentic voice of revolutionary terror.[115]

After the death of Major Stathatos, conditions in the Evros region deteriorated rapidly. Desperate to stop the slaughter, a local com-

319

munist travelled secretly to Macedonia to meet party officials. By the time he arrived back with a new leader, on 17 February, several hundred people had been killed by 'Odysseus' and his death squads, often for no other reason than because they had expressed misgivings about what the *andartes* were doing, or because some *andarte* had a personal grudge against them. It was reckoned that hundreds of others had been saved by the Party's intervention, since 'Odysseus' had prepared a long list of local Anglophiles to be executed.

'Athinodoros', the new leader, was a confident and well-educated party man, and he moved quickly to bring Evros's ELAS back into conformity with the national line. With the aid of several local resistance figures, he arrested 'Odysseus' and tried him publicly before a People's Court in the village of Lefkimi. 'Odysseus' was found guilty of being an enemy of the Party and the People, and was shot immediately. An OSS post-mortem summed up the situation: 'We think that the Communist leadership got out of hand, drunk with the power they had gained in the region, and overplayed their hand. We also believe they are now seeing their mistake.'[116]

What had pushed 'Odysseus' so far? Some believed there was 'no doubt the man went mad'. His successors spread the rumour that he had, in fact, been a Bulgarian agent, for the Left as well as the Right liked to keep its image of Hellenism pure. But there was no evidence for any Bulgarian connection, and if 'Odysseus' was mad it was only in the sense that applies to the behaviour of all ideological fanatics when offered unlimited power. Operating out on the north-eastern borderlands, he had temporarily enjoyed greater freedom from party supervision than other ELAS *kapetans*. Once he was executed, the *andartiko* in Evros returned to its main task of trying to make life as difficult as possible for the local German garrisons.[117]

*

The region 'Odysseus' terrorised was so isolated from the rest of Greece that it had been impossible for the Party or ELAS GHQ to keep an eye on him: for a long time, indeed, they were uncertain who he really was. But in this respect 'Odysseus's story was only an extreme illustration of the autonomy which many local ELAS commanders enjoyed throughout the war: even after the creation of the General HQ there was enormous variation in the behaviour – and in particular the repressiveness – of ELAS units in different districts. The 13th Division in central Greece, close to Aris's watchful eye, was notorious for terrorising the local population, for men like 'Odysseus' and 'Aris' suffered from a strange narrowness of political vision – able to accept that men might be motivated by the class struggle, but not by patriotism – which detached them from the emotional reality of many other *résistants*. At the same time, units in Evvia, for example – barely a hundred miles away – clearly enjoyed popular support under more moderate leadership, as did those in parts of Thessaly and southern Macedonia.[118]

The 'Odysseus' episode had a double meaning: it revealed the possibilities for revolutionary terror that ELAS's power offered its local commanders; yet it showed once again the national leadership's preference for moderation. Although neither ELAS's military commander General Sarafis, nor the 'Old Man' Siantos was the sort to provide strong and consistent leadership, ultimately both men recognised that ELAS was not really a communist army. In this they demonstrated their political realism. It was the violent and authoritarian ideologues, fanatical *kapetans* like Aris, 'Odysseus' or 'Perikles' – men strikingly similar to Cobb's revolutionary *commissaires* – who were truly naive in believing that the revolutionary purity of their vision was shared by most of their fellow-*andartes*. For if the proud, hungry guerrillas of ELAS were radical in their social aspirations, they were clearly democrats so far as politics was concerned. Their decision to take up arms was an assertion of everything that was most admirable in the Greek spirit – a fierce patriotism, a refusal to calculate where matters of honour were concerned, a stoic acceptance of enormous hardship and a determination to act together against overwhelming odds. It was not motivated by the desire to install a one-party state after the war.[119]

CHAPTER TWENTY-TWO

'A Cemetery Awash in Blood': the Counter-Revolution

When Ioannis Rallis became Prime Minister in April 1943 a new phase began in Graeco-German relations. In Berlin Goebbels was beginning to emphasise Germany's role as Europe's protector against Bolshevism, and both Neubacher and Kaltenbrunner were keen to build up anti-communist forces in the Balkans. So it is not surprising that in his first speech Rallis stressed that his goal was 'the restoration of order and the protection of our social status quo'. His government would help the Axis in its war against communism abroad, and would gather together all 'disciplined citizens' to restore order at home. Nowhere in his speech was there any mention of a New Order for Europe. This was to be an essentially conservative, anti-communist regime which, like the Nazis themselves, would present the war in terms of stark alternatives: 'People of Greece! Just as Hercules had to choose between virtue and vice, you must choose today between Europe and Bolshevism.'[120]

The appeal of this message was reinforced by the rise of EAM/ELAS and by the growing apprehensions, especially among better-off sections of the urban population, of its ultimate goals. Public opinion in Athens had begun to shift against the Left. In 1942 it was estimated that 90 per cent of students at the university supported EAM; by 1944 the figure had dropped to under half. These might have been crude estimates, but they indicated a trend. The middle ground of social radicalism which had emerged in the early period of the occupation under the strain of the famine was now disappearing again, as Greek politics became polarised.[121]

Stimulated, financed and supported by the Germans, there now emerged a patchwork alliance of Greek anti-communists who were in general motivated less by sympathy for National Socialism than by fear of Bolshevik revolution. This counter-revolution soon acquired a momentum of its own, and since it was an integral part of the internecine conflict that was tearing Greece apart by 1944 – and that would continue until the Right triumphed, with British and American support, in 1949 – we must now examine its origins.

58. Prime Minister Rallis (on the right) reviews detachments of the Evzone Battalions outside the Tomb of the Unknown Soldier in the presence of Greek police and army officers and German officials: Athens, 1944.

*

Rallis was an elderly, polished, rather world-weary man of considerable political experience. He came from one of Greece's most famous royalist families, and had been in politics since 1906, holding several ministerial posts though never quite making it to the top. Monocled and urbane, he spoke German well and through his White Russian wife (his third) he had long frequented *émigré* anti-Bolshevik circles in Athens. This background obviously attracted the Axis, and he in turn appears to have been tempted by their offers as early as 1941 when a relative reported that 'the Italians are trying to set up my disgusting cousin John Rallis in the place of Tsolakoglu'.[122] But he was reluctant to make the leap prematurely. Only when leaders of the prewar political parties gave him their tacit backing for an anti-EAM regime, urging him to 'sacrifice' himself for the sake of Greece, and when the Germans agreed to permit the formation of armed volunteer militias did he agree to take over.[123]

On 7 April 1943 the Rallis government passed a law providing for the formation of four Security Battalions, and appealed for volunteers. The new formations were slow to develop, however: neither the Germans nor the Italians were keen to give the Greeks arms, while few Greeks were prepared to enlist. Many of the early recruits were either the very poor, who joined as an alternative to going to work in the Reich, or criminals wanted by the Greek police, and men on the run from the resistance. There was also a less predictable reason for potential recruits to hesitate: the Battalions' organisers clearly hoped they would be used, not just against the Left, but to block the eventual return of the King. To understand why, we need to look more closely at who was actually behind the Battalions scheme.

In the interwar period, anti-communism had been an increasingly prominent feature of Greek politics as royalists and republicans began to sink their differences in defence of the 'bourgeois world'. It had actually been Venizelos's Liberal government which had introduced the repressive 'Special Law' in 1929 to defend the 'social status quo', jailing large numbers of KKE members and trades unionists. Now, though Rallis was a former royalist, it was a clique of notorious republican army officers who had masterminded the Battalions, including the megalomaniac, wily former dictator General Pangalos – a tough, short and excitable man, 'half-mad' in the opinion of one British diplomat who remembered the fiasco of his short-lived putsch in 1925. Grigorakis, the new Minister for Labour in Rallis's Cabinet was a follower of Pangalos and the leading recruiter of republican officers for the Battalions.[124]

Unfortunately, most republican officers were not prepared to fight against the British, as they might have to do if King George's return was to be prevented. In time, therefore, the original anti-royalism behind the Battalions was dropped. In May 1944, indeed, an emissary arrived in the Middle East on a secret mission to persuade the Allies that the Security Battalions were patriotic organisations playing their part in the 'national struggle'. By then it was clear that the Security Battalions would not resist the British when the Germans withdrew.[125]

The Battalions began to develop into a substantial force only after the Italians withdrew from the war. From September 1943, the Wehrmacht realised that Greek auxiliaries could be useful in the war against the resistance. At the same time, Higher SS-and-Police Führer (HSSPF) Schimana started to reorganise the gendarmerie and police forces, while the Gestapo penetrated Greece's specialist anti-communist surveillance units and gave them expanded executive powers. The growing influence of the Germans was eased by a series of reshuffles which left more of Pangalos's republican followers in key positions in the Greek security apparatus: one became Chief of Gendarmerie while the new head of the anti-communist Special Security unit, Alexandros Lambou, was another. Professional gendarmes grew alarmed: of the 300 gendarmes employed in Special Security, 194 were new, untrained appointees; of 90 new recruits in February 1944, 19 were actually convicted criminals. The Minister of the Interior made the problem worse by issuing Special Security ID cards to anti-communist vigilante squads which operated largely beyond effective political control.[126]

Towards the end of 1943 several hundred men were recruited in Athens, and three Battalions were formed. In January 1944 Rallis stepped up the pressure on army officers, threatening to penalise any serving officer who refused to 'volunteer' by stopping his pay and food cards. On 22 May the government published a three-page list of such men and announced that they had been placed on the retired list and had forfeited all pension rights. For the first time, regular army NCOs were posted to battalion units. Men were deliberately dismissed from the gendarmerie without rations to force them into the Battalions. Under duress, large numbers of gendarmes and army officers complied; others escaped to the Middle East, or took to the hills.[127]

Dressed in their distinctive traditional Evzone gear – complete with fustanellas and pom-pom shoes – and lightly armed, the new Battalions were sent out of Athens to central and southern Greece. On 20 January a detachment arrived in Patras, where it paraded through the streets, apparently to some popular acclaim, before being billeted in the town's schools. To drum up local volunteers, officers told their men to visit the tavernas and impress the public with their pay, rations and good living conditions. The result, however, was that most new recruits were hungry, poor and unemployed – not always those who held 'the healthiest ideas and beliefs about the social order,' complained one officer. The better-off citizens successfully avoided sending their own sons.[128]

In April, ELAS units forcibly dissolved the last remaining rival resistance group in central Greece, EKKA, and killed its leader, Colonel Psarros. This event, perhaps more than any other, drove men into the Battalions who would otherwise not have collaborated. EKKA's survivors, still in British uniform and carrying British guns, made the short journey to Patras and enlisted in the Battalion there. This now started to 'clean up' Patras of communists, and threw suspects and their families into a detention camp. It also helped the SS to guard Jewish deportees on their way to Athens and Auschwitz.[129]

Another Security Battalion was sent to Evvia at the beginning of 1944. This was a hilly and thickly wooded region where the

Germans were pinned to the capital, Chalkis. Rallis appointed a new governor for the area, Major-General Liakos, and assigned him a battalion detachment. Reinforcements were sent out from Athens, and by the end of January, Liakos's force amounted to some 400 men. Calling up villagers by year-group, Liakos managed to increase his strength even further in the course of a series of operations, conducted jointly with the Germans, against the guerrillas.[130]

Liakos's men soon acquired an unpleasant reputation and he himself won little acclaim in Evvia itself for his 'patriotic' activities. When, for example, he rode one day into the main square of the village of Xirochori, the streets emptied instantly. Standing in front of a newspaper stand, Liakos shouted: 'What are you running for? Do you think I'm going to eat you? Am I not Liakos, your patriot, your general?' But the villagers were lucky if they got away with these words, or with his habitual tirade against the 'vagabonds and gangsters', the 'shameful and wretched criminals and terrorists' he was going to chase out of the country.[131]

Usually his speeches were the prelude to burning and looting by his ill-disciplined troops, accompanied by some active 'recruiting' among the terrified inhabitants. When Liakos visited the market-town of Ayia Anna on 19 March, several local men agreed to carry arms as civil guards on his behalf. Meanwhile his troops burned a factory and the town library, looted the chemist's, and made several arrests before going off. Some time later, the town received another visit – this time from the *andartes*, who surrounded it and attacked the school where Liakos's men were billeted. After a brief fight, they and the three German soldiers with them were shot, and their families' houses were burned down.[132]

Although the villagers were caught in the cross-fire, what tilted their sympathies away from the Battalions, even more than their shameful association with the Germans, was their almost total lack of discipline. After a fight at the hamlet of Attali, for example, battalion men pillaged the houses in the village, making off eventually with 1,000 okes of olive oil, 5 sewing machines, 200 okes of cheese, and 30 dowry collections. They needed sixty mules to carry the load away. As a result of such raids, the population of Evvia looked upon the Battalions – in the words of one observer – 'one hundred percent as enemies'.[133]

The central Peloponnese, the third region where the Security Battalions were stationed, offered more fertile soil for anti-ELAS activity. The country population here was staunchly royalist, and the Left resistance had been slow to develop. During 1943 ELAS had forcibly disbanded other resistance movements, led by popular local figures, and this created – as in the case of EKKA and Colonel

Psarros – groups of angry, disaffected men who had personal as well as professional or ideological reasons for wanting to take up arms in the nationalist cause. Among these was a well-to-do farmer called Leonidas Vrettakos, whose brother had been killed by ELAS in fighting on the slopes of Mount Taygetos during the autumn of 1943. Vrettakos wanted his revenge, and that December he formed the 'Leonidas Battalion', which was equipped with German weapons and a liaison officer. By February 1944 it was based in Sparta and, now known as the local Security Battalion, conducted bloody expeditions against ELAS units.[134] Further Battalions were formed under the command of Colonel Dionysios Papadongonas, a royalist who had also clashed with ELAS. Papadongonas's units were put under the command of the Ministry of the Interior and regarded as part of the gendarmerie. During the summer months they conducted reprisal operations together with other Battalions from their bases in Tripolis and the southern Peloponnese.[135]

The Security Battalions came to dominate large parts of southern and central Greece. By the end of the occupation they numbered around 8,000 men, and posed serious problems for EAM/ELAS. Yet the German attitude towards them was rather ambivalent, as the Wehrmacht was reluctant to allow too many arms to find their way into Greek hands. The main reason for the emergence of the Battalions was less military than political: Rallis's interest in mounting an effective nationalist challenge to the Left coincided with the German interest in promoting a partnership with the Greeks against communism. 'Hellenism is by its heritage and tradition opposed to the communist world-view', the governor of the Patras district told an approving audience of Germans in February 1944. 'Annihilate communism!' This was just the sort of sentiment General Löhr had in mind when he remarked that the purpose of German policy was to make sure 'that the anti-communist part of the Greek population must be fully utilised, revealing itself openly and obliged to display an undisguised hostility towards the communist side'.[136]

Here Löhr was largely following the lead given by the Foreign Office and the SS. It was the diplomat Neubacher and HSSPF Schimana, rather than the Wehrmacht, who encouraged Rallis to form the Security Battalions. Both men were pragmatists, prepared to allow the Greeks to form anti-communist units even if these were sympathetic to the British. So far as they could see, anti-communism was a force which would eventually bring together, not just the Greeks and the Germans, but ultimately the British as well. Neubacher was working closely with Himmler's deputy Kaltenbrunner in pursuit of this goal, and had been allowed by

Kaltenbrunner to make use of the SD's foreign intelligence service to this end. He had also received a special slush fund to support 'friends of Germany' in the Balkans.[137]

The only powerful critic of this coherent if cynical strategy was Walter Blume, the feared head of the SiPo/SD, who never gave up hope of reviving the rift between republicans and royalists, in order to turn the Security Battalions into an effective bulwark against the British. Such a strategy was politically short-sighted and over-estimated the usefulness of the particularly nasty republican groups the SD was bankrolling; but Blume was in a position to push his policy a long way. During 1944 he mounted a series of in-trigues to replace Rallis. He funded EEE, an extremist republican anti-communist party, and saw it as a possible future partner. Papadongonas and other royalists aroused his suspicion; so did those Security Battalion leaders who went around boasting of their contacts with the Allies in the Middle East.[138]

With growing disregard for the political designs of his associates, Blume tried to ram this policy home unilaterally. In May 1944 the head of the Security Battalions, Major-General Vasilios Dertilis, was arrested by the SD, on the grounds of his alleged links with Zervas and the British. Blume's men followed this up by seizing the archives of the Battalions and searching their offices, as well as that of their superior, the Minister for the Interior, Tavoularis. Dertilis was sent to Vienna for further interrogation, and Tavoularis was demoted to Minister without Portfolio. The Security Battalions' ammunition stores were placed under German guard. Athens buzzed with rumours and Rallis himself was furious at the SD's heavy-handed intervention.[139]

The SD's charges against Dertilis were disingenuous, to put it mildly, for he had made no secret of his pro-British orientation. Before his arrest, he had told a meeting of several hundred army officers in the Ministry of National Defence that the British were supporting the Battalions; Cairo's denunciations, he reassured them, were merely a blind. Such a view was echoed by none other than HSSPF Schimana himself, Blume's commanding officer. On the occasion of Hitler's birthday, Schimana told an audience of Greek officers that they must all support the Germans against communism: the British were in agreement, as they would shortly find out.[140]

What had heartened more politically astute German officials were the signs that the British were worried at the growth of the Left and might be sympathetic to the creation of a substantial anti-communist force in Greece. The Germans already had hard evidence for this. In November 1943, in one of the most extraordinary and potentially explosive episodes of the whole war, a young liaison officer called Don Stott secretly met the head of the German Secret Field Police in Athens to discuss the possibility of joint action against the Russians.

The official interpretation of this – how should one put it? – unfortunate affair is that Stott went on his own initiative and failed to inform his superiors in the British Military Mission in Greece; certainly he put their lives at risk by this meeting, which appeared to confirm ELAS's worst suspicions about British policy. His signals were, however, reaching SOE in Cairo, and were being read by Brigadier Keble, who commanded SOE's operations in the Middle East. Shortly afterwards, Keble was sacked and Stott reprimanded. The true weight to be attached to this bizarre affair can only be gauged in the light of documents which remain under wraps in Whitehall, but it does indicate that at least some Allied officials were prepared to follow the implications of an anti-communist position to its logical end-point – negotiations with the Germans. For the premiss behind British policy, as Germans like Neubacher well knew, was that expressed by a British intelligence officer in May 1944: 'our long term policy towards Greece is to retain her as a British sphere of influence, and . . . a Russian dominated Greece would not be in accordance with British strategy in the Eastern Mediterranean.' The consequence of this appraisal was Britain's search for a counterweight to EAM/ELAS.[141]

As potential allies for the British in an anti-communist crusade the Germans and the Security Battalions were obviously less politically palatable than ELAS's resistance rivals, even though these were increasingly powerless and confined to the area of Athens. As well as contacting the GFP, Stott had also met representatives of all the Greek resistance organisations *except* EAM/ELAS to discuss how British arms could be supplied to them. These contacts, unlike those with the Germans, were carefully maintained, chiefly through the Greek government in exile, in the months leading up to Liberation, by which time the non-communist resistance was being seen as an essential buffer against the Left.

By 1944, hostility to EAM/ELAS had pushed several of these right-wing 'resistance' groups closer to the Security Battalions and their German sponsors. Here we find ourselves in the murky atmosphere of underground 'nationalist' politics, a highly duplicitous and dangerous world where resistance did not rule out collaboration, and where service alongside the Wehrmacht was justified on the grounds that it was necessary to save Greece from the Left. In Athens, for example, members of EDES enlisted in the Battalions, while several prominent leading EDES officials cultivated close ties with the Rallis government. Under pressure from EAM/ELAS, the

British insisted that Zervas personally break off all ties with his renegade colleagues in the capital, and in December 1943 he did so. For how long, however, remains a moot point. He did sign a joint denunciation of the Battalions in February 1944, which called upon all those who had joined to quit immediately. On the other hand, Dertilis – the Battalions' commander – was widely regarded as Zervas's 'alter ego' for the two men had been friends for over twenty years. Moreover, Zervas himself was playing a double game up in the mountains by refraining from attacking local German troops and keeping a liaison officer at their headquarters in Jannina. The only point that remains unclear is whether the British liaison officers with Zervas knew of these links.[142]

The Allies' condemnations of the Battalions appear to have had little effect inside Greece, at least until the very eve of Liberation. ELAS noted with alarm that the Battalions' members claimed that 'they are serving the interests of England with her consent'. An American OSS agent who interviewed captured Battalionists in Evvia, estimated that 35–40 per cent of them believed that they had Allied backing. 'Next time we will come back with the English,' one warned the villagers of Pili after a raid in July. Some thought that England and America had a secret agreement to wage war on Russia as soon as the conflict with the Germans was ended. According to one: 'Our leaders give us lectures and tell us that we are chasing the *Andartes* of the EAM/ELAS, and that way we are going to avoid Communism; and that the leaders of the Security Battalions act after orders of the King with whom they are in contact.'[143]

Were such claims completely unfounded? Despite Cairo's public denunciations of the Battalions, in private Allied attitudes were rather less clear-cut. There can be no doubt that many members of the exile government positively welcomed the Battalions as a counterweight to EAM/ELAS. A long intelligence report passed on from Cairo to the director of Military Intelligence in London reflected that whilst 'there is nothing to be said in their favour' from the military point of view, politically they 'seem useful to a considerable proportion of Greeks both at home and abroad in that they prevent a complete predominance of EAM/ELAS'. The fact that many British policy-makers shared such a view was not spelled out. But in June, following requests from the Greek government and the British Foreign Office, the Allies suspended the dropping of leaflets into Greece attacking the Battalions, and a British official commented confidentially that 'the Battalions may well contain as many as 70% Allied well-wishers whom it would be a pity to alienate'. The BBC was instructed by the Foreign Office to cease direct attacks on the Battalions, and at the end of September 1944 British officials in Cairo went so far as to censor certain radio broadcasts from the Greek Ministry of Information for being unduly harsh on the Battalions.[144]

By this point, with a German withdrawal only days away, outright condemnation of the Battalions was a thing of the past. Greek politicians and army officers in the Middle East had old friends and colleagues serving in them. British army planners were reluctant to reject a useful ally against a potentially hostile ELAS. American observers regarded British policy towards the Battalions as 'muddled' and 'confused'. In fact, the underlying tenor of British policy had long been anti-communist; EAM/ELAS was seen as a communist-led movement with whom coexistence in peacetime was likely to prove impossible. Military considerations had necessitated offering British support and encouragement to ELAS for a time, and had obscured the fundamental antagonism between them. As Liberation approached, this antagonism became more visible, with the Security Battalions one of the chief beneficiaries. When a new British liaison officer landed in Greece in August 1944 the first thing he was told by the man who met him was that 'all our best chaps are in the Battalions'.[145]

*

In March 1944 a proclamation was issued by George Siantos in his capacity as PEEA Secretary of the Interior offering battalion members an amnesty:

> ... I address myself to you, the Security organisations, to say that you too are children of the Greek people, that you should not remain unmoved by the people's desires nor hold aloof from its longings. . . .
>
> The conquerors are making treacherous efforts to keep you in the opposing camp, and they have found accomplices for this devilish work in certain of your leaders who are their tools. They disseminate filthy slanders and represent the struggling people and its leaders as evil-doers, anti-Christ, your enemies. But it is they who are the evil-doers, anti-Christ, the people's enemies and yours. . . . Do not listen to them when they say we are your enemies. We are the enemies only of the conquerors and traitors. . . . Come to our side! Do not carry out orders dictated by the conquerors.[146]

For many recruits into Rallis's security units, the overriding difficulty had been knowing whom to listen to. Moderate nationalism was vanishing as the country became polarised. The head of the gendarmerie in Volos instructed his men to steer clear of all political organisations. But did this apply to the Battalions? Gendarmerie officers in Macedonia sent a petition to the Greek government in exile asking for guidance. By obeying their original orders to remain at their posts they now found themselves 'protecting not the interests of the Greek people, but simply of the Germans and their agents and creatures, who hold the lives and property of the nation at their mercy while wearing the cloak of nationalism [and] anti-communism'. They found themselves, they wrote, 'in a very difficult position. To what conclusion should National Duty and the National Honour lead?'[147]

Under overwhelming pressure from the Rallis government, and given the ambiguous signals coming from abroad, many army officers and gendarmes had been left little choice in the matter. Village men who had been called up could either serve or flee into the hills; but in the latter case, their families might be brought before the local tribunal of the Committee for Public Security – an institution dating back to before the war – and sent into internal exile. If they joined up, their families were liable to be abducted and held as hostages by ELAS.[148]

Many recruits were driven into service under the Germans by poverty and hunger, just as others had been pushed into the resistance. Some were no more than fifteen or sixteen years old, orphans off the Athens streets who had somehow survived the famine. ELAS dismissed them as 'vagabonds', 'shoeblacks', and 'lumpenproletarian scum'. Some were on the run from the Greek police – like Giannis K., the clerk in the Ministry of Marine Affairs who had been discovered stealing money – or were EDES men captured by the Germans and then handed over to local battalion commanders. (ELAS men were, of course, shot.)[149]

Personal and family animosities were at least as important as class or political convictions in deciding whether a man went Left or Right. Kostandi, the proud peasant in Kevin Andrews's memorable study *The Flight of Ikaros*, could easily have joined ELAS when he returned from Albania. But the fact that his detested brother Spyro was already a member stopped him; and when an ELAS man from a neighbouring village killed his other, beloved, brother Pandeli he joined the local Battalion.[150]

In Alexandros Kotzias's novel of collaboration, *The Siege*, a former *andarte* called Anastasis describes how he had actually moved over from ELAS to the Right. At the time of the Italian surrender, Anastasis tells a fellow collaborator, the villagers had seized the local garrison's weapons and taken them to be blessed by the priest.

59.   Members of the Security Battalions in detention under British guard at a camp near Patras shortly after Liberation. Note the extreme youth of some of the Battalionists.

The village schoolmaster told them to 'make an organisation', and introduced them to a student from the 'Headquarters of the Struggle and Freedom'. Anastasis was put in charge of the village reserve and thus became a member of the resistance.

A month later the student returned, now wearing a red hand-kerchief round his neck and new boots, 'to show his rank'. Taking Anastasis aside, he showed him a 'catalogue' of names and told him to arrest local 'reactionaries'. Anastasis was shocked and tempers soon reached boiling point. 'Do you dare to judge the decisions of the central committee?' the young man demanded angrily. 'I don't judge any directives,' replied Anastasis, 'but we have been brought up differently here.' Before long, Anastasis faced arrest for 'extreme treachery'. Hunted by his former comrades in ELAS, he escaped from the village and eventually arrived in Athens. Several months later he had found refuge in an anti-communist squad.[151]

In such a story one can see the coercion, desperation and fear which had forced many men into a shameful association with the Germans and which perhaps helped explain why, by the summer of 1944, the Battalions had become notorious for their brutality and lack of discipline. They shot suspected EAM members and assaulted women who had family ties with the resistance. They looted villages, bringing away bread, cheese, grain and wine, as well as sheep or goats the villagers had not had time to take up into the hills.[152] Their commanders levied 'taxes' on the remaining farmers, and asked for 'contributions' towards the anti-communist cause. The notorious 'General' Papathanasopoulos together with his 'business adviser', a local lawyer called Oikonomidis, controlled what little economic activity continued in Evvia. For example, they forced a well-known shipowner to pay 800 million drachmas to the 'cause'; then they arrested one of his captains on a charge of supplying food to the communists, and invited him to pay for his captain's release. They also profited from the supplies of cigarettes which the Ministry of Finance gave for their men, diverting half on to the black market.[153]

'We ask the Greek people,' ran a message from Rallis in January 1944, 'to show affection for the men of the Security Corps, who place their lives at risk in order to assure the lives, honour and property of the citizens.' But few of the 'peace-loving citizens' to whom Rallis directed such appeals trusted the Battalions or felt any affection for them, and by the end of the occupation their name had become synonymous with arbitrary violence and appalling brutality. They were 'sincerely hated' and behaved as if in 'enemy country', wrote Sandstrom.[154]

Popular attitudes towards them could be gauged from a curious discussion which took place shortly after Liberation as British officers in Italy drew up proposals for the creation of new Greek internal security forces. One staff officer proposed the formation of forty new 'internal security battalions'. Another, more familiar with the situation in Greece, pointed out that 'Security Battalion' was an unfortunate expression, and emphasised that it was essential that 'no reference to the term "Security" be made in the title of the new units'. At his suggestion, the term 'National Guards Battalions' was eventually adopted. But though the name changed following Liberation, many of the faces did not. Hundreds of men who had fought in the Security Battalions alongside the Germans found their way without any difficulty into the postwar National Guard.[155]

The Death Squads

While the Battalions preyed upon the villagers of central Greece and the Peloponnese, the formation of anti-communist auxiliary units in the north was leading to even greater bloodshed. Much of the evidence surrounding these units has been destroyed, but enough survives to point to a deliberate policy by the German authorities of countering the rise of ELAS by financing what would later become known as 'death squads', whose mission was to reduce the country-side to a state of total terror by more or less random killings. Here we can find the first faltering steps towards what American military specialists would later define as 'counter-terror' – a doctrine employed by US client states in South-east Asia and central America to combat otherwise unreachable guerrilla forces.[156]

In Thessaly, for example, which was an ELAS stronghold, the local German security police backed an organisation called EASAD (National Agricultural Federation of Anti-Communist Action) which suddenly appeared in the spring of 1944, loudly proclaiming its loyalty to National Socialism. The organisation's leaders described Greece as a 'cemetery awash in blood' and said the new movement had been founded by 'pure Greeks' to 'ward off the possibility of the Red Flag being planted on the ruins of our land'. Radio Athens announced that EASAD would wipe out communism in Thessaly. Its several hundred recruits were mostly young farmers from the area, who had personal grievances against the *andartes*. Grouped into several bands, and identified only by green armbands, they hunted none too scrupulously for 'communist trash' in the streets of the local towns.[157]

By mid-May EASAD's murderous anarchy had stunned the port of Volos; gangs of thugs, carrying clubs and guns, roamed the streets, picking on passers-by and looting shops. Only old men and women were safe out of doors. Young men were shot in cold blood, or made to execute prisoners themselves. Tortures were carried out in the old tobacco warehouse that was used as a jail: its walls and floor were stained with blood. EASAD's leader, a former gendarme called Takis Makedon, could barely control the various units under his command.

Municipal officials tried in vain to reassure local opinion. A public announcement in May 1944 told people not to flee when their homes were surrounded by EASAD and German troops. They were to remain 'calmly' at work, for if they ran away they might be shot at. These units were simply liberating the country-side from 'communist elements'. Such advice did not save people like the President of Co-operatives in the village of Kazaklar who was killed by four EASAD men in June, when they broke into his house during a raid.[158]

Volos's mayor, a supporter of Zervas, had been instrumental in bringing EASAD to Volos in the first place. But by the summer he was deeply worried, and at an emergency session of the town council in early August, he discussed his concerns:

> It is true that the Nationalist squads pursue their military tasks out of limitless patriotism, nobility and self-sacrifice. . . . However, their leaders' lack of military and political training, the lack of a programme with a concrete goal and specially the lack of political advisers . . . and the unmethodical style of their activities have made these squads a thorn in the flesh of Volos and the environs. Arrests are often at random, interrogations are generally conducted without preparation and by unqualified men, with no guarantee of their impartiality; the executions are inhuman, an affront to the public spirit of the inhabitants of Volos. . . . Often arrests are accompanied by the seizure of valuables from a prisoner's family, which are then shared out among the men of the group. . . .
>
> This manner of making arrests, interrogations, confiscations and executions has terrified all the inhabitants, many of whom have left Volos, the more wealthy heading for Athens, others to the villages on Pilion. It is no exaggeration to say that at least 5,000 people have left Volos, one-twelfth of the prewar population.[159]

The mayor reported with relief that the SD in Volos had agreed to control the activities of these groups more tightly, but if he really believed this, he was simply deluding himself. The SD had their own interest in perpetuating the internecine killing, and a climate of terror persisted until the German withdrawal. Takis Makedon himself was captured by ELAS in the winter of 1944, and 'committed suicide' in captivity before he could be brought to trial. Many EASAD members had crossed over to ELAS by this point to save their skins, but others were to continue their anti-communist vendetta in the region after 1945. Within six months of Liberation they were back in the streets, helping National Guardsmen to arrest former *andartes*.[160]

*

Further north in Macedonia, Wehrmacht counter-intelligence and SS police officers were also using right-wing Greek paramilitaries to keep the *andartes* at bay. The town of Giannitsa, lying to the west of Salonika in the Axios valley, was a centre of resistance activity, and it was there that a massacre took place in September 1944 which demonstrated the truly horrific nature of this policy. Overseen by German officers, the killings were nevertheless carried out by Greeks, under the command of a pair of infamous anti-communists, the republican Colonel George Poulos, and a Greek-speaking Wehrmacht sergeant called Fritz Schubert.[161]

On 13 September the inhabitants of the town had – without warning – been ordered into their homes. At dawn next morning, Poulos's and Schubert's men ordered all males over ten years old to gather in the square in front of the school building where the local German garrison was lodged. Women and children were herded together in another square nearby. After a short address from Father Papagrigoriou, the priest who rode alongside the squad, it was Schubert who began to speak in his heavily accented Greek: '*Poustides* ["Faggots"], ruffians, pimps, arse-lickers . . . I'll wipe out the lot of you,' he bawled.[162] Then he gave the orders to his men. For them, already compromised beyond redemption by their association with the Germans, murder had become a routine and perhaps even a sport. In ten minutes they beat a town clerk to death with clubs and iron bars before everyone's eyes. By the time Poulos appeared, in Greek army uniform, six other men had been battered to death. Poulos simply made a short speech to the terrified civilians, and left again. By mid-afternoon many more people had been murdered, among them a woman who worked as an interpreter for the German commander. The final death toll amounted to at least seventy-five, not including people who were shot at random as they worked in their fields. Poulos's men took the victims' clothes, shoes, money and valuables, and burned many houses. All this time German officers from the local garrison stood by watching and taking photographs.

As soon as the paramilitaries drove away, the survivors fled into the countryside. Wenger, a Swiss Red Cross worker, arrived in the town two days later, and found himself in a 'dead city'.[163] Walking through the deserted streets, he noted that a third of the town had been burned down. As he travelled across the plain, he heard about other atrocities – in Verria, where twelve women had been raped; in the village of Skylitsi, where Poulos's men had shot whomever they met; and, most horrible of all, in the village of Hortiatis, just a few miles from the comfortable HQ of General Löhr himself, where dozens of villagers had been slaughtered. Wenger finally caught up with Poulos at his heavily fortified headquarters in the village of Krya-Vrysi just outside Salonika. He found the stocky colonel in a combative mood. Poulos told Wenger to take his complaints to the *andartes*, who were responsible for 'the entire situation'. He showed no remorse, and made his low opinion of the Red Cross clear.

60.   Colonel Poulos harangues villagers in a northern Greek village, 1944.

*

Poulos, a short, overweight reserve army engineer from Salonika, was one of the few out-and-out collaborators in Greece. Like many of the most fanatical anti-communists he was a republican. Working for Sonderkommando 2000, a German counter-intelligence operation, he had started out organising networks of informers and spies to infiltrate the resistance. He also helped to run an anti-Semitic organisation called the National Union of Greece (EEE), which the SS had revived.[164]

The liquidation of abandoned Jewish properties brought him ample funds. In the summer of 1943, when the Wehrmacht allowed him to organise a Greek volunteer detachment, conditions should have been favourable for recruitment, for EAM/ELAS had forcibly disbanded several non-communist bands in central Macedonia. Yet Poulos was able to recruit no more than 300 men. Marching through Salonika in German uniforms they attracted cat-calls and hostile remarks. On at least one occasion they reportedly exchanged shots with the Greek police. Undiscouraged, Poulos and his men took part in sweeps of the hills of western Macedonia alongside the Wehrmacht.[165]

In early 1944 they were joined by an equally violent unit of former convicts and village recruits led by a Greek-speaking GFP sergeant called Schubert. Formed on Crete in the autumn of 1943 to combat the resistance, the *Schubertiani* had caused such uproar by their brutality – which included indiscriminate executions, torture and the shooting of women and children – that they were sent off the island and posted to northern Greece. By the time they joined up with Poulos they were already responsible for the murder of hundreds of innocent victims.[166]

In April 1944 ELAS mounted a direct assault on Poulos and his men while they were dining in a school in the town of Verria. A special unit of about twenty *andartes* infiltrated the neighbourhood and opened fire with automatic weapons. Catching the group completely off guard, they missed Poulos but killed his second-in-command, and over a hundred of his men.[167]

As ELAS became increasingly threatening, Poulos's 'nationalists' seemed fearful, trigger-happy and prone to acts of unpredictable savagery. Whenever they were rumoured to be approaching, entire villages and towns would empty in panic, as their inhabitants ran into the fields to hide. These killings, of which Giannitsa was the culmination, were part of a deliberate German policy of using terror on a massive scale – Poulos had actually been provided with a German police liaison officer who reported to the head of the SS in Greece – and all that saved Macedonia from further atrocities was the German withdrawal in October.[168]

After Giannitsa, Poulos led his men northwards together with the Germans, and ended up forming a Greek Police Volunteer Battalion in Slovenia, before surrendering to the Americans in April 1945. Two years later, Schubert was put on trial in Athens and Poulos was the subject of proceedings in Salonika. Still in detention, he wrote a letter to the Greek government, declaring that he had only acted out of love of his country, and offering – in view of the fact that events had borne out his warnings about communism – to find volunteers to fight the Left in Greece. In the right-wing climate of the times it was not a foregone conclusion that such an offer would be rejected. But the Greek public was so horrified by their crimes that the two men were among the very few war criminals to be executed in Greece after the war.[169]

CHAPTER TWENTY-THREE

'Tired Out by History': Athens '44

The bitter fighting that took place in liberated Athens in December 1944 between EAM/ELAS and the British – a time known in Greece simply as *ta dekemvriana* (the December events) – was a unique episode in the Second World War. It was the only time British troops actually fought against the resistance. That fighting has come to be seen as one of the key events in the early stages of the Cold War and a decisive moment in the suppression of wartime radicalism. But in fact the *dekemvriana* began long before December. The fighting then was really the culmination of a bitter struggle that had been going on in the city between EAM/ELAS and collaborationist Greek forces throughout 1944. This struggle is largely forgotten today, but it was fresh in the minds of every Athenian when Liberation came. The daily street battles, the labour round-ups and assassinations that took place under the eyes of the Germans had constituted a virtual civil war of their own, in which the clash between EAM/ELAS and the Right was fought out at closer quarters than anywhere else in Greece.[170]

*

When the Italian collapse took place in early September 1943, something changed in the popular mood in the capital: with the Italians went the last traces of the feelings of national unity which had emerged at the time of the Albanian campaign. Memories of having humiliated the Italians had formed the core of a fierce patriotism that ran across party and ideological boundaries; now that the Italians were gone, and the Red Army was beginning to push the Wehrmacht back into Europe, that patriotism fragmented under the pressure of ideological passions. People talked anxiously about civil war. EAM and its opponents clashed openly in the city streets. 'As I was walking one day in Stadion Street next to another pedestrian,' an Athenian later recalled when asked what event had made the greatest impression on him during the war, 'someone took out a pistol and shot him on the spot.' According to another: 'Occasional hand grenades and frequent machine-gun fire were normal and the whole city took on the air of a field of battle.' At a time when many Greeks agreed on basic postwar political goals – democratic freedoms and moderate socialist reform – there was a tragic paradox in these bitter hatreds and growing fanaticism. Theotokas commented sadly: 'From this one may judge the importance which programmes and theories have in our times – they are nothing but a crust hiding inflamed and irreconcilable passions.'[171]

By the end of 1943 EAM/ELAS had established a well-organised armed presence in Athens, virtually independent of ELAS GHQ in the mountains and with little similarity to the *andartes*. The young men fighting for EAM/ELAS in the city were street fighters who wore civilian clothes, carried forged ID cards and based themselves in the generally sympathetic poorer quarters that ringed the more affluent city centre. Children in the youth movement EPON passed them information, as did the street vendors. Some kiosk owners, either voluntarily or as a result of threats, reserved the use of their telephones for EAM.

The gendarmerie and the Security Battalions found that they were up against a virtually invisible, well-informed enemy. As Beirut and Belfast have since demonstrated, relatively small numbers of armed men, supported by a basically sympathetic population, can exercise tight control over movement in and out of specific quarters. There were only about 200 street fighters (mostly under twenty-five years old) in Vyrona, and just over 100 in the pathways of Kaisariani, 'Little Stalingrad', by the summer of 1944 – yet these were among the most dangerous neighbourhoods of Athens for Rallis's men.[172]

During February 1944 an ELAS captain had ordered his men to disarm all the gendarmes and Security Battalionists in the Kokkinia quarter. Kokkinia was a warren of dirty alleys and one-roomed shacks which had sprung up in the interwar period on the southwest of the city to house refugees from Asia Minor.[173] With its open sewers, mounds of refuse and dingy hovels, it was typical of the refugee quarters. Its inhabitants had endured the worst of the famine in 1941–42, and earned their reputation as one of the capital's 'red' neighbourhoods. Now they were to witness the first of innumerable clashes between Left and Right.

At 9 a.m. on Sunday, 5 March, an EAM patrol in the quarter spotted a gendarmerie lieutenant in a barber's shop. When the officer refused to hand over his revolver, he was shot dead. Next day, a larger group of gendarmes was attacked with grenades by an EAM group as they drove into the area. Thus goaded, the gendarmerie commander in Athens decided to mount a full-scale assault on the quarter, and on the evening of 7 March the public crier of EAM walked through Kokkinia, announcing that 'there would be a great battle the following day'.[174]

At dawn on 8 March, a force of over a thousand gendarmes and Security Battalionists surrounded the quarter to conduct investigations. When German SS forces arrived on the scene they were prevented from taking part by Greek officers, who insisted that it was a purely Greek affair. Gendarmerie officials arrested several hundred people as hostages, and shot four suspected EAM members in front of the barber shop where the gendarme had been killed.[175]

Several days later, the Germans played a more active part in the next major policing operation, which took place in the northern suburbs of Nea Ionia and Kalogreza. The Ministry of the Interior requisitioned several buses and lorries and ordered the entire force of gendarmes in the Athens area – just over 2,000 men – to be on hand. Before dawn on 13 March, 500 of them were driven out to the refugee quarters. Thus started one of the first 'bloccos' (round-ups), which were to become the constant nightmare of many Athenians until Liberation.

The sleeping inhabitants were abruptly woken by the sound of megaphones ordering all males in the neighbourhood to make their way immediately to the main square. Gendarmes and battalion men began house-to-house searches, with orders to shoot anyone they found hiding. In the cold grey light of early morning, thousands of men sat on the ground, while hooded informers picked out EAM sympathisers. The gendarmes checked men's ID cards against a list of communist suspects, and arrested 300. One was killed straight away, and others were interrogated by the head of the gendarmerie and by 'General' Alexandros Lambou, of the much-hated Special Security branch, an anti-communist force which had received SS advice on policing methods. Most of the prisoners were detained in Haidari, and either sent to Germany or kept as hostages to be shot whenever ELAS claimed another victim.

Lambou ordered eighteen of the men to be shot there and then by firing squad. As the condemned men were executed, SS personnel looked on and took photographs. Then Lambou made a speech to the hundreds of terrified people in the square; icon in hand, he denounced the Left and told them that he was working for the Christian faith and for the good of Greece. Behind him, gendarmes and battalion men ran wild. They broke into shops and burned a couple of shacks because they belonged to 'communists'. Several girls were stripped naked and beaten in an unsuccessful effort to make them confess that they were associated with EAM/ELAS.[176]

Over the following months such nightmarish scenes were to

61. Woodcut of the blocco at Kokkinia, Athens, on 17 August 1944. A masked informer points out suspects from among the men to German troops and Greek collaborators. Some have been killed on the spot; others sit with their heads bowed.

become a regular if unpredictable feature of life in the refugee quarters of Athens and Piraeus. 'No one knew whether that evening they would return home or whether next morning they would be going back to work,' wrote one Athenian. Life and death were ruled by sheer chance, a matter of the whims of ill-disciplined Evzones and their sinister, masked informers. The Security Battalions sealed off and searched the 'red quarters', arresting hundreds of people and executing others on the spot. The horror and violence of these events imprinted themselves on the popular memory of the occupation. The 'frenetic scenes of the blocco at Kaisariani' made 'an unforgettable impression' on one Athenian. Another described how the 'endless bloccos forced me to travel home [from work] through unfamiliar and what I judged to be the least dangerous neighbourhoods. Once I spent eight hours amid scenes of inhuman tortures which still make me tremble.' For a third, 'the most vivid

343

62. Collaborationist Security Battalions lead workers away from their factory to be held as hostages or deported for forced labour in the Third Reich. Athens, 1944.

picture' that remained from the occupation was of 'the roughness of the men in the bloccos. . . . the men with masks who wandered among the masses gathered there, pointing out those they recognised.' 'You heard the blocco,' another recalled, 'and ran like crazy.'[177]

Although the fundamental conflict may have been a Greek affair, as the gendarmes had insisted at Kokkinia, there can be no doubt that the outcome was in accord with German policy, and reflected in particular the growing confidence of SS officials like Walter Blume.[178] To the alarm of Special Envoy Neubacher, Blume became keener and keener on these 'bloccos'; by summer he was ordering them on a massive scale, bringing thousands of civilians into the Haidari concentration camp to be perfunctorily interrogated, and then shot, held or transported to Germany. Wehrmacht and SS troops took part in the round-ups, alongside the Greek security forces. One rough Viennese thug at Blume's headquarters joined in as often as he could, since it reminded him of the butchery in which he had participated in occupied Russia. If German troops occasionally refrained from intervening, it was precisely because the main purpose of building up the Security Battalions and other

344

anti-communist Greek forces had been to 'save precious German blood'. HSSPF Schimana admitted openly that his aim was to sow dissension among the Greeks in order to allow the Germans to sit back and 'watch the fight in peace'. Civil strife was the inevitable outcome.[179]

Furthermore, the human by-product of the 'bloccos' – hundreds and sometimes thousands of ordinary civilians who were arrested and driven away to Haidari and other prison camps – fulfilled one of Himmler's obsessions during 1944: the forcible conscription of Europe's manpower for German military and economic ends. Prisoners from the refugee quarters would be packed off in trains northwards, and if the numbers never matched SS expectations the fault lay not with the method of collection, but with Greece's choked and limited railway capacity.

A prominent role in the 'bloccos' was played by Lambou's Special Security branch which, by the summer of 1944, had virtually escaped effective political control. The mere appearance of Special Security units provoked panic among the residents of Athens. One afternoon, EAM seized two Security men as they entered a taverna round the corner from their office in downtown Athens. To retaliate, Lambou searched the area along Vouliagmenis Street where they had disappeared. As his gendarmes fired off their guns, inhabitants of the area fled into the backstreets. On another occasion Special Security agents reduced the inhabitants of one suburb to abject terror during their search for the missing son of one of their colleagues; only the little boy's unexpected reappearance – it turned out he had simply got lost – saved many people from imprisonment, deportation or execution.[180]

The torture chambers at Special Security HQ in Stournara Street were as notorious as those of the SS itself. Each dawn revealed the corpses of men killed by Lambou's forces and dumped on street corners. 'As soon as it gets dark,' wrote Theotokas, 'the city scents murder.' At 10.30 one August evening, Special Security raided the Hesperos Hotel and took away three men; two were later released, the third was shot and wounded. Two nights later they seized two men as they left the Panhellenion café. The body of a twenty-three-year-old worker from Piraeus was discovered whom they had shot. In all, there must have been at least several hundred victims of these official killers.[181]

The randomness of such assaults was a source of concern to the Athens City police, who tried to keep their distance from the other security services. Sometimes, indeed, the police almost came to blows with gendarmes or Battalionists. One afternoon, for example, two uniformed battalion men, already the worse for drink, reeled into a taverna for more wine. 'Here come Rallis's stool-pigeons,' muttered one of the customers. Unsure who had spoken, the two men rounded on the nearest drinker, dragged him out of the shop and beat him with their guns in order to make him confess to the remark. Their victim showed them his papers and assured them he had not even heard the remark. But by the time they dumped him at the local police station he was almost senseless. When the duty officer told them to leave him alone, they turned on him too. 'We'll kill you, you fag,' they shouted before being pulled away. Still swearing, and threatening to burn down the police station, they left, accusing the police loudly of not executing enough communists.[182]

The police's moderation won respect from ELAS. When captured, individual policemen were usually disarmed, interrogated and then set free. One was surrounded one morning by five armed men – none more than twenty years old – whilst he supervised a council employee who was scrubbing graffiti off a wall. The gang searched him, took away his papers and led him into a vacant lot behind the Osram factory where several other men from EAM interrogated him. After half an hour, satisfied that he did not belong to the hated battalions, or to Special Security, they gave him back his documents and let him go.

Other collaborators were more harshly treated. A thirty-three-year-old taxi driver who worked for the Germans was shot dead after stopping at a crossroads. The body of an unidentified man was discovered by the police lying near Liosion Street and bearing a placard with the words: 'This is the punishment for informers. ELAS.' ELAS attacks on battalion men were a daily occurrence.

Such assaults provoked an immediate response from the Right. The body of an unknown man discovered one evening at the end of Nikomideias Street carried a placard which read: 'He is a communist. Executed as reprisal for the nationalists murdered by ELAS.' An EAM attack upon Nikolaos Papageorgiou, leader of the notorious right-wing Pankrati group, on the morning of 2 September was swiftly answered. At midday two young men were found dead in the road where the original attack had taken place; placards round their necks read: 'Papageorgiou – 2 for 1'. On the morning of the 4th, Papageorgiou's men pulled a young carpenter off the tram in Plateia Kondylis, and shot him in the chest; they then shot three other men and hung placards round their necks too. By 6 that evening, the death toll had risen to ten.

Imitating their German masters, Special Security officers and the Security Battalions even carried out mass executions of hostages to avenge the deaths of their colleagues. 'The execution took place on

63. Battalionist stands guard by the corpse of a member of the resistance: Athens, 1944.

the German model,' commented a colonel of gendarmerie after the shooting of seventeen civilians by Security men on the afternoon of 22 April. Like the Germans, the Greek authorities often carried out such shootings in full view of the public, to ensure the maximum deterrent effect. Photographs from these months show bodies dangling from acacia trees on streets in central Athens, while horrified civilians hurry past. Guarded by Battalionists to stop them being taken down and properly buried, they stayed in the minds of many Athenians for years afterwards. One woman could not forget seeing 'five corpses hanging in the square and two killed in front of the police station'. Another remembered 'the execution one sunny day of three young men in Kyriakou Square'. 'What made the greatest impression on me,' another Athenian recalled, 'was that life is such a cheap thing, cheaper than a pound of maize.'[183]

It was out on the fringes of Athens that most clashes took place, in the dangerous hours between dusk and dawn; here too the 'bloccos' cordoned off the most notorious trouble spots. From their expensive flats in Kolonaki round the slopes of Lykavettos, well-

347

off Athenians heard the crackle of gunfire in the poorer quarters through the night. Even the city centre, however, was increasingly unsafe. Going for an afternoon stroll in the Zappeion Gardens, one unsuspecting pedestrian was caught up in the firing between a group of Evzones and their quarry, and shot in the stomach. The National Gardens, which verged on Constitution Square within sight of the Grande Bretagne hotel, turned into a jungle where gunmen stalked one another through the dense greenery.[184]

Looting by Rallis troops occurred all the time. Lambou announced that no house searches were permitted except in the presence of uniformed officers with official papers: 'All searches by persons not showing the official service ID do not constitute official business by our organs.'[185] This announcement changed nothing. Late in the evening of 20 August, for example, four armed Greek youths, brandishing what they said was a pass from the SS, broke into a block of flats in the centre of Athens claiming to be searching for hidden Jews. They did not find any, but took away the residents' clothes, and seized two radios and other goods. The unidentified men who broke into the house of Gerasimos Loukatos's girlfriend on the evening after a battalion raid in the neighbourhood did not bother to present their search warrant; nor were the terrified inhabitants, cowering in an upstairs bedroom behind locked doors, in a mood to demand it.[186]

EAM gangs also had their targets for 'contributions', and these became particularly important as EAM started to run short of money. A soap manufacturer was visited one afternoon in his office in the centre of Athens by two youths, who demanded 200 gold pounds for the 'struggle' and threatened him with a gun when he denied he had the money on him. Only when someone shouted that the Germans were coming did they panic and run away. A bomb wrecked the Oasis cabaret in the Zappeion Gardens after its owner had refused to give money to EAM; the proprietor of the Piccadilly restaurant was shot dead for the same reason. According to the uncomplicated moral arithmetic of the Left, such men were collaborators who had enriched themselves by association with the occupiers and now refused to help 'the People'.[187]

EAM also used the threat of force to ensure the success of strikes and demonstrations. The evening before the strike of 24 August, five armed men entered the offices of the newspaper *Proia*, seized the plates for the front page, and ordered the workers home. 'We belong to ELAS,' they told them, 'and because there's a strike tomorrow, the papers must not appear.'

In the violent chaos it was impossible to keep track of the many organisations that emerged, especially on the Right. Pangalos's followers in the Ministry of the Interior backed various anti-communist groups. There were the Panoliascu brothers holed up in Kerameikos, and the Papageorgiou band which operated in Pankrati. Colonel Grivas, who would become better known in the 1950s as leader of the EOKA movement in Cyprus, headed an underground royalist organisation called 'X', which had started out fighting the Germans but by 1944 was spending more time in clashes with EAM from its bastion in the Theseion area beneath the Acropolis. In the side streets below the Theseion temple, 'X' gunmen exchanged shots with ELAS patrols and took part in major operations alongside the Security Battalions. 'Today [they are] with the Germans, tomorrow when the blessed King returns, with those bringing him back,' was one observer's assessment of their loyalties.[188]

By the summer of 1944 city life was approaching complete anarchy. 'It seems odd to us when we *can't* hear shooting,' observed one Athenian. The whole city had 'run amok'. 'Today's situation looks one way from the centre of the city, another from the suburbs and another from the refugee quarters,' Alekos Rodoulis wrote in July, in one of the most fair-minded assessments of the fighting to come out of Athens.[189] As Rodoulis put it, one had to question 'whether man is a logical animal or something which is to be found only in a jungle'. Theotokas echoed the same sentiment: 'What if humanity isn't rational, but really crazy?' The prudent course of action in such circumstances was that followed by the village president of Markopoulo, just outside Athens. He was reported to be 'friendly with all the organisations'. He had given large sums to EAM, but had also joined EDES and other nationalist organisations; he was even a personal friend of Lambou at Special Security. He was, in other words, 'on the right side of whoever is on top tomorrow'.[190] Few people, however, had the sang-froid or good fortune to emulate that impressive achievement. Most simply looked for an end to the violence, and were becoming sufficiently exhausted to support whoever promised to bring that about. 'We are tired out by History,' Theotokas wrote as Liberation beckoned, 'tired and uneasy. We fear the peace as much as the war. The world is sick, and no one can see a remedy close at hand.'[191]

*

In the final month of the occupation there were signs that some elements of Rallis's anti-communist coalition were looking for insurance after Liberation. The 'bloccos' and indeed the fighting continued unabated under German supervision through August and September, but Battalionists occasionally displayed an unfamiliarly humane side of their character.

The inhabitants of Kokkinia who watched gendarmerie officers and Evzones as they led captives away after a round-up on 12 August, were surprised to see them letting some of the men slip away. When several prisoners offered a battalion major money to let them escape, he replied: 'I'm not such a monster that I need to be bribed.' As soon as a nearby SS officer walked away, he allowed them to run off.[192]

At dawn on 28 August the Germans and the Security Battalions surrounded the Koukaki quarter in what had become the usual fashion. They also cordoned off the area around Nea Smyrni, gathering together thousands of inhabitants. Hooded informers picked out several people: 21 were executed on the spot, and 3–4,000 were herded together to be taken to Haidari. At this point, however, Colonel Plytzanopoulos, the commander of the Security Battalions, came up and told the prisoners not to worry – none of them would be going either to Haidari or to Germany; he would not allow it. And indeed, after a hurried, angry conversation with the senior German officer present, they were set free.

At Kokkinia events took a dramatic turn when SS men noticed that prisoners were being allowed to escape as they were being escorted to prison. Shooting broke out between the Germans and the Battalionists and one SS and three battalion men were killed. Many prisoners also died in the cross-fire. After that many Battalionists protested to their officers that they could not continue such work. Plytzanopoulos told the Germans that his men could no longer agree to round up innocent Greek citizens to be sent to Germany.

By the end of the summer the Germans were evacuating their lodgings in Athens, and nervously bracing themselves for the journey north. After the sudden collapse of Romania, their departure from Greece was evidently just a matter of time. They were eager, as one German officer put it, to get out of 'the mouse-trap'.[193] Colonel Plytzanopoulos could afford to disregard his plummeting reputation in German eyes, and try to regain some support amongst the Greek public. His theme now was national reconciliation. On 6 September he told a crowd of detainees that the Germans should be allowed to depart in peace, since any attack on them would only lead to further bloodshed. He went on to say that he and his officers had always been loyal to the Cairo government, and would work for understanding with their former enemies. Was it only four months ago, his listeners must have wondered, that the SD had chosen him to head the Security Battalions in place of the pro-British Dertilis?

Teams of battalion men began visiting EAM positions. Over roast lamb and shared bread, they suggested negotiating terms for joint action against the Germans. People were overjoyed at the prospect of an end to the killing, and news of the moves towards reconciliation swept the capital. But EAM rejected their offer, suggesting instead that the Battalions and gendarmes should either enlist in ELAS or hand over their weapons and return to their homes: 'there could never be unification with the murderers of the people, for they would all have to pay for their actions'.

By the night of 10 September things had returned to normal, with fighting between the two sides in Kaisariani, Vyrona and elsewhere. Three days later, the funeral of a dead battalion man was interrupted by an EAM attack: while the service went on, the mourners exchanged fire with EAM sharpshooters in the hills. Gun battles on the deserted streets between Battalionists and the guerrillas soon reached such a pitch that many people remembered the summer as a time of relative tranquillity. Street fighting continued right up until Liberation itself in October, and did not stop even then.

*

This, then, was the history of razzias, 'bloccos', public hangings and summary executions, which had traumatised and terrified people in the months before Liberation and which had irredeemably tainted the official security forces in their eyes. Only against this background of widespread suffering – so poorly and haphazardly appreciated by the British and other forces that entered Greece as the Germans left – can we understand the tragic events of December 1944.

So strong was the popular loathing of the gendarmerie, in particular, that at Liberation that body had 'ceased to exist as an effective force', leaving the British-backed Papandreou government with the problem of how to rebuild the country's internal security forces. This was probably the thorniest question the government faced, for Left and Right alike suspected the other of planning to monopolise control of whatever body eventually emerged. Pressure to confront this problem came from the British military, who wished to withdraw their troops as quickly as possible from Greece for use elsewhere. Together with the Greek general staff they decided to set up new apolitical National Guard battalions, which would supervise the disarming of all resistance organisations over a period of six to nine months before general elections. During this time, a new gendarmerie would be established to take over civil policing, leaving the battalions to form part of the country's future armed forces.[194]

In the middle of November 1944 the first National Guard battalions were set up, recruiting conscripts from the 1936 class. The

Left suspected with some justification that battalion commanders were being drawn from right-wing circles. Significantly, the man picked by the Papandreou government as the new military commander of Greek forces in Attica was an ardently anti-communist gendarmerie officer. The communist paper *Rizospastis*, affirming its faith in the idea of an impartial police force as the 'first guarantee of the normal development of the situation', accused the deputy Minister of War of appointing a majority of Guard officers who were 'Security Battalionists, Fascists, disguised Fascists or supporters of the Metaxas dictatorship' and warned that this was part of 'a premeditated plan for domination by the forces of Reaction'. In some areas EAM/ELAS disarmed National Guard units; in others, however, they urged their supporters to join up. The overall situation – like EAM policy itself – was highly confused.[195]

When EAM ministers finally resigned from the Papandreou government on 2 December, the issue of internal security was in everyone's minds. At the large EAM protest demonstration which was organised for the following day in Constitution Square, the only police units available to the government apart from British troops were the Athens city police, whose relatively neutral stance during the occupation had meant they were not disbanded immediately. Now, tragically, they stood as the last visible remnants of the hated wartime terror system. Shortly before 11 a.m., as thousands of EAM demonstrators entered Constitution Square, several policemen panicked and fired directly into the crowd from the police station which stood at one corner of the square. People fled, but it was discovered later that at least ten had been killed and over fifty injured. The initial reaction of the British 23rd Armoured Brigade, whose men moved in and cleared the square, was that the Greek police had lost their nerve: they had 'dealt rather wildly with the demonstration' and had 'fired unnecessarily'.[196]

The shootings in Constitution Square sparked off a popular uprising against the police. Within hours, crowds were reported to be besieging police stations and trying to capture them. At first EAM/ELAS refrained from firing on British soldiers and clearly regarded the conflict as an internecine one. But Churchill was convinced that he was seeing the Left's long-awaited attempt to seize power and he backed British commanders to the hilt, instructing them to treat Athens as they would 'a captured city where a local rebellion is in progress'. RAF Spitfires strafed the suburbs of Athens, and the fighting widened across the city to include British units. It ended, in early January, with the defeat of the Left, marking the re-ascendancy of the Right in Greek politics and further fuelling official anti-communism.[197]

Despite Churchill's belief that he had forestalled a communist attempt to seize power, there is no sign that the uprising in Athens was anything other than a spontaneous popular movement which took the party leadership wholly by surprise. Had the Party wanted to seize power, it could have done so easily two months earlier, as soon as the Germans left. The hand of Moscow was nowhere to be seen, for Stalin was content to let the British create a precedent in Greece that he could then use elsewhere in Eastern Europe. The causes of the wave of attacks in Athens against local police stations, following the shootings in Constitution Square, become more obvious when we realise how bitter were the hatreds and memories of police brutality during the occupation months. In the *dekemvriana*, above all, political actions have to be seen in their social context.

The fighting, of course, rendered impossible the formation of a politically impartial police force. Royalist army commanders urged the British to rearm Security Battalionists and Special Security men who were being held in camps in Athens. British military police officers, who had little idea of what had been happening in Athens earlier that year, sympathised with the plight of these detainees, many of whom – as they naively saw it – were just professional policemen 'out of a job through no fault of their own'. Hemmed in for days in the centre of Athens, the British were in no position to refuse offers of assistance and during the fighting, former gendarmes, Battalionists and right-wing collaborators were given arms and incorporated into National Guard units.[198]

Once the fighting stopped, screening procedures for entry into the National Guard were used to exclude candidates of the Left rather than the Right. According to General Tsakalotos, a senior army commander, the National Guard was built up 'only from nationally minded reservists and volunteers who had proved themselves during the December events'. The Guards' strength grew rapidly, to a maximum of around 60,000 by the middle of the year, but they soon proved to be an ill-disciplined and brutal force. Stationed in their home areas and often acting out of personal motives, they searched homes without warrants, ransacked left-wing offices, and beat people with impunity. The Peloponnese in particular witnessed the onset of a wave of violence in which the National Guards abandoned any pretence of impartiality and allied themselves with right-wing bands, releasing Security Battalionists from local jails and attacking suspected Leftists and their families. British observers became worried that such indiscriminate repression was making the situation worse and forcing the Left underground once more. In a sign of the increasingly right-wing attitudes of the Greek authorities, it was announced in August 1945 that a leader of the Security Battalions who had died in the fighting in December was to receive a posthumous promotion. Within months, former *andartes* had taken the 'road to the mountains' again for their own protection, and full-scale civil war spread across the country. The Democratic Army proved very successful at first against the British-backed government in Athens, and only the imposition of martial law in many areas, the displacement of thousands of civilians from zones held by the guerrillas, and a massive programme of American military aid eventually allowed the government to prevail.[199]

EPILOGUE

'No Peace Without Victory'

Why do you stand there, orphaned children, like strangers, like
*   passers-by? . . .*
Why do your eyes not run like a quiet river,
so that your tears become a lake and make a cool spring,
for the unwashed to be washed, for the thirsty ones to drink?
Greek folk lament

In August 1944 the Red Army threatened to cut off the
Wehrmacht forces in Greece as it overran Romania and swept
across the Balkans. Army Group E in Salonika was forced, finally,
to order its units northwards. They faced a long retreat across
partisan-infested mountains; the Reich seemed very distant. According to resistance sources, the Germans felt 'completely isolated'
and dreaded the arrival of the Russians at any minute. 'We can't
stay here any longer,' wrote Lance-Corporal Herbert Brehmer
to his wife Marianne on 18 September. 'Today we heard that
the Russians are on the Bulgarian–Yugoslav border.' Military discipline began to fray: the men shouted down their officers, and
cinemas were put out of bounds in punishment. 'Dear wife,' an
NCO wrote from Salonika, 'Our officers and sergeants are very
quiet around us. No more loud commands – they seem to be
worried.' General Löhr himself – prevented earlier by Hitler from
preparing a more orderly withdrawal – confided to Neubacher that
the situation was 'hopeless'.[1]

Isolated acts of desertion over the summer months betrayed the
troops' uncertainty. During an exchange of fire round the Kaisariani
cemetery, a German soldier suddenly ran towards the ELAS positions. As he was surrounded by resistance gunmen, his hands held
aloft, his words poured out nervously in an urgent jumble of
languages: 'Ego kalos syntrophos. Ego kommounistas. Hitler skata.
Stalin extra prima . . . ego ochi fasistas' (I good comrade. I communist. Hitler shit. Stalin extra fine. I no Fascist). Not wanting

64. The swastika is taken down from the former German Vice-Consulate on Vathy, Samos. October 1944.

anything to do with him, the ELAS detachment waved him away; he stumbled away across the hillside past a group of armed collaborators, shouting, 'EAM kalo. Esy ochi kalo. Esy skata' (EAM good. You no good. You shit). A medley of assorted Wehrmacht units – notably Caucasians, Silesian 'Germans' now identifying themselves as Poles, and Russians – deserted to the *andartes*.[2]

A few desperate optimists, like one Corporal Rettenhaber, still believed that 'we will win the war', and that 'so long as the Führer lives, so too will our beloved Homeland'. But others were worried by Hitler's silence. 'It would be a disgrace,' one soldier wrote bitterly, 'for a people which placed such a trust in its leaders to be led so astray, after all it has suffered – fathers, sons, homes destroyed – and still with a great belief in a better future after the war.' Their sole consolation was the evident tension that had sprung up between the English and the Russians. Perhaps, one speculated, 'the English will join us against the Russians'. Few soldiers thought much about the country they were leaving: they were much more concerned with what lay ahead.[3]

While a dense stream of 'trucks, wireless vans, ambulances, artillery, staff cars and motor cycles' bumped along the dusty main road northwards, frequently waved on their way by the villagers they passed, a special train left Athens on 2 October with prominent Greek collaborators, Italian Fascists and German civilians on board.[4] The big fish who had already fled north included ex-Premier Logothetopoulos, who reached Vienna in good time with his German wife and elder daughter (the younger one stayed in Athens). Among the small fry were the opportunists, men like Perikles Nikolaides, who had run gambling dens for the SD in Salonika, and now checked into the Hotel Meteor in Prague under the cover name 'Peter Speckbacher'. The 'Dr Paul Weber' who was captured by the Americans near Salzburg in May 1945 turned out to be a Greek translator and SD contact called Papadopoulos. At about the same time Constantine Tsimbas, a former agent for the GFP, pimp and black-marketeer, handed himself over to American troops in Bavaria and promptly denounced several high-ranking Nazis living in the vicinity. 'Tsimbas is an unprincipled opportunist,' wrote his disgusted interrogator. 'Feeling no allegiance to any cause or country, he tries to ally himself with whomever may be in power.'[5]

Also fleeing to the safety of central Europe were Colonel Poulos and several hundred of his vicious 'nationalist' thugs, who formed a Greek police volunteer battalion under German auspices in Ljubljana. When Poulos refused to order his men against US troops in Austria, he was relieved of his command and ordered to report to the so-called Greek National Committee, which had been set up in the spring of 1945 in the Grand Hotel at Kitzbühl.[6] On Neubacher's orders, a bizarre group of nervous Balkan quislings had already been escorted there: His Holiness Gavrilo, the magnificently bearded Patriarch of the Serbian Orthodox Church; former Serbian Prime Minister Nedić, various Bulgarian and Romanian sympathisers, and a small huddle of Greek collaborationist politicians. Though Rallis had stayed behind in Athens, Tsironikos, the last Finance Minister and Neubacher's confidante, was there; so too was Tavoularis, who had filled the gendarmerie with anti-communist extremists. But by the time this pathetic assortment of failures set up the National Committee the snow was melting in the Austrian Alps, and Greece had already been liberated: only a few days later, Hitler killed himself. Their 'government in exile', needless to say, existed on paper only, and made a suitably surreal finale for men who had never had a firm grasp of Greek political realities.[7]

*

Those Greeks who fled north were either genuine pro-Nazis, notorious killers, or simply too stupid to have taken the precaution of maintaining contacts with Cairo. Most collaborators, after all, had worked with the occupiers out of convenience, not conviction. Their sympathies were basically pro-British, and so they remained in Greece, waiting nervously for the Allies to land to protect them from the vengeance of ELAS.

Chief among them were the Security Battalions, left behind to garrison the Peloponnese when the last Wehrmacht troops pulled out early in September. In the town of Tripolis their commander, Colonel Papadongonas, held brief talks with representatives of the ELAS 3rd Division, but these quickly broke down. Battalion officers grew jittery as their ammunition ran out. Some proposed retreating northwards; others deserted to the *andartes*, who had come down from the hills and surrounded the town. Roads out of the town were mined by the guerrillas and the water supply was cut off.[8]

Increasingly desperate, Papadongonas ruled Tripolis through 'real terror'. People suspected of any sort of link with the *andartes* were imprisoned, and Papadongonas threatened to blow them up if he was attacked. Battalionists carried out executions in the streets, and laid mines everywhere. The *andartes'* surrender ultimatum ran out on 16 September, but Papadongonas's men clung on, desperately, for two more weeks before surrendering with the aid of the Red Cross to a British unit.[9]

Elsewhere, besieged battalion units clashed with the *andartes*. On 10 September Kalamata fell in the south, followed five days later by Meligala. Battalion forces collapsed in Pyrgos after a two-day battle. 'Wholesale massacres' of collaborators by the *andartes* were reported. Numbers were exaggerated, but in the tense, excited, vengeful atmosphere the reality turned out to be violent enough. After all, up to 1,500 people had been executed in the Kalamata area during the German occupation, and thousands of homes had been burned. Battalionists had carried out a last round of reprisals only a few weeks earlier, and now their victims sought their revenge. On Sunday, 17 September the former governor of Messenia and other officials were brought back under ELAS guard from Meligala to Kalamata. As soon as they were marched into the main square, frenzied onlookers broke loose of the ELAS civil police and in ten minutes beat some of the prisoners to death, and strung the others up from lamp-posts. An American radio operator had a good view of the crowd: 'All of [them] wanted to get in some kind of a blow. Canes, clubs, knives, shoes, rocks and everything anyone could strike a blow with were used on the group. This was their first chance at vengeance and they took it.'[10]

For months, conservative Greeks had been sure that EAM/ELAS would seize power, or at least would try to, as soon as the Germans withdrew. One senior gendarmerie officer had predicted a black future for Salonika when Liberation came: 'The programme of communism aims, immediately after the withdrawal of occupation forces, at stirring up the masses . . . to general looting and disorder, while its large, well-armed and well-organised units seize power, and overthrow their opponents, neutralising all existing or potential reaction to the communist regime.' Events, however, took a very different course: generally, faced with emotional public demands for instant vengeance, the hard-pressed officials of EAM/ELAS in towns like Kalamata struggled to impose order and a rudiment-ary rule of law in the vacuum of power created by the German withdrawal.[11]

On Mytilene, where the last German troops sailed away at dawn on 10 September, EAM/ELAS immediately took over the island and prevented any rioting or looting. Police and gendarmes were usually disarmed, while ELAS units arrested collaborators and trai-tors, but resisted popular pressure to execute them on the spot. According to an observer: 'It is impossible to imagine more effec-tive management than that established by EAM and enforced by ELAS.'[12] In the Macedonian town of Naoussa, where the retreating German soldiers had blown up the school building before leaving, ELAS insurgents entered four hours later. They made a few arrests, and requisitioned houses and supplies much as any occupying force might have done: again there was little disorder or looting, though there was considerable local fear of the *andartes*. The Greek flag was immediately run up, alongside those of Serbia, the Soviet Union, England and the USA.[13]

Against members of the Security Battalions or Zervas's EDES, the *andartes* were keen to settle accounts, but elsewhere ELAS rule was as orderly as was to be expected in the extraordinary circum-stances that prevailed. Passions ran high, and intense suspicions were mingled with euphoria. 'In some districts the [ELAS] Civil Guard are maintaining order fairly and impartially,' ran the report of a British observer in the Peloponnese. 'In others, they are abus-ing their position.' What such observations point to is the looseness of the overall organisation of EAM/ELAS, and the variety of behaviour at a local level. Did the 'looting of private goods and property, injury to and intimidation of the civil population, and unjustified arrests' which took place in some villages constitute the first indications of a systematic takeover of power? It seems unlikely. Signs of communist domination of the *andartes* were not difficult to find, but at the same time there was no indication that the KKE desired to seize power by force. On the contrary, what evidence there is suggests that the KKE – in so far as its divided leadership was capable of any decisions at all in the absence of a clear lead from Moscow – had decided *not* to seize power at a time when it could easily have done so.[14]

*

Nowhere was this more evident than in Athens itself, which was 'liberated' on Thursday, 12 October, before British troops had reached the city. Here, if ever, was the time for EAM/ELAS to seize power; but it did not. EAM activists had spread news of the expected German withdrawal the night before by shouting messages across the rooftops through their megaphones. On the 12th, the sun rose on hundreds of blue-and-white Greek flags which people had draped over their balconies. That morning, as crowds gathered in Syntagma Square, a German unit took down the swastika from the Acropolis, and gave a last salute at the Tomb of the Unknown Soldier. Their officer told the mayor they were handing the city over to him, and marched off. 'We found the streets filled with a sea of humanity, so dense that our car could only push its way through with difficulty,' recalled one of the last German officials to leave. 'I have never seen people in the grip of such joy and enthusiasm.' By noon Syntagma Square was packed; people kissed and embraced one another. Bells rang out over the city.[15]

Now came the capital's first glimpse of the extraordinary social changes that had been unfolding in the mountains of Free Greece over the past two years. 'Today we feel an enormous, uncontrollable popular wave lifting us and carrying us off,' Theotokas wrote. 'What this mass wants exactly, no one knows, not even its most articulate members. This is not the industrial proletariat of the great European centres with the concrete socio-economic demands of scientific socialism. Here we have to do with incalculable forces. The Russian Revolution is in the air, but also the French Revolution and the Paris Commune, a national liberation war, and who knows what other confused elements.' A column of priests marched through the streets chanting the EAM slogan 'Laokratia!' (People's Rule). Rough-looking youths from the Piraeus slums carried a cardboard Hitler on a pole. More shocking to many Athenians even than the groups of bearded *andartes*, a young woman rode through the crowds, sitting astride her horse like a man, her face burned brown from the sun: she had wrapped a red shawl round her head and shoulders and waved a Greek flag. To cap it all, there was a parade of children clutching wooden rifles, the so-called 'Children's

65.   The Liberation of Athens: October 12, 1944.

Front' of EAM. Celebrations, march-pasts and victory services took the place of the widely feared EAM *coup d'état*.[16]

In among the celebrating and curious crowds was a thirty-one-year-old Frenchman called Roger Milliex, a philhellene who had spent the war in Athens working for the Institut Français. Behind the scenes he had also been active in EAM. The whole of that unforgettable autumn day he wandered in a daze through the streets, clutching his four-year-old son in one hand, and a Free French flag in the other. After lunch he joined a group of EAM intellectuals in Kolonaki, the 'Mayfair' of Athens, where they chanted communist slogans 'to scare the bourgeois'. Running along behind, his tiny son copied them as loudly as he could: 'Laokratia, laokratia kai ochi vasilia!' (People's Rule, People's Rule, No to the King!).[17]

Spirits were high among the young ELAS fighters; they were boisterous, confident and full of their own prowess. Milliex recalled the wonderful atmosphere of Paris in 1936, the heyday of the Popular Front – 'the same popular participation (women and children), the same jubilation, the same enthusiasm'. But this was wishful thinking and perhaps also political naivety, for Athens in 1944 was a far tenser city than Paris eight years earlier. When EAM supporters gathered outside the headquarters of nationalist organisations shouting slogans, the mood of rejoicing vanished with astonishing speed. 'It only needs a match for Athens to catch fire like a tank of petrol,' wrote Theotokas.[18]

*

Some days later, disturbing news came from the north, where ELAS troops marched into Salonika in defiance of orders from their commander-in-chief. 'We are the boys of the mountains and we are afraid of nothing,' they yelled. 'An incredible number of soldiers of all ages, wearing different uniforms and various weapons fills the streets,' wrote an amazed onlooker. 'There is an incessant stream of these men, whose clothes bear the traces of the hardships of their fugitive existence. Many of them, alone or in groups, march about, or head for mysterious destinations, loaded down with catridge belts, carrying a rifle or machine gun on their shoulder or under their arm, not to mention the grenades and knives.'[19]

In Salonika, as it turned out, the *andartes'* guns were mostly for display. ELAS units combed the dirty, booby-trapped streets for collaborators, but there was little of the sniping that continued in Athens. A small detachment of British Empire troops – 7 Indian Infantry Brigade – arrived and paraded through the town. Thanks to the efforts of the Brigade's officers and senior EAM/ELAS officials, by the middle of November the two sides were co-operating, if with some mutual watchfulness.[20]

In Athens, however, events followed a different and ultimately more tragic course. Suspicion grew between EAM/ELAS and the other politicians until Papandreou's fragile Government of National Unity fell apart. By December Athens was again at war, and ELAS units were fighting British troops for control of the capital. The

66. Liberation: Greek villagers in Xylokastron welcome a British jeep as it passes through en route to Athens, October 1944. Carpets have been laid in the road for the cars to drive over.

question of who bore the responsibility for this sequence of events was to become one of the most bitterly contested issues of modern Greek history.

Lincoln MacVeagh, the experienced American minister in Greece and as close to a neutral figure as was to be found in Athens in the weeks after Liberation, noted the tactics of both sides with foreboding. EAM's movements he described as 'threatening', while the response of the British was 'verging on the kind of thing which might be pointed to by the leftists as savoring of foreign interference with Greek liberties – imposition of dictatorship by foreign force'. While EAM/ELAS made no overt bid for power and EAM ministers actually remained in the Papandreou government until 2 December, the Left was continually challenging the government's authority on the streets and in the workplace. But this was at least in part because many EAM supporters suspected that one occupation had merely given way to another, and that the independence they had been fighting for was being compromised for the sake of British imperial interests.[21]

Ordinary British soldiers arriving in Athens got an overwhelmingly friendly reception: 'Men and women surrounded the Tommies with the intention of bestowing kisses on them,' wrote an observer, 'while the Tommies like bashful puppies tried to pass through the crowd.'[22] But British policy at higher levels was less well received. Did the Allies intend to punish the Battalionists and gendarmes now in their custody, or to protect them, and even use them against the Left? Did they intend to reimpose the King upon the Greek people? As British policy-makers themselves were badly divided on these most sensitive of issues, it is scarcely surprising that many in EAM/ELAS suspected the worst.

What strained relations further was the lack of sympathy or understanding some British diplomats and senior military commanders displayed towards EAM. This was partly a cultural matter: imperial mentalities as well as the regular soldier's low opinion of irregulars – particularly when the latter were unshaven, loquacious and prone to fire off their weapons for no discernible reason – both contributed to this tendency. It was widely noted by a number of American observers and inevitably infuriated the *andartes* who after all saw themselves as having fought for national self-determination, and who took great pride in their wartime exploits. MacVeagh criticised what he saw as 'the handling of this fanatically freedom-loving country as if it were composed of natives under the British Raj'. Unfortunately the officer commanding the Allied forces, General Ronald Scobie, was a stiff, abrasive and taciturn military man with no natural finesse for the subtleties of politics: his was not the type of personality capable of identifying, let alone defusing, the lively suspicions of the ELAS officers he had to work with.[23]

But Scobie was only one man in a complex policy-making network which linked the armed forces, the Foreign Office and – crucially – members of the Greek government in exile. Official British policy was that collaborators would be punished. Yet over the previous year several fiercely anti-Left Greeks, friendly to many Battalionists, had been appointed to key posts in the Ministry of War, thereby determining the political complexion of their country's future police and army. Colonel Spiliotopoulos, whom the Papandreou government had appointed to the key post of military commander of the Athens area, had actually been helping to coordinate right-wing anti-communist groups during the occupation and was regarded by ELAS as a collaborator. The presence of such men in the official government made an impartial solution to Greece's security problems virtually impossible, and largely undermined the moral basis for the British doctrine of non-interference in internal Greek affairs.[24]

It was not merely that the British now found themselves supporting some anti-communist Greeks with doubtful pasts. The

British Foreign Office was also fearful of Soviet influence in Greece, while Churchill, increasingly prone to intervening directly in Greek affairs and one of the King of Greece's foremost supporters, exhibited an imperious contempt for the resistance: when they were not Bolsheviks, they were – in a celebrated phrase – 'miserable banditti'. Having already privately agreed with Stalin that Greece lay in Britain's sphere of influence, he was in no mood for compromise with the Left. 'I fully expect a clash with EAM,' Churchill noted as early as 7 November, 'and we must not shrink from it, provided the ground is well chosen.' One week later, Churchill instructed Scobie to make 'maximum use' of the troops at his disposal 'to show the flag'. He was to ensure the security of Athens, if necessary by declaring it a military area and ordering all ELAS troops to pull out. Scobie's instructions closed on an uncompromising note: 'In the event of an attack on British troops, or an attempted coup d'état, you have full authorisation to use such force . . . as may be required to crush ELAS.'[25]

By this point – just a few weeks after Liberation – some factions within EAM/ELAS were becoming increasingly concerned about the ultimate goals of British policy, and more extreme elements were pushing strongly for a clean break with the Papandreou government. On 17 November – in an episode which indicated the tensions within the resistance – ELAS's leading *kapetans* met in Lamia, the first and last time that such a gathering took place. Aris, ever ready to read the worst into British actions, warned the others that General Scobie was planning a surprise attack, which ELAS should pre-empt. But his warnings were rejected by a majority of those present on the grounds that 'there was no reason to worry . . . neither the British nor the reactionaries will have the force to realise [a coup]'. At this stage it is clear that the *andartes* were very far from planning the show of force which Churchill expected. Indeed, ELAS, which certainly had enough men to seize power, had no fixed policy and little clear leadership with the result that local officials were increasingly taking matters into their own hands. 'I have doubts,' the British ambassador informed his American counterpart on the day the ELAS *kapetans* met, 'as to whether the national leaders of the organisations are really able any longer to control their men.' The British, meanwhile, led from the top by an almost gung-ho Prime Minister, had adopted an uncompromising approach, which would test their scanty forces to the limit.[26]

*

The social and economic hardships caused by the occupation did not cease with the Germans' withdrawal. Indeed it was only now that the full extent of the physical destruction became apparent. In the Peloponnese, children attending village schools were using rocks for desks. Visiting Kalavryta, George Skouras noticed the absence of men, and learned about the mass killings there the previous year by Le Suire's 117 Jaeger Division. On the road to Karpenisi he passed through eight small towns, 'all of them entirely destroyed by fire'. Thousands of acres of land in north Greece lay uncultivated. Wherever he went, he was shocked by the condition of the inhabitants, their lack of dental care, their poor diet and ragged appearance.[27]

Winter approached, but the peasants lacked mules to bring in wood from the countryside. Jewish survivors from the tiny port of Preveza came down from the hills to find their property stacked up in a warehouse, being sold off to the profit of local notables. Backlogs of mail had accumulated in provincial offices, and postal staff – like most civil servants – were 'disheartened and somewhat demoralised following a long period of hardship and privation'. Inflation continued unabated. 'Today in Larissa money is of no value,' reported a visitor in November.[28]

Red Cross delegates could now travel more freely than before to gauge the extent of the relief task ahead. A daunting prospect faced them. At the end of November, for example, UNRRA (United Nations Relief and Rehabilitation Agency) officials visited the Peloponnesian village of Doxa for the first time since it had been burned down by Axis troops in August 1943. They found few signs that the villagers had resumed a normal life: 'they live, together with the cattle, in miserable shelters raised among the ruins'. In hundreds of other villages the situation was no better.[29]

The relief workers found that vehicles were liable to be requisitioned by the *andartes* or the British; caiques were not yet available. The railways would remain unusable for some time. Roads and ports had been mined, slowing down the delivery of supplies. Unemployment actually increased as workers employed by the Wehrmacht lost their jobs. Endless deputations called on UNRRA and Red Cross personnel demanding special treatment in the distribution of food, and hurling accusations of Fascism at them when they were denied. 'Things were quite lively when we distributed clothing in various parts of the town,' reported Judge Emil Sandstrom, head of the Swedish Red Cross team. 'Large queues were formed which shouted and demonstrated, forced their way into the district office. . . . Shoes and clothing represent such values in present circumstances that feeling runs high and disorderliness occurs spontaneously.'[30]

By the end of November, however, there were encouraging

67.   A little girl looks at her first pair of new shoes: Athens, 1945.

signs. Food rations were increased, and relief staff were paid in money for the first time, not in kind, indicating confident expectations that inflation was slowing. In the country towns, ELAS officials proved generally co-operative with the relief workers, and checked the inhabitants' demands.

A revealing and touching episode took place on the barren island of Kea when US naval personnel landed one day in November to distribute relief supplies. Villagers queued up with their donkeys outside the warehouse from 4.30 in the morning. Around 9 o'clock a young American officer, Lieutenant Bailey, began distributing blankets and coats. The islanders' response took him by surprise. As he reported later: 'The people brought token gifts in appreciation of the supplies issued, and a quantity of almonds, oranges and eggs were deposited, a few at a time, at the doors of the warehouse.'[31]

Not even the deprivations of the past few years had obliterated popular traditions of honour and reciprocity, and Bailey was profoundly moved: 'The expression of gratitude had a deep emotional effect on the few Americans present. It was a rare privilege to be able to assist in even a partial and temporary fulfilment of one of the Four Freedoms for this small island,' he wrote, adding with understandable emotion: 'At least one island in the Aegean will not suffer from cold this winter; at least one community has shown that it can forget politics to meet common needs; at least 2,500 Greek people have had a chance to note the difference between Axis tyranny and Allied concern for human suffering.'

*

But while the young Lieutenant Bailey was recalling the optimistic language of the Four Freedoms, the Atlantic Charter and the United Nations, Churchill's notorious 'Percentages Agreement' with Stalin – whereby the two men privately agreed, among other details, to give Britain a '90 per cent' share of the influence in Greece – revealed that the calculus of Great Power interest and ideological conflict still held the Balkans in thrall. In the months ahead, Greece's desperate social and economic needs were to be completely over-shadowed by the political conflict between EAM/ELAS and the British-backed government.

On 2 December EAM ministers resigned from Papandreou's Cabinet after negotiations broke down over the terms upon which the *andartes* would demobilise and a new provisional national guard would be formed. The break, so long dreaded, had at last occurred, and each side now suspected the other of preparing the ground for a coup d'état. On the 3rd, the dispute exploded into open violence when police opened fire (for reasons which still remain unexplained) on unarmed EAM demonstrators in Syntagma Square in central Athens. It may be that the police were simply intimidated by the sight of thousands of demonstrators advancing towards them; or it may be, as some eyewitnesses alleged, that the shooting was a deliberate provocation. If so, it worked: EAM supporters, mindful of the brutality of Greek security forces during the occupation, replied almost immediately by blockading and attacking police stations throughout the capital. The poet Seferis summed it up sadly: 'Blood brings blood and more blood.'[32]

Catching the national leadership of EAM/ELAS off guard, the Athens rank and file seem to have been motivated initially at least by a more or less spontaneous desire to wreak their revenge on the last remnants of those forces who had collaborated with the SS throughout 1944. A full-scale offensive to seize the capital, which would have implied taking on the British, was not uppermost in their minds, and this gave the early fighting a sporadic and dis-organised character. ELAS gunmen were at first reluctant to fire on British soldiers, whom they did not regard with hostile feelings. A

68. Scenes from the December fighting: (*top*) Civilians rush a wounded man to safety: 4 December 1944; (*bottom*) A British sniper fires on ELAS positions from the Acropolis, held by men of the 5th Battalion Scottish Para Regiment: 10 December 1944.

battalion of *andartes* marching into the capital from Thebes allowed itself to be disarmed without a struggle by British soldiers. There was an even stranger episode when 23rd Armoured Brigade, the main British unit in the capital, found that most of its rations were held in a warehouse in an ELAS area. Not only were the lorries they sent out not attacked *en route*, but ELAS sympathisers actually helped British soldiers load up the supplies when they reached their destination. For the Left, the quarrel was not with the British, but with the collaborators who they believed were returning to power and deliberately provoking them under British protection.[33]

Mistakenly, General Scobie anticipated that his forces could clear the city without much ado in two or three days. He was quickly disabused. ELAS snipers successfully pinned down the British for some time to a tiny area of central Athens. In the south of the city, and in the 'Red' suburbs like Kaisariani – EAM's 'Little Stalingrad' – there was bitter, drawn-out street fighting. But once the British forces survived the initial shock there could be only one outcome. In the long run the Left's courage and subterfuges were unable to match the disciplined tactics of trained soldiers; nor could EAM gunmen rival their opponents' superior firepower. In a show of force, RAF Spitfires and Beaufighters strafed ELAS positions in the pine woods and apartment blocks overlooking the centre of Athens, and towards the end of December a sustained counter-offensive by the British and pro-government Greek forces broke the back of the Left. On 10–11 January, after Churchill had finally changed his mind about the Greek King and agreed to back the idea of a regency, negotiations finally brought to an end the tragic spectacle – unparalleled during the war – of Allied soldiers fighting against resistance forces.

Churchill defended British policy before an angry House of Commons by insisting that Greece had been saved from Bolshevik dictatorship, warning his critics that: 'there was . . . as we can now see, a fairly well organised plot or plan by which ELAS should march down upon Athens and seize it by armed force'.[34] This thesis was not widely accepted at the time, and fails to convince today. To be sure, there were some intransigents in ELAS itching for the chance to 'exterminate . . . fascist elements', but the party leadership had certainly not abandoned hope of finding a political solution. Most *andartes* were still deployed far from Athens and ELAS had not concentrated its forces in the capital; nor – more damningly for Churchill's argument – had it attempted to seize power in Athens eight weeks earlier at the time the Germans withdrew. During the fighting, in fact, EAM/ELAS made several efforts to open talks with the British; but reversing a well-known slogan of Woodrow

Wilson from the First World War, Churchill now claimed that there could be 'no peace without victory'. His intransigence was matched only by that of some conservative Greeks, who sensed the opportunity to finish off ELAS with British help.

Athens itself was divided by the fighting more deeply than at any time since the occupation. Terrified non-combatants in EAM-held areas, subjected to attacks from the RAF, felt great bitterness and 'cold hatred' against the British. The wounded women and children brought in for medical treatment after British planes strafed a square in Pankrati said despairingly that 'they had liked the English, but now they knew that the Germans were gentlemen'.[35] Barely a mile away, but at the opposite end of the political spectrum, bourgeois Athenians were convinced that large groups of *andartes* had infiltrated the city centre, and believed that ELAS was planning an assault on the prosperous Kolonaki district – 'the Mayfair of Athens'. British soldiers grew tired of the reports they received of 'concentrations' or 'nests' of bearded mountain guerrillas which turned out upon investigation to be figments of frightened civilian imaginations. It all amounted to a 'considerable nerve war', observed one British officer.[36]

Out of these fierce hatreds and hysterical fears emerged the very real horrors of something akin to class war. On one side, the young street fighters of EAM fought on, in the words of their opponents, 'with a courage and tenacity of purpose which at times reached the equal of the Germans . . . coupled with fanatical political convictions'. They were by now utterly convinced that the British planned to 'force the King back on the people together with the dictatorship for which they hold him personally responsible'. Against them were ranged not only the British, but loyalist Greeks, 'intensely bitter against the ELAS fighters and . . . nearly all ardent monarchists'. The struggle took a particularly nasty turn after the British rounded up and interned 15,000 suspected left-wing sympathisers, 8,000 of whom were actually deported, after rudimentary enquiries, to camps in the Middle East. ELAS units responded in a brutal fashion by executing hundreds of members of 'reactionary' families in Athens and burying them in mass graves.[37] Thousands more 'enemies of the people' were seized as 'hostages' from their homes in Athens and Salonika and marched despite freezing conditions into the hills. A group of 400 men, for instance, was seen stumbling away through the January mists out of Salonika along a snowy, muddy road, without coats or shoes, their feet clad in sacking. The *andartes* guarding them sometimes protected them from the stones of villagers, at other times encouraged the country people they passed to humiliate their frozen, weeping and exhausted 'bourgeois' captives. More than any other action, the abduction and killing of these hostages – often selected for no better reason than that their relatively prosperous homes had aroused the envy or suspicion of some class-conscious *andarte* – destroyed much of the moral credibility which EAM/ELAS had enjoyed in the eyes of the world until then.[38]

One OSS operative who had fought alongside ELAS in the final months of the occupation caught both sides of this tragedy. On 2 January he was making his way to Athens from central Greece. By then, ELAS and the British had virtually stopped fighting in the capital. But outside Levadia he ran into a 'flood' of hostages who were still being shepherded northwards by ELAS guards. They 'presented a terrifying sight with their great numbers, holding blankets over their heads, their lack of clothing and shoes,' he wrote. 'Upon approaching they would make wild gestures of being hungry, cold, of demanding salvation. Their voices, sobs and staring eyes were an accusation to all civilisation. There were young boys and girls, old men and women, what was left of intellectuals and businessmen.'

But the same observer went on to take a closer look at their captors. 'One could hardly distinguish the "hostages",' he wrote, 'from the refugees and disguised ELAS soldiers also streaming north.' Many ELAS men wanted no more to do with the war, least of all with hostages. Few guerrillas were unaffected by the news of the fighting with the British. 'All along the road one could see the demoralisation of ELAS. . . . The ELAS soldiers, dressed in civilian clothes, were hiking through the mountainsides, and some were anxious to give up their guns to anybody that came along.' Now that the war was over, the *andartes* wanted simply to return home as quickly as possible. People listened anxiously for the news from Athens; when the truce was announced between ELAS and the British 'they cheered wildly'.[39]

*

'Which side, then, has committed more crimes, the Right or the Left?' a young American student asked an elderly farmer as Greece's bitter civil war neared its end several years later. His companion responded carefully: 'I can only tell you that the side which happens to be in power has more opportunity to commit them.' In attempting to ascertain responsibility for the tragic imbroglio of Greek politics in the 1940s, the historian can scarcely hope to improve on this formulation.[40]

Although EAM survived into the postwar period, its power was broken by the fighting in Athens. Early in 1945, according to the

69.   The end of the *andartiko* in early 1945: despondent *andartes* in Epiros learn over the radio of the Varkiza Agreement which not only brings the fighting in Athens to an end but calls for ELAS to be demobilised.

agreement which ended their clash with the British, most *andartes* handed over their weapons to the authorities. One of those to refuse was Aris; taking to the hills, he was denounced by the Communist Party. After a few months he was hunted down by government troops, and his severed head was displayed in the main square in Trikkala. But what he had predicted came to pass: during 1945 former *andartes* were exposed to the full force of a right-wing backlash. A White Terror made normal life impossible for them, and bands of resistance fighters reformed in the hills. With the British and then the Americans backing them, Greece's anticommunist politicians regained the power they had forfeited during the occupation.

   Almost immediately there began an official effort to rewrite the history of those years. As the Civil War raged, large parts of the occupation experience were passed over and forgotten as quickly as possible. The Greek authorities showed little interest in pursuing war criminals, and war crimes trials petered out more quickly in Greece than anywhere else in Europe, whilst over-conscientious prosecutors were buried in provincial postings. This becomes easier to understand when we bear in mind that the Civil War had turned many former *andartes*, soon regrouped into a powerful new guerrilla movement called the Democratic Army of Greece, into the main threat to the British-backed government, while personal and professional ties linked the postwar ruling *élites* in Athens with men who had served the Germans.

British protégés were constantly causing their patrons embarrassment as details of their wartime activities came to light. General Plastiras, for example, who succeeded Papandreou as Prime Minister in 1945, was actually forced to resign following the leak of a letter he had written four years earlier in which he had offered to head a pro-German government in Athens. Napoleon Zervas resigned from the Cabinet in 1947 after details emerged at Nuremberg about his contacts with German officers.

Although fate dealt a mixed hand to the most important German and Austrian figures, few were put on trial by the Greek authorities – with the exception of several former military commanders on Crete and the death squad leader Schubert. After successfully overseeing the retreat of most of his 300,000 soldiers back from the Balkans, the stoic, asthmatic Lieutenant-General Löhr volunteered to join those of his troops who had been captured by the Yugoslavs. Tito's attitude towards war crime trials differed sharply from that in Athens: Löhr was tried in Belgrade and hanged in 1947. Generals Lanz, Speidel and Felmy were tried at the so-called 'Trial of the Southeastern Generals' at Nuremberg, and served prison terms of seven to ten years for their part in the execution of hostages, and reprisals. Walter Schimana, the last commander of the SS, committed suicide in prison in Salzburg in 1948. Eichmann's assistant Dieter Wisliceny gave a lengthy account of what he knew of the Final Solution before being handed over to the Czechs and hanged.

Few other German or Austrian officials were ever punished for their crimes in Greece: SS-Standartenführer Walter Blume, for example – a man with the blood of thousands of civilians on his hands – was sentenced to death at Nuremberg in the 'Einsatzgruppen Trial', had his sentence commuted to life imprisonment and was eventually released after serving just 3 years in Landsberg prison. From 1957 he worked as a businessman in the Ruhr, re-married in 1958, and had six children (including 2 by adoption). Despite repeated investigation into his involvement in the deportation of the Jews from Athens, he was never brought before a German court and died a natural death in 1977 in Dortmund, the town where he had been born 71 years earlier. West German and Austrian police conducted an investigation into the slaughter at Komeno in the 1970s, but no one was ever tried for the killing of the 307 villagers there: 1st Mountain Division's chief intelligence officer returned to civilian life and resumed his law practice in the Federal Republic, while the Division's chief operations officer became a corps commander in the new Bundeswehr. The 'little men' of 12 Company became bakers, mechanics, builders and drivers in West Germany and Austria; it is unlikely that the subject of Komeno often came up during their annual reunions in Bavaria and the Tyrol. Dr Max Merten, who had been involved in the deportation of Salonika's Jews and then profited from the disposal of their properties, returned to Greece as a tourist in 1959. He appears to have possessed incriminating information about the wartime past of members of Karamanlis's government, for despite being found guilty of war crimes by a Greek court he was allowed to return to the Federal Republic after a brief stay in prison. Hermann Neubacher served one year of a 20-year term in Belgrade before moving out of the limelight to Addis Ababa, returning to Vienna in 1956 to take up a directorship of a leading industrial concern. An ambitious young intelligence officer called Kurt Waldheim, stationed in Greece for the last eighteen months of the war, rose to become Secretary-General of the United Nations and President of Austria.

This story of benign judicial neglect of Nazis and collaborators forms a striking contrast with the systematic repression of the Greek Left, which lasted for over two decades. As early as the beginning of 1945, all thoughts of allowing former *andartes* to enter the new National Guard were abandoned, while former Security Battalionists were given the most perfunctory screening before being re-employed. By the end of 1945 – in other words, before the formation of the Democratic Army of Greece – ten times more *andartes* had been convicted by the courts than collaborators, and the figures steepened as the Civil War escalated. A typical case was that of Thomas Venetsanopoulos, a gendarmerie officer who was tried by a court martial in 1945 on the extraordinary charge of deserting his station without authority in 1943 to join the *andartes*. On being acquitted, he was immediately rearrested and charged with two wartime murders. Rex Leeper, the British ambassador, was appalled and wrote that his case was 'one of many . . . where people who undoubtedly did good work for the Allied cause are nevertheless accused of crimes against the Greek penal code'.[41]

As late as the 1960s, Greece's prisons were packed with hundreds of men and women whose only crime was to have fought against

375

the Germans. During the Civil War many former *andartes* were executed while others fled behind the Iron Curtain, and only returned – old men and women – during the 1980s; under Greek law, Slavophone *andartes* are still prevented from returning. Typical of many was the fate of a regular artillery officer who had joined ELAS in 1943 and died a political exile in Tashkent in the 1970s without ever seeing his wife and child again. Equally harrowing were the experiences of a former police officer, John Palavos, who had joined the *andartes* after refusing to take orders from a German officer. Persecuted by the Greek authorities after the war, he was sentenced to a long prison term. His wife too was exiled and imprisoned. Released in 1963, Palavos was arrested again three years later, and jailed after singing resistance songs in a demonstration marking the anniversary of the Liberation.[42]

In what one Greek film-maker termed the 'stone years' which followed the end of the Civil War in 1949, the country was dominated by conservative politicians and the armed forces. Behind them lurked the mysterious 'para-state', a loose network of shadowy right-wing paramilitary organisations dedicated to protecting Greece with covert American assistance from the Left. While the economic 'miracle' transformed society, Greece's cultural and intellectual life was held back by the sterile nationalist phobias of the Right. The imaginative social and educational innovations of the wartime resistance were regarded with suspicion, and the old sophistication and vitality of prewar Greek culture slowly atrophied. This process reached its nadir during the dictatorship of the Colonels (1967–74), when a law was passed which defined EAM/ELAS *andartes* as 'enemies', while making former Security Battalionists eligible for state pensions. Not coincidentally, several members of the Colonels' regime had served in the Battalions during the war.

Only after the collapse of the dictatorship in 1974 were the first tentative steps taken to approach the country's recent past in a more open spirit. History conferences were convened to discuss the wartime years, and museums and memorials were unveiled acknowledging the part played by all sides in the resistance. Today, the services of EAM/ELAS fighters have been officially recognised by the state, and the old debates between Left and Right have lost much of their venom. In an astonishingly short period of time, the occupation has come to seem to a younger generation a matter of some antiquity, of little relevance to their own concerns. To the visitors, of course, who flock to Greece each summer, it is practically invisible as they lie on sunny beaches or familiarise themselves with ruined temples and amphitheatres. In Greece, as elsewhere, the postwar world hides its origins well; but for those who know where to look – behind the fences of abandoned Jewish mansions in Salonika, in the suburb of Haidari where new apartments screen the site of the once-notorious 'Bastille of Greece', or behind the thick shrubbery concealing the abandoned and derelict concrete German bunkers that line the winding mountain road from Jannina to Arta – traces of its wartime scars still survive.

Notes

ACS	Archivio Centrale dello Stato (Rome)
ADAP	*Akten zur Deutschen Auswärtigen Politik* Serie E: 1941–45; i–iii, Göttingen, 1969–74
AK	Armeekorps
AOK	Armeeoberkommando
BA/K	Bundesarchiv (Koblenz)
BA–MA	Bundesarchiv–Militärarchiv (Freiburg im Breisgau)
BDC	Berlin Document Centre
BdS	Befehlshaber der Sicherheitspolizei und des SD
BG	Bank of Greece Archives
CEH	*Central European History*
CEWA	Combined Economic Warfare Agencies
DDI	*Documenti diplomatici italiani* 9 ª serie: 1939–43; i–viii (Rome, 1954–88)
Deas archive	Benaki Museum (Athens)
EK	*Efimeris Kyverniseos* (Athens)
EV	*Eleftheron Vima*
FO	Foreign Office files (Public Record Office, Kew, London)
GFP	Geheime Feldpolizei
Gray Coll.	Christ Church Library, Eric Gray Newspaper Collection
HGrE	Heeresgruppe E
I.D.	Infantrie Division
IfZ	Institut für Zeitgeschichte
IWM	Imperial War Museum (London)
JCH	*Journal of Contemporary History*
JGHQ	Joint General Headquarters
KCL	King's College, London
KTB/LLGS	Kriegstagebuch
LDG	Archives of the League for Democracy in Greece (King's College, London)

Mbfh	Militärbefehlshaber
MFA/AD	Ministère des Affaires Etrangères, Archives Diplomatiques (Nantes)
MFA/ASD	Ministero degli Affari Esteri, Archivio Storico Diplomatico (Rome)
NA	USA National Archives (Washington, DC)
NCA	International Military Tribunal, Nuremberg Trials, *Nazi Conspiracy and Aggression*, i–x (Washington, DC, 1947–9)
NG	Document prepared for the Nuremberg War Crimes Trials
NOKW	Document prepared for the Nuremberg War Crimes Trials
NSFO	Nationalsozialistischer Führungsoffizier
OKW	Oberkommando der Wehrmacht
OMGUS	Office of the Military Government, United States
OSS, R and A	Office of Strategic Services, Research & Analysis branch
PAAA	Politisches Archiv, Auswärtiges Amt (Bonn)
PWE	Political Warfare Executive
Rochlitz	J. Rochlitz *The Righteous Enemy: Document Collection* (Rome, 1988)
SME US.DS	Stato Maggiore dell'Esercito V Reparto, Ufficio Storico (Rome)
SSGM	*Actes et documents du Saint Siège relatifs à la Seconde Guerre Mondiale*, i–ix (Vatican City, 1965–75)
StA.	Mussolini Papers (formerly held at St Antony's College, now at Foreign and Commonwealth Office, London)
Thames documents	Documents and interviews prepared for *Waldheim: A Case to Answer* (1988)
TMWC	*The Trial of the Major War Criminals before the International Military Tribunal*, i–xlii (Nuremberg, 1947–9)
TWC	*Trials of War Criminals Before the Nuremberg Military Tribunals under Control Council Law no. 10*, i–xv (Washington, DC, 1951–53)
URO	United Restitution Organization, *Judenverfolgung in Italien, den italienisch besetzten Gebieten und in Nordafrika* (Frankfurt a. Main, 1962)
WO	War Office files (Public Record Office, Kew, London)
ZSt.	Zentrale Stelle der Landesjustizverwaltungen (Ludwigsburg)

Introduction

1. NA, RG 226/120, 29/203, 'Greece: Censorship', 21 April 1944.
2. NA, RG 226/120, 29/204, 'Greece: Censorship', 7 Oct. 1944.
3. R. Paxton, *Vichy France: Old Guard and New Order, 1940–44* (New York, 1972).
4. F. Fukuyama, *The End of History and the Last Man* (London, 1992), esp. pp. 254–75.
5. D. George Kousoulas, *Revolution and Defeat: the Story of the Greek Communist Party* (London, 1965); E. O'Ballance, *The Greek Civil War* (London, 1966); B. Sweet-Escott, *Greece: A Political and Economic Survey, 1939–1953* (London, 1954); F. Voigt, *The Greek Sedition* (London, 1949); S.G. Xydis, *Greece and the Great Powers* (Thessaloniki, 1963). Among the key British first-hand accounts are R. Capell, *Simiomata: A Greek Note Book 1944–45* (London, 1946); G. Chandler, *The Divided Land: An Anglo-Greek Tragedy* (London, 1959); R. Leeper, *When Greek Meets Greek* (London, 1950); E.C.W. Myers, *Greek Entanglement* (London, 1955); C.M. Woodhouse, *Apple of Discord: A Survey of Recent Greek Politics in their International Setting* (London, 1948).
6. T. Coloumbis, J. Petropulos and H.J. Psomiades, *Foreign Intervention in Greek Politics: An Historical Perspective* (New York, 1976); D. Eudes, *The Kapetanios: Partisans and Civil War in Greece, 1943–1946* (New York, 1972); J. Hondros, *Occupation and Resistance: The Greek Agony, 1941–44* (New York, 1983); A. Kedros, *La résistance grecque, 1940–1944* (Paris, 1966); H. Richter, *Griechenland zwischen Revolution und Konterrevolution (1936–1946)* (Frankfurt am Main, 1973); C. Tsoucalas, *The Greek Tragedy* (London, 1969); L. Wittner, *American Intervention in Greece, 1943–1949* (New York, 1982).
7. A pioneering account is J.O. Iatrides, *Revolt in Athens: the Greek Communist 'Second Round', 1944–1945* (Princeton, 1972). See also the essays in Iatrides (ed.), *Greece in the 1940s: A Nation in Crisis* (London, 1981); C.M. Woodhouse, *The Struggle for Greece, 1941–1949* (London, 1976), which marks a notable shift from his earlier views; P. Papastratis, *British Policy towards Greece during the Second World War 1941–1944* (Cambridge, 1984); G. Alexander, *The Prelude to the Truman Doctrine: British Policy in Greece, 1944–1947* (Oxford, 1982); H. Vlavianos, 'The Greek Communist Party: in Search of a Revolution', in T. Judt (ed.), *Resistance and Revolution in Mediterranean Europe, 1939–1948* (London, 1989), pp. 157–213.
8. In addition to the works mentioned above, see: P. Auty and R. Clogg (eds), *British Policy towards Wartime Resistance in Yugoslavia and Greece* (London, 1975); E. Barker, *British Policy in South-Eastern Europe during the Second World War* (London, 1976); E. Barker, F.W. Deakin and J. Chadwick (eds), *British Political and Military Strategy in Central, Eastern and Southern Europe in 1944* (London, 1988); H. Fleischer, *Im Kreuzschatten der Mächte: Griechenland 1941–1944*, 2 vols. (Frankfurt a. Main, 1986).
9. J. Gross, *Polish Society under German Occupation: the Generalgouvernement, 1939–1944* (Princeton, 1979).
10. In this connection, I cannot help recalling the comments of a fine historian of the French resistance: 'Local conditions and initiative be-

came major determinants if only for a short period. This fact. . . . reminds the historian that Communists must be placed not only within the context of the Party but also within the context of their locality, *métier* and other conditioning factors. The belief that a Communist is fully defined by his Communism is *a priori*

rather than empirical': H.R. Kedward, 'Behind the Polemics: French Communism and the Resistance, 1939–1941', in S. Hawes and R. White (eds), *Resistance in Europe, 1939–1945* (Harmondsworth, 1976), 103–4. For Greece, the brilliant new study by G. Margaritis, *Apo tin itta stin exegersi* (Athens, 1993).

PROLOGUE: Swastika over the Acropolis

1. G. Theotokas, *Tetradia imerologiou (1939–1953)* (Athens, n.d.), 260.
2. Ibid., 250–1.
3. MFA/AD, box 54, Lecureul–Maugras, 30 April 1941; L. White, *The Long Balkan Night* (New York, 1944), 330–1.
4. Theotokas, *Tetradia imerologiou*, 260.
5. MFA/AD box 54, Lecureul–Maugras, 30 April 1941.
6. Ibid.
7. MFA/AD, box 9, Syra file: report 'Avril 1941–Octobre 1944. Syra sous l'occupation italienne, puis allemande'.
8. P. Argenti, *The Occupation of Chios by the Germans and their Administration of the Island, 1941–1944* (Cambridge, 1966), 9–11, 252.
9. R. Schnabel, *Missbrauchte Mikrofone: Deutsche Rundfunkpropaganda im Zweiten Weltkrieg* (Vienna, 1967), 353–67.
10. E. Papadimitriou (ed.) *O koinos logos*, iii (Athens, n.d.), 71; L.G. Marcantonatos, *A Athènes Pendant La Guerre* (Thessaloniki, 1976), 228, 234.
11. Ch. Christides, *Chronia katochis* (Athens, 1971), 1–3.
12. Theotokas, *Tetradia imerologiou*, 260–2.
13. Wrede's account is in *Jahrbuch des Auslands-Organisation der NSDAP*, iv (Berlin, 1942), 49–66.
14. A photo of the two men on the Parthenon is to be found in R. Barthe and E. Glodschey, *Der Kampf um den Balkan* (Berlin, 1942), 225.
15. NA, T–120/1174/468908, Hitler–Mussolini, 6 Aug. 1942.

PART ONE   The Chaos of the New Order: 1941–43

1. J. Hondros, *Occupation and Resistance: the Greek Agony* (New York, 1983), 41–50; J. Koliopoulos, *Palinorthosi, diktatoria, polemos, 1935–1941* (Athens, 1985), 212–14. Among such politicians was the republican general, Plastiras: in late 1940 he offered to organise a pro-German coup in Athens; by 1945 he was Prime Minister under the British. Hondros, 42–3; T–120/379/285975–6, 14 Jan. 1941.
2. NA, T–120/292/223086–7, 12 March 1941.
3. C. Buckley, *Greece and Crete 1941* (repr. Athens, 1984), 114.
4. NA, T–120/157/127476–82, 'Aufzeichnung über die Besprechungen betr. die Kapitulation

der griechischen Epirus-Armee mit der italienischen Wehrmacht-führung', 23 April 1941.

5. D. Irving, *Hitler's War: 1939–1942* (London, 1983), 228.

6. Ibid., notes to p. 227; MFA/AD, box 54, Lecureul – Athens, 30 April 1941.

7. Ministero degli Affari Esteri, *I documenti diplomatici italiani, Nona serie, 1939–43*, vi (29 Oct. 1940–23 Mar. 1941) (Rome, 1986), 892–4; NA, T–821/128/139, Marras (Berlin) – Guzzoni (Rome), 24 April 1941.

8. *I documenti diplomatici italiani*, (hereafter *DDI*). 9, vii (24 April 1941–11 Dec. 1941) (Rome, 1987), 17–18.

9. Generaloberst Franz Halder, *Kriegstagebuch. Tägliche Aufzeich-nungen des Chefs des Generalstabes des Heeres 1939–1942* H.-A. Jacobsen, ed. 3 vols (Stuttgart, 1962–64) ii, 356ff.; G. Andri-kopoulos, 'Synthikologisi kai katarrevsi tou metopou', in H. Fleischer and N. Svoronos (eds), *H Ellada 1936–1944: diktatoria, katochi, antistasi* (Athens, 1989), 196–7.

10. NA, RG 59/868.00/1143, 'Greece during the Occupation' (n.d.).

11. NA, T–120/157/127503, Benz-ler–Ribbentrop, 29 April 1941.

12. *EK*, 29 April 1941; T–120/157/127516, Altenburg–Berlin, 2 May 1941.

13. BA–MA, N 449, 'Vortragsnotiz für Herrn Oberst von Millenthin', Athens, 18 May 1941; NA, T–120/157/127527, Altenburg–Berlin, 5 May 1941.

14. *DDI*, 9, vii, 130, 409.

15. Ibid., 540.

16. FO 371/32467 W9765/62/49, Osborne (Holy See)–London, 26 June 1942.

17. FO 371/29840 R7541/96, Letter from Mrs. H.W. Davis; FO 371/29841 R8094/96, Noel Baker–Cadogan, 30 Aug. 1941; MFA/AD, box 27, Haimet (Saloniki)–

Athens, 5 Oct. 1942; cf. A Kyrou, *Oneira kai pragmatikotitis. Chronia diplomatikis zois (1923–53)* (Athens, 1972), 207.

18. NA, RG 59/868.00/1126, 'Notes on the German Army's Methods of Acquiring Property in Greece', G.L. Jones, 5 June 1941; D. Vogel, 'Der Kriegsalltag im Spie-gel von Feldpostbriefen (1939–1945)', in W. Wette (ed.), *Der Krieg des Kleinen Mannes: Eine Militärgeschichte von unten* (Munich, 1992), 200–1; K. Delopou-los (ed.), *To imerologio tou Minou Dounia* (Athens, 1987), 50.

19. NA, T–120/157/127596, 25 May 1941.

20. NA, T–77/1435/927–8, 'Leben-smittellage in Griechenland', 5 June 1941.

21. P. Argenti, *The Occupation of Chios by the Germans and their Administration of the Island, 1941–1944* (Cambridge, 1966), 12; BA–MA, RW 40/159, Anlage 9, KTB des Befehlshaber Sal./Aegäis, 17 June 1941; *Ravittaille-ment de la Grèce pendant l'occupa-tion 1941–44 et pendant les premiers cinq mois après la libération* (Athens, 1949), 39.

22. FO 371/29841 R8099/96, Inter-view with Mr James Schafer, 4 Aug. 1941.

23. D. Eichholtz 'Oikonomiki poli-tiki germanikon dynameon kato-chis stin Ellada', in Fleischer and Svoronos (eds), *H Ellada, 1936–1944*, 225–6.

24. Hondros, *Occupation and Resist-ance*, 62–3; NA, RG 59/868.00/1126, 'Notes on the German Army's Methods of Acquiring Property in Greece', 5 June 1941; K. Zavitzianos, 'I dioikisis tis Ethnikis Trapezis tis Ellados kata ta eti 1941 kai 1942', 13, mss in author's possession; MFA/AD, box 68, 'Compagnie Française du Laurium'. The most thorough study of German economic penetration is by R. Eckart,

'Grundzuge der faschistichen deutschen Okkupationspolitik in der von Deutschland besetzten Gebieten Griechenlands vom Beginn der Okkupation bis zur Schlacht von Stalingrad (6 April 1941 bis Februar/März 1943), dissert., Zentralinstitut für Geschichte, Berlin, 1984.

25. Eichholtz, 'Oikonomiki', 225. The activities of the Wehrmacht Economics Stuff, as well as other special missions like the Sonderkommando von Künsberg, which collected diplomatic archives, and the anti-Jewish (& anti-Masonic) Sonderkommando Rosenberg, are described in H. Fleischer, 'Searching for the Fruits of Victory: the Activities of the German "Sonderkommandos" following the Wehrmacht in the Newly Occupied Greek Territories', in *Greece & the War in the Balkans (1940–41)* International Conference (Thessaloniki, 1992), 101–11.

26. Zavitzianos, 'I dioikisis tis Ethnikis Trapezis', 19–20.

27. *DDI*, 9, vii, 86.

28. Ibid.; St A. (Mussolini Collection), job 11, 005441–7, 'Interessi dell'AMMI nei Balcani', 24 March 1944.

29. *DDI*, 9, vii, 254; see also NA, T–84/102/1396169–72 'Monatsbericht July/August 1941: Griechenland'.

30. A. Sen, *Poverty and Famine: An Essay in Entitlement and Deprivation* (Oxford, 1981), and A. Sen and J. Drèze, *Hunger and Public Action* (Oxford, 1989), ch. 6.

31. FO 371/32460, 'Note sur la production agricole et d'elevage en 1941 et previsions sur celle de 1942'.

32. See e.g. BA–MA, RW 40/159, Anlage 7, 18 A.K./Chief of Staff – 12 AOK, 1/6/41 on the manner of searches for 'war booty' in the countryside.

33. MFA/AD, box 33 (Salonique), 'Situation en Grèce du Nord', 28 Oct. 1941; *Tachydromos* (Volos), 15 Feb. 1942.

34. MFA/AD, box 33 (Salonique), 'Situation en Grèce du Nord', 28 Oct. 1941; NA, T–821/354/753ff., 'Relazione sull'opera svolta . . .', 43.

35. FO 371/36485 W182/3/49, 'Exposition of the Food Situation in Greece', dated 12 Nov. 1942, Cairo.

36. FO 371/32475 W14201/62/49 Mallet (Stockholm)–London, enclosing 'Preliminary Survey of the Olive Oil Situation in Greece', 1 Oct. 1942.

37. NA, T–821/354/753 ff. 'Relazione sull'opera svolta . . .'.

38. FO 371/32460 W3831/62/49, 'Rapport sur la situation en Grèce', 31 Jan. 1942; Hondros, *Occupation and Resistance*, 70–1.

39. MFA/AD, box 104 (Salonique), 20 June 1941.

40. B. Helger, *Ravittaillement de la Grèce pendant l'occupation 1941–44 et pendant les premiers cinq mois après la libération* (Athens, 1949), 39.

41. League of Nations, *Food Rationing and Supply, 1943/44* (Geneva, 1944), 38–9.

42. PAAA, R29612/175, Altenburg–Berlin, 25 May 1941; NA, T–120/2423, 19 July 1941.

43. NA, T–120/2423/E226769, 24 July 1941.

44. NA, T–120/157/127691–3, 'Aufzeichnung betreffend Lebensmittelversorgung Griechenlands', 15 Sept. 1941.

45. NA, T–120/157/127707, 10 Oct. 1941.

46. NA, T–821/249/829–32, 'Situazione economica e organizzazione civile nei territori occupati', 1 Nov. 1941.

47. NA, T–120/2423/E226826–8, 24 Oct. 1941; T–120/157/127733, 15 Nov. 1941.

48. *Ciano's Diary, 1939–1943*, ed. M.

Muggeridge (London, 1947), 379.

49. League of Nations, *Food Rationing*, esp. 37–40, 52–4. The mentality behind German occupation policy is revealed by Göring's speech of 6 Aug. 1942, reproduced in J. Noakes and G. Pridham (eds.) *Nazism: A History in Documents and Eyewitness Accounts, 1919–1945*, vol. II: Foreign Policy, War and Racial Extermination (New York, 1988), 901–902.

50. NA, T–821/354/739ff., pp. 47–8.

51. Ch. Christides, *Chronia Katochis* (Athens, 1971), 10, 51, 93; FO 371/29841 R8094/96, Young–'Andrea' (Lisbon), 7 Aug. 1941.

52. Ibid.; Delopoulos (ed.) *To imerologio katochis tou Minou Dounias*, 61; Argenti, *Occupation of Chios*, 47.

53. FO 371/29842 R9761/96 Censorship (Bermuda).

54. FO 371/29841 R8428/96; extracts from a letter by Mme. Constantakos, 16 and 17 Aug. 1941; FO 371/29841 R8464/96, Interview with Ralph Kent, 3 August 1941.

55. FO 371/32460 W3831/62/49, Morgan (Ankara) – FO, 20 Feb. 1942, enclosing 'Report on distribution of food & on the situation in Greece' Dr M. Junod, 31 Jan. 1942.

56. WO 204/8753, 'Financial Conditions in Greece (Feb. 1944) and Survey of Textile and Chemical Industries'.

57. FO 371/32460 W3831/62/49.

58. FO 371/32463 W6860/62/49, Osborne (Vatican)–London, 7 April 1942.

59. Christides, *Chronia katochis*, 171.

60. Examples from the report by Marcel Junod cited in n. 55.

61. H. Fleischer, *Im Kreuzschatten der Mächte: Griechenland 1941–1944*, 2 vols (Frankfurt a. Main, 1986) i, 118.

62. Cf. F. Skouras et al., *Psychopathologia tis peinas, tou fovou kai tou*

anchous: nevroseis kai psychonevroseis (Athens, 1947; repr. 1991), 288–9.

63. Ibid., 290.

64. B. Helger, *Ravittaillement de la Grèce*, 618–19.

65. Ibid., 625; K. Sosnowski, *The Tragedy of Children Under Nazi Rule* (Warsaw, 1962), 119–25, makes it clear that Greece was one of the countries worst affected from the demographic point of view by Nazi Occupation.

66. Delopoulos (ed.), *To imerologio katochis tou Minou Dounias*, 124; Christides, *Chronia katochis*, 185; on beliefs about death and burial, see C. Stewart, *Demons and the Devil: Moral Imagination in Modern Greek Culture* (Princeton, 1992), 103–4; M. Alexiou, *The Ritual Lament in Greek Tradition* (Cambridge, 1974).

67. *Tachydromos* (Volos), 10–11 Jan. 1942.

68. FO 371/32460 W3831/62/49; BA–MA, N 449, Athens, June/July 1942; Christides, *Chronia katochis*, 222–3.

69. R. Milliex, *Imerologio kai martyries tou polemou kai tis katochis* (Athens, 1982), 38–45.

70. Ibid., 46; cf. Alexiou, *Ritual Lament*, 38.

71. Skouras et al., *Psychopathologia*, 326; Milliex, *Imerologio*, 39.

72. FO 371/32480 W17196/62/49, Allard–Stockholm, 20 Nov. 1942; FO 371/33175 R610/281, 17 Jan. 1942.

73. Skouras et al., *Psychopathologia*, 327.

74. Christides, *Chronia katochis*, 172; I. Tsatsou, *Fylla katochis* (Athens, 1987), 27.

75. NA, T–77/1435/807–11, 'Lagebericht', 10 Jan. 1942; BDC, Dörhage personal file.

76. WO 204/8869, 'Notes on the Relief Services of the Greek Resistance Organisation EAM', 30 Dec. 1943; FO 371/33175 R610/281, 'Conditions in Salonika', 14

Jan. 1942.

77. BA–MA, N 449, Berlin, 13 May 1942.

78. See G.A. Kazamias, 'Allied Policy towards Occupied Greece: the 1941–44 Famine', D.Phil., University of Bradford, 1990. Among those in Britain disturbed by reports of the starvation in Greece were the founders of the Oxford Committee for Famine Relief, later better known as Oxfam: M. Black, *A Cause for Our Times: Oxfam, the First Fifty Years* (Oxford 1992), 5–21.

79. P. Papastratis, *British Policy towards Greece during the Second World War, 1941–1944* (Cambridge, 1984), 115–18.

80. O. Chadwick, *Britain and the Vatican during the Second World War* (Cambridge, 1988), 191–2; cf. P. Hoffmann, 'Roncalli in the Second World War: Peace Initiatives, the Greek Famine and the Persecution of the Jews', *Journal of Ecclesiastical History*, 40, 1 (1989), 74–99.

81. *Tachydromos* (Volos), 8 Feb. 1942.

82. FO 371/32479 W16977/62/49, encl. Courvoisier Report dated 2 Nov. 1942; FO 371/43679, R2844/9, 14 Feb. 1944.

83. MFA/AD, box 9 (Athens), Rigouzzo–de Vaux St Cyr, 24 Nov. 1945, enclosing 'Avril 1941–octobre 1944. Syra sous l'occupation italienne, puis allemande', 18 Oct. 1944; another source for the same subject is the special issue of *Syriana Grammata*, 15 (July 1991), devoted to the subject of the occupation.

84. D. Varthaliti, 'I kinisi tou plithismou tis Syras kata tin Katochi', *Syriana Grammata*, 15 (July 1991), 251–2.

85. FO 371/32460, 'Télégramme du Métropolite de Syra Philaretos et du maire d'Hermoupolis Th. Carakala'.

86. FO 371/32460 W3831/61/49, 20 Feb. 1942; FO 371/36485 W182/

3/49, 'Exposition of the Food Situation in Greece', 12 Nov 1942.

87. WO 204/8601, 21 May 1942; according to the *Südost Echo* of Vienna, 'the black market has replaced normal trade' (29 Aug. 1941).

88. R. Cobb, *The Police and the People* (Oxford, 1970), pt 3.

89. G. Zaroyianni, *Anamniseis apo tin ethniki antistasi (ELAS), 1940–1944* (Athens, n.d.), 44; *Tachydromos* (Volos), 2 Dec. 1942; Argenti, *Occupation of Chios*, 35.

90. WO 204/9172, 'Economic Conditions, Mani'; FO 371/32473, W12720/62/49, encl. 'Report by the International Red Cross Committee on distribution of relief in the Greek Islands of Chios, Samos & Mytilene', Aug. 1942.

91. Cf. Sen and Drèze, *Hunger and Public Action*, 89–90.

92. WO 208/3361 142035, 'Aleppo Report no. 1: George Petropoulakos', 26 Aug. 1944.

93. *Panevvoikon Vima*, 6 May 1943.

94. FO 371/32467, W9765/62, Osborne (Vatican)–London, 26 June 1942; WO 208/3357, A. Masopoulos Report, April 1942; FO 371/36501, HM Consul-General (Izmir)–Ankara, 23 Aug. 1943; WO 208/3356, 'Report on N. Katsareas', interrogated 13 March 1942.

95. NA, RG 226/190, box 3/34, 'Pliroforiai', 8.

96. WO 204/8718, 'Aegean Islands: Economic and Social Conditions', 2 Oct. 1943; FO 371/36504 W15436/3, Mallet–FO, 26 Oct. 1943, enclosing 'General Report on Red Cross Activity on Crete during the Period February to August 1943'.

97. *EV*, 28 June 1941.

98. *SSGM*, viii, 241: Roncalli (Athens)–Maglione (Vatican), 6 Aug. 1941; *Tachydromos* (Volos), 15 March 1942; *To Kerdos*, 31 Oct. 1942.

99. For the procedure at checkpoints, see NA, RG 226/154, box 39/596, 'Report of Activity in the Field' (Triforos Report).

100. WO 204/8888, 'Cyclades', 15 Aug. 1943.

101. Argenti, *Occupation of Chios*, 254–5; BA–MA RW 40/198, 'Ergebnisse der Feldpostprüfung', 2 Jan. 1942.

102. FO 371/42366 W13772/6/75, Mallet (Stockholm)–London, 12 Sept. 1944.

103. FO 371/33176 R5368/281 Madrid–London, 11 Aug. 1942; WO 204/8718, 'Currency, Finance & Economics', 20 Aug. 1943; Tsatsou, *Fylla katochis*, 26.

104. Cf. *Syriana Grammata* (July 1991), 252 for the figures on Ermoupolis.

105. G. Loukatos, *Athinaïka tou polemou kai tis katochis* (Athens, 1989), 104.

106. *SSGM*, viii, Roncalli–Maglione, Athens, 30 Nov. 1942.

107. G. Theotokas, *Tetradia imerologiou (1939–1953)* (Athens, n.d.), 387.

108. NA, RG 59/868.00/1256, Berry–State, 30 July 1943.

109. NA, RG 226/120, box 29/203, 'Greece: Censorship'.

110. NA, T–81/543/531429–30, 'Griechenland: Stimmungsbericht', early Dec. 1941.

111. IWM, 181/2, E. Thomashausen, *Beiträge zur Geschichte Griechenlands während des zweiten Weltkrieges*, Ergänzungsband, i (1947), 55.

112. Christides, *Chronia katochis*, 233, 256–7; NA, RG 226/190, box 2/25, 'GEDEFI Archive', 11 July 1945; Rochlitz, 119–20: 'Notiziario', 8 July 1942; 171–4: 'Notiziario del 14 Ottobre 1942'.

113. *EV*, 28 March 1942.

114. *To Kerdos*, 3, 10, 31 Jan. 1942, 31 Oct. 1942.

115. Delopoulos (ed.), *To imerologio tou Minou Dounias*, 101, 129.

116. *Larissaikos Typos*, 1 April 1942; 19–20 March 1942, 8 April 1942;

Tachydromos (Volos), 1 Feb. 1942; 3 March 1942.

117. E. Cowling and J. Mundy, *On Classic Ground: Picasso, Lèger, de Chirico and the New Classicism, 1910–1930* (London, 1990).

118. FO 371/48311 R12647/52/19 encl. 'Rapport sur mon activité en Thessalie en qualité de Delegué de la Mission de la Croix-Rouge Suisse en Grèce,' Dr. Oberhausli; WO 204/8718 Intelligence Reports, vol. 1; 9172, Economic Reports, Greece & Crete; Argenti, *Occupation of Chios*, 36.

119. *EK*, 5 June 1942; NA, RG 226/190, box 8/Athens file 80, 'Greece: Economic', 12 Feb. 1944; *DDI*, ix, 700, 21 June 1942.

120. NA, T–120/166/81309, Altenburg–Berlin, 23 July 1942.

121. NA, T–120/2481/E259713–715, 'Promemoria', 23 Sept. 1942.

122. NA, T–120/1174/468908, 6 Aug. 1942.

123. NA, T–120/166/81392, 4 Sept. 1942.

124. BG: 'Relazione sulle condizioni economiche e delle finanze pubbliche della Grecia', 5 Sept. 1941; Gotzamanis–Ghigi, 24 June 1942; Gotzamanis–Ghigi, 23 July 1942; *EV*, 18 April, 24 June 1942. An analysis of the fiscal situation, together with unpublished budget estimates of the first three wartime budgets is contained in WO 204/8850B, 'CSDIC Reports: Allied/CD/27'.

125. NA, T–120/166/81313–15, 'Aufzeichnung betreffend griechische Besatzungskosten', 23 July 1942; BG, Sofoulis (and others)–Tsolakoglu, 18 Aug. 1942.

126. NA, T–120/166/81370–5, Altenburg–Berlin, 22 Aug. 1942.

127. NA, T–120/166/81392–3, Rintelen–Berlin, 4 Sept. 1942.

128. NA, T–120/166/81559, Ribbentrop–Rome, 17 Oct. 1942.

129. NA, T–120/166/81558–62, Ribbentrop–Rome, 17 Oct. 1942.

130. Cited in IWM, Thomashausen, *Beiträge*, i, 75; also see *TMWC*, vol. xi (Nuremberg, 1947), 425–30.
131. NA, T–120/166/81563–4, 19 Oct. 1942.
132. Hondros, *Occupation and Resistance*, 65–6.
133. MFA/AD, Athens, box 6, Salonika–Athens, 16 June 1942.
134. *EK*, 2 Dec. 1942.
135. NA, T–120/166/81678, Altenburg–Berlin, 2 Dec. 1942.
136. NA, T–120/166/81725–7, Neubacher, 9 Jan. 1943; T–120/166/81730, Neubacher, 9 Jan. 1943.
137. NA, T–120/166/81739–42, 14 Jan. 1943.
138. NA, T–120/166/81803–5, 'Aufzeichnung', 8 Feb. 1943; 81861–2, 'Besatzungskosten Griechenland', 21 March 1943.
139. Figures from D. Mangriotis, *Thysiai tis Ellados kai englimata katochis kata ta eti 1941–44* (Athens, n.d.), 35.
140. NA, RG 226/120, 29/203, 'Summary of Greek Captured Mail', 17 July 1944; ibid., 29/204, 'Greece: Censorship', 7 Oct. 1944; RG 165/179, 651, 'IR on a German POW from 18 Fortress Infantry Bn. 999', 11 Sept. 1944.
141. FO 898/153, 28 April 1943.
142. E.L. Homze, *Foreign Labor in Nazi Germany*, (Princeton, 1965), 81.
143. Ibid., 57, 65.
144. Hondros, *Occupation and Resistance*, 76; OSS, R and A 1174, 'Population Movements in Greece', 31 July 1943; *Tachydromos* (Volos), 4 April 1942;

Rochlitz, 109–10: 'Notiziario della settimana', 27 May 1942.
145. MFA/AD, Athens, box 6, Haimet (Salonika)–Athens, 16 Aug. 1942.
146. OSS, 'Population Movements in Greece', 31 July 1943.
147. C. Hadziiosif, 'Griechen in der deutschen Kriegsproduktion', in U. Herbert (ed.), *Europa und der 'Reicheinsatz': ausländische Zivilarbeiter, Kriegsgefangene und KZ-Häftlinge in Deutschland, 1938–1945* (Essen, 1991), 225; BA/K, R 58/176, 'Stimmen zum Einsatz von griechischen Arbeitskraften', n.d., which is the main source for what follows.
148. *NCA*, iii, L–26, 771–2.
149. BA/K, R 58/186, 'SD Berichte zu Inlandsfragen: Erfahrungen mit griechischen Zivilarbeitern im Reich', 1 July 1943.
150. Ibid.
151. Ibid.
152. Homze, *Foreign Labor*, 148; Hadziiosif, 'Griechen in der deutschen Kriegsproduktion', 226–8.
153. N. Kazantzakis, *Report to Greco*, (London, 1973), 445.
154. MFA/AD, Athens, box 6, French consul (Salonika)–Athens, 9 May 1942.
155. NA, T–120/1174/468819–20, Gotzamanis's schedule in Berlin; T–120/166/81625, 'Aufzeichnung', 31 Oct. 1942; T–120/1174/81920, Altenburg–Berlin, 10 April 1943.
156. 'La Nuova Europa' in StA., 306/097810–26.
157. *DDI*, viii, 410: Luciolli–D'Ajeta, 14 March 1942.

PART TWO 'This Heroic Madness': 1942–43

1. Cited in Ch. Christides, *Chronia katochis* (Athens, 1971), 18–19.
2. FO 916/213, Consul-Gen.

(Lisbon)–POW Dept. (London), 9 Aug. 1941.
3. WO 208/3358, 'Statement by 2nd

Lt. Constantine Altzerinakos of Ayeranos, Lakonia'; FO 916/702.

4. I. Tsatsou, *Fylla katochis* (Athens, 1987), 14–15.

5. Christides, *Chronia katochis*, 55–7.

6. *EK*, 10 May 1941; K. Antoniou, *Istoria tis Ellinikis Vasilikis Chorofylakis*, iii (Athens, 1965), 1910; WO 208/3365, 'German Counter-espionage Activity in Crete: June 1941–May 1942', 29 May 1942; PAAA, R 101082, Altenburg–Rademacher, 26 Aug. 1941.

7. Hondros, *Occupation and Resistance: The Greek Agony, 1941–44* (New York, 1983), 95–6.

8. Ibid., 97–100; MFA/ASD, Grecia AAPP., B22 (1939–43), f1, 3 Aug., 20 Sept. 1941; NA, T–315/1474/496–8, 164 I.D./1a, 20 Oct. 1941, 511–12; also BA–MA RH 20–12/198, 'Tagesmeldungen von Befh.Sal/Agäis', 26 Oct. 1941.

9. MFA/AD, Athens box 6, Haimet–Athens, 27 and 29 Nov. 1941; H. Fleischer, *Im Kreuzschatten der Mächte: Griechenland 1941–1944*, 2 vols. (Frankfurt a. Main, 1986), i, 130; M. Vafeiades, *Apomnimonevmata*, ii (Athens, 1985), 46–7.

10. MFA/AD, Athens box 33, 28 Oct. 1941; StA. 238/063607–11, 'Grecia: relazione sulla situazione economica', 20 Jan. 1942; *SSGM*, v (Vatican, 1969), 102; *Ciano's Diary 1939–1943* M. Muggeridge, ed. (London, 1947), 382.

11. *The Goebbels Diaries*, ed. L.P. Lochner (New York, 1948), 104.

12. G. Theotokas, *Tetradia imerologiou (1939–1953)* (Athens, n.d.), 277, 332; *SSGM*, v, 100: Roncalli–Maglione, 24 July 1941.

13. B. Wason, *Miracle in Hellas: the Greeks Fight On* (London, 1943), 9; *SSGM*, v, 100.

14. V. Tsitsanis, *I zoi tou, to ergo tou* (Athens, 1979), 20.

15. Christides, *Chronia katochis*, 322.

16. K. Delopoulos (ed.), *To imerologio katochis tou Minou Dounias* (Athens, 1987), 66–7, 118–19; Christides, *Chronia katochis*, 82, 105.

17. Christides, *Chronia katochis*, 322.

18. Karl L. Rankin Papers, Mudd Library, Princeton, box 6, 'The Reopening of the American Embassy at Athens', Feb. 1945; NA, T–311/188/993.

19. G. Theotokas, *Tetradia imerologiou (1939–1953)* (Athens, n.d.), 291.

20. I. Persakis, *Istories tis kathe meras* (Athens, n.d.) 12; Vlachou cited in K.N. Hadzipateras and M.S. Fafaliou, *Martyries 40–44* (Athens, 1988), 343.

21. *To imerologiou katochis tou Minou Dounia* (Athens, 1987), 110.

22. Theotokas, *Tetradia imerologiou*, 390.

23. A. Sikelianos, *Pezos Logos*, iv: *1940–1944* (Athens, n.d.), 48, 105–7.

24. A. Sikelianou, *I zoi mou me ton Angelo* (Athens, n.d.), 148.

25. Tsatsou, *Fylla katochis*, 37.

26. Interview with Mario M., Jan. 1988.

27. Fleischer, *Kreuzschatten*, i, 100; Christides, *Chronia katochis*, 21–2.

28. A. Mazarakis-Ainian, *Apomnimonevmata* (Athens, 1948), 623.

29. Cited in P. Kanellopoulos, *Ta chronia tou megalou polemou, 1939–1944* (Athens, 1964), 198.

30. FO 371/43674 R226/9.

31. Kanellopoulos, *Ta chronia tou megalou polemou*, 197; Fleischer, *Kreuzschatten*, i, 100–3.

32. Glinos cited in Th. Chadzis, *I nikifora epanastasi pou chathike*, i (Athens, 1982), 107.

33. Chadzis, *I nikifora epanastasi pou chathike*, i, 208–13.

34. Ibid., 107.

35. G. Katsoulis, *Istoria tou KKE*, v (1941–45) (Athens, n.d.), 40–7.

36. NA, RG 226/57515, 'Greece Underground Movement:

Corfu', 12 Oct. 1943; RG 226/57516, 'Greece: Underground Organisations – concerning Boeotia (Levadeia)', 12 Oct. 1943.

37. Fleischer, *Kreuzschatten*, i, 95–8; Chadzis, *I nikifora epanastasi pou chathike*, i, 213–14; Hondros, *Occupation and Resistance*, 104–7. A valuable recent account of EDES based on unpublished documents is H. Petimezas, *Ethniki antistasi kai koinoniki epanastasi: Zervas kai E.A.M. O agonas 1941–44 vasei ton archeion tis antistasiakis omadas 'Nikitas'* (Athens, 1991).

38. *SSGM*, v (Vatican, 1969), 100: Roncalli–Maglione, 24 July 1941.

39. NA, T–821/354/770, 'Relazione sull'opera svolta dal Commando Superiore FF.AA. Grecia nel campo politico–economico durante il primo anno di occupazione (Maggio 1941–Maggio 1942)', 3 Aug. 1942.

40. NA, T–821/248/305, 'Relazione sulla Grecia, relativa al mese di maggio 1943'.

41. FO 371/42356 W6834/6, Mallet (Stockholm)–London, 14 April 1944; FO 371/43674 R226/9 Leeper–Eden, 22 Dec. 1943.

42. G. Beikos, *I laiki exousia stin Eleftheri Ellada*, i (Athens, 1979), 135–40; *Tachydromos* (Volos), 9 Jan., 4 Feb., 26 Feb. 1942.

43. *Gynaikes stin Antistasi: Martyries* (Athens, 1982), 100–15; FO 371/43674 R225, 15 Nov. 1943.

44. L. Arseniou, *I Thessalia stin antistasi* (Athens, 1966), 29–32.

45. Ibid., 24–7.

46. V.K. Lazaris, *Politiki istoria tis Patras* iii: 1940–1944 (Athens, 1989), 68–9.

47. The Vlachs were a minority found chiefly in the Pindos range who spoke a Romance language akin to Romanian. WO 208/3358, June 1942; FO 371/37201 R2569, 17 March 1943.

48. Antoniou, *Istoria*, iii, 1902–3; WO 204/8890, 'General Administrative Questions'; WO 204/

9172, 'Record of Information Received up to 4 July 1943'; LDG archives, INFO XI, 'Prisons, 1945–67: Individual Dossiers'.

49. NA, RG 226/135385, 'Greece – Underground and Quisling Organisations', 14 April 1943; RG 226/57516 'Greece: Underground Organisations – concerning Boeotia (Levadeia)', 12 Oct. 1943.

50. Chadzis, *I nikifora epanastasi pou chathike*, i, 249–51, 344–5; Katsoulis, *Istoria tou KKE*, v, 86–7; *EK*, 17 April 1942; *EV*, 18 April 1942.

51. Chadzis, *I nikifora epanastasi pou chathike*, i, 251; Katsoulis, *Istoria tou KKE*, v, 87–8.

52. NA, T–120/2481/E259694, 10 Sept. 1942.

53. Christides, *Chronia katochis*, 318; FO 371/42360, 'Aspects financiers', 31 April 1944.

54. NA, T–821/248/355 'Notizie della Grecia Relative al Mese di Gennaio 1943', 19 Feb. 1943.

55. Theotokas, *Tetradia imerologiou*, 374–5; Hondros, *Occupation and Resistance*, 115.

56. FO 371/37201 R1416/4, 'Situation in Greece', 21 Jan. 1943; Christides, *Chronia katochis*, 352.

57. FO 371/43679 R2697/9, 3 Feb. 1944; FO 371/43674, R226/9, 'Alignment of the Politicians on the Constitutional Question'.

58. Ch. Sakellariou, *I Paideia stin Antistasi* (Athens, 1984), 27–9; LDG archives, INFO XI, 'Prisons, 1945–67: Individual Dossiers'.

59. Theotokas, *Tetradia imerologiou*, 429, 406–8; E. Fourtouni, *Greek Women in Resistance* (New Haven, Conn., n.d.), 29, 40–2; for previous unrest at the university, see Theotokas, *Tetradia imerologiou*, 310–11.

60. NA, T–821/248/344–5, 'Notizie dalla Grecia relative al mese di Febbraio U.S.', n.d.

61. Ibid.

62. Hondros, *Occupation and Resist-

ance, 116.

63. NA, T–821/248/349–50, 'Notizie dalla Grecia', 24 Feb. 1943.
64. Theotokas, *Tetradia imerologiou*, 402.
65. K.N. Hadzipateras and M. Fafalios, *Martyries 40–44* (Athens, 1988), 374.
66. Ibid. 375.
67. Christides, *Chronia katochis*, 366–8; Theotokas, *Tetradia imerologiou*, 405–6; Hondros, *Occupation and Resistance*, 116–17; NA, T–821/248/333, 'Notizie dalla Grecia', 1 April 1943.
68. Christides, *Chronia katochis*, 367; Hondros, *Occupation and Resistance*, 116.
69. Christides, *Chronia katochis*, 384; FO 371/37204 R8423/4, 'Interrogation of Three EAM Members Who Left Greece, 11 July 1943'.
70. NA, T–821/248/279–82, 'Grecia: sciopero generale del 25 giugno', 14 July 1943.
71. NA, T–821/354/848–50, 25 March 1942.
72. E. Papadimitriou (ed.) *O koinos logos*, i (Athens, 1975), 108.
73. *Tachydromos* (Volos), 25, 28 Feb., 15, 25 March 1942; 4 April 1942.
74. NA, T–821/354/794–5, 'Relazione sull'opera svolta . . .'.
75. *Larissaikos Typos*, 7, 13, 23, 25 Aug. 1942; *Tachydromos* (Volos), 15 Aug. 1942.
76. Lazaris, *Patras*, iii, 68–9, 86–7.
77. *Tachydromos* (Volos), 24, 29 Dec. 1942; *Larissaikos Typos*, 16 Jan. 1943.
78. LDG archives, INFO XI: 'Prisons, 1945–1967: Individual Dossiers'.
79. Ibid.; Antoniou, *Istoria*, iii, 1702.
80. E.C.W. Myers, *Greek Entanglement* (Gloucester, 1985 revised ed. [orig. ed. 1955]), 62; WO 204/8991A, 'Greece: Medical Summary', 30 July 1944; FO 371/37211, PWE, Weekly Directive BBC Greek Service (23–30 April 1943).
81. [A. Sevastaki] Kapefan Boukouvalas, *To andartiko ippiko tis Thessalias* (Athens, 1978), 31.
82. NA, T–821/248/337–8 'Nota informativa circa le constatazioni fatte presso la banda di "Andartes" capitanata dal Maggiore Custopulos, nella regione Triccala–Calabaca'.
83. Myers, *Greek Entanglement*, 36, 40–1; W. Jordan, *Conquest without Victory* (London, 1969), 80.
84. Myers, *Greek Entanglement*, 60–2.
85. FO 371/43687 R8298/9, 'Food Conditions in the Guerrilla Areas', n.d.; WO 204/9172, 'Economic Reports, Greece and Crete'.
86. Myers Papers (KCL), 1/3, *Instructions*, National Band of Rebels, JGHQ, no. 10 (24 Aug. 1943); 12 (25 Aug. 1943).
87. Myers, *Greek Entanglement*, 166.
88. Myers Papers (KCL), 1/2, 'Stevens Report', 15 Aug. 1943, 14–15.
89. FO 371/36503 W14787/3, Mallet (Stockholm)–London, 14 Oct. 1943.
90. Myers Papers (KCL), 1/1, 'The Crisis in Greece', n.d.; 'Inside Greece: A Review', 25 Aug. 1943; 1/2, 'Report of Lt. Col. J.M. Stevens on Present Conditions in Central Greece', 15 Aug. 1943; FO 371/43676 R1149/9, Leeper–Eden, 14 Jan. 1944.
91. WO 204/9004, 'Periodic Summary of Non-operational Intelligence of Medical Interest no. 6: Month Ending March 31, 1944'.
92. Interview with Alexandros Mallios, Feb. 1988.
93. WO 204/8869, 'Notes on the Relief Services of the Greek Resistance Organisation EAM', 30 Dec. 1943; Myers Papers (KCL), 1/3, *Instruction*, no. 18 (29 Aug. 1943).
94. A. Flountzis, *Stratopeda Larrisas Trikalon 1941–1944: i yennisi tou andartikou sti Thessalia* (Athens,

1977), 214–42; NA, T–821/248/337; FO 371/37201 R2569/4, 'Guerrilla Activities in Greece', 17 March 1943; Lazaris, *Patras*, iii, 106–7.

95. WO 204/8890, 'General Administrative Questions', 9 Aug. 1943; *EK*, 1 Aug. 1942: the decree was backdated to 3 July.

96. NA, T–315/1474/452, 'Tätigkeitsbericht der Abt.Ic vom 1.9.–15.9.1941', 164 I.D./Ic, 19 Sept. 1941.

97. MFA/ASD, AAPP. Grecia, B20 (1942), Ghigi (Athens)–Rome, 1 Nov. 1942; Flountzis, *Stratopeda*, 206–9; Antoniou, *Istoria*, iii, 1702.

98. NA, T–821/248/342, 'Notizie dalla Grecia relative al mese di Febbraio u.s.', n.d.; T–821/248/330, 'Notizie dalla Grecia', 16 April 1943.

99. WO 208/698A, 'Summary of Guerrilla Activity in Greece: Sept. 1942 – Feb. 1943'.

100. Ibid.; large clashes had occurred as early as September 1942 near Amfissa: SME US.DS (CSFFAA. Grecia) (11a Armata), B1054, 19 and 29 Sept. 1942.

101. WO 208/698A; WO 204/8852, CEWA: Economic Warfare Reports, no. 16, 15 Aug. 1944.

102. NA, T–821/248/341–3; WO 208/698A, 'Summary of Guerrilla Activity – Feb.–March 1943', 31 March 1943.

103. NA, T–821/248/309–10, 'Condizioni dell'ordine e della sicurezza pubblica', 21 May 1943; T–821/248/329–31, 'Notizie dalla Grecia', 16 April 1943.

104. NA, T–821/248/330, 'Notizie dalla Grecia', 16 April 1943.

105. Myers, *Greek Entanglement*, 139.

106. Theotokas, *Tetradia imerologiou*, 416.

107. FO 371/43676 R1487/9, 'The Guerrilla Movement in Greece', n.d.; Myers Papers (KCL), 1/1, 'The Crisis in Greece: a Review of its Causes', 13, 17; NA, T–821/248/273, 'Grecia: dislocazione masse ribelli dalla data del 30.6.1943'.

108. FO 371/43685 R6180/9, 'The Andarte Movement in Epirus', 30 March 1944; C.M. Woodhouse, *Apple of Discord: A Survey of Recent Greek Politics in their International Setting* (London, 1948), 72–3.

109. Hondros, *Occupation and Resistance*, 106.

110. Woodhouse, *Apple of Discord*, 74; Myers, *Greek Entanglement*, 128; C.M. Woodhouse, 'The National Liberation Front and the British Connection', in J. Iatrides (ed.) *Greece in the 1940s: A Nation in Crisis* (London, 1981), 81–101. Cf. the same author's 'Early British contacts with the Greek Resistance', *Balkan Studies*, 12 (1971), 347–63.

111. Hondros, *Occupation and Resistance*, 107, 146, 148; cf. FO 371/37202 R4209/4, 'Greek Resistance Movement', 6 May 1943. According to this report, 59,774 lbs of arms had been dropped to EDES since 24 Jan., and 34,072 lbs to ELAS. The same report estimates that ELAS forces had inflicted 2,865 casualties on Axis forces in the previous three months, whilst 'apart from one attack on the Arta–Amfilochia road, there are no reports of attacks by Napoleon Zervas on the Axis'.

112. P. Papastratis, *British Policy Towards Greece during the Second World War, 1941–1944* (Cambridge, 1984), 129–43; B. Sweet-Escott, 'SOE in the Balkans'; C.M. Woodhouse, 'Summer 1943: the Critical Months' and R. Clogg ' "Pearls from Swine": the Foreign Office Papers, S.O.E. and the Greek Resistance', in P. Auty and R. Clogg (eds.) *British Policy towards Wartime Resistance in Yugoslavia and Greece* (London, 1975).

113. Papastratis, *British Policy*, 142–3; Hondros, *Occupation and Resistance*, 150–1.

114. M. Howard, *British Intelligence in the Second World War*, v: *Strategic Deception* (London, 1990), 71–103.

115. L. Craig, 'German Defensive Policy in the Balkans. A Case Study: the Buildup in Greece, 1943', *Balkan Studies*, 23,2 (1982), 403–19.

116. Ibid., 419.

117. SME US.DS (CSFFAA. Grecia), B1054, allegato 6, 19 Oct. 1942; SME US.DS, Commando Supremo, B1442, 22 Nov. 1942; ACS/Segretaria Particolare del Duce, B174 (1942–43), 'Promemoria per il Duce', 13 May 1943.

118. SME US. DS B634, Geloso – all commandos, 7 Feb. 1942; ibid., B736, 'allegati', 4 March 1942, 23 March 1942; ibid., B840, 'allegato 6', 12 June 1942.

119. NA, T–821/249/1040, 'Addestramento', 11 May 1941.

120. WO 208/3353, 23 Oct. 1941; WO 208/3355; WO 208/3357, 8 June 1942; FO 371/37211, R113/13, PWE Weekly Directives (12–19 March 1943).

121. FO 898/152, Min.State (Cairo)–London, 21 Nov. 1942; ibid., 4 Nov. 1942.

122. FO 371/29840, R7541/96; J. Steinberg, *All or Nothing: the Axis and the Holocaust, 1941–43* (London, 1990), 101; FO 371/29841 R8099/96, 28 Aug. 1941.

123. FO 371/32463 W6719/62, 23 April 1942; IWM, 181/2, E. Thomashausen, *Beiträge zur Geschichte Griechenlands während des zweiten Weltkrieges*, Ergänzungsband i (1947), 49–50.

124. SME US.DS (CSFFAA. Grecia), B966, 'allegato 7', 22 July 1942; ibid., B1098, 'allegato 4', 20 Nov. 1942.

125. BA–MA RH 19 VII/7, OKdo HGrE/OBSüdost, KTB/Ia, 20 March 1943; Office of U.S. Chief of Counsel for Prosecution of Axis Criminals, *Nazi Conspiracy and Aggression*, vii (Washington, 1946), D–740.

126. BA–MA RW 4/682, OKW/WfSt., 'Protokoll über Besprechung in Schloss Klessheim', 9 April 1943; for the background, see F.W. Deakin, *The Brutal Friendship: Mussolini, Hitler and the Fall of Italian Fascism* (London, 1966), 289–307.

127. BA–MA RH 19 VII/53, Altenburg–Berlin, 15 June 1943; SME US.DS, B1393A, 'Due Anni in Grecia', 2 July 1943.

128. Theotokas, *Tetradia imerologiou*, 431.

129. StA. 309/09861–9, 'Rapporto sulle Isole Ionie' (n.d.); FO 371/36501 W13506/3, Knatchbull–Hugessen (Ankara)–London, 13 Sept. 1943, enclosing 'Mr. Courvoisier's Visit to the Islands: 17 to 31 July 1943'; FO 371/37204 R7730/4, 'Situation in East Aegean Islands', 5 Aug. 1943.

130. Woodhouse Papers (KCL), 1/11, no. 311, 18 July 1943; Hondros, *Occupation and Resistance*, 88.

131. MFA/AD, box 9; Such celebrations, though, were often inspired by more than one motive. According to Maria Cavallari, an Italian teacher on the island, 'our soldiers immediately dispersed the crowd and quiet returned at once to the island'. The Simiotes – she wrote – confessed later that they had meant to 'celebrate the peace' by 'ransacking the shops and the stores of hoarders and profiteers': NA, T–315/2275/299–303, 'Relazione sugli avvenimenti di Simi fra il giorno 8 settembre – data dell'armistizio – e il 2 novembre – giorno dell'occupazione dell'isola delle forze tedesche'.

132. Theotokas, *Tetradia imerologiou*, 438–9.

133. NA, T–311/175/615.

134. The two chief sources for this account are: the Kriegestagebuch (KTB) of the German General Staff in Athens, BA–MA RH 31 X/1, and BA–MA RH 31 X/2, 'Die Vorgänge des italienischen Abfalls in Athen am 8. und 9. September 1943', 14 Sept. 1943.
135. BA–MA RH 31 X/1, 11 Sept. 1943.
136. Ibid., 13 Sept. 1943.
137. The definitive study of this controversial subject is G. Schreiber, *Die italienischen Militärinternierten in deutschen Machtbereich, 1943–1945* (Munich, 1990).
138. NA, T–315/175/1121, 12 Sept. 1943; T–315/2275/381ff.; StA. 309/098961–9, 'Rapporto sulle Isole Ionie' (n.d.).; BA–MA RH 24–22/2, 22 AK/1a, Kriegstagebuch, 24/8 – 31/12/43 provides a full account of the battles for Cefalonia and Corfu. The verdict is in Schreiber, *Die italienischen Militärinternierten*, 157.
139. NA, T–315/2275/379, Stormdiv. Rhodos/1c–HGrE,Ic/AO, 18 Sept. 1943.
140. On Carta, see StA., 168/049557, 'Relazione sugli avvenimenti in Creta dopo l'8 settembre 1943', 15 March 1944; on Rhodes, NA, T–315/2275/661, n.d.; T–315/2275/259–60, Gen. Kleemann, 14 Oct. 1943; cf. StA. 300/095172–3, Ant.Cocchieri–Pavolini, 2 May 1944. On the number of Blackshirts: an Italian source in December 1943 gave an estimate of 3–4,000, StA. 107/029414–15; a British War Office estimate put the total of Italian volunteers on Rhodes and Crete in April 1944 at 10,000; another 10,000 Italians were reckoned to be employed as labourers in the rest of Greece, WO 204/8850A, 'Troops Left Behind in Event of Axis Withdrawal' (April 1944).
141. NA, RG 165/179, box 650, 'Interrogation Reports of Paolo Chiriati and Giocondo Biancalana'.
142. StA. 309/098968–9.
143. StA. 13/005924, 15 April 1944; BA–MA RH 24–22/20, 22AK/1c–HGrE, 1c/AO, 28 April 1944.
144. StA. 107/029414, 16 Dec. 1943. On the plight of the Pinerolo men see J. Mulgan, *Report on Experience* (Oxford, 1947), 84–7, and Woodhouse's comments in Auty & Clogg (eds.) *British Policy*, 245–6; 'General Report' by Major R.R. Prentice (n.d.), 7, 12–13, in author's possession. For estimates of the numbers of Italians in the hills see StA. 11/005565–6, 6 Sept. 1944 (sets an upper limit of 25,000, lower of 4–5,000); WO 204/8850A 'Troops Left Behind in Event of Axis Withdrawal' (April 1944).
145. BA–MA RH 31 X/1, 26 Sept. and 4 Oct. 1943.

PART THREE The Logic of Violence and Terror: 1943–44

1. On Löhr, see J. Diakow, *Generaloberst Alexander Löhr* (Freiburg, 1964), and the biographical material in BA–MA, Msg 1/919.
2. NA, T–311/175/909, 6 Dec. 1943; ZSt. AR 418/63, Loos affidavit, 97: a Wehrmacht report estimated that 4,785 civilians had been shot as 'hostages' in addition to 20,650 'enemy dead' (i.e. guerrillas) in the period between June 1943 and September 1944. In fact, civilian casualties were higher than this, and guerrilla

casualties lower: document reproduced in H. Fleischer, 'Nazistiki eikona yia tous (neo)-ellines kai i antimetopisi tou amachou plythismou apo tis germanikes arches katochis', in V. Kremmidas *et al.* (eds), *Afieroma ston Niko Svorono*, ii (Rethymno, 1986), 392; cf. J. Hondros, *Occupation and Resistance: The Greek Agony 1941–44* (New York, 1983), 162–3.

3. H. Krausnick, *Hitlers Einsatzgruppen: Die Truppen des Weltanschauungskrieges 1938–1942* (Frankfurt a. Main, 1985). See also O. Bartov, *The Eastern Front, 1941–45: German Troops and the Barbarisation of Warfare* (New York, 1986), and *Hitler's Army* (New York, 1992).

4. NA, T–315/1299/352–9, 117 Jg.Div./1a, 'Besprechung am 28/4 beim Befehlshaber Südgriechenland'.

5. Ibid.; on the historical background see R.C. Fattig, 'Reprisal: the German Army and the Execution of Hostages during the Second World War', (University of California, San Diego, Ph.D., 1980), ch. 1; G. Best, *Humanity in Warfare* (London, 1980), 166–200. An officer who served in Serbia, Lt.-Gen. Friedrich Stahl, admitted after the war that: 'during my thirty-eight years in a military career I was never trained in the combating of partisans . . . from a military-tactical point of view we were not equal to the partisan situation.' NA, T–1119/23/0227.

6. On Speidel's philhellenism, see IWM 181/2, E. Thomashausen, *Beiträge zur Geschichte Griechenlands während des zweiten Weltkrieges* (1947), 278; on Felmy, IWM 343/FO 646 'Case vii: Hostages', document book 1 for defence: R. Geornandt affidavit, 8 July 1947; Lanz, NA, RG 338, H. Lanz, 'Partisan warfare in the Balkans', MS. P-0551, p. 56. (I am grateful to Nigel Clive for bringing this document to my attention).

7. *Trials of War Criminals before the Nuremburg Military Tribunals*, ix ('The Hostage Case') (Washington, 1950), 801–3; Hitler believed that Löhr's Austrian background qualified him to understand the Balkans: 'Protokol über den Verhör des kriegsgefangen deutschen Generals Alexander Löhr, verfasst am 24. Mai 1945 in der Kanzlei des Lagers Banjica-Belgrad.' 24 May 1945, 9; [I thank Dr. Jonathan Steinberg for making available a copy of this document], on the ideological war against the partisans, see M. Cooper, *The Nazi War against Soviet Partisans: 1941–44* (New York, 1979), Bartov, *The Eastern Front*.

8. Lanz, 'Partisan Warfare', 8, 10; ibid., introduction by Hans von Grieffenberg, viii; also, *TWC*, ix, 890–2, 1056; Günther Müller-Fritz Scheuering, *Sprung über Kreta* (Oldenburg, 1944), 26 cited by Fleischer, 'Nazistiki eikona', 383.

9. IWM 350/FO 646, NOKW–1132, Chief of General Staff, Commander/Serbia – 704 Inf.Div./1a, 16 Jan. 1943: 'The Führer has banned the term "Partisans".... In the southeast area it is to be replaced by the word "Communists" or "Communist bands"'; Löhr's addition to the Führer Befehl of 18 Oct. 1942, in BA–MA, RA 19 XI/7; NA, T–315/1542/709, 68 AK/1a, 31 May 1944.

10. IWM 343/FO 646, Case vii: 'Hostages', doc. book 3 for Defence, Erhard Glitz affidavit, 13 Oct. 1947.

11. NA, RG 165/179, box 651, 'Interrogation Report on 5 German POWs'; C. Couvaras, *OSS with*

the Central Committee of EAM (San Francisco, 1982), 48; H. Franz, *Gebirgsjäger der Polizei: Gebirgsjäger-Rgt. 18 und Polizei-Geb.-Artillerieabteilungen: 1942–1945* (Bad Nauheim, 1963), 150.

12. Lanz, 'Partisan Warfare', 24, 26, 72, IWM 344/FO 646, Doc. book 4 for Defence, Kleykamp affidavit, 25 Oct. 1947, 8.; NA, T–315/1300/378, 'Abschlussbericht', 18 Dec. 1943.

13. NA, T–312/465/8053722, Obfh. 12 Armee/1a, 'Richtlinien für die Behandlung der Aufständischen in Serbien und Kroatien', 19 March 1942; ZSt. AR 12/62, vii, Walter V. affidavit, 68–9.

14. Hans Wende, 'Die Griechische Widerstandsbewegung im Urteil der Deutschen Heeresführung', unpublished typescript. (My thanks to Richard Mitten for providing me with a copy of this document.)

15. NA, T–501/331/425; T–311/179/1073.

16. IfZ 18/14, 'Auszug aus der Meldung eines zur Aufklärung in das Bandengebiet angesetzten Unteroffiziers'.

17. NA, T–314/1540/330, 68 AK/1c, '1c–Lagebericht', 27 Nov. 1943.

18. NA, T–315/1474/512; P. Argenti, *The Occupation of Chios by the Germans and their Administration of the Island, 1941–1944* (Cambridge, 1966), 78.

19. NA, RG 226/120–29/203, 'Greece: Censorship', 21 April 1944.

20. Lyall Wilkes typescript (Private Papers); NA, T–315/1300/374.

21. On the GFP, about which little is known, the best available study is K. Gessner, *Geheime Feldpolizei: zur Funktion und Organisation des Geheimpolizeilichen Exekutivorgens der Faschistichen Wehrmacht* (Berlin (DDR), 1986); on the Abwehr in Greece, see NA, RG 165/179, box 739, 'CIR no. 13: Asts. in the Balkans'; quotes from RG 226/190, 3/30.

22. BA–MA RH 24–22/19; 1c–Aussenstelle Korfu–Korpsgruppe Jannina/1c, 'Feindlagebericht', 25 April 1944.

23. This section based on NA, T–315/2275/521–61.

24. NA, T–315/2275/402, 'Massnahmen zur Bandenbekämpfung', 13 Nov. 1943.

25. NA, T–501/331/438, Deutsch. Generalstab beim ital. AOK. 11/1c, '1c–Lagebericht', 4 Sept. 1943.

26. Hondros, *Occupation and Resistance*, 154–5; Lanz, 'Partisan Warfare in the Balkans', 60–1, 80–5; on Salminger, see NA, T–315/65/359, 'Bericht über die Säuberung vom 22.–26.7.1943'.

27. NA, T–501/331/59, Deutsch Gen. Stab. beim ital. AOK 11/1a–HGrE/1a, 7 Aug. 1943; T–501/331/47–8, Deutsch. Gen. Stab. beim ital. 11 AOK–HGrE/1a, 19 Aug. 1943.

28. NA, T–311/175/1071, HGrE/1a–OBSüdost/1a, 26 Oct. 1943; T–311/180/1295–6, HGrE/1c/AO, 'Lagebericht für die Zeit vom 1.–8.11.43'; T–311/180/1297–8, HGrE/1c/AO, 'Lagebericht für die Zeit vom 9.–17.11.43'.

29. Deas archive, 4/76, 'Report on the Destruction and Military Activity Which Took Place in the Kalabaka Area by Occupation Forces.' (n.d.); Hondros, *Occupation and Resistance*, 156.

30. NA, T–314/671/288–94, SS.Pol. Pz.Gren.Rgt.1/1c, 'Feindlagebericht', 30 Oct. 1943; T–314/1540/330, 68 AK/1c.

31. Lanz, 'Partisan Warfare', 68–9.

32. Hondros, *Occupation and Resistance*, 155–6; Franz, *Gebirgsjäger der Polizei*, 81–84.

33. Hondros, *Occupation and Resistance*, 81–2. See chapter 22 (*below*) on the Security Battalions & counter-terror units. The de-

velopment of US counter-
insurgency doctrine during the
Cold War is superbly analysed
by Michael McClintock in
Instruments of Statecraft (New
York, 1992). Among the studies
of German anti-partisan tactics
commissioned by the US Army
were D.M. Condit, *Case Studies
in Guerrilla War: Greece during
World War Two* (Washington,
1961); H.M. Gardner, *Guerrilla
and Counterguerrilla Warfare in
Greece, 1941–1945* (Washington,
1962); R.M. Kennedy, *German
Antiguerrilla Operations in the
Balkans, 1941–1944* (Washington,
1954).

34. IfZ 1043/53, HGrE, 1c/ AO,
'Feindnachrichtenblatt (Griechische Banden), nr. 9: April/Mai
1944', 9.

35. *TWC*, ix, 799.

36. BA–MA, RH 28–5/4b, 'Vergel-
tungsmassnahmen', 31 May
1941; also, M. von Xylander, *Die
deutsche Besatzungsherrschaft auf
Kreta, 1941–1945* (Freiburg, 1989),
32–3.

37. NA, T–315/1474/497–8, 512;
on List, see C. Browning,
'Wehrmacht Reprisal Policy and
the Mass Murder of Jews in
Serbia', *Militärgeschichtliche Mit-
teilungen*, 331, (1983), 34–55.

38. See now C. Browning, *Ordinary
Men: Reserve Police Battalion 101
and the Final Solution in Poland*
(New York, 1992), 161; M.
Cooper, *The Nazi War against
Soviet Partisans, 1941–44* (New
York, 1979), 53–94; R.B.
Asprey, *War in the Shadows: the
Guerrilla in History*, ii (New York,
1975), 858–74, 1313–40.

39. NA, T–315/65/787–8, 'Div-
isionsbefehl für Säuberungsunternehmen Augustus', 7 Aug.
1943; on the 1st Mountain Division in Yugoslavia see the vivid
account of F.W. Deakin, *The
Embattled Mountain* (London,
1971), 29–30.

40. NA, T–315/65/747.

41. NA, T–315/1299/361, 117
Jg.Div./1a, 28 April 1943; for the
importance of the civilian population to the guerrillas, see Lanz,
'Partisan Warfare', *passim*; NA,
T–315/1541/800, 117 Jg.Div.,
'Massnahmen zur Bekämpfung
der Komm. Bewegung', 3 May
1944: NA, RG 226/144, 100/
1051, Moyers Diary, entry for 16
Aug. 1944.

42. IWM 350, NOKW 1079, Löhr –
1 Pz. Div./1a, 14 July 1943;
TWC, ix, 1306 (NOKW 155).

43. Hondros, *Occupation and Resistance*, 154; C. Browning, 'Wehrmacht Reprisal Policy'.

44. IWM 351, NOKW 864, 18 Oct.
1943; C. Burdick, *Hubert Lanz:
General der Gebirgstruppe, 1896–
1982* (Osnabruck, 1988), 210–11;
NA, T–314/1541/759–60, 68
AK/1a–HGrE/1a, 26 April 1944;
T–314/1542/742, 68 AK/1c, 28
April 1944.

45. See ZSt. AR 2415/67, Alwin A.
affidavit, 145; *TWC*, ix, 1307.

46. Hondros, *Occupation and Resistance*, 175–81.

47. FO 371/37209 R13295/4, 8 Dec.
1943.

48. IfZ 1043/53, 'Bericht über meinen
Aufenhalt in Athen vom 2.4. bis
6.4.44', Hans Wende; Wende,
'Die Griechische Widerstands-
bewegung', 22. See also O.
Heilbrunn, *Partisan Warfare*
(London, 1962), 150–52.

49. NA, T–315/1300/291.

50. NA, T–311/179/1256–65,
Speidel–Löhr, 8 Jan. 1944.

51. *TWC*, ix, 826; NA, T–311/175/
929, 'Vortrag des Chef des Generalstabes über die allgemeine
Lage'.

52. NA, T–315/1300/39, 117
Jg.Div./1a, 'Tätigkeitsbericht', 5
Nov. 1943; T–311/179/1267,
Feldkomm. 1042, 'Lagebericht',
31 Dec. 1943; T–315/1300/341–
4, 117 Jg.Div./Komm., 20 Dec.
1943.

53. NA, T–315/1541/800; BA–MA, RW 40/149, Mbfh/Griechenland, 'Lagebericht für die Zeit vom 16.5 bis 15.6.1944'.

54. IfZ, 1043/53, 'Bericht über meinen Aufenthalt in Athen vom 2.4 bis 6.4.44'; H. Neubacher, *Sonderauftrag Südost, 1940–1945* (Göttingen, 1956), 139–44.

55. NA, T–314/1541/800, 'Massnahmen zur Bekämpfung', 3 May 1944; IWM, 352, NOKW–1377, 14 Aug. 1944.

56. NA, T–314/671/99, 'Abschlussmeldung über Unternehmen "Hubertus"', 13 Nov. 1943; T–314/671/295, 'Erfolge des SS-Pol.Pz.Gren.Rgt. 1 beim Unternehmen Panther', 30 Oct. 1943.

57. NA, T–315/671/875–81, 22AK/1c, '1c–Lagebericht', 26 Oct. 1943; T–315/671/850, 22AK/1c, '1c–Lagebericht', 26 Nov. 1943; T–311/179/1184, 'Ergebnisse des Unternehmens "Maigewitter" nach bis 28.4 vorliegenden Meldungen' (n.d.); NA, T–311/178/332–3, 22 Aug. 1944.

58. BA–MA, RH 24–91/10, 91 AK/1a, 'Führungshinweise', 27 Oct. 1944.

59. FO 371/43674 R382/9, Leeper–Eden, 26 Dec. 1943.

60. Greek Government, Office of Information, *Ruins of Modern Greece, 1941–1944* (Washington, n.d.), 12; an important source of information is the interim list contained in FO 371/43677, 'Atrocities Committed in Greece by the Occupying Forces', 15 Jan. 1944; FO 371/42351 W1466/6, Mallet (Stockholm)–London, 18 Jan. 1944; FO 371/42356 W6272/6, Mallet (Stockholm)–London, 8 April 1944; FO 371/42362 W10312/6, Mallet (Stockholm)–London, 13 June 1944; Deas archive, 4/9, 'Report of Mrs Elly Adosidou and Messrs Chr. Vasmatzidou and Theodoros Papadimitriou on the Situation of the Burned Areas of Epiros and Aitoliakarnania', 4 Jan. 1944.

61. Deas archive, 5/89, 'Destruction in Western Macedonia', 15 March 1944; WO 204/8869, 'Greece: Political Situation'; WO 204/8890, 'Greece and Crete: Local Government Layout'; see also FO 371/42363 W11160/6, 'Damage Caused in Western Macedonia owing to the Development of Military Operations,' enclosed in Leeper–London, 9 June 1944; NA, RG 226/120, 29/203, 'Summary of Captured Greek Mail', 17 July 1944.

62. Deas archive 5/87, 'Rapport de M. Wenger à M. Sandstrom sur la situation alimentaire actuelle du province de Macedoine', 1 March 1944; Deas archive 5/89, 'Destruction in W. Macedonia', 15 March 1944; FO 371/42352 W2497/6, Red Cross reports sent by Leeper–London, 5 Feb. 1944; FO 371/48308 R10270/52, Mallet (Stockholm)–London, 7 June 1945.

63. Deas archive, 4/24, 'Report on the general situation in the Region of Arta'.

64. Deas archive, 4/9, 'Report of Mrs Elly Adosidou and Messrs Chr. Vasmatzidou and Theod. Papadimitriou on the Situation of the Burned Areas of Epiros and Aitoliakarnania', 4 Jan. 1944.

65. NA, RG 226/144, 100/1051, Moyers Diary, 16 Aug. 1944.

66. Deas archive, 4/24, 'Report on the general situation in the region of Arta'.

67. Deas archive, 4/9, 'Report of Mrs. Elly Adosidou...' 4 Jan. 1944. Cf. K. Sosnowski, *The Tragedy of Children Under Nazi Rule* (Warsaw, 1962), 164–85.

68. P. Simha, *Oikoyeneia 'Dimitriou'* (Thessaloniki, 1988), 39.

69. LDG, INFO XI, 'Prisons, 1945–67: Individual Dossiers'.

70. *Gynaikes stin Antistasi: Martyries* (Athens, 1982), 11–12. The forth-

coming work by Janet Hart will shed light on this important subject.

71. Theotokas, *Tetradia imerologiou*, 467; Simha, *Oikoyeneia 'Dimitriou'*, 64–5.

72. K. Papakongos, *Archeio Person* (Athens, 1977), esp. the photograph opposite page 144. WO 204/8991A, 'Periodic Summary of Non-operational Intelligence of Medical Interest, no. 7'; Deas archive, 4/4, 'Note sur la situation alimentaire de l'Epire et des Cyclades', 16 Sept. 1943.

73. Frantz Fanon, 'Colonial War and Mental Disorders' in *The Wretched of the Earth* (New York, 1968), 249–310. On puerperal psychoses, RG 226/144, 100/1051, Moyers diary, 20 Dec. 1943 and Fanon, *op. cit.*, 278–79.

74. RG 226/190, 2/19, Stygia Mission, 24; Frantz Fanon, *The Wretched of the Earth* (New York, 1968); on Anna K., *Gynaikes stin antistasi*, 62.

75. NA, T–315/66/457, 1 Geb.Div./ 1a – Deutsch. Gen. Stab. beim ital.11 Armee, 'Tagesmeldung', 12 Aug. 1943; T–315/2305/1527, 'Mittagsmeldungen der Truppe', 12 Aug. 1943; T–501/331/212–13, Deutsch. Gen. Stab. beim ital. AOK 11/1a–OBSüdost/1a, 'Tagesmeldung vom 13.8.43'.

76. V. Klemperer, *LTI: Lingua Tertii Imperii. Die Sprache des Dritten Reiches* (Leipzig, 1991 [orig. ed. Halle, 1957]) Larissa ref. from NA, T–311/175/1083, HGrE/ 1a–OBSüdost/1a, 'Tagesmeldung', 14 Oct. 1943; Vianos ref., BA–MA, RH 26–22/79, 22 Inf.Div.KTB, 15 Sept. 1943.

77. Details of the names on the monument from S. Pappa, *I sfagi tou Kommenou* (Athens, 1976), 37–45.

78. ZSt. AR 1462/68, 201–3.

79. Interview with Alexandros Mallios, Komeno, Feb. 1988.

80. ZSt. AR 1462/68, 105.

81. Ibid., 163; G. Papakonstantinou, *Enthymimata potismena me aima kai dakrya* (Athens, 1985), 148–9.

82. ZSt. AR 1462/68, 86–7.

83. Ibid., 43, 53–4, 81, 107, 182.

84. NA, T–315/66/422, 'Mittagsmeldungen der Truppe', 16 Aug. 1943.

85. NA, T–315/66/423, 'Abendmeldungen der Truppe', 16 Aug. 1943.

86. NA, T–315/66/425, 1 Geb.Div./ 1a–Deutsch. Gen. Stab. beim ital.11 Armee, 'Tagesmeldung 16.8.43'.

87. The lack of fire from the village is confirmed by the following affidavits: ZSt. AR 1462/68, 58, 60, 79.

88. BA/MA, RH 31 X/1, Deutscher Generalstab beim ital. A.O.K. 11, entry for 17 Aug. 1943; NA, T–501/331/220, Deutsch. gen. Stab. beim ital. AOK 11/1a–HGrE/1a, 17 Aug. 1943; T–501/331/438, 'Deutsch. Gen. Stab. beim ital. AOK 11/1c, '1c-Lagebericht', 4 Sept. 1943.

89. Interview with Kurt R., Hamburg, 1 April 1988.

90. ZSt. AR 1462/68, 76–7. Between 1969 and 1971 the West German and Austrian police interviewed every surviving member of 12 Co. as part of an investigation into the Komeno massacre. Nobody, however, was ever brought to trial.

91. Bartov, *The Eastern Front, passim.*

92. ZSt. AR 1462/68, 57.

93. Ibid. 56, 43.

94. Ibid., 43–5, 58–9, 182; NA, T–315/72/1259, 'Tätigkeitsbericht für die Zeit vom 21/6 – 30/9/43', 15 Oct. 1943; Herr S. to author, 20 July 1989.

95. ZSt. AR 1462/68, 115, 105, 182.

96. Ibid., 76–7, 164, 213. For further discussion of these issues see my 'Military Violence & National Socialist values: the *Wehrmacht* in Greece, 1941–1944', *Past & Present*, 134 (Feb. 1992), 129–59.

97. Wiener Library, P.111.g.470, 'Interview with Non-Jewish ISK Member', 9, 26 Oct. 1955.
98. On the 999ers, see H.-P. Klausch, *Die 999er* (Frankfurt a. Main, 1986). There was, however, some tension between Germans from the Altreich and others from border areas, or from Eastern Europe, cf. NA, T–315/1300/102; T–315/1299/1051; on the generally good treatment of Polish Germans, see NA, RG 165/179, 650.
99. NA, T–315/1299/358, 117 Jg. Div./1a, 'Besprechung am 28/4 beim Befehlshaber Südgriechenland'.
100. Cited in F. Husemann, *Die guten Glaubens waren: Geschichte der SS-Polizei-Division*, ii (Osnabruck, n.d.), 201, 204.
101. NA, RG 226/120, 29/203, 'Captured Mail from Amorgos–Ios' 20 June 1944; NA, T–78/134/6062773–82, Feldpostprüfstelle beim Okdo.H.Gr.E., 'Bericht'.
102. NA, RG 226/120, 29/203, 'Captured Mail from Amorgos–Ios', 20 June 1944.
103. Husemann, *Guten Glaubens*, ii, 222–3; on Schilling, Hana Vondra, 'Malariaexperimente in Konzentrationslager und Heilaustalten während der Zeit des Nationalsozialismus' (Diss., Med. Hochschule, Hannover 1989); Franz, *Gebirgsjäger der Polizei*, 84; cf. 'Chronik der Nachrichten-Abteilung der 4 SS.Pol.Pz.Gren.Division' (unpublished mss written in 1987: copy in the Military History Research Institute, Freiburg).
104. NA, T–315/2275/592, 624.
105. NA, T–315/1474/571–2.
106. NA, T–315/1474/474–5, 799–800, 861; ZSt. AR 2415/67, 440–5 (Diary of Kurt L.).
107. Husemann, *Guten Glaubens*, ii, 221, 602; NA, T–315/2275/589.
108. NA, T–315/1474/568–9.
109. NA, T–315/1299/358.
110. NA, T–315/2275/585.
111. NA, T–315/2275/620.
112. E.g. NA, T–315/2275/590; R.L. Quinnett, 'The German Army Confronts the NSFO', *JCH*, 13 (1978), 53–64; M. Messerschmidt, 'The Wehrmacht and the *Volksgemeinschaft*', *JCH*, 18 (1983), 719–44.
113. Ibid.; Bartov *The Eastern Front, passim*; in Greece, the NSFO was slow to get off the ground; see BA–MA, RH 24–68/35, 'Tätigkeitsbericht 1c vom 1/1–30/6/44'.
114. NA, T–315/1474/469, 573–4; T–315/1300/246. Letter from Herr K., March 1990.
115. NA, T–311/175/925; T–315/1474/467.
116. NA, T–315/64/56; T–315/2275/588.
117. NA, T–315/1299/1051; cf. T. Copp and B. McAndrew, *Battle Exhaustion: Soldiers and Psychiatrists in the Canadian Army, 1939–1945* (Montreal and London, 1990), 126–7.
118. NA, T–315/1299/358–9, 1051.
119. NA, T–315/1474/573, 466; T–315/2275/598. Bartov, in *Hitler's Army*, chapter 3, has emphasized the importance of harsh military discipline in maintaining cohesion in the Wehrmacht. Undoubtedly this was more important for front-line troops than for those on occupation duties in relatively quiet areas like Greece. Deserters were shot, and mutineers arrested, but in general the troops in Greece do not appear to resemble the 'very frightened' men, kept in check by a 'terroristic system of discipline' depicted by Bartov (p. 104).
120. BDC, personnel files on Fritz Lautenbach and Georg Weichenrieder.
121. Ibid., file on Josef Salminger.
122. NA, T–315/1299/935.
123. NA, T–315/1299/362; NA, M–893/4/247.

124. NA, T–315/69/1119, 1247.
125. NA, T–315/72/187; Husemann, *Guten Glaubens*, ii, 308; ZSt. AR 2415/67, 183.
126. Husemann, *Guten Glaubens*, ii, 604; ZSt. AR 2415/67, 314.
127. ZSt. AR 2415/67, 413; ZSt. AR 1763/62, 139–40.
128. H.-P. Klausch, *Die 999er: von der Brigade 'Z' zur Afrika-Division 999* (Frankfurt a. Main, 1986) 138–40.
129. ZSt. AR 2056/67, 20, 98–9, 110–13.
130. On the role of the GFP in investigating anti-partisan 'excesses', see ZSt. AR 418/63, 96–8; most of the Distomo correspondence is to be found in IWM, 352, FO 646 (case vii 'Hostages'), book 21.
131. ZSt. AR 301/5–VU5, iii, 218–21.
132. Information on Lautenbach, Schmedes and Schümers from BDC personnel files; Schümers is also described in the post-mortem on the Klisura massacre, NOKW-469, IWM 352/FO 646, Defence doc. book 21.
133. Klausch, *Die 999er*, 138–40; IWM, 345, FO 646, Defence doc. book 1, Georg Lipp affidavit, 12 July 1947.
134. NA, T–315/64/57.
135. NA, T–315/64/20–23.
136. NA, T–311/188/984–5.
137. NA, T–311/188/1003.
138. NA, T–311/188/985, 1002; T–311/179/1266.
139. NA, T–311/179/1269.
140. IWM, 343, FO 646, Defence doc. book 3, Franz Fritsch affidavit, 28 Sept. 1947.
141. NA, T–311/188/1004; T–311/179/1266–7.
142. NA, T–311/179/1266–7.
143. PAAA, R 27542, Vogel–Berlin, 1 May 1941, and ibid., 30 April 1941; ibid. R 29612, Altenburg–Berlin, 1 May 1941.
144. PAAA, R 29614, Altenburg–Berlin, 3 Dec. 1942; R 101082,

'Vortragsnotiz', 12 Dec. 1942; BDC, Dörhage personnel file; Thames Documents: Interview with Walter Kraushaar, 16 March 1988, and with Erhard Gudrich, 18 March 1988, two former members of the Abwehr, based in Athens.
145. NA, M–893/4/469–71; BA/K, NS 7/99–1, 27 May 1944.
146. ZSt., Verschiedenes, 8, 2190–1; K. Moczarski, *Gespräche mit dem Henker* (Düsseldorf, 1978), 290–304.
147. *TWC*, ix, 1307, NOKW–1438, 7 Sept. 1943.
148. Moczarski, *Gespräche*, 296–8.
149. *TMWC*, xi, 237, 422; H. Ritter, 'Hermann Neubacher and the Austrian Anschluss Movement, 1918–1940', *CEH* (Dec. 1975), 348–70; R. Luza, *Austro-German Relations in the Anschluss Era* (Princeton, 1975), 153–254; NA, RG 165/179, box 738, 'IIR no. 36: Dr H. Neubacher', 29 Jan. 1946.
150. ZSt. AR–Z, 26/63, Blume affidavit, 1159–63; BDC, Stroop personnel file.
151. FO 645, box 8: doc. 1919–PS; IfZ Zs 1420, 'Vernehmung von Walter Schimana', 25 April 1947, 7.
152. BDC, Walter Schimana, personnel file; Blume affidavit, ZSt. AR–Z 26/63, 1163; RG 165/179, 'IIR no. 6: Walter Schimana', 31 July 1945.
153. IWM, Thomashausen, *Beiträge*; Hitler's support for Neubacher is outlined in BA–MA, RH 19 XI/82, HGrF 1c/AO, 4 Nov. 1943.
154. See Schimana's remarks in IfZ, Zs 1420, 'Vernehmung des Walter Schimana', 3 Feb. 1947, 14–15. On relations generally between the SiPo/SD and the HSSPF see A. Buchheim, *Die SS-das Herrschaftsinstrument, Befehl und Gehorsam* (Munich, 1989 ed.) 113–45.
155. 'Mia Katathesis', *Istorikon Archeion Ethnikis Antistaseos*, 25–

6 (Athens, 1960), 81–102; BA/K, NS 19/3695, also R 70 Griechenland/1–3.

156. ZSt. AR–Z 26/63, 1077, Karl S. affidavit; NA, T–175/475/9–49, n.d.; ZSt. AR–Z 26/63, 1134, Alfred S. affidavit; P. Enepekides, *Oi diogmoi ton Evraion en Elladi, 1941–1944* (Athens, 1969), 147–9.

157. ZSt. AR–Z 26/63, 1028; IWM, 352, NOKW–1245 (117 Jg.Div. round-ups in the Peloponnese); on the GFP, Gessner, *Geheime Feldpolizei*.

158. T–501/258/602, 'Entwurf eines Befehls über Sühnemassnahmen', 16 Jan. 1944; ZSt. AR 1798/67, Ioannis Papassiopoulos affidavit, 23–4.

159. ZSt. AR 1798/67, Carl T. affidavit, 42–9; Skouras *et al.*, *Psychopathologia*, 122–3, 126.

160. Skouras, *Psychopathologia*, 136.

161. Mary Henderson, *Xenia – A Memoir: Greece, 1919–1949* (London, 1988), 74.

162. NA, M–893/4/760–1.

163. Skouras *et al.*, *Psychopathologia*, 121.

164. Cf. ibid., 131; 'Haidari' in *Anexartisia* (Athens), 14–15 Oct. 1944.

165. NA, T–175/474/2996172, BdSD/Gr.–RSHA, Athens, 5 June 1944.

166. NA, T–175/474/2996134, 2996156–8, 2996164–5, and 2996172.

167. BDC, P. Radomski personnel file.

168. Ibid.

169. Ibid., Hans Dörhage personnel file.

170. See Gellatelly, *The Gestapo and German Society*, 50–1, and the apposite comments of M. Burleigh and W. Wippermann in *The Racial State: Germany 1933–1945* (Cambridge, 1991), 98.

171. BDC, Walter Blume personnel file; further details in IfZ Zs 2389.

172. *TWC*, iv, 139–40, 529–32; the full transcript of Blume's pre-trial interrogation is IfZ Zs 2389, 'Vernehmung: Walter Blume,' 29 June 1947; also FO 646: (case vii: 'Einsatzgruppen, Sept. 15–Oct. 7, 1947', book 1, 158, 345.

173. *TWC*, iv, 531.

174. ZSt, AR–Z, 26/63, 1150, affidavit of Karl M.

175. NA, RG 226/L47196, 'Personalities and Political Manoeuvring in the Rallis Government', 1 Oct. 1944.

176. PAAA, R 99260, Neubacher–Kaltenbrunner, 27 Nov. 1943; PAAA R 99230, 'Notiz für den Herrn RAM', Berlin, 7 Nov. 1943; Schimana affidavit, IfZ Zs 1420, p. 38.

177. PAAA, R 27301/75, 110, 157–8; R 27302/78.

178. PAAA, R 27302/74.

179. PAAA, R 27302/8, 9.

180. PAAA, R 27301/26; R. Hampe, *Die Rettung Athens im Oktober 1944* (Wiesbaden, 1955), 17–50.

181. The point is well made by Burleigh and Wippermann in *The Racial State*, chs 3 and 4.

182. PAAA, R 99419, Rademacher–Athens, 22 July 1940.

183. FO 645/303, USA–371, Rosenberg–Bormann, 23 April 1941; BA/K, NS 30/75, 'Abschlussbericht über die Tätigkeit des Sonderkommandos Rosenberg in Griechenland', 15 Nov. 1941; *NCA*, iii (Washington, 1946), 200–3.

184. Report by Isaac Matarasso, 'L'occupation allemande de Salonique et les juifs', Jan. 1945, American Joint Distribution Committee, Jerusalem, Israel. (My thanks to Steve Bowman for providing me with a copy of this document.)

185. Rochlitz, 'Notiziario della settimana', 27 May 1942; ZSt. AR–Z 139/59, 216–21.

186. *Apoyevmatini*, 8 July 1942; Matarasso, 'L'occupation allemande de Salonique et les juifs'; M. Novitch, *To Perasma ton Var-*

varon (Athens, 1985), 101.

187. Rochlitz, 'Notiziario' 184–93; NA, RG 226/65281, 'Note on the Labor Battalions of Jews Sent from Salonica in 1942 and 1943', 18 March 1944.

188. M. Molho & J. Nehama, *In Memoriam-Homage aux victimes juives des Nazis en Grèce* (Salonika, 1975 ed.), 386.

189. *TMWC*, iv (Nuremberg, 1947), 355–8; this is a summary. The complete series of Wisliceny interrogations is to be found in the Imperial War Museum, FO 645/162. See also, L. Rothkirchen, 'Vatican Policy and the "Jewish Problem" in "Independent" Slovakia (1939–1945),' *Yad Vashem Studies*, vi (1967), 41.

190. E. Sevillias (trans. N. Stavroulakis), *From Athens to Auschwitz* (Athens, 1983), 5.

191. ZSt. AR–Z 139/59 (Merten trial), 217: Friedrich Heine testimony; Steinberg, *All or Nothing*, p. 86; FO 645/162, 'Testimony of Dieter Wisliceny at Nurnberg, 2/4/46'.

192. Rochlitz, 'Notiziario', 19 Feb. 1943; ibid., 'Notiziario', 25 Feb. 1943; ibid., 'Misure contro gli ebrei di Salonicco', 27 Feb. 1943; *Apoyevmatini*, 27 Feb. 1943.

193. PAAA, R 100870/76–7, Schönberg–Berlin, 15 March 1943.

194. PAAA, vol. 66 (Deutsche Gesandtschaft–Athen), Wisliceny–Merten, 15 April 1943.

195. ZSt. AR–Z 139/59, 566–7.

196. NA, RG 226/41745, 'Interview with a Young Jewess Who Left Salonica July 8, 1943', 7 Aug. 1943; Steinberg, *All or Nothing*, 100; Molho, *In Memoriam*, 326; Danuta Czech gives the figure of 45,853 arrivals from Salonika, of whom 35,762 were immediately gassed, 'Deportation und Vernichting der Griechischen Juden im KL Auschwitz', *Hefte von Auschwitz*, 11 (1970), 5–37.

197. *Apoyevmatini*, 9 Nov. 1942.

198. ZSt. AR–Z 139/59, ii, 186; Molho, *In Memoriam*, 133, 137.

199. NG–5050, von Thadden, 24 July 1943; PAAA, R 100871, 'Aufzeichnung', von Thadden, 21 July 1943; on von Thadden, see H.-J. Döscher, *SS und Auswärtiges Amt im Dritten Reich*, (Frankfurt, 1991) 276–81; PAAA, R 100871, 26 July 1943.

200. Steinberg, *All or Nothing*, 97–102; MFA/AD, Athens Embassy, box 152, no.36 (19 March 1943), and no.50 (6 April 1943).

201. NA, T–821/248/189, 'Campagna antisemita in Macedonia', 28 April 1943; PAAA, R 100871, von Thadden–Eichmann, 19 June 1943; NA, RG 226/13270, 'Anti-Semitic Measures', in 'The Jews in Greece, 1941–1944', *Journal of the Hellenic Diaspora*, 12,2 (1985), 30–1; NA, RG 226/120, box 29/203, 'Greece:Censorship', 11 May 1944.

202. G. Ioannou, *To Diko Mas Aima* (Athens, 1978), 60–1.

203. ZSt. AR–Z 139/59, ii, 244–5.

204. Greek Ministry of Justice, Archives of the Service for the Disposal of Jewish Property: 'Ekthesis', 13 June 1943.

205. Greek Ministry of Justice, 'Praktikon synedriaseos tis 31is Maiou 1943'.

206. ZSt. AR–Z, 139/59, 270, 294.

207. Ibid., 248–51.

208. Ibid., 252.

209. Matarasso, 'L'occupation allemande de Salonique et les juifs'; NA, RG 59/868.00/1324, Berry (Istanbul)–State, 6 Dec. 1943, enclosing 'Memorandum of Dim. Andreades, Nomarch of Drama, Concerning the Situation in Macedonia', 18 Oct. 1943.

210. Yad Vashem archives: YV/M, 4–5 (Rescue Committee of the Jewish Agency for Palestine), 'State of the Jews in Greece, April, 1945'.

211. On this whole question, see Steinberg, *All or Nothing, passim.* Geloso's story is in his 'Due anni in Grecia al Comando dell'11 Armata', copy in Archives du Centre de Documentation Juive Contemporaine, (ACDJC) CCCLXXX–10. Eichmann found Italian proposals unacceptable. URO, *Judenverfolgung,* 165, Rademacher–Ribbentrop, 19 March 1943.

212. ACDJC, CXXVII–12, NG–5048, Henke 'Memorandum', 12 May 1943

213. BA/K, R 70 (Griechenland), RSHA/1a–Bfh.SiPo/SD in Athens, 24 Sept. 1943; Moczarski, *Gespräche,* 293–301; Yad Vashem archives, DIV/54–1, Wisliceny affidavit, 5.

214. NA, RG 226/190, 73/27, 'Statement on the Jews in Greece and Their Present Situation', E. Barzilai, 14 June 1944.

215. Simbi testimony in Novitch, *To Perasma,* 42–3; a slightly different account is provided in the interview with S.M. July 1977, Hebrew University, Institute of Contemporary Jewry, Oral History Division. My thanks to Steve Bowman for making this document available to me; also S. Bowman 'Joseph Matsas and the Greek Resistance', *Journal of the Hellenic Diaspora,* 17,1 (1991), 60, for yet another version.

216. Moczarski, *Gespräche,* 301; URO, *Judenverfolgung,* 195; OSS, R and A, 2500.4 'German Military Government over Europe: Greece', 1 Dec. 1944.

217. PAAA, vol. 69, Rallis–Altenburg, 7 Oct. 1943.

218. PAAA, R 99419, 'Vortragsnotiz', 22 Oct. 1943; von Thadden, 'Vermerk', 26 Jan. 1944; FO 645, box 162, 'Wisliceny Testimony', 23 Nov. 1945, 18; PAAA, R 100870, von Thadden–Eichmann, 2 Dec. 1943; R 100871, Graevenitz–Berlin, 3

April 1944.

219. FO 645/162, 'Wisliceny Testimony', 23 Nov. 1945.

220. ZSt. AR–Z 26/63, 937, 1175, Linnemann affidavit; D. Czech, *Kalendarium der Ereignisse im Konzentrationslager Auschwitz–Birkenau, 1939–1945* (Hamburg, 1989), 754.

221. On disposal of Jewish property in Jannina and Preveza, see WO 204/9349 'Jannina: Intelligence' (n.d.).

222. Interview with Armandos Aaron, March 1988.

223. Thames documents, Athens bundle, pp. 251–6; 1c–Aussenstelle Korfu – Korpsgruppe Joannina/1c, 25 April 1944; ZSt. AR–Z 26/63, 947–8.

224. BA–MA RH 24–22/23, Jaeger–Gen.Kdo.22 AK, 14 May 1944; cf. Steinberg, *All or Nothing,* 174–5.

225. ZSt. AR–Z 26/63, 948.

226. Interview with Armandos Aaron, March 1988.

227. ZSt. AR–Z 26/63, 475, Rekanati affidavit.

228. Interview with Perla Soussi, March 1988.

229. NOKW–855, 12 May 1944; ZSt. AR–Z 26/63, 478, Rekanati affidavit.

230. Danuta Czech, 'Deportation und Vernichtung der Griechischen Juden im KL Auschwitz', *Hefte von Auschwitz,* 11 (1970), 5–37; Höss in *NCA,* vii (Washington, 1946), 608; Wisliceny in FO 645/162, 'Testimony of Dieter Wisliceny taken at Nurnberg', 17 Nov. 1945.

231. Czech, 'Deportation und Vernichtung', 5–37.

232. Sevillias, *Athens–Auschwitz,* 1; Ioannou, *To Diko Mas Aima,* 51.

233. Reuven Dafni and Yehudit Kleiman (eds), *Final Letters from the Yad Vashem Archive* (London, 1991), 122.

234. BA/K, NS 30/75, 'Abschlussbericht', 15 Nov. 1941; Hondros,

Occupation and Resistance, 93;
Larissaikos Typos, 4 April 1943;
Novitch, *To Perasma*, 56.

235. L. Poliakov and J. Sabille, *The Jews under the Italian Occupation* (Paris, 1955), 158–9; NA, RG 226/50292, 'An Appeal Issued in Athens on Behalf of Jews', 20 Nov. 1943; RG 226/49692, 'Information Concerning Jews in Greece', 11 Nov. 1943; RG 226/65281, 'The Present Status of Jews in Greece', 18 March 1944.

236. NA, RG 226/67911, 'Occupied Greece: Fate of Jewish Communities and Assistance Given to Them by the Greek Christians', 27 March 1944.

237. The Jewish Museum of Greece, *Newsletter*, 28 (winter 1990), 8.

238. NA, RG 226/190, 73/27, 'Statement on the Jews', E. Barzilai, 14 June 1944; Novitch, *To Perasma*, 75–6.

239. NA, RG 226/120, 29/203, 'Captured Mail from Amorgos–Ios', 20 June 1944; RG 226/65281, 'The Present Status of Jews in Greece', 18 March 1944; RG 226/49692, 'Information Concerning Jews in Greece', 11 Nov. 1943.

PART FOUR   A Society at War: 1943–44

1. L. Baerentzen (ed.), *British Reports on Greece: 1943–1944* (Copenhagen, 1982), 2–3.

2. FO 371/43690 R11347/9; G. Kolko, *The Politics of War: the World and US Foreign Policy, 1943–1945* (New York, 1990; first published 1968), 173.

3. FO 188/438, 22 Nov. 1944; FO 371/43674 R226/9, 'General Notes on Public Opinion', 22 Dec. 1943.

4. Kolko, *Politics of War*, xxii.

5. FO 371/43676 R1046/9, 'Periodical Intelligence Summary: Greek Internal Situation', 9 Jan. 1944; *Protoporoi*, 1 (Dec. 1943), Gray Coll.

6. R. Kapuscinski, *The Soccer War* (London, 1990), 108; NA, RG 226/80220, 'Comments on the Situation in Greece by Recent Arrivals', 21 June 1944; *Eleftheros Ellin*, year 2, 12 (n.d.), 'To Pistevo Mas', Gray Coll.

7. NA, RG 226/120, 30/208, 2 Dec. 1944.

8. M. Antonopoulou, 'I ekdochi tou "exeliktikou marxismou" stin Ellada kai i amfisvitisi tis (1930–1945)', *Ta Istorika*, 10 (June, 1989), 139; G. Katsouli, *Istoria tou* *Kommounistikou Kommatos Elladas*, (Athens, n.d.), 98; H. Fleischer, *Im Kreuzschatten der Mächte: Griechenland 1941–1944*, 2 vols (Frankfurt, 1986), i, 493ff.

9. G. Theotokas, *Tetradia imerologiou (1939–1953)* (Athens, n.d.), 511.

10. See G. Beikos, *I laiki exousia stin Eleftheri Ellada*, i (Athens, 1979), *passim* and G. Beikos, *EAM kai Laiki Autodioikisi* (Thessaloniki, 1976).

11. Beikos, *I laiki exousia*, i, 387–9, 499–510.

12. D. Zepos, *Laiki Dikaiosyni eis tas eleftheras periochas tis ypo katochin Ellados* (Athens, 1945), 4–5; L. Stavrianos, 'The Greek National Liberation Front (EAM): A Study in Resistance Organization and Administration', *Journal of Modern History*, 24 (March, 1952), 47.

13. Stavrianos, 'Greek National Liberation Front (EAM)', 50–1.

14. NA, RG 226/144, 100/1051, Moyers Diary; RG 226/XL 975, 'ELAS and EAM in Euboea', 26 June 1944; Stavrianos, 'Greek National Liberation Front (EAM)', 51; Th. Tsouparopoulos, *Oi laokratikoi thesmoi tis ethnikis antistasis* (Athens, 1989), 260.

15. NA, RG 226/144, 100/1051, Moyers Diary, 19 March 1944.

16. NA, RG 226/190, 3/34, 'Pros ta laika dikastiria: syntomes odigies yia ton tropo tis leitourgias tous.' (n.d., but Aug. 1944).

17. Stavrianos, 'Greek National Liberation Front (EAM)', 48–9.

18. This and the following paragraphs draw upon N. Koliou, *Agnostes ptyches katochis kai antistasis 1941–44*, ii (Volos, 1986), 1013–21.

19. On crime in the first year in Argastali, see *Tachydromos* (Volos), 11 April 1942.

20. G. Kotzioulas, *Theatro sta vouna* (Athens, 1976), 157–82.

21. R. Stites, *Revolutionary Dreams: Utopian Vision and Experimental Life in the Russian Revolution* (New York, 1989).

22. See also L. Myrsiades, 'Resistance Theatre and the German Occupation', *Journal of the Hellenic Diaspora* (1992), 5–36.

23. Kotzioulas, *Theatro*, 359, 308–9, 252–3.

24. Ibid., 350–1.

25. C. Couvaras, *OSS with the Central Committee of EAM* (San Francisco, 1982), 26, 74, 118–21; NA, RG 226/190, 2/26, 'Ap'ti drasi tis EPON Stereas Elladas'; RG 226/190, 3/40, 'Voice of Youth', Serres, 23 Dec. 1943; see also J. Hart, 'Women in the Greek Resistance: National Crisis and Political Transformation', *International Labor and Working-Class History*, 38 (Fall 1990), 46–62.

26. P. Antaios, *Symvoli stin istoria tis EPON*, 3 vols (Athens, 1977–79).

27. Myrsiades, 'Resistance Theatre', 18; Koliou, *Agnostes ptyches*, ii, 836–8.

28. Koliou, *Agnostes ptyches*, i, 141–2; Hart, 'Women in the Greek Resistance' 46–62.

29. P. Roussos, *H Megali Pentaetia, 1940–1945*, i (Athens, 1978), 355–9; FO 371/43674 R14531/7185,

'Introductory Report on Sub-Area Vitsi by Captain P.H. Evans', 7 Aug. 1944.

30. Tsouparopoulos, *Laokratikoi thesmoi*, 235–51.

31. Kotzioulas, *Theatro*, 37–8.

32. Myrsiades, 'Resistance Theatre', 12–13; M. Djilas, *Wartime: with Tito and the Partisans* (London, 1977), 59.

33. NA, RG 226/190, 3/44, 'KKE: Internal Party Bulletin no. 13, Dec. 1943'.

34. M. Djilas, *Wartime*, 88.

35. 'I dychroni drasi tou EAM' (n.d.), Gray Coll.

36. *Eleftheriotis*, 1, 5 (17 Aug. 1943), Gray Coll.; Karl L. Rankin Papers, Mudd Library, Princeton, box 6, 'OPLA – The Greek Gestapo'.

37. *Foni tou Moria*, 1, 5 (10 July 1944), Gray Coll.

38. *Eleftheriotis*, (30 Jan. 1944), ibid.

39. NA, RG 226/154, 39/580, Hartmeister Report; *Eleftheriotis*, 1, 6 (22 Aug. 1943), Gray Coll.; *Odigitis* (1 Feb. 1944), ibid.; NA, RG 226/56828, 'A Greek Underground Paper'.

40. NA, RG 226/144, 9/976, Interrogation of John Liapes; ibid., Interrogation of Evangelos Beltzios, 27 Oct. 1943.

41. FO 371/43691 R12720/9, 2 Aug. 1944; NA, RG 226/154, 39/576, 'Operational Report of Capt. Edward N. Kimball, Jr. Greece, 24 July to 11 Nov. 1944'; RG 226/154, 39/580, 'Report of Activities in Greece by Lt. Joel T. Hartmeister'.

42. A. Zaoussis, *Anamniseis enos antieroa (1933–1944)* (Athens, 1980), 137, 161, 257–8.

43. Hadzis, *I nikifora epanastasi pou chathike*, iii (Athens, 1982), 314; RG 226/154, 39/576, 'Operational Report of Capt. Edward N. Kimball, Jr. Greece, 24 July to 11 Nov. 1944,; NA, RG 226/154, 39/580, 'Report of Activities in Greece by Lt. Joel T.

Hartmeister'.

44. *Lefteria*, 5 (15 Dec. 1943), Patras.
45. Roussos, *Megali Pentaetia*, i, 541; Svolos had many misgivings, NA, RG 226/120, 30/208.
46. Roussos, *Megali Pentaetia*, ii, 54–5.
47. Lars Baerentzen, 'I laiki ypostirixi tou EAM sto telos tis Katochis', *Mnimon*, 9 (1984), 159.
48. Ibid., 160.
49. Ibid., 162–3; Stavrianos, 'Greek National Liberation Front (EAM)', 53.
50. NA, RG 226/L43800, 'National Council and Election of Councillors', 15 Aug. 1944.
51. On Setta, see Couvaras, *OSS*, 23–6; NA, RG 226/L43800.
52. NA, on the National Council, see *Ethniko Symvoulio: Periliptika praktika ergasion tis protis synodou tou* (Koryschades, 1988).
53. Couvaras, *OSS*, 22–3; Theotokas, *Tetradia imerologiou*, 511.
54. C.M. Woodhouse, *The Struggle for Greece 1941–1949* (London, 1976), 85; Hadzis, *I nikifora epanastasi pou chathike*, iii (Athens, 1982), 292–304, quotes from pp. 292, 300. Hadzis' account is put into perspective by Michael S. Macrakis, 'Russian Mission on the Mountains of Greece, Summer 1944 (A View from the Ranks)' *Journal of Contemporary History*, 23 (1988), 387–408.
55. NA, RG 226/80220.
56. K. Papasteriopoulos, *O Moreas sta opla*, ii (Athens, 1965), 43, 46, 48–9.
57. NA, RG 226/190, 3/40.
58. NA, RG 226/120, 29/203, 'Greece: Censorship, 27 Aug. 1944 (Letters)'; A. Zaoussis, *Anamniseis*, 212; WO 204/8312, 'History of 23rd Armoured Brigade in Greece'; D. Hamilton-Hill, *SOE Assignment* (London, 1975), 141.
59. For Siantos's explicit reservations about the *andartiko* in December 1942, see his speech in *Kom-

mounistiki Epitheorisi: tis epochis tis fasistikis katochis, 1941–1944* (Athens, 1976), 289–90.
60. S. Sarafis, *ELAS: Greek Resistance Army* (London, 1980), 100–1. For a suggestive discussion of the Yugoslav case, see F.W. Deakin, *The Embattled Mountain* (Oxford, 1971), 87–91, 98–100.
61. [A. Sevastaki], Kapetan Boukouvalas, *To andartiko ippiko tis Thessalias* (Athens, 1978), 47–59; also M. Vafiades, *Apomnimonevmata* (Athens, 1985), ii, 115.
62. Th. Mitsopoulos, *To 30° Syntagma tou ELAS* (Athens, 1987), 68–106.
63. Ibid., 96.
64. Cf. Sarafis, *ELAS*, 156.
65. On Tsavelas, see G. Kotzioulas, *Otan imouna me ton Ari: anamniseis* (Athens, 1965), 177–8, n. 4.; Boukouvalas, *Andartiko ippiko*, 72–3, 262–8; NA, RG 226/120, 30/208, 'ELAS Personalities', 23 Jan. 1945.
66. Vafiades, *Apomnimonevmata*, ii, 75–9.
67. Ibid.
68. Boukouvalas, *Andartiko ippiko*, 370–2.
69. D. Eudes, *The Kapetanios: Partisans and Civil War in Greece, 1943–1949* (New York, 1972).
70. S. Veopoulos, *To Sfalma* (Athens, 1961), 73; G. Zaroyiannis, *Anamniseis apo tin ethniki antistasi (ELAS), 1940–1944* (Athens, n.d.), 43–7, 149; Sarafis, *ELAS*, 168; Woodhouse, *Struggle for Greece*, 25, 45.
71. G. Chandler, *The Divided Land: An Anglo-Greek Tragedy* (London, 1959), 16; Vafiades, *Apomnimonevmata*, ii, 113, 146, 196–221; NA, RG 226/154, 39/586, 'Feasibility of the Formation of a "National Army" in Greece', 24 June 1944.
72. Vafiades, *Apomnimonevmata*, ii, 46; Sarafis, *ELAS*, 159–60.
73. Mitsopoulos, *30° Syntagma*, 109, 258–9.

74. NA, RG 226/144, 100/1051, Moyers Diary, entry for 10 Feb. 1944; RG 226/120, 30/154, Triforos Report.

75. Sarafis, *ELAS*, 402; Couvaras, *OSS*, 58–61.

76. J. Mulgan, *Report on Experience*, (Oxford, 1947), 100–1.

77. H. Fleischer and A. Stergellis (eds) 'Imerologion Phaidona Maidoni (24.6–10.9.44)', *Mnimon*, 9 (1984), 110.

78. Mitsopoulos, *30° Syntagma*, 561, 628–9.

79. LDG archives, INFO IV, 'Bulletin of Press, no. 3', Athens 5 Nov. 1946; cf. the brilliant study by G. Margaritis, *Apotin itta stin exegersi* (Athens, 1993), ch. 1.

80. LDG archives, INFO XI: 'Prisons, 1945–67: Individual Dossiers'.

81. Koliou, *Agnostes ptyches*, ii, 423–4.

82. For Lakonia, see Papasteriopoulos, *O Morias sta opla*, iii, 253–4; Thessaly, Koliou, *Agnostes ptyches*, ii, 457–9, 377 (Papastafidas family).

83. Mitsopoulos, *30° Syntagma*, 62–9.

84. Ibid., 265.

85. NA, RG 226/190, 3/34, ELAS letter sent 25 Aug. 1944 to a gendarme in Karystos.

86. For examples from Patras, see V.K. Lazaris, *Politiki Istoria tis Patras: 1940–1944*, iii (Athens, 1989), 170; for Evvia, G. Douatzis, *Oi tagmatasfalites tis Evvias* (Athens, 1982), 182–3.

87. LDG archives, INFO IV, 'Bulletin of Press. No. 3', Athens, 5 Nov. 1946; RG 226/154, 39/564, 'Report of Capt. Winston Ehrgott on Greece'.

88. C. Jecchinis, *Beyond Olympos* (Athens, repr. 1988), 93; Novitch, *To Perasma ton Varvaron* (Athens, 1985), 75–6; N. Hammond, *Venture into Greece* (London, 1983), 21.

89. Couvaras, *OSS*, 61–9; Djilas, *Wartime*, 127.

90. Portraits from a variety of accounts, including D. Dimitriou, *Gorgopotamos* (Athens, 1975), 12–19; NA, RG 226/190, 2/19, 24 July 1944.

91. G. Papakonstantinou, *Enthymimata potismena me aima kai dakrya* (Athens, 1985), 140, Zaroyiannis, *Anamniseis*, 50–1; NA, RG 226/190, 3/40, 8 June 1944.

92. Koliou, *Agnostes ptyches*, ii, 374; Papakonstantinou, *Enthymimata*, 290.

93. K. Papasteriopoulos, *O Morias sta opla*, ii, 19.

94. Papasteriopoulos, *O Morias sta opla*, ii, 19; Koliou, *Agnostes ptyches*, ii, 472; WO 106/3158; Boukouvalas, *Andartiko ippiko*, 368–9; Mitsopoulos, *30° Syntagma*, 216.

95. This draws heavily upon Riki van Boeschoten, 'From Armatolik to People's Rule: Investigations into the Collective Memory of Rural Greece, 1750–1949' (University of Amsterdam, Ph.D., 1989).

96. Boukouvalas, *Andartiko ippiko*, 31, 36; van Boeschoten, 'Armatolik to People's Rule', 157.

97. See the case of Georgios Davidis, a farmer from near Florina, who moved from prewar involvement in the co-operative movement into the *andartiko*, LDG archives, INFO XI, 'Prisons, 1945–67: Individual Dossiers'.

98. NA, RG 226/190, 3/40, 'Ekthesis yia ta gegonota tis 3/6/44'; RG 226/190, 3/40, 'Day's Command', II/87, 8 June 1944.

99. Van Boeschoten, 'Armatolik to People's Rule', 243–4; Couvaras, *OSS*, 69; Makriyiannis cited in K. Andrews (ed.), *Athens Alive* (Athens, 1979), 218; NA, RG 226/190, 1/5, 'Odysseus'–Georgiades, 7 Dec. 1943.

100. NA, RG 226/144, 100/1051, Moyers Diary, entry for 12 Jan. 1944; for the clashes between

Aris and the KKE leadership, see e.g. Hadzis, *I nikifora epanastasi pou chathike*, iii, 77, 83.

101. Papakonstantinou, *Enthymimata*, 142–3; Couvaras, *OSS*, 120–1.

102. OSS, NA, RG 226/144, 100/1051, Moyers Diary, 25 March 1944; Papasteriopoulos, *O Morias sta opla*, ii, 276; I adzis, *Chnikifora epanastasi*, iii, 37.

103. B. Davidson, *Scenes from the Anti-Nazi War* (New York, 1980), 152; NA, RG 226/112837, 22 Feb. 1945.

104. NA, RG 226/154, 39/564; cf. Deakin's comments on the ideology of the Yugoslav partisans in *Embattled Mountain*, 107.

105. IWM, 88/6/1, Hudson, 'A Valley in Greece'; Mitsopoulos, *30° Syntagma*, 56; RG 226/154, 39/564.

106. NA, RG 226/154, 39/579, 'Report of Lt. Wallace C. Hughling, AC on Activities in Greece'.

107. Boukouvalas, *Andartiko ippiko*, 183; WO 204/8869, 15 Feb. 1944.

108. Zaroyianni, *Anamniseis*, 226–9.

109. Couvaras, *OSS*, 120–2.

110. Papakonstantinou, *Enthymimata*, 384–5; R. Cobb, *The People's Armies*, trans. by M. Elliott (New Haven & London, 1987), 221.

111. Boukouvalas, *Andartiko ippiko*, 34–5, 140–1.

112. Ibid., 78–9; for the mentality at work, cf. Vafiades, *Apomnimonevmata*, ii, 153–6; WO 204/8312.

113. NA, RG 226/190, 1/15, Aleko–Rodney, 12 Dec. 1943.

114. NA, RG 226/190, 1/5, Odysseus–Greek Consulate in Adrianople, 10 Sept. 1943, and Odysseus–Georgiades, 7 Dec. 1943, and 'Exact Copy of a Letter Received by Aleko from ODYSSEUS', 6 Feb. 1944.

115. Ibid., Petritzikis statement.

116. NA, RG 226/190, 1/13, 'Present Conditions in Evros'.

117. NA, RG 226/190, 1/5, 'New Conditions of Evros Antartika and My Trip to Limeria – My Impressions', (Aleko), n.d.; cf. V. Kasapis, *Ston Korfo tis Gymbrenas: chroniko tis ethnikis antistasis ston evro*, 2 vols (Athens, 1977).

118. Veopoulos, *Sfalma*, 363; on Roumeli, NA, RG 226/154, 39/580.

119. Cf. Cobb, *People's Armies*, 223.

120. *EK*, 7 April 1943; *SSGM*, vii, Testa–Maglione, (15 May 1943), 339–45; WO 204/6096, Radio Athens, 17 Feb. 1944.

121. FO 371/43685 R6253/9, 'Technical Personnel in Athens under the Occupation'.

122. NA, RG 59/868.00/1143 'Greece during the Occupation'; NA, RG 226/120, 29/199, 'Quisling Greek Government', 15 Sept. 1944.

123. On the backing of the political mainstream, see N. Karkanis, *Oi dosilogoi tis Katochis* (Athens, 1985), 109–10; also NA, T–821/248/255–8, Pieché–Rome: 'Grecia – il governo di Rallis', 16 July 1943.

124. FO 371/43677, Leeper–Eden, 24 Jan. 1944; Pangalos 'half-mad' in FO 371/37205, R10400; WO 208/713, 'Greek Security Battalions', App. 'H'; Fleischer, *Kreuzschatten*, i, 459–60.

125. WO 208/713.

126. Antoniou, *Istoria tis Ellinikis Vasilikis Chorofylakis*, iii (Athens, 1965), iii, 1871–93.

127. WO 208/713; FO 371/43690, 'Periodical Intelligence Summary to 30 June 1944'.

128. Lazaris, *Patras*, iii, 141–2.

129. Ibid., 148.

130. WO 208/713; Douatzis, *Oi tagmatasfalites tis Evvoias*.

131. Douatzis, *Oi tagmatasfalites tis Evvoias*, 38, 91, 118.

132. Ibid., 92.

133. Ibid., 101; NA, RG 226/190, 2/19, Stygia Mission, 24 July 1944.

134. Fleischer, *Kreuzschatten*, i, 459.

135. NA, RG 165/179, box 651, 'Members of the German Military Mission to the Greek Security Battalions in Greece' (9

Oct. 1944).

136. Lazaris, *Patras*, iii, 136; Fleischer, 'Nea stoicheia yia ti schesi germanikon archon Katochis kai Tagmata Asfaleias', *Mnimon*, 8 (1980–82), 193.

137. NA, RG 165/179, box 738, 'IIR: Hermann Neubacher', 29 Jan. 1946.

138. NA, RG 165/179, box 651, App. A 'History of the Volunteer Movement of Col. Papadongonas and his Security Battalions'; *ADAP*, v, 222 (Graevenitz–Neubacher, 7 Sept. 1944).

139. NA, RG 226/XL 39252, 28 June 1944.

140. NA, RG 226/190, 5/51 'Greek Security Battalions', 18 May 1944.

141. H. Fleischer, 'The Don Stott Affair: Overtures for an Anglo-German Local Peace in Greece', in M. Sarafis (ed.), *Greece: From Resistance to Civil War* (Nottingham, 1980), 91–103; Interview with C.M. Woodhouse, 27 Jan. 1992; WO 106/3225, 'Paper on Greece's Strategic Position in the Eastern Mediterranean by Force 133 M.E.F.', 3 May 1944. For a more balanced assessment than Fleischer's, see L. Baerentzen, 'British Strategy towards Greece in 1944', in E. Barker, J. Chadwick & F.W. Deakin (eds), *British Political and Military Strategy in Central, Eastern & Southern Europe in 1944* (London, 1988), 130–151.

142. FO 371/43674, R224/9, 'Biographical Note on "General" Napoleon Zervas', 2 Jan. 1944; For the background, see WO 204/8871, 'Greece: Political Situation'; on the links between Zervas and Dertilis, see Waldheim Documents: IfZ 1043/53, Wende Report, 'Bericht über meinen Aufenhalt in Athen vom 2.4. bis 6.4.44'; H. Petimezas, *Ethniki antistasi kai koinoniki epanastasi: Zervas kai EAM* (Athens, 1991), 346–53. On SIS ignorance of the Zervas-Lanz negotiations, see N. Clive, *A Greek Experience, 1943–1948* (Salisbury, 1985), 75.

143. WO 208/713; NA, RG 226/154, 40/601, 'Statement of Expedition inside Evvia, Feb. 25 to March 18, 1944'; RG 226/190, 2/19, Stygia Mission; RG 226/190, 78/101, 'Vlach' Mission.

144. WO 208/713, 'Greek Security Battalions', 18 July 1944; FO 898/152, Cairo–London, 14 June 1944; FO 371/43706 R8041, 22 June 1944, cited in Sarafis, *From Resistance to Civil War*, 115, fn.; NA, RG 226/L47184, 1 Oct. 1944; J.L. Hondros, 'I Megali Vrettania kai ta ellinika Tagmata Asfaleias, 1943–1944' in H. Fleischer and N. Svoronos (eds), *I Ellada 1936–1944* (Athens, 1989), 262–77.

145. NA, RG 226/L47184; L47310, 11 Oct. 1944; Lyall Wilkes, 'ELAS, the Germans and the British', *The New Statesman and Nation*, 9 March 1946; L. Wilkes, 'British Missions and Greek Quislings', *The New Statesman and Nation*, 1 Feb. 1947.

146. WO 208/713, 'Greek Security Battalions', Appendix 'M'.

147. WO 208/713, Appendix 'Q'; Volos gendarmerie referred to in an ELAS 54th Regt. intelligence bulletin, NA, RG 226/190, 3/30, 'Ekthesis genikon pliroforion', n.d.

148. NA, RG 226/190, 3/40, 13 July 1944; RG 226/XL 975, 'ELAS and EAM in Euboea', 26 June 1944.

149. On Giannis K., see NA, RG 165/179, 650/2; on EDES men in the Battalions, WO 204/8837, Lamia HQ, Force 133 – HQ, 3 Corps, 29 Nov. 1944.

150. K. Andrews, *The Flight of Ikaros* (London, 1959), 159.

151. A. Kotzias, *Poliorkia* (Athens, 1953), 95–9.

152. Based on the loot from Pili, in NA, RG 226/190, 2/19, Stygia

153. Mission, 24 July 1944; orders from battalion and gendarme commanders in the Peloponnese, in I. Papasteriopoulos, *O Morias sta opla*, ii, 260, 274.

153. NA, RG 226/L44672, 26 Aug. 1944.

154. WO 204/6094, Radio Monitoring Dept, Radio Athens, 15 Jan. 1944; Sandstrom quoted in FO 371/42363 W11214/6, Mallet–London, 13 June 1944.

155. NA, RG 226/L45701, 3 Sept. 1944; WO 204/5604, 5 Nov. 1944, 8 Nov. 1944, 14 Nov. 1944, 20 Nov. 1944.

156. M. McClintock, *Instruments of Statecraft* (New York, 1992) and the same author's 'American Doctrine and Counterinsurgent State Terror' in A. George (ed.) *Western State Terrorism* (Oxford, 1991), 121–54.

157. Karkanis, *Dosilogoi*, 225–6; WO 208/713; FO 371/43687, 9 May 1944; *Larissaikos Typos*, 20 May 1944, 20–22 June 1944.

158. *Larissaikos Typos*, 13 May 1944, 22 June 1944.

159. N. Koliou, *Agnostes ptyches Katochis kai Antistasis, 1941–44*, i (Volos, 1985), 109–10.

160. NA, RG 226/XL 43787, 7 July 1944; RG 226/190, 9/77; FO 371/48271 R10009/4, 31 May 1945; FO 371/48267, R7138/4, 11 April 1945.

161. Deas archive: 5/94, 'Report on Our Journeys in the Provinces from 15 to 21 Sept. 1944', E. Wenger, 23 Sept. 1944.

162. Deas archive: 5/107, 17 Sept. 1944; cf. the account in Ath.I.Chrysochoou, *I katochi en Makedonia*, i (Thessaloniki, 1949), 148–9. Chrysochoou, who was inspector-general of gendarmerie in Macedonia during the occupation, claims that the Giannitsa massacre was provoked by an ELAS attack on German soldiers, and says that retaliation was carried out by *German* troops.

163. Deas archive, 5/94, 'Report on Our Journeys'.

164. OSS, NA, RG 226/135385; On Poulos's connections with the Abwehr and the SD, see NA, RG 165/179, box 721A, 'PIR: Poulos', box 737, 'FIR:Tsimbas', and 'FIR:Papadopoulos'.

165. FO 371/37204 'Resistance Organisations in Salonika', 20 July 1943; NA, T–821/248/185, 'Notizie dalla Macedonia tedesca', 24 June 1943.

166. M. von Xylander, *Die deutsche Besatzungsherrschaft auf Kreta, 1941–1945* (Freiburg, 1989), 117–18; BA–MA, RH 26–22/79, KTB, 1c Anlagen, 20 Sept. 1943 and 8 Oct. 1943.

167. NA, RG 226/154, 39/568, Maclean Report.

168. Poulos's German liaison officer was a member of the Hamburg police force called Kurt Tobias: BA/K, R 19/135, 'Nachweisung über Samtliche Verwaltungsbeamte im Bereich des Befehlshabers der Ordnungspolizei Griechenland nach dem Stande vom 1.7.44'.

169. Karkanis, *Dosilogoi*, 384–8; on Poulos, FO 371/78416, R6082/10152, Chancery (Athens)–London, 15 June 1949.

170. The key source for this chapter are the extracts from daily reports of the Athens police contained in NA, RG 226/190, 3/34.

171. F. Skouras *et al.*, *Psychopathologia tis peinas, tou fovou kai tou anchous: nevroseis kai psychonevroseis* (Athens, 1947; repr. 1991), 133; FO 371/43677, Leeper–Eden, 24 Jan. 1944; Theotokas, *Tetradia imerologiou*, 444–5, 447, 463.

172. Numbers from a police source for August 1944 in NA, RG 226/190, 3/34, 'Aetos', 13 Sept. 1944; cf. O. Makris, *O ELAS tis Athinas*, (Athens, 1985), 40.

173. L. Leontidou, *Poleis tis Siopis* (Athens, 1989).

174. NA, RG 59/868.00/1388, 'Events

in Nea Kokkinia, Kalogreza and other Refugee Districts', 15 April 1944.

175. Ibid.

176. Ibid.

177. Skouras *et al.*, *Psychopathologia*, 123, 125–6. The atmosphere of the 'blocco' is brilliantly evoked in Odysseus Elytis's poem *To Axion Esti* (Pittsburgh, 1974), 74–76.

178. *ADAP*, v, no. 222 (7 Sept. 1944, Graevenitz–Neubacher).

179. Fleischer, 'Nea stoicheia', 196; PAAA, R27301/8–75; FO 188/438, 'Summary of a Letter dated Athens 22nd November 1944, from Mr Justice Sandstrom, Chairman of the Greek Relief Commission to the Supervisory Board of the Swedish Red Cross'.

180. NA, RG 226/190, 3/34, 'Pliroforiai', n.d. These reports of the Athens City Police, passed on to the OSS, are the main source for the next four pages.

181. Karkanis, *Dosilogoi*, 188; Theotokas, *Tetradia imerologiou*, 457.

182. NA, RG 226 L45701, 'Political Situation in Athens', 3 Sept. 1944.

183. Karkanis, *Dosilogoi*, 192; Skouras et al., *Psychopathologia*, 122, 133.

184. Theotokas, *Tetradia imerologiou*, 468–9; Karkanis, *Dosilogoi*, 193–4.

185. *Athinaïka*, 21 Feb. 1944.

186. G.S. Loukatos, *Athinaïka tou polemou kai tis katochis*, (Athens, 1989), 189–91.

187. S.R. Zervos, *One Woman's War: A Diary of an English Woman living in Occupied Greece, 1939–1945* (Athens, 1991), 97; NA, RG 226 L45701, 'Political Situation in Athens', 3 Sept. 1944.

188. NA, RG 226/190, 3/34, 'Ekthesis', 28 July 1944; RG 226, R and A Report no.2500.4, 'German Military Government over Europe: Greece', 1 Dec. 1944, 53; P. Papastratis, *British Policy towards Greece during the Second World War, 1941–1944* (Cam-

bridge, 1984), 205; WO 204/4483, Force 133 – Force 140, 28 Sept. 1944.

189. Theotokas, *Tetradia imerologiou*, 488; NA, RG 226/190, 3/34, 'Ekthesis', 28 July 1944.

190. Theotokas, *Tetradia imerologiou*, 423; NA, RG 226/190, 3/34, 'Pliroforiai'.

191. Theotokas, *Tetradia imerologiou*, 486.

192. NA, RG 226/190, 3/34, 'Tassos'.

193. NA, RG 165/179, 651, 'CSDIC Interrogation Report on 2 German POWs', 29 July 1944.

194. FO 371/48365 R1918/1918, 21 Jan. 1945; the debate on the formation of the National Guard may be followed in: WO 204/8974; WO 204/5604. A brief but suggestive comparative discussion of the demobilisation issue in other European countries is to be found in P.J. Stavrakis, *Moscow and Greek Communism, 1944–1949* (Ithaca & London, 1989), 42–47.

195. *Rizospastis* article from end Nov. 1944 enclosed in WO 204/8837; for the situation outside Athens, see 'Account of Military & Political Events in Western Greece during the Independent Mission of 11 Indian Int. Brigade: Nov. 1944–Jan. 1945', WO 204/8301; WO 170/581 'War Diary: 23rd Armoured Brigade 1 Nov.–30 Nov. 1944' FO 371/48365 R1918/1918, 21 Jan. 1945.

196. The definitive study is L. Baerentzen, 'The Demonstration in Syntagma Square on Sunday the 3rd of December 1944', *Scandinavian Studies in Modern Greek*, 2 (1978), 3–53; WO 170/581, 'Internal Security', 3 Dec. 1944. Stavrakis, *Moscow & Greek Communism*, 37 concludes that by 3 Dec. the KKE had not decided to seize power.

197. J. Iatrides, *Revolt in Athens* (Princeton, 1972), 201.

198. C. Foley (ed.), *The Memoirs of*

General Grivas (London, 1964), 10; Th. Tsakalotos, *Saranta chronia stratiotis tis Ellados* (Athens, 1960), 598–600; 916.

199. Tsakalotos, *Saranta chronia*, 715; FO 371/48271 R9941/4, Leeper–London, 8 June 1945 ('The Excesses of the National Guard Must Be Punished'); FO 371/48271, R9355/4, 'Situation in Greece: AGIS Weekly Report no. 31: 13–19 May 1945'; H. Richter, *British Intervention in Greece: from Varkiza to Civil War* (London, 1986), 145–52.

EPILOGUE   'No Peace without Victory'

1. Army History Directorate, Athens, Mitsou archive, 'Salonika Intelligence Bulletin, no. 22', 15 Aug.–15 Sept. 1944; no. 16, 15 Feb. 1944; NA, T–78/134/6063175–6, Feldpostprüfstelle beim Okdo. H.Gr.E, 'Tätigkeitsbericht für den Monat September 1944', 1 Oct. 1944; 6063180–1, 'Zwischenbericht', 19 Sept. 1944; FO 371/43692 R14792, Boxshall–Laskey, 'Report on the Failure of Operation "Kitchenmaid"', 12 Sept. 1944; NA, RG 165/179, box 738, 'IIR: Hermann Neubacher', 29 Jan. 1946.

2. NA, RG 226/190, 2/40, 'Ekthesi yia ta gegonota tis 3–6–44 (Savvato)', 5 June 1944.

3. NA, T–78/134/6063175–7.

4. P.O. Hudson, 'A Valley in Greece', IWM 88/6/1; StA. 11/005550–9, 'Rimpatrio dalla Grecia con treno speciale di funzionari del Consolato e di altri connazionali', 8 Jan. 1945.

5. NA, RG 165/179, box 737, 'FIR: Konstantinos Tsimbas', 6 Aug. 1945; RG 165/179 box 739, 'CIR no. 13. Asts. in the Balkans'; RG 165/179, box 736, 'USFET no. 16: Panajiotis Papadopoulos', 13 July 1945.

6. NA, RG 165/179, box 721A, 'PIR, APO 758: Georg Poulos', 27 June 1945.

7. NA, RG 165/179, box 738, 'IIR no. 36: Hermann Neubacher', 29 Jan. 1946, annexe 51, 'List of Personalities in the Grand Hotel, Kitzbuehl'.

8. NA, RG 165/179, box 651, 'Detailed Interrogation Report on Six German POWs', 9 Oct. 1944.

9. FO 371/48308, R10293/52/19, Millet (Stockholm)–London, 7 June 1945, enclosing A. and E. Persson, 'Survey of Activities of the Tripolis Bureau during the Last Six Months 1944': L. Baerentzen, 'The Liberation of the Peloponnese, September 1944' in J. Iatrides (ed.) *Greece in the 1940s: A Nation in Crisis* (London, 1981), 131–141.

10. FO 371/43692, R14436/9; NA, RG 226/190, box 8/61, 'Report Submitted by Charles W. Kanes', n.d.; FO 371/58844, R738/728, Wilkes–Bevin, 10 Jan. 1946, enclosing 'Memorandum on Pending Trial of George Dallas'.

11. NA, RG 226/190, box 3/30, 'Synoptiki ekthesis', 1 April 1944; for an overall judgement, see Iatrides (ed.), *Ambassador MacVeagh Reports: Greece, 1933–1947*, ed. J. Iatrides (Princeton, 1980), 652–3.

12. NA, RG 226/L47219, 'Mitilini after Departure of Germans', 30 Sept. 1944.

13. Deas archive, 5/94, E. Wenger, 'Ekthesis epi ton taxeidion mas eis tas eparchias apo 15–21 Septemvriou 1944', 23 Sept. 1944.

14. On the Civil Guard in the Peloponnese, see WO 170/581,

'23 Armoured Brigade GP: OP. Instruction no. 1', 6 Nov. 1944; Archiv na Makedonskya, *Egeyske Makedonskya vo Noj, 1944–1945*, i (Skopje, 1971), 468 (Siantos–Stringos, 12 Sept. 1944); see also C.M. Woodhouse, *The Struggle for Greece, 1941–1949* (London, 1976), 99.

15. G. Theotokas, *Tetradia imerologiou (1939–1953)* (Athens, n.d.), 505; R. Hampe, *Die Rettung Athens im Oktober 1944* (Wiesbaden, 1955).

16. G. Theotokas, *Tetradia*, 507, 509.

17. R. Milliex, *Imerologio kai martyries tou polemou kai tis katochis* (Athens, 1982), 56.

18. Theotokas, *Tetradia*, 509.

19. WO 208/3362, I. Stampadakis, 'Report of Things Happened during the Voyage 25/8/44–20/1/45'; MFA/AD, Ambassade de France à Athènes: box 6, 5 Nov. 1944.

20. W. Byford-Jones, *The Greek Trilogy* (London, 1945); G.M. Alexander, 'British Perceptions of EAM/ELAS Rule in Thessaloniki 1944–45', *Balkan Studies*, 21 (1980), 203–16.

21. Iatrides (ed.), *Ambassador MacVeagh Reports*, 650.

22. FO 188/438 Mallet (Stockholm)–London, 24 Dec. 1944, encl. report dated 22 Nov. 1944 by E. Sandstrom, President of Greek Relief Commission to the Swedish Red Cross.

23. Iatrides (ed.) *Ambassador MacVeagh Reports*, 660.

24. C. Couvaras, *OSS with the Central Committee of EAM* (San Francisco, 1982), 110–11; see also the disturbing analysis by Lyall Wilkes, 'British Missions and Greek Quislings', *The New Statesman and Nation*, 1 Feb. 1947, 88–9; on Spiliotopoulos, see FO 371/43684 R5591, 26 March 1944; S. Sarafis, *ELAS: Greek Resistance Army* (London, 1980), 385; Senior Greek army officers in Italy were openly sympathetic to the Secur-

ity Battalions and criticised the Papandreon Govt. for its association with EAM, going so far as to discuss the overthrow of the Papandreou Government, and its replacement by an extreme rightwing administration: see e.g. WO 170/3812, 'Political Activities: Greek Medn. Base', n.d.

25. G. Alexander, *The Prelude to the Truman Doctrine: British Policy in Greece, 1944–1947* (Oxford, 1982), 66; WO 204/8832, SACMED–Scobie, 15 Nov. 1944.

26. M. Vafiadis, *Apomnimonevmata*, ii (Athens, 1985), 24–7; Th. Chadzis, *I nikifora epanastasi pou chathike*, iii (Athens, 1982), 245–52; Leeper quoted in G. Kolko, *The Politics of War: the World and US Foreign Policy, 1943–1945* (New York, 1990), 184.

27. NA, RG 226/190, 8/61, 'Report' G. Skouras, 27 Jan. 1945.

28. WO 204/9349, 'Jannina: Intelligence', n.d.; WO 204/8573, Civil Posts Dept, 'Report Concerning the Period from D-Day to 31 March 1945'; WO 204/8810, 'Report by Lt Barnwell. Larissa and Pelion Area', 9 Nov. 1944.

29. FO 371/48308, R10293/52/19, Millet (Stockholm)–London, enclosing A. and E. Persson, 'Survey of Activities of Tripolis Bureau during the Last Six Months 1944'.

30. FO 188/438, Mallet (Stockholm)–London, 24 Dec. 1944, enclosing report dated 22 Nov. 1944 by E. Sandstrom, President of Greek Relief Commission to the Swedish Red Cross.

31. NA, RG 226/190, 8/63, 'Relief Distribution on Kea', 27 Nov. 1944.

32. The best primary sources for the *Dekemvriana* are the British Civil Police Liaison log book, in WO 170/4049, and the subsequent account by 23rd Armoured Brigade in WO 204/8312. There is also an

excellent article by L. Baerenzten, 'The Demonstration in Syntagma Square on Sunday the 3rd of December, 1944', *Scandinavian Studies in Modern Greek*, 2 (1978), 3–53; G. Seferis, *A Poet's Journal: 1945–1951*, trans. A. Anagnostopoulos (Cambridge, Mass., 1974), 5.

33. WO 204/8312, '23rd Armoured Brigade: Operations in Greece: Oct. 15 1944–Jan. 7 1945'.

34. Cited by J.O. Iatrides, *Revolt in Athens: the Greek Communist 'Second Round', 1944–1945* (Princeton, 1972), 207.

35. WO 170/4049, 'Report on Visit to Greek Red Cross F.A.P., Platia Kastalia, Kypseli. 12 Dec. 1944' on the panic among non-combatants caused by the RAF raids.

36. WO 204/8312, '23rd Armoured Brigade. Operations in Greece:

Oct. 15 1944–Jan. 7 1945'.

37. Iatrides (ed.) *Ambassador MacVeagh Reports*, 660; WO 204/8301, 'The Fighting in Piraeus'; WO 204/9380, 'Report by Capt. W.E. Newton on a Visit to Kokkenia [*sic*] on 12th January 1945', 13 Jan. 1945.

38. FO 996/1, 'Report on Hostages Seen by Major T. Aitken, HLI and Capt. J.A. Wyke, R.A. on 15/1/45', 28 Jan. 1945; Rapp (Salonika)–Athens, 12 Feb. 1945.

39. NA, RG 226/190, 9/72, 'A Report on the Activities of the "Ellas" Mission by Lt. C. Kantionis, USNR'.

40. K. Andrews, *The Flight of Ikaros* (London, 1959), 194.

41. FO 371/48286, R20262/4, Leeper –FO, 30 Nov. 1945.

42. LDG archives, INFO XII, INFO XI: 'Prisons, 1945–1967: Individual Dossiers'.

Archival Sources

GREECE (Athens)

Army History Directorate:

Agoros archive
'Apollo' archive
PAO (Mitsou) archive
Moatsou archive
Sarantis archive
Triantaphyllides archive
Italian 11th Army files

Bank of Greece:

Financial correspondence, 1941–42

Central Board of Jewish Communities:

Files from the Service for the Disposal of Jewish
Properties (originally held at Ministry of Justice)

Benaki Museum:

Nikolaos Deas archive
Heraklis Petimezas archive

Archival Sources

UNITED KINGDOM

Public Record Office (Kew):

FO 188:   Embassy and Consular, Sweden
FO 371:   General Correspondence (Political)
FO 837:   Ministry of Economic Warfare
FO 898:   Political Warfare Executive
FO 916:   Consular (War) Dept: POWs and Internees
FO 939:   Control Office: POWs
FO 996:   Embassy and Consular, Greece

WO 106:   Director of Military Intelligence (Operations)
WO 204:   War of 1939–45, Military HQ Papers: Allied Forces HQ
WO 208:   Directorate of Military Intelligence
WO 224:   POW camps

Public Record Office (Holborn):

TS 26:   Treasury Solicitor, War Crimes

Liddell Hart Centre for Military Archives: King's College, London

Myers Papers
Woodhouse Papers
League for Democracy in Greece, archives

Wiener Library, London:

Unpublished testimonies
'Thames documents': a collection of documents and interviews prepared
   for *Waldheim: a Case to Answer* (1988)

Foreign and Commonwealth Office Library, London:

Italian Documents Collection (formerly housed at St Antony's College,
   Oxford)
German Foreign Ministry microfilms

Imperial War Museum, London:

Foreign Documents Collection
'A Valley in Greece', P.O. Hudson, unpubl. mss.

Christ Church, Oxford:

Eric Gray newspaper collection

Private Papers:

Eric Gray (in possession of Patrick Gray)
Arthur Wickstead
Lyall Wilkes (in possession of Margaret Wilkes)

GERMANY

Berlin Document Centre:

Personal files:
    Walter Baach
    Walter Blume
    Friedrich Crome
    Hans Dörhage
    Paul Krocker
    Fritz Lautenbach
    Roman Loos
    Paul Radomski
    Kurt Rickert
    Walter Schimana
    Werner Schlätel
    Fritz Schmedes
    Franz Schönfeldt
    Ferdinand Schörner
    Karl Schümers
    Jürgen Stroop

Bundesarchiv, Koblenz:

R 19   Hauptamt Ordnungspolizei
R 43   Reichskanzlei
R 58   Reichssicherheitshauptamt
R 63   Südosteuropa-Gesellschaft
R 127   Deutsch-Griechische Warenausgleichsgesellschaft

NS 7   SS-und-Polizeigerichtsbarkeit
NS 19   Persönlicher Stab Reichsführer SS
NS 30   Einsatzstab Reichsleiter Rosenberg

Bundesarchiv-Militärarchiv, Freiburg:

RH 19–VII   Army Group E
RH 19–IX   Army Group F
RH 24–68   68 Army Corps
RH 24–91   91 Army Corps
RH 26–22   22 Inf. Division
RH 28–5   5 Mtn. Division
RH 28–6   6 Mtn. Division
RH 53–18   Wehrkreis XVIII

RW 5   Abwehr
RW 40   Territorial Commanders, Greece
RW 48   Secret Field Police

N 60   Nachlass Ferdinand Schörner
N 449   Nachlass Christian Clemm von Hohenberg
N 527   Nachlass Wilhelm List

MSg 1/919, 924 Sammlungsgut Löhr

Politisches Archiv, Auswärtiges Amt, Bonn:

Athens Embassy:
Vols. 66–79 Bevollmächtigter des Reichs für Griechenland

Signatur:
27201   Chef der Auslandsorganisation
27301–321   Sonderbevollmächtigter Südost
27532–551   Sonderkommando v. Künsberg

29612–614   Staatssekretär (Griechenland)
29880   Unterstaatssekretär (Griechenland)

Inland II a/b: 99419, 99517–20, 99230–1, 99259–60
Inland IIg: 100718, 100741–44, 100746, 100750, 100767, 100826,
               100870–1, 101081–2

105896–897:   Handelakten Clodius
106155:   Handelakten Wiehl

Institut für Zeitgeschichte, Munich:

Zs 1420   Zeugenschrifttum: Walter Schimana
Zs 2389   Zeugenschrifttum: Walter Blume

Zentrale Stelle der Landesjustizverwaltungen, Ludwigsburg:

AR   12/62   (Police Battalion 64)
AR   418/63   (Loos case)
AR   743/68   (Kalabaka)
AR 1116/68   (Kalamata)
AR 1187/68   (Epiros)
AR 1293/68   (Kalavryta)
AR 1462/68   (Komeno)
AR 1604/64   (Epiros)
AR 1763/67   (Tripolis)
AR 1798/67   (Lamia)
AR 2056/67   (Argos)
AR 2415/67   (Distomo)
AR–Z 26/63   (Final Solution)
AR–Z 139/59   (Merten proceedings)
301/5–VÜ5   (Distomo)

FRANCE

Archives Diplomatiques, Ministère des Affaires Etrangères,
Nantes:

Ambassade de France à Athènes (boxes 4, 6, 9, 33, 37, 40, 51, 54, 68, 76,

101, 103, 104, 106, 115, 152)
Consulat de France à Salonique (boxes 8, 25, 27, 28, 37, 50, 96)

Centre de Documentation Juive Contemporaine, Paris:

Misc. files

ISRAEL

Yad Vashem, Jerusalem:

DIV/54–1, Wisliceny affidavit, Bratislava, 1947

Hebrew University, Jerusalem:

Institute of Contemp. Jewry, Oral Histories

ITALY

Archivio Centrale dello Stato (Rome):

Segreteria Particolare del Duce (B. 174)

Ministero degli Affari Esteri: Archivio Storico Diplomatico (Rome):

B. 22   Rapporti politici

Stato Maggiore dell'Esercito V Reparto: Ufficio Storico (Rome):

B. 634, 736, 840, 966, 1054, 1098, 1226, 1442

USA

National Archives, Washington, DC:

Captured Enemy Documents (microfilm series) (roll no.):

T–77   (Armed Forces High Command): Abwehr (1435)
T–78   (Armed Forces High Command): Misc. files (102)
T–81   (Records of Deutsches Ausland–Institut): Misc. files, incl. Greece (348, 543, 562, 564)
T–84   (Misc. records) Misc. economic files (102)
T–120   (Records of the German Foreign Ministry): Buro des Staatsekretärs: Griechenland (157, 166, 292)
        Inland D.II. Geheim. Griechenland (379)
        Ha.Pol. Wiehl: Griechenland (1174)
        Ha.Pol. Clodius: Griechenland (2423)
        German Embassy, Rome (2481)
        Inland II 'Juden in Griechenland' (2721)
T–175   (Records of the Reich Leader of the SS and Chief of the German Police):
        Misc. Correspondence (75, 474, 475)
T–311   (Records of German Field Commands) (Armies):
        Army Group E (175–85, 286)
        Army Group F (187–97, 285–6)
T–314   (Records of German Field Commands) (Corps):
        22 Army Corps (670–73)
T–315   (Records of German Field Commands) (Divisions):
        1st Mountain Division (64–72, 2305)
        117 Jaeger Division (1299–1300)
        164 Infantry Division (1474)
        Sturmdivision Rhodos (2275)
T–501   (Records of German Field Commands) (Rear Areas):
        Armee Sudgriechenland (330–31)
        Befehlshaber Saloniki-Aegaeis (48, 245–51)
        Militärbefehlshaber Griechenland (252, 254–5)
T–586   (Records of the Italian Foreign Ministry):
        Misc. files (412, 454, 1064, 1282)
T–821   (Records of Italian Armed Forces):
        Political situation in Greece (248, 249)
        Commando Supremo, Greece (354, 355, 356)

Nuremberg War Crimes Trials (microfilm series):

M–893:   USA v. Wilhelm List *et al.* (Case VII)

Archival Sources

US Department of State (RG 59):

Decimal file 740.00 (1940–41)
Decimal file 868.00 (1936–44)

War Dept: General and Special Staffs (RG 165):

7th Army Interrogation Reports (Boxes 650, 651, 654, 721A, 736–9)

OSS (RG 226):

Pt 1:   numbered files (41745–135385)
Pt 2:   L and XL files (XL 813–21026, L 39254–51881)
Pt 3:   CIA's OSS archive:
           Washington CI and OSS files (entry 120, boxes 29, 30)
           Washington/Field Office misc. (entry 144, boxes 91, 100)
           OSS Field Offices (entry 154, boxes 39, 40)
           OSS NY Secret Intell. Branch (entry 160, box 34)
           Director's Office and Field Station Records (entry 190, boxes 1–3, 8, 9, 73, 77–8)
Pt 4:   Research and Analysis (R & A) Reports

Seeley Mudd Library, Princeton University (Princeton, New Jersey):

Karl L. Rankin Papers

Note on Sources

The state of Greece's archives is a national disgrace: for over twenty years, while valuable documents moulder in ministry basements, scholars have been waiting for a modern public records building to be completed. Even with the assistance offered by patient and dedicated archivists struggling against official indifference, sustained research into the wartime period is almost impossible on the basis of Greek archives alone.

The starting-point for my research into Axis occupation policy was the massive microfilmed collection of captured German documents held at the National Archives in Washington. These microfilms include series of reports and telegrams by Foreign Office officials, Nazi party members stationed in Greece, and records of Wehrmacht and Waffen-SS units. The military records alone provide an extraordinarily detailed picture of Greece as seen by the occupiers, covering – in addition to operational matters – intelligence concerning the guerrillas, assessments of popular opinion, interrogations of captured prisoners, and detailed analysis of economic activity.

These microfilm collections should be supplemented with other materials. I drew, first, upon the documents collected for the Nuremberg trials, which are available at the Imperial War Museum, London. Personal files of SS officers from the Berlin Document Centre revealed information that could not have been gleaned from the Wehrmacht records. The Central Office of the Federal Ministry of Justice for the Prosecution of Nazi War Crimes in Ludwigsburg made available to me affidavits collected since the war from German and Austrian ex-servicemen. They contained revealing information on troop morale within the Wehrmacht, attitudes towards reprisals, the mechanics of the Final Solution, and the structure of SS activity in Greece. Ludwigsburg also holds materials collected by the Greek National War Crimes Office, whose files are not available in Greece.

Two microfilmed collections of captured Italian documents were indispensable for this book: one set seized by the Germans after the

Italian surrender and later microfilmed by the Americans, contains various documents from military and *carabinieri* officials in Greece; the other, captured at the end of the war by the Allies and available at the Foreign and Commonwealth Office in London, includes files from Mussolini's secretariat concerning Fascist Party activity in Greece. Conditions in Salonika were analysed in the weekly reports compiled by the Italian consul-general there, Guelfo Zamboni, recently published by Joseph Rochlitz in *The Righteous Enemy: Document Collection* (Rome, 1988).

In comparison with other countries in Eastern Europe, wartime Greece was surprisingly open to foreign observers: from Swiss Red Cross delegates to American OSS operatives, they have left records of what they found. This makes the Greek experience a valuable one for the historian, since it allows us to glimpse something of what life must have been like in far less accessible parts of Eastern Europe, where Axis policy ran along similarly horrific lines to that in Greece.

One valuable source for the relatively obscure early period of the occupation are French diplomatic files. In particular, the Archives Diplomatiques in Nantes house the reports received by the French Embassy in Athens from consuls and other correspondents living in Greece. The honorary consul on Syros, for example, left a 90-page account of his family's experiences on the island throughout the war; he sent this to Athens when the legation opened again late in 1944, together with a claim for expenses arising from bomb damage to his house. Consul Lecureul in Patras sent Athens an eyewitness account of the arrival of the Germans; so did his colleague in Salonika. The Ecole des Soeurs in Volos described the difficulties of continuing with school classes in 1943; the Ecole des Filles de la Charité in Salonika wanted support in running their soupkitchen.

Swiss and Swedish Red Cross delegates travelled throughout the country in 1943–44 to distribute food supplies, and wrote reports which are vital for understanding socio-economic conditions in the provinces. They are available upon special request in the Nikolaos Deas archive in the Benaki Museum; many from the Swedish side are also to be found in the files of the British Embassy in Stockholm, deposited in the Public Record Office in London (FO 188). They got there because Swedish Red Cross delegates sent duplicates to their Foreign Office, which allowed British diplomats to copy the reports out by hand. Some Swiss Red Cross documents, by a similar route, ended up in the files of the British Ministry of Economic Warfare (FO 837).

On the British side, the files of SOE are currently unavailable for research, thanks to Britain's absurdly restrictive official secrecy laws. Many SOE reports and telegrams, however, were passed on to the Foreign Office, and can therefore be found in the Public Record Office. The Foreign Office archives also contain intelligence brought out of occupied Greece by agents of Prime Minister Tsouderos, and passed on by him to British diplomats. More SOE material is available in the papers of the two heads of the British (later Allied) Military Mission to Greece, E.C. Myers and C.M. Woodhouse. These are deposited at the Liddell Hart Centre for Military Archives in King's College, London. Another valuable British source consists of the files of the War Office, including military intelligence (WO 106, WO 208), Allied Forces HQ/Middle East (WO 204), and POW conditions (WO 224). WO 204, in particular, covers SOE operations, economic and political intelligence, administrative and medical conditions in enormous detail.

The American OSS played the role of junior partner to the British in Greece, but their intelligence is no less useful. In fact, so long as the SOE files remain under wraps, the OSS view remains indispensable. OSS operatives included many Greek-Americans who were more sympathetic than the British to what EAM/ELAS was trying to do. The OSS archives, catalogued in the National Archives in Washington as RG 226, have recently been swollen by the addition of hundreds of boxes of documents released from the custody of the CIA. The new accessions to RG 226 include some remarkable documents: the complete diaries of R.E. Moyers, which provide one of the most perceptive glimpses of village life under EAM; the final reports of OSS officers serving alongside ELAS units; analyses of resistance newspapers and of captured Greek postal mail; internal Communist Party bulletins; and perhaps most importantly of all, documents passed over by sympathetic officials in the quisling governments, including a series of intelligence reports which appear to emanate from the Athens police. Their cumulative effect is to transform our understanding of the roots of the Civil War.

The National Archives also holds OSS films, including the one made by George Skouras in November 1944 (RG 226 H 6524). Another record group, RG 165/179, contains interrogation reports of POWs by the US 7th Army. Among the POWs were German and Italian servicemen who escaped from Greece, Greek collaborators captured in 1945 in central Europe, and senior Axis officials in Greece. Some of the interrogations provide information on a very obscure but important subject: the German secret services' use of Greek collaborators during the war.

These foreign archival sources, together with published collections of diplomatic papers (German, Italian and Vatican), provided the foundations for my research. Yet despite the paucity of official Greek archives, I wanted to add Greek viewpoints as far as possible. Papers held at the Bank of Greece gave insights into Italo-German economic policies. The *Government Gazette* of the quisling governments was available at the British Library – I have not come across a copy in Greece. Four grimy sacks from the Ministry of Justice which were handed over to the Central Board of Jewish Communities in Athens turned out, when I opened them, to contain papers concerning the handling of property left behind by the Jews ·of Salonika after they were deported. In the uncatalogued mass of torn bills, receipts and petitions I found the list of Jewish shops and premises which was drawn up by members of the community under German orders, and the minutes of meetings held by the Greek body set up under German auspices to handle the property after the deportations began. Copies of some of these documents may be consulted at Yad Vashem in Jerusalem.

On the resistance side, a few EAM/ELAS and KKE documents have been published. Some ELAS material appears to be held in archives in Skopje. Other resistance documents are published in Thanasis Mitsopoulos's very valuable *To 30° Sytagma tou ELAS* (Athens, 1987, 4th edn), in the three volumes of Petros Antaios's study of the youth movement EPON, *Symvoli stin istoria tis EPON*, 3 vols (Athens, 1977–79), and in Nitsa Koliou's account of the Volos area during the war, *Agnostes ptyches tis katochis kai antistasis, 1941–1944*, 2 vols (Volos, 1986). Primary material for the study of EAM is included in the appendices to Thanasis Tsouparopoulos's *Oi Laokratikoi Thesmoi tis Ethnikis Antistasis* (Athens, 1989), and in the classic work by Georgoulas Beikos, *I laiki exousia stin Eleftheri Ellada*, 2 vols (Athens, 1979). The archives of the League for Democracy in Greece, now held at King's College, London, contain moving, brief autobiographies of many ELAS fighters, written while they were held as political prisoners in the two decades after the war ended.

There are all too few diaries or collections of letters available. The OSS file RG 226/120 includes extracts from private mail captured by Allied submarines. FO 371 files also contain extracts from intercepted private mail addressed abroad. The reports of the Wehrmacht censors on troop morale include excerpts from letters sent to and from soldiers in Greece in the second half of 1944. A great literary achievement, as well as a first-rate primary source, is the diary of the novelist George Theotokas, *Tetradia imerologiou (1939–1953)* (Athens, n.d.). Two other excellent first-hand accounts are the diaries of Ch. Christides, *Chronia katochis* (Athens, 1971) and of the musicologist Minos Dounias, *To imerologio katochis tou Minou Dounias* ed. K. Delopoulos (Athens, 1987).

The Greek press provided a valuable glimpse of life under occupation. Censorship in the Italian zone was not very strict, and papers such as *Eleftheron Vima*, while they could not be openly critical of the authorities, did discuss many of the problems of daily life. Specialist papers, like the economics daily, *To Kerdos*, were sometimes surprisingly outspoken. The best view of concerns in the provinces is provided by the local dailies. Despite the scarcity of newsprint, each town had its official paper, like *Larissaikos Typos* or *Tachydromos* (Volos), and they were often even more outspoken than their Athens counterparts. I have hardly tapped the possibilities of this genre in this book: more than any other source, it may help transform our understanding of the origins of the resistance.

The resistance press was much more extensive than the official press, but I have used it here chiefly for the light it sheds on the mentality and outlook of the resistance itself. For this purpose it is rich and varied, giving a sense of the emotions involved as well as the differences of approach and attitude across the country. To draw any broader conclusions on the basis of the information it presents would be in my view to risk confusing propaganda with reality.

The published literature, primary and secondary, on this topic is now enormous and expanding all the time. I do not intend to offer a guide to it here, as several excellent bibliographical studies are available. My own view is that many authors remain so polarised in their convictions that any serious student of the period must base his or her work upon the very ample contemporary material that exists. It may, however, be helpful to mention one or two works in English which may interest anyone who wishes to explore the subject further.

Among the most vivid first-hand accounts of the occupation are *OSS with the Central Committee of EAM* (San Francisco, 1982), by the former OSS agent Costas Couvaras; George Psychoundakis's *The Cretan Runner* (London, 1955), which brilliantly captures the popular view of the resistance; and John Mulgan's *Report on Experience* (London, 1947), which together with Edmund Myers' *Greek Entanglement* (Gloucester, 1985 edn), provides the most penetrating and sympathetic account of the impact of the resistance on country life.

John Hondros's *Occupation and Resistance: The Greek Agony, 1941–1944* (New York, 1983) remains an excellent analysis, while Procopis Papastratis's lucid study, *British Policy towards Greece during the Second World War, 1941–1944* (Cambridge, 1984) will give the

British reader pause for thought. The volume of essays edited by
John Iatrides, *Greece in the 1940s: A Nation in Crisis* (Hanover,
NH, 1981) is also valuable. Meanwhile, the most detailed and
exhaustive study of the politics of the occupation period remains
Hagen Fleischer's *Im Kreuzschatten der Mächte: Griechenland 1941–
1944*, 2 vols (Frankfurt, 1986). Let me end by drawing the reader's
attention to a unique and fascinating work written by four Greek
psychiatrists at the end of the war. Their brilliant dissection of
the impact of occupation on the minds of their compatriots has
recently been republished in Greece, though it remains unavailable in translation. *I psychopathologia tis peinas, tou fovou kai tou anchous: nevroseis kai psychonevroseis* [The Psychopathology of Hunger,
Fear and Anxiety: Neuroses and Psychoneuroses] (Athens, 1947;
repr. 1991) is by F. Skouras, A. Hadzidimos, A. Kaloutsis and G.
Papadimitriou.

Index

NB: there are no entries for Athens, EAM/ELAS, Germany, Greece, Hitler.

Aaron, Armandos 255
Abwehr 24, 163–4, 219, 247
Aegina 34
Aegion 152, 297, 314
Agrafa 135
Agrinion 95, 137, 148
Albania 15–16, 125, 145
Alexis Zorbas 78
Algeria 161, 169, 176, 188, 268, 315
Alikianos 173
Altenburg, Günther 19, 22, 24, 30,
    68–71, 147, 219, 251
Altzerinakos, Constantine 86
Ambrosio, General Vittorio 145–6
Amfikleia 135
andartes 113, 125–9, 131–43, 152,
    158–9, 161–2, 192, 298–321, 326,
    354, 356, 358–65, 370, 372–6
    and Albanian campaign 123,
    125–6, 305–6; and klephtic
    traditions 311–3; social
    composition of 311–13.
Andrews, Kevin 332
Andros 50
Animals, Operation 143–4
anti-communism 13–14, 99–100,
    218, 222, 232, 297–8, 322–4, 327,
    329–30, 338, 352, 359–60, 364–5
anti-guerrilla operations 48, 130–32,
    146–8, 169–72, 190–91, 196–8,
    215–18, 225
    social impact of 182–9.
anti-Semitism in Greece 257–8
Apostolou, Levteris 105
Apoyevmatini 242
Arcangelo 165
Argalasti 274–6

Argos 28, 54, 216
Aris 125–7, 138, 270–71, 290, 298,
    300–301, 313–14, 316, 320–21, 365,
    373
Arkadia xv
Arta 137, 142, 178, 184, 191–3, 377
Ataturk *see* Mustafa Kemal
Athanasiades, Themistokles 4
'Attic' 63
Attica 163
Auschwitz-Birkenau 244, 252–3,
    256–7
Axis, Operation 146–50, 170
Ayeranos 86

Badoglio, Marshal Pietro 147–8, 150
Bakirtzis, Colonel Evripidis 291–2
Bank of Athens 64
Bank of Greece 67, 115
Barzilai, Grand Rabbi Elias 250, 259
Bathgate, Major P. 140
BBC 38, 41, 330
Beikos, Georgoulas 270
Belgium 31, 157
Belgrade 242, 245
Benekos, Georgios 163
Bengal famine (1943) 26
Bergen-Belsen 245
Berry, Burton 23
black market 30, 53–64, 164, 318
bloccos 225–6, 232–4, 342–4, 349–
    52
Blume, Standartenführer Dr Walter
    222, 224–5, 229, 231–2, 250–51,
    261, 328, 344, 374–5
Bodosakis munitions works 25
Boeotia 104, 111

Bormann, Martin 237
Bosnia 155
'Boukouvalas', *Kapetan* 299, 301–2, 311
Bozika 163
Brauchitsch, Field Marshal Walter von 7, 157
brigandage 288, 312
British Army (and associated units): 7th Indian Infantry Brigade 362; 23rd Armoured Brigade 352, 370; 14th Hussars 3.
Brunner, Alois 241
Bubat, Hanhelmuth 206
Bulgaria 15, 20–22, 31, 74, 320
Burger, Hauptsturmführer Toni 252, 254

Campione, Inigo 51
Canada 48
Carrà, Carlo 65
Carta, General 150
Casablanca 70
Cassini, Major Fernando 150
Cavafy, Constantine 1, 3
Cefalonia 150
Chadzis, Thanasis 105
Chadzivasileiou, Chrysa 104
Chalkidiki 58
Chalkis 56, 325
Chania 11
Charon 43
children 36–7, 40, 185–9, 279–80, 360–62
China 267
Chios 4, 21, 24, 33, 58, 66, 163, 216
Christides, Christos 4, 99
Chrysanthos, Archbishop 19
Churchill, Winston xv, 101, 142, 144, 352–3, 365, 368, 370
Ciano, Count Galeazzo 18, 25, 32, 89
Civil War, Greek xvi, 281, 301, 372–6
Clauberg, Professo Carl 257
Cobb, Richard 317, 321
Cold War xvi, 340
Comintern, dissolution of 268, 296
Communist Party, Greek *see* KKE
Constantakos, Mrs 34
Constantinidis, Dimitri 115
Corfu 72, 104, 150, 152, 164, 253, 256, 261

Corinth 3, 180, 217–18, 297
corruption, official 56–64
counter-terror *see* death squads
Couvaras, Costas 295, 309, 317
Crete 11, 28, 56–8, 87, 104, 106, 162, 173, 180, 183, 191, 253, 339, 374 battle for 20; Jews deported from 256.
crime 64, 123–5, 127, 272–3, 288
Croatia 88
Cyclades 22, 31
Czech, Danuta 256

Dachau 103, 203
Damaskinos, Archbishop 94–6, 117, 233, 259
Daphni 226
Davidson, Basil 314
Davis, Mrs Homer 33
death squads, anti-communist 172, 334–9 (*see also* Poulos, EASAD)
death squads, resistance 319 (*see also* OPLA)
Deighton, Len xiv
Dekemvriana 340, 352–4, 362–5, 368–72
Delabona, General 148
Deleri 124
Delphi 152, 180, 290, 317
Democratic Army of Greece xvi, 301, 354, 374–5
Denmark 251
Dertilis, Major-Gen. Vasilios 328, 330, 350
Despotopoulos, Kostas 293
Deter, Walter 25
Dhenousa 57
Disaster, Asia Minor (1922) 11–12, 35, 117 (*see also* refugees)
Distomo, massacre at 180, 209, 212–15
Djilas, Milovan 285–6, 309
doctors 66, 177
Dodecanese 253
Domokos 135
Donauzeitung 75
Dörhage, Kriminalrat Hans 44, 230
Dounias, Minos 23, 33, 64, 91, 93
Dourgouti 37
Douros, Elias 246–8
Dunkirk xiv

EA 100
EASAD 335–6 (*see also* anti-
communism)
economy (*see also* expropriation,
famine, food, inflation)
pre-war 12–13; state of at
Liberation 365–7; wartime
disintegration of 7, 26–8, 35–6,
54, 72.
EDES xvii, 106, 140–42, 265, 289–
90, 329–30, 332, 338, 359
EEE 238, 328, 338
Efharpia 163
Ehrgott, Winston 309, 315
Eichmann, Sturmbannführer Adolf
230, 240–42, 250–51, 256, 261, 374
EKKA 142, 290, 292, 304, 319, 325
El Alamein xiv, 113
Elassona 130, 134, 203
Elytis, Odysseus 83, 93
Engonopoulos, Nikos 93
EOKA 349
Epiros 11, 31, 125, 129, 142, 148, 176,
178, 183, 188, 273, 276
EPON 114, 279–80, 341
Eudes, Dominique 302
Evros 310, 318–21
Evrytania 269–71
Evvia 188, 261, 291, 293, 321
Evzones *see* Security Battalions
expropriation, Axis 24–6, 46

Fallmerayer, J. 158
family unit 36, 40, 114–15, 185–9
famine xiii, xviii, 26–30, 32–49, 64
and political radicalisation 34,
51–2, 108–10, 112–14, 267.
Fanon, Frantz 188
Farsala 108, 135
Fascist Party (Italian) in Greece 151
Fatherland (transmitter) 4
Felmy, General Hellmuth 177, 211,
215, 374
Flight of Ikaros, The 332
food, diplomacy of 46–8
andartiko and 129–31; supply of
at Liberation 366–8.
Foreign Ministry, German 25, 30–31,
69–72, 219, 235–7, 244
Foreign Ministry, Italian 18, 25
Fourni 148
France, Vichy xv, 113, 201, 245

Franco-Prussian War 157
Franz, Hermann 159
French Revolution 34, 297, 317, 360

Gambetas, Kostas 109–110
Geissler, Sturmbannführer 219
Geloso, General Carlo 32, 106, 124,
135, 145–7, 241, 248–9
gendarmerie 111, 123, 125–7, 134–5,
270, 288, 307–8, 324–5, 332, 339,
341–54, 359, 375–6
postwar reconstruction of 334,
351–2.
George II, King of the Hellenes 2,
13–14, 18, 46, 89, 97–8, 101–2, 141,
289, 291, 324, 365
Georgiou, Panteli 85
German army *see* Wehrmacht
Gestapo 76–8, 207–8, 217, 219, 225,
230–31, 233, 245, 252, 260, 290,
324–5
GFP 163–4, 166–9, 212, 220, 225,
253, 329, 339, 357
Ghigi, Pellegrino 22, 30–32, 67–8,
248
Giannitsa massacre 336–7
Glinos, Dimitri 100–101, 299
Glitz, Erhard 159
Gyldenfeldt, General Heinz von 149,
170
Goebbels, Josef 89, 93, 322
Goering, Hermann 9, 31
Gonatas, General Stylianos 101, 106
Gorgopotamos viaduct 113, 135, 138,
310
Gotzamanis, Sotirios 63–4, 67–9,
79–82, 110–13
Goumas, Dionysios 306, 309
graffiti 91–2, 113
Greek War Relief Association 47
Grevena 136, 183
Col. Grivas, George 349
Guernsey xiv
Günter, Ludwig 159

Hadzimikalis, Platon 19, 62
Hadzis, Thanasis 295–6
Haidari 226–30, 233, 252, 256,
344–5, 350, 377
Hamilton-Hill, Donald 298
Heine, Sonderführer H. 24
Heydrich, Reinhard 229, 231

Himmler, Heinrich   xiv, 174, 203, 229, 222–3, 231, 240, 251, 254, 327, 345
Hohenberg, Clemm von   43
Holland   31, 82
Houtas, Stylianos   137, 140
Hubertus/Operation   181
Hungary   229
hunger *see* famine

I.G. Farben   24, 70, 223
Ikarya   49, 148, 163
Imvriotis, Rosa   281
Indochina, French   xviii
inflation   xiii, 26–7, 65–72, 108, 120–21, 267
Interpol   225
Ioannides, Ioannis   295–6
Ioannou, Giorgios   245, 257
Ionian islands   22, 31, 197
Ionian Bank   79
Ireland, Northern   161
Istanbul   245
Italian Army   xv, 1, 24
    11th Army   22; Pinerolo Division   152.

Jaeger, Oberst Emil   253, 261
Jannina   16, 134, 137, 144, 164, 170, 178, 190, 192, 197, 204, 377
    Jews deported from   252–4.
Jannina, Bishop of   148
Jecchinis, Christos   309
Jewry, Greek   xiii, 55–6, 244–5, 248–9, 250–53
    abandoned property of   246–8; Italian policy towards   240–41; SS policy towards   223, 225.
Junod, Marcel   36, 40, 42–3, 53
Junta, Colonels' (1967–74)   xvi
justice, resistance   269–73

Kafandaris, George   100
Kaisariani   226, 343, 351, 355, 370
Kalabaka   109, 134–5, 170, 183
Kalabalikis, Brigadier   303
Kalamata   48, 111, 186, 358–9
Kalavryta   xv, 179, 366
Kaltenbrunner, Ernst   223, 233, 251, 322, 327
Kandanos   173
Kanellopoulos, Panayiotis   102

Kapuscinski, Ryzard   268
'Karaïskakis'   127
Karalivanos   127–8, 301
Karamanlis, Constantine   375
Karatula   162
Karditsa   72, 124–5, 135, 270–71, 289
Karitena   161–2
Karoplesi   269
Karpenisi   170, 176, 184, 269–71, 291, 294, 366
Karyotakis, Konstantinos   12
Karystos   308
Kastellorizo   72
Katsareas, Nikolaos   56
Katyn massacre   74
Kazantzakis, Nikos   12, 78
Kazantzis, Kostas   117
Kea   55, 367–8
Keble, Brigadier   329
Keitel, Field Marshal Wilhelm   18, 71–2, 146–7, 153
Kemal, Mustafa   11
Kent, Ralph   34
Kerzilion, Ano and Kato   87, 174
Kiev   229
Kissavos, Mount   309
Kithnos   55
KKE   xvi, 97–8, 103–6, 112, 138, 268–70, 291, 293, 295–6, 298–300, 302, 311, 314, 324, 353, 360, 373
Kleedorfer, Franz   221
Kleemann, General Ulrich   151
Kleitsos   270
Klemperer, Victor   190–91
Kleykamp, Gunther   160
Klisura   180
Kokkinia   64, 341–4, 350
Kolko, Gabriel   267
Kolonaki   347, 362, 371
Komeno   191–200, 375
Kondomari   173
Koretz, Chief Rabbi Zvi   242–3
Koroyiannakis, Alexandros   65
Koryschades   294
Koryzis, Alexandros   98
Kosmidou, Anna   188
Kotzias, Alexandros   332
Kotzioulas, Georgios   276–80, 283
Kozani   87, 209
Krech, General   178
Krenzski, General Kurt von   79, 238–41

Kreuzotter, Operation 181
Krupp 24
Kuklesi (near Filippias) 190

Lambou, Alexandros 325, 342, 345, 348–9
Lamia 135, 365
Lanz, General Hubert 142, 158, 171–2, 177–8, 207–9, 215, 374
Larissa 55, 64, 121, 109, 132, 191, 204, 253, 259, 289, 366
Lautenbach, Hauptstürmführer Fritz 209, 212–15
Laval 82
Lavrion silver mines 25
Le Suire, General Karl 177, 179, 207–11, 265, 366
League of Nations 30
Lecureul, Xavier 2–3
Leeper, Rex 375
Lefkada 254–5
Leibstandarte Adolf Hitler 3, 16, 18, 214 (*see also* Waffen-SS)
Lemnos 22
Leros 216
Lesbos *see* Mytilene
Levadia 111, 134, 178, 290, 372
Liakos, Major-General Dimitrios 326
Liberal Party 12, 105, 291, 294
List, Wilhelm 1, 16–19, 173–4
Logothetopoulos, Constantine 19, 71, 75, 116–20, 357
Löhr, Lieutenant-General Alexander 144–9, 155, 158–9, 177, 179–81, 223, 234, 241, 327, 337, 355, 374
Lokris nickel mines 25
Loos, Roman 225
Louvaris, Nikolaos 259
Luftwaffe 155

Macedonia 11, 27–8, 87, 106, 129, 136, 163, 182–3, 298, 305, 317–18
MacNabb, Capt. Richard 86
MacVeagh, Lincoln 363–4
Makedon, Takis 335–6
Makriyiannis, General 313
malaria 65, 145, 203–4
Malaya 169
Mallios, Alexandros 193–5
Mangani, General 148
Mani 55

Maniadakis, Constantinos 98
Mantakas, General Manolis 292
Marathon reservoir 4
Marita, Operation 15
Mazarakis-Ainian, General Alexandros 99–100
Megalopolis 161–2
Melandrina 217–18
Melas, Spiros 98
Meligala 358
Mengele, Dr Josef 252, 257
Merbaka 211
Merten, Dr Max 241–48, 375
Mesolonghi 273
Messenia 306, 358
Metaxas, General Ioannis 13–15, 19, 79, 97–8, 101, 103, 170–71, 238, 269, 281, 295, 352
Metsovo 16, 136, 152, 170–71
Michos, Dimitri 133
Mihailovic, Draza 88
Milliex, Roger 43, 361
Mincemeat, Operation 144
Mitsialis, George 255
Mitsopoulos, Thanasis 299, 307
Molaos 178
Molho, Michael 244
mortality rates 48–50
Mulgan, John 304
Mussolini, Benito 1, 15–18, 32, 67–8, 79, 89, 91, 145, 147, 222
Myers, Brigadier Edmund 129, 138, 142, 144
Mytilene 22, 28, 57–8, 109, 359
Mytilene, Bishop of 56

Naoussa 359
National Bank of Greece 25, 243
National Committee, Greek (1945) 357
National Mortgage Bank 246
National Socialism xix, 6–7, 80–81, 155, 160, 322, 335
    Greek imitators of 87; and
    Wehrmacht 204–8.
Naxos 49
Nea Evropi 75
Nehamas, Itzchak 243–4
Neubacher, Hermann 69–72, 113, 120, 179–80, 212, 222–4, 232, 251, 322, 327, 329, 344, 355, 357, 375
Nikolaides, Perikles 357

Norway 31, 82
NSFO 207

occupation costs, Axis 66–72
'Odysseus', *Kapetan* 310, 313, 318–21
OPLA 288
OSS 304, 317, 320, 372

Paikos, Mount 299, 303
Palamas, Kostas 11, 117–18
Palavos, John 376
Pangalos, General Theodoros 99, 101,
  106, 119, 140, 232, 324, 348
Papadakis, Nausicaa 109
Papadongonas, Col. Dionysios
  327–8, 358
Papageorgiou, Nikolaos 346, 349
Papanaum, Laskaris 247
Papandreou, George 99–100, 291,
  295, 351, 362–4, 374
Papayiannis, Stefanos 125
Parnes, Mount 137
partisans, Italian xviii, 315
partisans, Yugoslav xviii, 88, 158
Patras 2–3, 18, 75, 109–111, 125,
  216, 255, 268, 325
Paxton, Robert xv
PEEA 291–3, 331
Peloponnese xiv, 19, 33, 49, 55,
  109–11, 131, 133, 144, 160–61, 163,
  172, 200, 311, 316
People's Committees (1941–2) xviii,
  108
Pericles 157
Persaki, Julia 92
Petinis, Colonel 16
Petropoulakos, George 55–6
philhellenism, Nazi 157
Philippines 267, 315
Picasso 65
Pièche, General Giuseppe 107, 116,
  119
Pietro Band 164–9
Pilion 110, 178
Pindos mountains 15, 49, 170, 181,
  183, 185, 298–9
Piraeus 4, 20, 24, 31–2, 36, 40, 47,
  54, 60, 87, 92–3, 121, 266, 360
Plastiras, General Nikolaos 106, 140,
  374
Plytzanopoulos, Col. 350
Poland 18, 33, 241, 245

police, Greek (*see also* gendarmerie)
  during *Dekemvriana* 368–70; and
  Final Solution 243, 255.
policing, German and the SiPo/SD
  230–31
Polychronopoulos, Ioannis 56
Populist Party 268
Poros 298
Porta, Captain Mario 150
Poseidon Code 271
Poulos, Georg xv, 246–7, 337, 339,
  357
POWs, British 85–7, 107
POWs, Italian 149–52
Preveza 366
price movements *see* inflation
priests 124, 271, 314–15
propaganda, Allied 38, 78
propaganda, resistance 113, 116,
  277–9, 283–8
Psaromialos, Dimitri 124
Psarros, Col. Dimitrios *see* EKKA
Psychiko 37, 64
Pyrgi 163
Pyrgos 297
Pyromaglou, Komninos 141

Radomski, Sturmbannführer Paul
  221, 227, 229–30
Rallis, Ioannis 71, 99, 120–21, 179,
  223, 232, 242, 251, 259, 329–32,
  331–2, 334, 357
Rangavis, Alexandros 87
Rankin, Karl 92
Red Cross 29, 41, 49, 65, 107, 148,
  184, 337, 355, 358, 366
  and Final Solution 250, 254;
  International 47–8, 70, 131.
refugees 11, 20, 34–5, 71, 341
Rekanati, Constantin 252, 254
reprisals 173–81, 210–11, 226–8
Rhodes 149–50, 164–9, 206, 216, 256
Ribbentrop, Joachim von 31, 69, 146
Rigouzzo, Mario 49
Rintelen, Enno 16
Ritsos, Iannis 93
Rizospastis 106, 352
Rodoulis, Alekos 349
Roman Legion 110
Romania 15, 70, 229, 281, 308, 350,
  355
Rommel, General E. 69–70, 92, 147

Roncalli, Angelo Giuseppe (later Pope John XXIII) 57, 89, 106
Rosenberg, Alfred 237–8, 258
Röser, Lieutenant 194–5, 199
Rotas, Vasilis 283
Roumeli 136
Roussos, Petros 282
RSHA 219, 229, 251
rumours 44–6, 60, 92, 113, 266

Salerno xiv
Salminger, Col. Josef 170, 177, 193, 198–9, 207, 209
Salò, puppet Government of 149–51
Salonika xv, 1, 11, 16, 18, 20, 25, 28–9, 31, 33, 43, 45, 48, 58, 62, 74–5, 79, 87, 90, 125, 144, 147–9, 151, 164, 170, 207, 258, 299, 338, 355, 359, 362, 371
    Jews deported from 55, 235–6, 246–8, 377.
Salzburg 146
Samos 22, 55, 72, 111, 148
Sandstrom, Justice Emil 267, 334, 366
Sarafis, General Stefanos 298, 301, 303, 304, 321
Sarantis, Theodoros 133
Saüberungen, see anti-guerrilla operations
Sauckel, Fritz 74–5
Schafer, James 24
Schilling, Prof. Claus 203
Schimana, HSSPF Walter 220, 223–4, 251, 324, 327, 345, 374
Schlätel, Werner 210
Schmedes, Brigadeführer Fritz 204, 214
Schubert, Fritz 337–9, 374
Schümers, Standartenführer 207, 210–11, 214–15
Scobie, Lieutenant General Sir Ronald 364–5, 370
Security Battalions xv, 120, 172, 308, 324–34, 341–54, 358–9, 375–6
    British policy towards 328–31, 353, 364–5; and Greek Jews 325; postwar rehabilitation of 354.
Seferis, George 93, 368
Sen, Amartya 26
Serbia 155, 244–5
Serres 87
Servia 183

Setta 279
Sevillias, Errikos 240, 257
Shell 25
Siantos, George 105, 268, 292–3, 296, 299–300, 321, 331
Siatista 134–5, 211, 310
Sicily 144, 147
The Siege 332
Sifnos 58
Sikelianos, Angelos 93–6, 117–18
Sikelianou, Anna 95, 118
Simha, Pavlos 186
Simi 148
Simonides, Vasilis 246
Sinopoulos, Takis 90, 93
SiPo/SD 219–25, 230, 232–4, 247, 328–9, 357
    and death squads 336.
Sironi, Mario 65
Skouras, George 366
Smokovo 136
SOE 135, 138–40, 329
Sofoulis, Themistoklis 100–101, 233
Sonderkommando 7a (Eastern Front) 222, 231
Sonderkommando 2000 (Greece) 338
Sonderkommando Rosenberg *see* Rosenberg
Sontis, Ioannis 219–20
soup kitchens 28–30, 36–7, 99
Soussi, Perla 255–6
Soviet Union, German invasion of 18, 30, 103, 174
Sparta 178
Speer, Albert 74, 76
Speidel, General Wilhelm 177, 374
Spilaios 134
Spiliotopoulos, General Panayiotis 364
SS 77, 157, 163, 219–20, 250, 261, 308, 344–5, 368
Stalin, Josef 268, 296, 353, 355, 365, 268
Stalingrad 69, 113, 137
Stefani 182
Stettin 229
Stettner, General Walter von 177, 207
Stevens, Col. J.M. 265
Stites, Richard 276
Stott, Capt. Don 329
Stroop, Jürgen 222–4, 250, 253
Strymon, River 87

Student, General Kurt   173–4
Stylida   124
Svolos, Prof. Alexandros   291
Sykourion   125
Syros   3, 49–52, 56, 63

Tassopoulos, Kostas   110, 125
Tavoularis, Anastasios   328, 357
Taygetos, Mount   86, 327
'Tempest'   318
terror policy   217–18, 347
Thadden, Obersturmführer Eberhard
   von   244
Thebes   159, 370
Theotokas, George   1, 3–5, 61, 83, 89,
   92–4, 113–14, 117, 186, 295, 341,
   349, 360–62
Theresienstadt   251
Thermon   135
Thessaloniki *see* Salonika
Thessaly   109, 113, 129, 136
The Third Wedding Wreath   90
Thrace   11, 88, 178, 183
Thucydides   263
Tinos   55
Tirana   164
Tito   88, 291, 294, 300, 374
Trikeri   274
Trikkala   123–4, 133, 135, 170, 259,
   373
Tripolis   161, 178, 358
Tsakalotos, General Th.   353
Tsaldaris, Constantine (Dino)   297
Tsangarada   135
Tsaousopoulos, Major A.   53
Tsatsou, Ioanna   44, 60, 86, 95
Tsimas, Andreas   106, 298, 300–301
Tsimbas, Constantine   357
Tsironikos, Hector   357
Tsitsanis, Vasilis   90–91
Tsolakoglu, General George   16,
   18–20, 57, 62–4, 67–71, 82, 89,
   98–9, 101, 109, 124, 132–3, 323
Tsouderos, Emmanouil   98
Turkey   xv, 21, 46–7, 56, 102, 261

Ukraine   155
UNRRA   366–8
Ustashe   88

Vafiades, Markos   301–4
Valtos   290

Vatican   47–8
Vatikiotis, Constantine   227–8
Vecchiarelli, General Carlo   147, 149,
   176
Velouchiotis, Aris *see* Aris
Venetsanopoulos, Thomas   134, 375
Venizelos, Eleftherios   11–14, 117,
   324
Verria   337, 339
Vidalis, Kostas   250
Vienna   69
Vietnam   161, 169, 176
Vlachou, Eleni   93
Volos   28, 42, 48, 55, 64–5, 108, 259,
   266, 274, 335–6
Volpi, Count   25
Vrettakos, Leonidas   327

Wacht auf Rhodos   206
Waffen-SS   xv, 155, 171, 181, 184,
   204, 207, 212–15, 229, 253
   4 SS Polizei Panzer Grenadier
   Div.   201, 204, 214–15.
Waldheim, Kurt   xiii, 161, 190–91,
   375
   and Komeno massacre   197–8.
war crimes trials   226, 339, 374–5
Warnstorff, Col.   180
Warsaw Ghetto   222
Wason, Betty   89
Wehrmacht   xiii, 1, 22–8, 67, 72, 87,
   144, 155–7, 162–3, 219, 297, 308,
   324, 327, 344
   Army Group E   155, 161, 170–
   72, 180–81, 190, 355; Commander
   Salonika/Aegean   87; Economics
   Staff   24–5; and the Final Solution
   238–54; Fortress Crete   22; and
   intelligence operations   161–3;
   and racial ideology   157–60;
   relations with Italians   17–22,
   145–9; and sex   202, 207, 216;
   sociology of   199–218;
   Sturmdivision Rhodos   150, 169,
   203; 1st Brandenburg Regiment
   149; 1st Mountain Div.   144, 150,
   170, 176, 190, 192–200, 204, 210,
   215, 375; 1st Panzer Div.   144,
   177; 22 Army Corps   142,
   170–71, 178, 181, 203, 253; 68
   Army Corps   162, 172, 178; 104
   Jaeger Div.   144; 117 Jaeger Div.

144, 157, 160, 163, 179, 210–11, 366; 164 Infantry Div. 174, 204–5, 207–8; 999 Battalions 200, 209, 216.
Weichs, Field Marshal Maximilian von 149
Weichenrieder, Georg 209
Weixler, Franz-Peter 173
Wende, Hans 161, 178
Wilson, General Sir Henry M. 142
Winter, General August 161, 179–81, 208
Wisliceny, Dieter 240–43, 248, 250, 256, 374
Woodhouse, Colonel Christopher M. 138, 141, 296

Wrede, Landesgruppenleiter Walter 5–8, 44

Yugoslavia 74, 88, 144, 149, 155, 173, 176, 267

Zachariades, Nikos 103, 105
Zakynthos 37, 148, 150–51, 259–60
Zamboni, Guelfo 241, 245, 248
Zante *see* Zakynthos
Zaralis, Nikos 317
Zaroyianni, *Kapetan* 311
Zervas, Napoleon 106, 133, 137–41, 178, 297, 302–3, 313–14, 328, 330, 335, 359, 374
Zisopoulos, Major Fotis 303